John A. Hobson

The Evolution of Modern Capitalism

A study of machine production

John A. Hobson

The Evolution of Modern Capitalism
A study of machine production

ISBN/EAN: 9783337237547

Printed in Europe, USA, Canada, Australia, Japan

Cover: Foto ©Suzi / pixelio.de

More available books at **www.hansebooks.com**

THE CONTEMPORARY SCIENCE SERIES.

EDITED BY HAVELOCK ELLIS.

EVOLUTION

OF MODERN CAPITALISM.

OF

MODERN CAPITALISM.

A STUDY OF MACHINE PRODUCTION.

BY

JOHN A. HOBSON, M.A.,

AUTHOR OF "PROBLEMS OF POVERTY."

LONDON:
WALTER SCOTT, LTD., PATERNOSTER SQUARE.
CHARLES SCRIBNER'S SONS,
153-157 FIFTH AVENUE, NEW YORK.
1897.

PREFACE.

IN seeking to express and illustrate some of the laws of the structural changes in modern industry, I have chosen a focus of study between the wider philosophic survey of treatises on Social Evolution and the special studies of modern machine-industry contained in such works as Babbage's *Economy of Manufactures* and Ure's *Philosophy of Manufactures*, or more recently in Professor Schulze-Gaevernitz's careful study of the cotton industry. By using the term "evolution" I have designed to mark the study as one of a subject-matter in process of organic change, and I have sought to trace in it some of those large movements which are characteristic of all natural growth.

The sub-title, *A Study of Machine-Production*, indicates a further narrowing of the investigation. Selecting the operation of modern machinery and motors for special attention, I have sought to enforce a clearer recognition of organic unity, by dwelling upon the more material aspects of industrial change which mark off the last century and a half from all former industrial epochs. The position of central importance thus assigned to machinery as a factor in industrial evolution may be—to some extent must be—deceptive, but in bringing scientific analysis to bear upon phenomena so complex and so imperfectly explored, it is essential to select some single clearly appreciable standpoint, even at the risk of failing to present the full complexity of forces in their just but bewildering interaction.

In tracing through the Business, the Trade, and the Industrial Organism the chief structural and functional changes which accompany machine-development, I have not attempted to follow out the numerous branches of social investigation which diverge from the main line of inquiry. Two studies, however, of "the competitive system" in its modern working are presented; one examining the process of restriction, by which competition of capitals gives way to different forms of combination; the other tracing in periodic Trade Depressions the natural outcome of unrestricted competition in private capitalist production.

In some final chapters I have sought to indicate the chief bearings of the changes of industrial structure upon a few of the deeper issues of social life, in particular upon the problem of the Industrial Town, and the position of woman as an industrial competitor.

A portion of Chapters VIII., IX., and X. have already appeared in the *Contemporary Review* and in the *Political Science Quarterly Review*, and I am indebted to the courtesy of the editors for permission to use them.

I have also to acknowledge most gratefully the valuable assistance rendered by Dr. William Smart of Glasgow University, who was kind enough to read through the proofs of a large portion of this book, and to make many serviceable corrections and suggestions.

JOHN A. HOBSON.

CONTENTS.

——•●•——

CHAPTER I.

PAGE

INTRODUCTION I

Section.

1. Industrial Science, its Standpoint and Methods of Advance.
2. Capital as Factor in Modern Industrial Changes.
3. Place of Machinery in Evolution of Capitalism.
4. The Monetary Aspect of Industry.
5. The Literary Presentment of Organic Movement.

CHAPTER II.

THE STRUCTURE OF INDUSTRY BEFORE MACHINERY . 10

1. Dimensions of International Commerce in early Eighteenth Century.
2. Natural Barriers to International Trade.
3. Political, Pseudo-economic, and Economic Barriers— Protective Theory and Practice.
4. Nature of International Trade.
5. Size, Structure, Relations of the several Industries.
6. Slight Extent of Local Specialisation.
7. Nature and Conditions of Specialised Industry.
8. Structure of the Market.
9. Combined Agriculture and Manufacture.

Section.   PAGE

10. Relations between Processes in a Manufacture.
11. Structure of the Domestic Business: Early Stages of Transition.
12. Beginnings of Concentrated Industry and the Factory.
13. Limitations in Size and Application of Capital—Merchant Capitalism.

CHAPTER III.

THE ORDER OF DEVELOPMENT OF MACHINE INDUSTRY   44

1. A Machine differentiated from a Tool.
2. Machinery in Relation to the Character of Human Labour.
3. Contributions of Machinery to Productive Power.
4. Main Factors in Development of Machine Industry.
5. Importance of Cotton-trade in Machine Development.
6. History refutes the " Heroic " Theory of Invention.
7. Application of Machinery to other Textile Work.
8. Reverse order of Development in Iron Trades.
9. Leading Determinants in the General Application of Machinery and Steam-Motor.
10. Order of Development of modern Industrial Methods in the several Countries—Natural, Racial, Political, Economic.

CHAPTER IV.

THE STRUCTURE OF MODERN INDUSTRY   .   .   .   88

1. Growing Size of the Business-Unit.
2. Relative Increase of Capital and Labour in the Business.
3. Increased Complexity and Integration of Business Structure.
4. Structure and Size of the Market for different Commodities.
5. Machinery a direct Agent in expanding Market Areas.
6. Expanded Time-area of the Market.
7. Interdependency of Markets.

8. Sympathetic and Antagonistic Relations between Trades.

9. National and Local Specialisation in Industry.

10. Influences determining Localisation of Industry under World-Competition.

11. Impossibility of Final Settlement of Industry.

12. Specialisation in Districts and Towns.

13. Specialisation within the Town.

CHAPTER V.

THE FORMATION OF MONOPOLIES IN CAPITAL.   .   . 117

1. Productive Economies of the Large Business.

2. Competitive Economies of the Large Business.

3. Intenser Competition of the few Large Businesses.

4. Restraint of Competition and Limited Monopoly.

5. Facilities for maintaining Price-Lists in different Industries.

6. Logical Outcome of Large-Scale Competition.

7. Different Species of "Combines."

8. Legal and Economic Nature of the "Trust."

9. Origin and *Modus Operandi* of the Standard Oil Trust.

10. The Economic Strength of other Trusts.

11. Industrial Conditions favourable to "Monopoly."

CHAPTER VI.

ECONOMIC POWERS OF THE TRUST   143

1. Power of a Monopoly over earlier or later Processes in Production of a Commodity.

2. Power over Actual or Potential Competitors.

3. Power over Employees of a Trust.

4. Power over Consumers.

5. Determinants of a Monopoly Price.

6. The Possibility of low Monopoly Prices.

7. Considerations of Elasticity of Demand limiting Prices.

8. Final Summary of Monopoly Prices.

CHAPTER VII.

MACHINERY AND INDUSTRIAL DEPRESSION . . . 167

Section.

1. The external phenomena of Trade Depression.
2. Correctly described as Under-production and Over-production.
3. Testimony to a general excess of Productive Power over the requirement for Consumption.
4. The connection of modern Machine-production and Depression shown by statistics of price.
5. Changing forms in which Over-supply of Capital is embodied.
6. Summary of economic relation of Machinery to Depression.
7. Under-consumption as the root-evil.
8. Economic analysis of " Saving."
9. Saving requires increased Consumption in the future.
10. Quantitative relation of parts in the organism of Industry.
11. Quantitative relation of Capital and Consumption.
12. Economic limits of Saving for a Community.
13. No limits to the possibility of individual Saving—Clash of individual and social interests in Saving.
14. Objection that excess in forms of Capital would drive interests to zero not valid.
15. Excess is in embodiments of Capital, not in real Capital.
16. Uncontrolled Machinery a source of fluctuation.

CHAPTER VIII.

MACHINERY AND DEMAND FOR LABOUR . . . 220

1. The Influence of Machinery upon the number of Employed, dependent on " elasticity of demand."
2. Measurement of direct effects on Employment in Staple Manufactures.
3. Effects of Machinery in other Employments—The Evidence of French Statistics.

4. Influence of Introduction of Machinery upon Regularity of Employment.
5. Effects of " Unorganised " Machine-industry upon Regularity.
6. Different Ways in which modern Industry causes Unemployment.
7. Summary of General Conclusions.

CHAPTER IX.

MACHINERY AND THE QUALITY OF LABOUR . . . 244

1. Kinds of Labour which Machinery supersedes.
2. Influence of Machine-evolution upon intensity of physical work.
3. Machinery and the length of the working day.
4. The Education of Working with Machinery.
5. The levelling tendency of Machinery—The subordination of individual capacity in work.

CHAPTER X.

THE ECONOMY OF HIGH WAGES 261

1. The Economy of Low Wages.
2. Modifications of the Early Doctrine—Sir T. Brassey's Evidence from Heavy Manual Work.
3. Wages, Hours, and Product in Machine-industry.
4. A General Application of the Economy of High Wages and Short Hours inadmissible.
5. Mutual Determination of Conditions of Employment and Productivity.
6. Compressibility of Labour and Intensification of Effort.
7. Effective Consumption dependent upon Spare Energy of the Worker.
8. Growth of Machinery in relation to Standard of Comfort.
9 Economy of High Wages dependent upon Consumption.

PAGE

CHAPTER XI.

SOME EFFECTS OF MODERN INDUSTRY UPON THE
WORKERS AS CONSUMERS 285
Section.

1. How far the different Working Classes gain from the
Fall of Prices.

2. Part of the Economy of Machine-production compensated
by the growing Work of Distribution.

3. The Lowest Class of Workers gains least from Machine-
production.

CHAPTER XII.

WOMEN IN MODERN INDUSTRY 290

1. Growing Employment of Women in Manufacture.
2. Machinery favours Employment of Women.
3. Wages of Women lower than of Men.
4. Causes of Lower Wages for Women.
5. Smaller Productivity or Efficiency of Women's Labour.
6. Factors enlarging the scope of Women's Wage-work.
7. " Minimum Wage " lower for Women—Her Labour
often subsidised from other sources.
8. Woman's Contribution to the Family Wages—Effect of
Woman's Work upon Man's Wages.
9. Tendency of Woman's Wage to low uniform level.
10. Custom and Competition as determinants of Low
Wages.
11. Lack of Organisation among Women—Effect on Wages.
12 Over-supply of Labour in Women's Employments the
root-evil.
13. Low Wages the chief cause of alleged Low " Value " of
Woman's Work.
14. Industrial Position of Woman analogous to that of Low-
skilled Men.
15. Damage to Home-life arising from Women's Wage-
work.

CHAPTER XIII.

MACHINERY AND THE MODERN TOWN 324

Section.

1. The Modern Industrial Town as a Machine-product.
2. Growth of Town as compared with Rural Population in the Old and New Worlds.
3. Limits imposed upon the Townward Movement by the Economic Conditions of World-industry.
4. Effect of increasing Town-life upon Mortality.
5. The impaired quality of Physical Life in Towns.
6. The Intellectual Education of Town-life.
7. The Moral Education of Town-life.
8. Economic Forces making for Decentralisation.
9. Desirability of Public Control of Transport Services to effect Decentralisation.
10. Long Hours and Insecurity of Work as Obstacles to Reforms.
11. The Principle of Internal Reform of Town-life.

CHAPTER XIV.

CIVILISATION AND INDUSTRIAL DEVELOPMENT . . 350

1. Imperfect Adjustment of Industrial Structure to its Environment.
2. Reform upon the Basis of Private Enterprise and Free Trade.
3. Freedom and Transparency of Industry powerless to cure the deeper Industrial Maladies.
4. Beginnings of Public Control of Machine-production.
5. Passage of Industries into a public Non-competitive Condition.
6. The *raison d'être* of Progressive Collectivism.
7. Collectivism follows the line of Monopoly.
8. Cases of " Arrested Development:" the Sweating Trades.

Section.   PAGE

9. Retardation of rate of Progress in Collective Industries.

10. Will Official Machine-work absorb an Increasing Proportion of Energy?

11. Improved Quality of Consumption the Condition of
Social Progress.

12. The Highest Division of Labour between Machinery and
Art.

13. Qualitative Consumption defeats the Law of Decreasing
Returns.

14. Freedom of Art from Limitations of Matter.

15. Machinery and Art in production of Intellectual Wealth.

16. Reformed Consumption abolishes Anti-Social Competition.

17. Life itself must become Qualitative.

18. Organic Relations between Production and Consumption.

19. Summary of Progress towards a Coherent Industrial
Organism.

INDEX 385

THE EVOLUTION
OF MODERN CAPITALISM.

THE EVOLUTION
OF MODERN CAPITALISM.

CHAPTER I.

INTRODUCTION.

§ 1. *Industrial Science, its Standpoint and Methods of Advance.*
§ 2. *Capital as Factor in Modern Industrial Changes.*
§ 3. *Place of Machinery in Evolution of Capitalism.*
§ 4. *The Monetary Aspect of Industry.*
§ 5. *The Literary Presentment of Organic Movement.*

§ 1. Science is ever becoming more and more historical in the sense that it becomes more studiously anxious to show that the laws or principles with whose exposition it is concerned not merely are rightly derived from observation of phenomena but cover the whole range of these phenomena in the explanation they afford. So likewise History is ever becoming more scientific in the sense that facts or phenomena are so ordered in their setting as to give prominence to the ideas or principles which appear to relate them and of which they are the outward expression. Thus the old sharp line of distinction has slipped away, and we see there is no ultimate barrier between a study of facts and a study of the laws or principles which dominate these facts. In this way the severance of History and Science becomes less logically justifiable. Yet it is still convenient that we should say of one branch of study that it is historical in the sense that it is directly and consciously engaged in the collection and clear expression of facts or phenomena as they stand objectively in place or time without any conscious reference to the laws which relate or explain them; of another branch of study that it is scientific because it is engaged in the discovery, formulation, and correct expression of the laws according to which facts are related, without affecting to give a full presentment of those facts.   The treatment in this book belongs in this sense to economic science rather than to industrial history as being an endeavour to discover and interpret the laws of the movement of industrial forces during the period of the eighteenth and nineteenth centuries.

It cannot, however, be pretended that any high degree of exactitude can attach to such a scientific study.

Two chief difficulties beset any attempt to explain industrial phenomena by tracing the laws of the action of the forces manifested in them.   The first is that only a limited proportion of the phenomena which at any given time constitute Industry are clearly and definitely ascertainable, and it may always be possible that the laws which satisfactorily explain the statical and dynamical relations of these may be subordinate or even counteracting forces of larger movements whose dominance would appear if all parts of the industrial whole were equally known.

The second difficulty, closely related to the first, is the inherent complexity of Industry, the continual and close interaction of a number of phenomena whose exact size and relative importance is continually shifting and baffles the keenest observer.

These difficulties, common to all sciences, are enhanced in sociological sciences by the impossibility of adequate experiment in specially prepared environments.

The degree of exactitude attainable in industrial sciences may thus appear to be limited by the development of statistical inquiry.   Since the collection of accurate statistics, even on those matters which are most important, and which lend themselves most easily to statistical description, is a modern acquirement which has not yet widely spread over the whole world, while the capacity for classifying and making right use of statistics is still rarer, it is held by some that in a study where so much depends upon accurate statements of quantity little advance is at present possible.

And it is, of course, true that until the advance of organised curiosity has provided us with a complete measurement of industrial phenomena over a wide area of commerce and over a considerable period of time, the inductive science of Economics cannot approach exactitude.

But a study which cannot claim this exactness may yet be a science, and may have its value. A hypothesis which best explains the generally apparent relation between certain known phenomena is not the less science because it is liable to be succeeded by other hypotheses which with equal relative accuracy explain a wider range of similar phenomena. It is true that in studies where we know that there exists a number of unascertained factors we shall expect a more fundamental displacement of earlier and more speculative hypotheses than in studies where we know, or think we know, that most of the phenomena with which we are concerned are equally within our ken: but the earlier scientific treatment, so far as it goes, is equally necessary and equally scientific.

In modern industrial changes many different factors, material and moral, are discernibly related to one another in many complex ways. According as one or other of the leading factors is taken for a scientific objective the study assumes a widely different character.

For example, since the end of Industry is wealth for consumption it would be possible to group the industrial phenomena accordingly as they served more fully and directly to satisfy human wants, or as they affected quantitatively or qualitatively the standard of consumption, and to consider the reflex actions of changed consumption upon modes of industrial activity. Or again, considering Industry to consist essentially of organised productive human effort, those factors most closely related to changes in nature, conditions, and intensity of work might form the centre of scientific interest; and we might group our facts and forces according to their bearing upon this. These points of view would give us different objective scientific studies.

Or, once more, taking a purely subjective standpoint, we might search out the intellectual expression of these industrial changes in the changing thought and feeling of the age, tracing the educative influences of industrial development upon (1) the deliberate judgments of the business world and of economic thinkers as reflected in economic writings; (2) politics, literature, and art through the changes of social environment, and the direct stimulation of new ideas and sentiments. The deeper and more important human bearings of the changes in industrial environment might thus be brought into prominence as well as the reaction by which, through the various social avenues of law, public opinion, and private organised activity, these intellectual forces have operated in their turn upon the industrial structure.

The crowning difficulty of an adequate scientific treatment consists in the fact that each and all of these scientific objects ought to be pursued simultaneously; that is to say, the whole of the phenomena — industrial, intellectual, political, moral, æsthetic—should be presented in their just but ever-changing proportions.

This larger philosophic treatment is only named in order that it may be realised how narrow and incomplete would be even the amplest fulfilment of the purpose indicated in the title of this book.

§ 2. Industrial science has not yet sufficiently advanced to enable a full treatment of the objective phenomena to be attempted.

The method here adopted is to take for our intellectual objective one important factor in modern industrial movements, to study the laws of its development and activity, and by observing the relations which subsist between it and other leading factors or forces in industry to obtain some clearer appreciation and understanding of the structure of industry as a whole and its relation to the evolution of human society. This central factor is indicated by the descriptive title peculiarly applied to modern industry, Capitalism. A clear view of the phenomena grouped together under the head of the Industrial Revolution cannot fail to give prominence to the changes that have taken place in the structure and functional character of Capital. Whatever transformations have taken place in the character of land, the raw material of industrial wealth, and of labour; or those abilities and faculties of man which operate upon the raw material, have occurred chiefly and directly through the agency of the enlarged and more complex use of those forms of material wealth which, while embodying some element of human effort, are not directly serviceable in satisfying human want.

Writers upon Political Economy have brought much metaphysical acumen to bear upon definitions of Capital, and have reached very widely divergent conclusions as to what the term ought to mean, ignoring the clear and fairly consistent meaning the term actually possesses in the business world around them. The business world has indeed two views of Capital, but they are consistent with one another. Abstractly, money or the control of money, sometimes called credit, is Capital. Concretely, capital consists of all forms of marketable matter which embody labour. Land or nature is excluded except for improvements: human powers are excluded as not being matter: commodities in the hands of consumers are excluded because they are no longer marketable. Thus the actual concrete forms of capital are the raw materials of production, including the finished stage of shop goods; and the plant and implements used in the several processes of industry, including the monetary implements of exchange. Concrete business capital is composed of these and of nothing but these.[1] In taking modern industrial phenomena as the subject of scientific inquiry it is better to accept such terminology as is generally and consistently received by business men, than either to invent new terms or to give a private significance to some accepted term which shall be different from that given by other scientific students, and, if we may judge from past experience, probably inferior in logical exactitude to the current meaning in the business world.

§ 3. The chief material factor in the evolution of Capital-

[1] Professor Marshall regards this restricted use of capital as "misleading," rightly urging that "there are many other things which truly perform the services commonly attributed to capital" (*Principles*, Bk. II., chap. iv.). But if we enlarge our definition so as to include all these "other things" we shall be driven to a political economy which shall widely transcend Industry as we now understand the term, and shall comprehend the whole science and art of life so far as it is concerned with human effort and satisfaction. If it is convenient and justifiable to retain for certain purposes of study the restricted connotation of Industry now in vogue, the confinement of Capital as above to Trade Capital is logically justified. For a fuller treatment of the question of the use of the term Capital in forming a terminology descriptive of the parts of Industry the reader is referred to Chapter VII., and in particular to Appendix I.

ism is machinery. The growing quantity and complexity of machinery applied to purposes of manufacture and conveyance, and to the extractive industries, is the great special fact in the narrative of the expansion of modern industry.

It is therefore to the development and influence of machinery upon industry that we shall chiefly direct our attention, adopting the following method of study. It is first essential to obtain a clear understanding of the structure of industry or "the industrial organism" as a whole, and of its constituent parts, before the new industrial forces had begun to operate. We must then seek to ascertain the laws of the development and application of the new forces to the different departments of industry and the different parts of the industrial world, examining in certain typical machine industries the order and pace of the application of the new machinery and motor to the several processes. Turning our attention again to the industrial organism, we shall strive to ascertain the chief changes that have been brought about in the size and structural character of industry, in the relations of the several parts of the industrial world, of the several trades which constitute industry, of the processes within these trades, of the businesses or units which comprise a trade or a market, and of the units of capital and labour comprising a business. It will then remain to undertake closer studies of certain important special outcomes of machinery and factory production. These studies will fall into three classes. (1) The influences of machine-production upon the size of the units of capital, the intensification and limitation of competition; the natural formation of Trusts and other forms of economic monopoly of capital; trade depressions and grave industrial disorders due to discrepancies between individual and social interests in the working of modern methods of production. (2) Effects of machinery upon labour, the quantity and regularity of employment, the character and remuneration of work, the place of women in industry (3) Effects upon the industrial classes in the capacity of consumers, the growth of the large industrial town and its influences upon the physical, intellectual, moral life of the community. Lastly, an attempt will be made to summarise the net influences of modern capitalist production in their relation to other social progressive forces, and to indicate the relations between these which seem most conducive to the welfare of a community measured by generally accepted standards of character or happiness.

§ 4. Since every industrial act in a modern community has its monetary counterpart, and its importance is commonly estimated in terms of money, it will be evident that the growth of capitalism might be studied with great advantage in its monetary aspect. Corresponding to the changes in productive methods under mechanical machinery we should find the rapid growth of a complex monetary system reflecting in its international and national character, in its elaborate structure of credit, the leading characteristics which we find in modern productive and distributive industry. The whole industrial movement might be regarded from the financial or monetary point of view. But though such a study would be capable of throwing a flood of light upon the movements of concrete industrial factors at many points, the intellectual difficulties involved in simultaneously following the double study, in constantly passing from the more concrete to the more abstract contemplation of industrial phenomena, would tax the mental agility of students too severely, and would greatly diminish the chance of a substantially accurate understanding of either aspect of modern industry. We shall therefore in this study confine our attention to the concrete aspect of capitalism, merely indicating by passing references some of the direct effects upon industrial methods, especially in the expansion and complexity of markets, of the elaborate monetary system of modern exchange.

§ 5. The inherent difficulty which besets every literary presentation of the study of a living and changing organism is here present in no ordinary degree. A book of physiology is necessarily defective in that it can neither present the just simultaneity of phenomena which occur together, nor the just sequence of phenomena which are successive. Diagrams may serve effectively to set forth tolerably simple simultaneity, but a complex diagram inevitably fails of its object; for it confuses the sight of one who seeks to simultaneously grasp the whole, and thus compels a successive examination of different parts which is generally inferior to skilled narration, in that it affords no security of the fittest order of examination of the parts. For certain simple

relations between the movements of a few definite objects
a working model may be serviceable; but when complex
changes of shape, pace, and local relations exist, when
intricate interaction takes place, and when new phenomena
arise affecting by their presence all former ones, little can
be effected by such visual presentment. Still less can a
succession of diagrams assist us to realise the continuity of
the working of such shifting forces as are presented in
industrial movements.

Thus while the impossibility of adequate experimentation,
the difficulties of scientific observations of phenomena so
vast in scope and so intricate in their relations, make the
student of sociological subjects more dependent upon
printed records for his material than is the case in most
other sciences, these printed records induce a sequence of
thought antagonistic to the grasp of a living and moving
unity. This cause is primarily responsible for the failure of
many of the ablest and subtlest economic treatises to impress
upon the reader a clear conception of the industrial world
as a single "going concern." Each piece of the mechanism
is clearly described, and the reader is informed how it fits
into the parts which are most closely related to it, but no
simultaneous grasp of the mechanism as a working whole is
attained. When we graft upon the idea of a mechanism
that character of continuous self-development which trans-
forms it into an "organism," the synthesis of the changing
phenomena is still more difficult to comprehend. These
difficulties can only be overcome by a recognition that
the scientific imagination must play a larger part here
than it does in those sciences whose subject-matter is more
amenable to direct observation. In the latter the chief
function of the imagination will be the increase of knowledge by means of hypotheses which tentatively transcend
the region of known facts.

In economic science, as Cairnes has ably shown, the use
of hypothesis is much wider, serving in large measure as a
substitute for experiment.[1] But the scientific imagination
has another constant service to perform. Its exercise is
constantly required by the economist, and in general by
the sociologist, to gather into true relations of time, space,

---

[1] *Logical Method of Political Economy*, p. 81, etc.

and causality those intricately connected phenomena which, though individually amenable to sensuous presentation, are not able to be thus presented as an aggregate in their right organic order.

The attempts to construct a deductive economic science upon a piece-meal basis by framing special and separate theories of wages, rent, value, the functions of money, and so forth, are now recognised to be in large measure failures precisely because they involve the fundamental scientific fallacy of supposing that the several parts of an organic whole can be separately studied, and that from this study of the parts we can construct a correct idea of the whole. As in economic theory so in the comprehension of industrial history, no detailed investigation of a number of different heaps of facts laboriously collected by intellectual moles will suffice for our purpose. To understand the evolution of the system of modern industry we must apply to the heaps of bare unordered facts those principles of order which are now recognised as the widest generalisations or the most valid assumptions derivable from other sciences, and endeavour without slavish conformity to the formulæ of these other sciences to trace in the growth of industrial organisms those general laws of development which seem common to all bodies of closely-related phenomena.

CHAPTER II.

THE STRUCTURE OF INDUSTRY BEFORE MACHINERY.

§ 1. *Dimensions of International Commerce in early Eighteenth Century.*

§ 2. *Natural Barriers to International Trade.*

§ 3. *Political, Pseudo-economic, and Economic Barriers— Protective Theory and Practice.*

§ 4. *Nature of International Trade.*

§ 5. *Size, Structure, Relations of the several Industries.*

§ 6. *Slight Extent of Local Specialisation.*

§ 7. *Nature and Conditions of Specialised Industry.*

§ 8. *Structure of the Market.*

§ 9. *Combined Agriculture and Manufacture.*

§ 10. *Relations between Processes in a Manufacture.*

§ 11. *Structure of the Domestic Business: Early Stages of Transition.*

§ 12. *Beginnings of Concentrated Industry and the Factory.*

§ 13. *Limitations in Size and Application of Capital— Merchant Capitalism.*

§ 1. In order to get some clear understanding of the laws of the operation of the new industrial forces which prevail under machine-production it is first essential to know rightly the structure and functional character of the "industrial organism" upon which they were destined to act. In order to build up a clear conception of industry it is possible to take either of two modes of inquiry. Taking as the primary cell or unit that combination of labour and capital under a single control for a single industrial purpose which is termed a Business, we may examine the structure and life of the Business, then proceed to discover how it stands related to other businesses so as to form a Market, and, finally, how the several Markets are related locally, nationally, internationally so as to yield the complex structure of Industry as a whole. Or reversely, we may take Industry as a whole, the Industrial Organism as it exists at any given time, consider the nature and extent of the cohesion existing between its several parts, and, further, resolving these parts into their constituent elements, gain a close understanding of the extent to which differentiation of industrial functions has been carried in the several divisions.

Although in any sociological inquiry these two methods are equally valid, or, more strictly speaking, are equally balanced in virtues and defects, the latter method is here to be preferred, because by the order of its descent from the whole to the constituent parts it brings out more definitely the slight cohesiveness and integration of industry beyond the national limits, and serves to emphasise those qualities of nationalism and narrow localism which mark the character of earlier eighteenth century industry. We are thus enabled better to recognise the nature and scope of the work wrought by the modern industrial forces which are the central object of study.

While the Market or the Trade is less and less determined or confined by national or other political boundaries in modern times, and nationalism is therefore a factor of diminishing importance in the modern science of economics, the paramount domination of politics over large commerce in the last century, acting in co-operation with other racial and national forces, obliges any just analysis of eighteenth century industry to give clear and early emphasis to the slight character of the commercial interdependency among nations. The degree of importance which statesmen and economists attached to this foreign commerce as compared with home trade, and the large part it played in the discussion and determination of public conduct, have given it a prominence in written history far beyond its real value.[1]

It is true that through the Middle Ages a succession of European nations rose to eminence by the development of navigation and international trade, Italy, Portugal, Spain, France, Holland, and England; but neither in size nor in

---

[1] A. Smith, *Wealth of Nations*, Bk. iv., chap. i.

character was this trade of the first importance. Even in the case of those nations where it was most developed it formed a very small proportion of the total industry of the country, and it was chiefly confined to spicery, bullion, ornamental cloths, and other objects of art and luxury.

It is important to recognise that in the first half of the eighteenth century international trade still largely partook of this character. Not only did it bear a far smaller proportion to the total industry of the several countries than does foreign trade to-day, but it was still engaged to a comparatively small extent with the transport of necessaries or prime conveniences of life. Each nation, as regards the more important constituents of its consumption, its staple foods, articles of clothing, household furniture, and the chief implements of industry, was almost self-sufficing, producing little that it did not consume, consuming little it did not produce.

In 1712 the export trade of England is officially estimated at £6,644,103,[1] or considerably less than one-sixth of the home trade of that date as calculated by Smith in his *Memoirs of Wool.* Such an estimate, however, gives an exaggerated impression of the relation of foreign to home trade, because under the latter no account is taken of the large domestic production of goods and services which figure in no statistics. A more instructive estimate is that which values the total consumption of the English people in 1713 at forty-nine or fifty millions, out of which about four millions covers the consumption of foreign goods.[2] In 1740 imports amounted to £6,703,778, exports to £8,197,788. In 1750 they had risen respectively to £7,772,339 and £12,699,081,[3] and ten years later to £9,832,802 and £14,694,970. Macpherson, whose *Annals of Commerce* are a mine of wealth upon the history of foreign commerce in the eighteenth century, after commenting upon the impossibility of obtaining a

---

[1] Macpherson, *Annals of Commerce,* vol. ii. p. 728.
[2] Smith, *Memoirs,* vol. ii., chap. iii. As the approximate calculation of a very competent business man these figures are more reliable than the official figures of imports and exports, the value of which throughout the eighteenth century is seriously impaired by the fact that they continued to be estimated by the standard of values of 1694.
[3] Whitworth's *State* quoted, Macpherson, vol. iii. p. 283.

just estimate of the value of home trade, alludes to a calculation which places it at thirty-two times the size of the export trade. Macpherson contents himself with concluding that it is "a vast deal greater in value than the

PROGRESS OF FOREIGN TRADE IN ENGLAND.

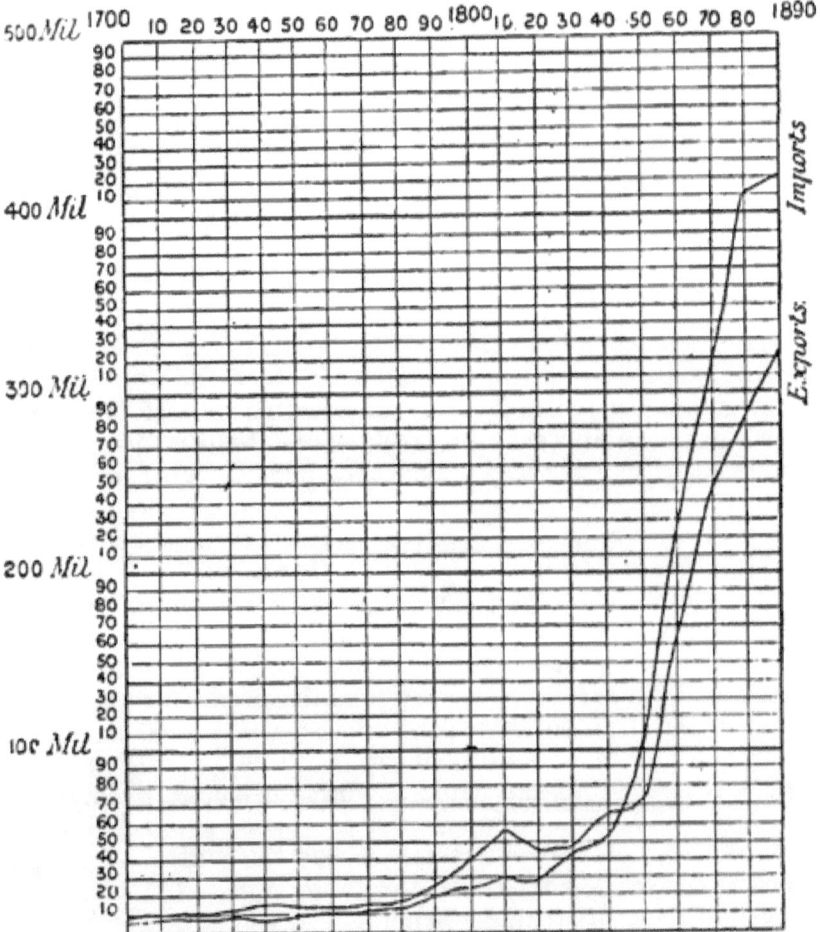

whole of the foreign trade."[1] There is every reason to believe that in the case of Holland and France, the only two other European nations with a considerable foreign trade, the same general conclusion will apply.

[1] *Annals*, vol. iii. p. 340.

The smallness of the part which foreign trade played in industry signifies that in the earlier part of the eighteenth century the industrial organism as a whole must be regarded as a number of tolerably self-sufficing and therefore homogeneous national forms attached to one another by bonds which are few and feeble. As yet there was little specialisation in national industry, and therefore little integration of national parts of the world-industry.

§ 2. Since the breaking-down of international barriers and the strengthening of the industrial bonds of attachment between nations will be seen to be one of the most important effects of the development of machine-industry, some statement of the nature of these barriers and their effect upon the size and character of international trade is required.

Though considerable advances had been made by England and Holland at the beginning of the eighteenth century in the improvement of harbours, the establishment of lighthouses, and the development of marine insurance,[1] navigation was still subject to considerable risks of the loss of life and of investments, while these "natural" dangers were increased by the prevalence of piracy. Voyages were slow and expensive, commerce between distant nations being necessarily confined to goods of a less perishable character which would stand the voyage. Trade in fresh foods, which forms so large a part of modern commerce, would have been impossible except along the coasts of adjoining nations. With these natural barriers to commerce may be reckoned the defective knowledge of the position, resources, and requirements of large parts of the earth which now fill an important place in commerce. The new world was but slightly opened up, nor could its known resources be largely utilised before the development of more adequate machinery of transport. We can scarcely realise the inconveniences, costs, and risks entailed by the more distant branches of foreign trade at a time when the captain of a merchant-ship still freighted his vessel at his own expense, and when each voyage was a separate speculation. Even in the early nineteenth century the manufacturer commonly shipped his surplus produce at his own risk, employing the merchant

<hr>

[1] Cunningham, *History of English Industry*, vol. ii. p. 287, etc.

upon commission, and in the trade with the Indies, China, or South America he had frequently to lie out of his money or his return freight of indigo, coffee, tea, etc., for as long as eighteen months or two years, and to bear the expense of warehousing as well as the damage which time and tide inflicted on his goods.

§ 3. Next come a series of barriers, partly political, partly pseudo-economic, in which the antagonism of nations took shape, the formation of political and industrial theories which directed the commercial intercourse of nations into certain narrow and definite channels.

Two economic doctrines, separate in the world of false ideas, though their joint application in the world of practice has led many to confuse them, exercised a dominant influence in diminishing the quantity, and determining the quality of international trade in the eighteenth century. These doctrines had reference respectively to the construction and maintenance of home industries and the balance of trade. The former doctrine, which was not so much a consciously-evolved theory as a short-sighted, intellectual assumption driven by the urgent impulse of vested interests into practical effect, taught that, on the one hand, import trade should be restricted to commodities which were not and could not with advantage be produced at home, and to the provision of cheap materials for existing manufactures; while export trade, on the other hand, should be generally encouraged by a system of bounties and drawbacks. This doctrine was first rigidly applied by the French minister, Colbert, but the policy of France was faithfully copied by England and other commercial nations and ranked as an orthodox theory of international trade.

The Balance of Trade doctrine estimated the worth of a nation's intercourse with another by the excess of the export over the import trade, which brought a quantity of bullion into the exporting country. This theory was also widely spread, though obviously its general application would have been destructive of all international commerce. The more liberal interpretation of the doctrine was satisfied with a favourable balance of the aggregate export over the aggregate import trade of the country, but the stricter interpretation, generally dominant in practice, required that in the case of each particular nation the balance should be favourable. In regarding England's commerce with a foreign nation, any excess in import values over export was spoken of as "a loss to England." England deliberately cut off all trade with France during the period 1702 to 1763 by a system of prohibitive tariffs urged by a double dread lest the balance should be against us, and lest French textile goods might successfully compete with English goods in the home markets. On the other hand, we cultivated trade with Portugal because "we gain a greater balance from Portugal than from any other country whatever." The practical policy prevalent in 1713 is thus summarised by one of its enthusiastic upholders—"We suffer the goods and merchandises of Holland, Germany, Portugal, and Italy to be imported and consumed among us; and it is well we do, for we export a much greater value of our own to those countries than we take from them. So that the consumption of those nations pays much greater sums to the rents of our lands and the labour of our people than ours does to theirs. But we keep out as much as possible the goods and merchandises of France, because our consumption of theirs would very much hinder the consumption of our own, and abate a great part of forty-two millions which it now pays to the rents of our lands and the labour of our people."[1] Thus our policy was to confine our import trade to foreign luxuries and raw materials of manufacture which could not be here produced, drawn exclusively from countries where such trade would not turn the balance against us, and, on the other hand, to force our export trade on any country that would receive it. Since every European nation was largely influenced by similar ideas and motives, and enforced upon their colonies and dependencies a like line of conduct, many mutually profitable exchanges were prevented, and commerce was confined to certain narrow and artificial grooves, while the national industrial energy was wasted in the production of many things at home which could have been more cheaply obtained from foreign countries through exchange.

The following example may suffice to illustrate the intricacy of the legislation passed in pursuance of this policy. It describes a change of detailed policy in support and regulation of textile trade :—

[1] Smith, *Memoirs of Wool*, vol. ii. p. 113.

" A tax was laid on foreign linens in order to provide a
fund for raising hemp and flax at home; while bounties
were given on these necessary articles from our colonies,
the bounty on the exportation of hemp was withdrawn.
The imposts on foreign linen yarn were withdrawn.
Bounties were given on British linen cloth exported ; while
the making of cambricks was promoted, partly by pro-
hibiting the foreign and partly by giving fresh incentives,
though without success, to the manufacture of cambricks
within our island.   Indigo, cochineal, and logwood, the
necessaries of dyes, were allowed to be freely imported." [1]

The encouragement of English shipping (partly for commercial, partly for political reasons) took elaborate shape in
the Navigation Acts, designed to secure for English vessels
a monopoly of the carrying trade between England and all
other countries which sent goods to English or to colonial
shores.   This policy was supported by a network of minor
measures giving bounties to our colonies for the exportation
of shipping materials, pitch, tar, hemp, turpentine, masts,
and spars, and giving bounties at home for the construction
of defensible ships.   This Navigation policy gave a strong
foundational support to the whole protective policy.   Probably the actuating motives of this policy were more
political than industrial.   Holland, the first to apply this
method systematically, had immensely strengthened her
maritime power.   France, though less successfully, had
followed in her wake.   Doubtless there were many clear-
thinking Englishmen who, though aware of the damage
done to commerce by our restrictive regulations about
shipping, held that the maintenance of a powerful navy
for the defence of the kingdom and its foreign possessions
was an advantage which outweighed the damage.[2]

The selfish and short-sighted policy of this protective
system found its culminating point in the treatment of
Ireland and the American plantations.   The former was
forbidden all manufacture which might either directly or
indirectly compete with English industry, and was compelled to deal exclusively with England; the American
colonies were forbidden to weave cloth, to make hats, or to

[1] Chalmers, *Estimates*, p. 148.
[2] Cf. Cunningham, *Growth of English Industry*, vol. ii. p. 292.

forge a bolt, and were compelled to take all the manufactured goods required for their consumption from England.

The freedom and expansion of international commerce
was further hampered by the policy of assigning monopolies
of colonial and foreign trade to close Chartered Companies.
This policy, however, defensible as an encouragement of
early mercantile adventure, was carried far beyond these
legitimate limits in the eighteenth century. In England
the East Indian was the most powerful and successful of
these companies, but the assignment of the trade with
Turkey, Russia, and other countries to chartered companies
was a distinct hindrance to the development of foreign
trade.

Our foreign trade at that period might indeed be classed
or graded in accordance with the degree of encouragement
or discouragement offered by the State.

Imports would fall into four classes.

1. Imports forbidden either (*a*) by legislative prohibition, or (*b*) by prohibitive taxation.
2. Imports admitted but taxed.
3. Free imports.
4. Imports encouraged by bounties.

Exports might be graded in similar fashion.

1. Prohibited exports (*e.g.*, sheep and wool, raw
hides, tanned leather, woollen yarn, textile implements,[1] certain forms of skilled labour).
2. Exports upon which duties are levied (*e.g.*,
coals[2]).
3. Free exports.
4. Exports encouraged by bounties, or by drawbacks.

The unnatural and injurious character of most of this
legislation is best proved by the notable inability to
effectively enforce its application. The chartered companies were continually complaining of the infringement of
their monopolies by private adventurers, and more than one
of them failed through inability to crush out this illegal
competition. A striking condemnation of our policy to-

---

[1] Smith, *Wealth of Nations*, Bk. iv., chap. viii.   [2] *Ibid.*

wards France consisted in the growth of an enormous illicit trade which, in spite of the difficulties which beset it, made a considerable part of our aggregate foreign trade during the whole of the century. The lack of any clear perception of the mutuality of advantage in foreign and colonial trade was the root fallacy which underlay these restrictions. Professor Cunningham rightly says of the colonial policy of England, that it "implied that each distinct member should strengthen the head, and not at all that these members should mutually strengthen each other."[1]

So, as we tried to get the better of our colonies, still more rigorously did we apply the same methods to foreign countries, regarding each gain which accrued to us as an advantage which would have wholly gone to the foreigner if we had not by firmness and enterprise secured it for ourselves.

The slight extent of foreign intercourse was, however, partly due to causes which are to be regarded as genuinely economic. The life and experience of the great mass of the population of all countries was extremely restricted; they were a scattered and rural folk whose wants and tastes were simple, few, home-bred, and customary. The customary standard of consumption, slowly built up in conformity with local production, gave little encouragement to foreign trade. Moreover, to meet the new tastes and the more varied consumption which gradually found its way over this country, it was in conformity with the economic theory and practice of the day to prefer the establishment of new home industries, equipped if necessary with imported foreign labour, to the importation of the products of such labour from abroad. So far as England, in particular, is concerned, the attitude was favoured by the political and religious oppression of the French government which supplied England in the earlier eighteenth century with a constant flow of skilled artisan labour. Many English manufacturers profited by this flow. Our textile industries in silk, wool, and linen, calico-printing, glass, paper, and pottery are special beholden to the new arts thus introduced.

Among the economic barriers must be reckoned the

---

[1] *Growth of English Industry*, vol. ii. p. 303.

slight development of international credit, and of the machinery of exchange.

§ 4. These barriers, natural, political, social, economic, against free international intercourse, throw important light upon the general structure of world-industry in the eighteenth century.

In this application they determined and strictly limited not only the quantity but the nature of the international trade. The export trade of England, for example, in 1730 was practically confined to woollen goods and other textile materials, a small quantity of leather, iron, lead, silver, and gold plate, and a certain number of re-exported foreign products, such as tobacco and Indian calicoes. The import trade consisted of wine and spirits, foreign foods, such as rice, sugar, coffee, oil, furs, and some quantity of foreign wool, hemp, silk, and linen-yarn, as material for our specially favoured manufactures. Having regard to the proportion of the several commodities, it would not be much exaggeration to summarise our foreign trade by saying that we sent out woollen goods and received foreign foods. These formed the great bulk of our foreign trade.[1] Excepting the woollen goods and a small trade in metals, leather is the only manufactured article which figured to any appreciable extent in our export of 1730. At that time it is clear that in the main English manufacture, as well as English agriculture, was for the supply of English wants. The same was true of other industrial countries. Holland and France, who divided with England the shipping supremacy, had a foreign trade which, though then deemed considerable, bore no greater proportion to the total industry of these countries than in the case of England. Germany, Italy, Russia, Spain, and even Portugal were almost wholly self-sustained.

Regarding, then, the known and related world of that time in the light of an industrial organism, we must consider it as one in which the processes of integration and of differentiation of parts has advanced but a little way, consisting as yet of a number of homogeneous and incoherent national cells.

This homogeneity is of course qualified by differences in production and consumption due to climate, natural pro-

---

[1] Macpherson, *Annals*, vol. iii. pp. 155, 156.

ducts, national character and institutions, and the development of industrial arts in the several nations.

§ 5. This consideration of the approximate homogeneity of the national units of world-industry gives a higher scientific value to the analysis of a single typical industrial nation such as England than would be the case in modern times, when the work of differentiation of industrial functions among the several nations has advanced much further.

Taking, therefore, the national industry of England as the special subject of analysis, we may seek to obtain a clear conception of the size, structure, and connections of the several branches of industry, paying special regard to the manufactures upon which the new industrial forces were chiefly to operate.

It is not possible to form a very accurate estimate of the relative importance of the different industries as measured either by the money value of their products, or by the amount of labour engaged in producing them. Eighteenth century statistics, as we saw, furnished no close estimate of the total income of the nation or of the value of home industries. Since no direct census of the English population was taken before 1805, the numbers were never exactly known, and eighteenth century economists spent much time and ingenuity in trying to ascertain the growth of population by calculations based upon the number of occupied houses, or by generalising from slender and unreliable local statistics, without in the end arriving at any close agreement. Still less reliable will be the estimates of the relative size and importance of the different industries.

Two such attempts, however, one slightly prior to the special period we are investigating, and one a little later, may be taken as general indications of the comparative importance of the great divisions of industry, agriculture, manufacture, distribution or commerce.

The first is that of Gregory King in the year 1688. King's calculation, however, can only be regarded as roughly approximate. The quantity of combined agriculture and manufacture, and the amount of domestic industry for domestic consumption, renders the manufacturing figures, however carefully they might have been collected, very deceptive. The same criticism, though to a less degree, applies to the estimate of Arthur Young for 1769.

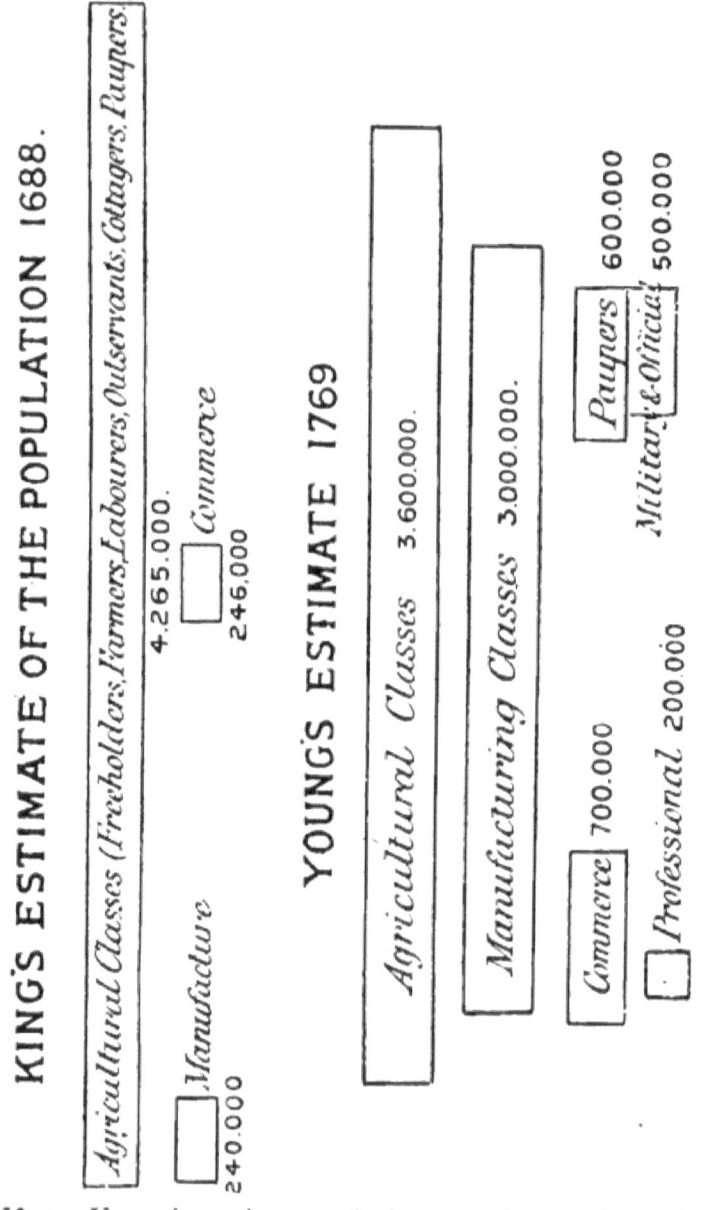

KING'S ESTIMATE OF THE POPULATION 1688.

Agricultural Classes (Freeholders, Farmers, Labourers, Outservants, Cottagers, Paupers) 4.265.000.

Commerce 246,000

Manufacture 240.000

YOUNG'S ESTIMATE 1769

Agricultural Classes 3.600.000.

Manufacturing Classes 3.000.000.

Paupers 600.000

Military & Official 500.000

Commerce 700.000

Professional 200.000

If to Young's estimate of the population dependent upon agriculture we add the class of landlords and their direct dependents and a proper proportion of the non-industrious poor, who, though not to be so classed in a direct measurement of occupations, are supported out of the produce of agriculture, we shall see that in 1769 we are justified in believing that agriculture was in its productiveness almost equivalent to the whole of manufactures and commerce.

In turning to the several branches of manufacture, the abnormal development of one of them, viz. the woollen, for purposes of foreign trade, marks the first and only con siderable specialisation of English industry before the advent of steam machinery. With the single exception of woollen goods almost the whole of English manufactures were for home consumption. At the opening of the eighteenth century, and even as late as 1770, no other single manufacture played any comparable part in the composition of our export trade.

According to Chalmers,[1] in the period 1699-1701, the annual value of woollen exports was over two and a half million pounds, or about two-fifths of the total export trade, while in 1769-71 it still amounted to nearly one-third of the whole, giving entire or partial employment to no fewer than "a million and a half of people," or half of the total number assigned by Young to manufacture.

Next to the woollen, but far behind in size and importance, came the iron trade. In 1720 England seems to have developed her mining resources so imperfectly as to be in the condition of importing from foreign countries 20,000 out of the 30,000 tons required for her hardware manufactures.[2] Almost all this iron was destined to home consumption with the exception of hardware forced upon the American colonies, who were forbidden to manufacture for themselves. In 1720 it is calculated that mining and manufacture of iron and hardware employed 200,000 persons.[3]

Copper and brass manufactures employed some 30,000 persons in 1720.[4]

Silk was the only other highly developed and consider-

[1] Chalmers, *Estimate*, p. 208. See, however, Baines, who gives a slightly smaller estimate, *History of the Cotton Manufacture*, p. 112.
[2] Macpherson, *Annals*, vol. iii. p. 114.
[3] *Ibid.*, vol. iii. p. 73.   [4] *Ibid.*, vol. iii. p. 73.

able manufacture. It had, however, to contend with Indian competition, introduced by the East India Company, and also with imported calicoes.[1] In 1750 there were about 13,000 looms in England, the product of which was almost entirely used for home consumption. Cotton and linen were very small manufactures during the first half of the eighteenth century. At the beginning of the century the linen trade was chiefly in the hands of Russia and Germany, although it had taken root in Ireland as early as the close of the seventeenth century, and was worked to some extent in Lancashire, Leicestershire, and round Darlington in Yorkshire, which districts supplied the linen-warp to the cotton weavers.[2] As for cotton, even in 1760 not more than 40,000 persons were engaged in the manufacture, and in 1764 the cotton exports were but one-twentieth of the value of the woollen exports.[3] The small value of the cotton trade and an anticipatory glance at its portentous after-growth is conveyed in the following figures :—

Home Market.		Export Trade.
1766	£379,241	£220,759 (Postletwayte)
1819-21	13,044,000	15,740,000
1829-31	13,351,000	18,074,000 } (Ellison[4])

The many other little manufactures which had sprung up, such as glass, paper, tin-plate, produced entirely for home consumption, and employed but a small number of workers.

§ 6. If we turn from the consideration of the size of English industry and the several departments to the analysis of its structure and the relation to the several trades, we shall find the same signs of imperfect organic development which we found in the world-industry, though not so strongly marked. Just as we found each country in the main self-sufficing, so we find each district of England (with a few significant exceptions) engaged chiefly in producing for its own consumption. There was far less local specialisation in industry than we

[1] Smith, Memoirs on Wool, vol. ii. pp. 19, 45.
[2] Smith, ibid., vol. ii. p. 270 ; cf. also Cunningham, Growth of English Industry, vol. ii. p. 300.
[3] Toynbee, Industrial Revolution, p. 50.
[4] Schulze-Gaevernitz, Der Grossbetrieb, p. 77.

find to-day. The staple industries, tillage, stock-raising, and those connected with the supply of the common articles of clothing, furniture, fuel, and other necessaries were widespread over the whole country.

Though far more advanced than foreign intercourse, the internal trade between more distant parts of England was extremely slight. Defective facilities of communication and transport were of course in large measure responsible for this.

The physical obstructions to such freedom of commerce as now subsists were very considerable in the eighteenth century. The condition of the main roads in the country at the opening of the century was such as to make the carriage of goods long and expensive. Agricultural produce was almost entirely for local consumption, with the exception of cattle and poultry, which were driven on foot from the neighbouring counties into London and other large markets.[1] In the winter, even round London, bad roads were a great obstacle to trade. The impossibility of driving cattle to London later than October often led to a monopoly of winter supply and high prices.[2] The growth of turnpike roads, which proceeded apace in the first half of the century, led to the large substitution of carts for pack horses, but even these roads were found "execrable" by Arthur Young, and off the posting routes and the neighbourhood of London the communication was extremely difficult. "The great roads of England remained almost in this ancient condition even as late as 1752 and 1754, when the traveller seldom saw a turnpike for two hundred miles after leaving the vicinity of London."[3]

Rivers rather than roads were the highways of commerce, and many Acts were passed in the earlier eighteenth century for improving the navigability of rivers, as the Trent, Ouse, and Mersey, partly in order to facilitate internal trade and partly to enable towns like Leeds and Derby to engage directly in trade by sea,[4] and to connect adjoining towns such as Liverpool and Manchester. In 1755 the first canal was constructed, and in the latter part of the century the part played by canals in the development of the

[1] Defoe, *Tour*, vol. ii. p. 371.
[2] *Ibid.*, vol. ii. p. 370.
[3] Chalmers, pp. 124, 125.
[4] Defoe, *Tour*, vol. iii. p. 9, etc.

new factory system was considerable. But in spite of these efforts to improve methods of transport in the earlier eighteenth century, it is evident that the bulk of industry was engaged in providing articles for local consumption, and that the area of the market for most products was extremely narrow.

The facile transport of both capital and labour, which is essential to highly specialised local industry, was retarded not merely by lack of knowledge of the opportunities of remunerative investment, but also by legal restrictions which had the influence of checking the free application and migration of labour. The Statute of Apprentices by requiring a seven years' apprenticeship[1] in many trades, and the Law of Settlement by impairing mobility of labour, are to be regarded as essentially protective measures calculated to prevent that concentrated application of capital and labour required for specialisation of industry.

Within the nation we had for the most part a number of self-sufficing communities, or, in other words, there was little specialisation of function in the several parts, and little integration in the national industry. With the single exception of Holland, whose admirable natural and artificial water communication seemed to give unity to its commerce, the other countries of Europe, France, Germany, Italy, Spain, Russia, were still more disintegrated in their industry.

§ 7. In regarding those districts of England in which strong indications of growing industrial specialisation showed themselves, it is important to observe the degree and character of that specialisation.

We find various branches of the woollen, silk, cotton, iron, hardware, and other manufactures allocated to certain districts. But if we compare this specialisation with that which obtains to-day we shall observe wide differences.

In the first place, it was far less advanced. The woollen industry of England, though conveniently divided into three districts—one in the Eastern Counties, with Norwich, Colchester, Sandwich, Canterbury, Maidstone, for principal centres; one in the West, with Taunton, Devizes, Bradford (in Wilts), Frome, Trowbridge, Stroud, and Exeter; and the third, in the West Riding, is in reality distributed over

---

[1] Smith, *Wealth of Nations*, vol. i., chap. x., part 2.

almost the whole of England south of the Thames, and over a large part of Yorkshire, to say nothing of the widespread

INDUSTRIAL ENGLAND IN 1830.

LARGE TEXTILE DISTRICTS | IRON CENTRES ●
TEXTILE CENTRES ■   TEXTILE AND IRON DISTRICTS
LARGE IRON DISTRICTS

production, either for private consumption or for the market, in Westmoreland, Cumberland, and indeed all the North of England. Where the land was richer in pasture or with easier access to large supplies of wool, the clothing manufactures were more flourishing and gave more employment, but over all the southern and most of the northern counties some form of woollen manufacture was carried on.

The only part of England which Defoe regarded as definitely specialised in manufacture is part of the West Riding, for though agriculture is carried on here to some extent, the chief manufacturing district is dependent upon surrounding districts for its main supply of food.[1]

Iron, the industry of next, though of far inferior importance, was of necessity less widely distributed. But in 1737 the fifty-nine furnaces in use were distributed over no fewer than fifteen counties, Sussex, Gloucester, Shropshire, Yorkshire, and Northumberland taking the lead.[2] So too the industries engaged in manufacturing metal goods were far less concentrated than in the present day. Though Sheffield and Birmingham even in Defoe's time were the great centres of the trade, of the total consumption of the country the greater part was made in small workshops scattered over the land.

Nottingham and Leicester were beginning to specialise in cotton and woollen hosiery, but a good deal was made round London, and generally in the woollen counties of the south. Silk was more specialised owing to the importation of special skill and special machinery to Spitalsfield, Stockport, Derby, and a few other towns. In Coventry it was only the second trade in 1727.[3]

The scattered crafts of the wheelwright, the smith, carpenter, turner, carried on many of the subsidiary processes of building, manufacture of vehicles and furniture, which are now for the most part highly centralised industries.

When we come presently to consider the structure of the several industries we shall see that even those trades which are allocated to certain local areas are much less concentrated within these areas than is now the case.

But though stress is here laid upon the imperfect differentiation of localities in industry, it is not to be supposed that the eighteenth century shows England a simple industrial community with no considerable specialisation.

[1] Defoe, *Tour*, vol. iii. p. 84.
[2] Scrivener, *History of the Iron Trade*.
[3] Defoe, *Tour*, vol. ii. p. 323.

Three conditions of specialised industry are clearly discernible in the early eighteenth century — conditions which always are among the chief determinants.

1. *Physical aptitudes of soil—e.g.*, since timber was still used almost entirely for smelting, iron works are found where timber is plentiful or where river communication makes it easily procurable. So the more fertile meadows of Gloucester and Somerset led these districts to specialise in the finer branches of the woollen trade. A still more striking example is that of South Lancashire. By nature it was ill-suited for agriculture, and therefore its inhabitants employed themselves largely in the cotton and woollen trades. The numerous little streams which flowed from the hills to the neighbouring sea gave plenty of water-power, and thus made this district the home of the earlier mills and the cradle of machine-industry.[1] The "grit" of the local grindstones secured the supremacy of Sheffield cutlery, while the heavy clay required for the "seggars," or boxes in which pottery is fired, helped to determine the specialisation of Staffordshire in this industry.[2]

2. *Facility of Market.*—The country round London, Bristol, and other larger towns became more specialised than the less accessible and more evenly populated parts, because the needs of a large town population compelled the specialisation in agriculture of much of the surrounding country; cottagers could more easily dispose of their manufactures; improved roads and other facilities for conveyance induced a specialisation impossible in the purely rural parts.

3. *The Nature of the Commodity.*—When all modes of conveyance were slow the degree of specialisation depended largely upon the keeping quality of the goods. From this point of view hardware and textiles are obviously more amenable to local specialisation than the more perishable forms of food. Where conveyance is difficult and expensive a commodity bulky for its value is less suitable for local

[1] Schulze-Gaevernitz, *Der Grossbetrieb*, p. 52.
[2] Cf. Marshall, *Principles*, p. 328. In the case of Staffordshire, however, there existed an early trade in wooden platters dependent on quality of timber and traditional skill. When the arts of pottery came in, the new trade taken up in the same locality ousted the old, though there was no particular local advantage in materials.

specialisation in production than one containing a high
value in small weight and bulk. So cloth is more suitable
for trade than corn;[1] and coal, save where navigation is
possible, could not be profitably taken any distance.[2]

The common commodities consumed, as food, fuel, and
shelter, were thus excluded from any considerable amount
of specialisation in their production.

§ 8. Turning from consideration of the attributes of
goods and of the means of transport which served to limit
the character of internal trade and determine the size of
the market, let us now regard the structure of the market,
the central object in the mechanism of internal commerce.

The market, not the industry, is the true term which
expresses the group of organically related businesses.
How far did England present a national market? How
far was the typical market a district or purely local
one?

The one great national market town was London. It
alone may be said to have drawn supplies from the whole
of England, and there alone was it possible to purchase at
any season of the year every kind of produce, agricultural
or manufactured, made anywhere in England or imported
from abroad. This flow to and from the great centre of
population was incessant, and extended to the furthermost
parts of the land. Other large towns, such as Bristol, Leeds,
Norwich, maintained close and constant relations with the
neighbouring counties, but exchanged their produce for
the most part only indirectly with that of more distant parts
of the country.

The improving communication of the eighteenth century
enabled the clothiers and other leading manufacturers to
distribute more of their wares even in the remotest parts of
the country, but the value paid for their wares reached the
vendors by slow and indirect channels of trade, passing for
the most part through the metropolis.

But while London was the one constant national
market-place, national trade was largely assisted by fairs
held for several weeks each year at Stourbridge, Winchester,
and other convenient centres. At the most important of

---

[1] Smith, *Wealth of Nations*, Book III., chap. iii.

[2] Westmoreland coal did not compete in the Newcastle market.—
Wealth of Nations, Book I., chap. xi. p. 2.

these the large merchants and manufacturers met their customers, and business was transacted between distant parts of the country, including all kinds of wares, English and foreign. Thus we had one constant and two or three intermittent avenues of free national trade. The great bulk of markets, however, were confined within far smaller areas.

In the more highly developed and specialised textile trades certain regular market-places were established of wide local importance. The largest of these specialised district markets were at Leeds, Halifax, Norwich, and Exeter. Here the chief local manufacturers of cloth, worsted, or crape met the merchants and factors and disposed of their wares to these distributing middlemen.

It was, however, in the general market-places of the county town or smaller centres of population that the mass of the business of exchange was transacted. There the mass of the small workers in agriculture and manufacture brought the product of their labour and sold it, buying what they needed for consumption and for the pursuance of their craft. Only in considerable towns were there to be found in the earlier eighteenth century any number of permanent shops where all sorts of wares could be bought at any time. The weekly market in the market-town was the chief medium of commerce for the great mass of the population.

Regarding the general structure of Industry we see that not only are international bonds slight and unessential, but that within the nation the elements of national cohesion are feeble as compared with those which subsist now. We have a number of small local communities whose relations, though tolerably strong with other communities in their immediate neighbourhood, become greatly weakened by distance. For the most part these small communities are self-sufficing for work and life, producing most of their own necessaries, and only dependent on distant and unknown producers for their comforts and luxuries.

Trade is for the most part conducted on a small steady local basis with known regular customers.

Outside of agriculture the elements of speculation and fluctuation are almost entirely confined to foreign trade.

Capital and labour are fixed to a particular locality and a particular business.[1]

§ 9. Turning to the structure of the several industries we find that different employments are not sharply separated from one another. In the first place, agriculture and manufacture are not only carried on in the same locality but by the same people. This combined agriculture and manufacture took several forms.

The textile industries were largely combined with agriculture. Where spinning was carried on in agricultural parts there was, for the most part, a division of labour within the family. The women and children spun while the men attended to their work in the fields.[2] Every woman and child above the age of five found full employment in the spinning and weaving trades of Somerset and the West Riding.[3]

This method prevailed more largely in the spinning than in the weaving trades, for before the introduction of the spinning-jenny the weaving trade was far more centralised than the other. For example, a large quantity of weaving was done in the town of Norwich while the earlier process was executed in the scattered cottages over a wide district. But even these town workers were not specialised in manufacture to the extent which prevails to-day. Large numbers of them had allotments in the country to which they gave their spare time, and many had pasture rights and kept their cattle on the common lands. This applied not merely to the textile but to other industries. At West Bromwich, a chief centre of the metal trade, agriculture was still carried on as a subsidiary pursuit by the metal workers.[4] So too the cutlers of Sheffield living in the outskirts of the town had their plot of land and carried on agriculture to a small extent, a practice which has lasted almost up to the present day. The combined agriculture and manufacture often

---

[1] Adam Smith, writing later in the century, observes with some exaggeration, "A merchant, it has been said very properly, is not necessarily the citizen of a particular country. It is in a great measure indifferent to him from what place he carries on his trade, and a very trifling disgust will make him remove his capital, and together with it all the industry which it supports, from one country to another."— Book III., chap. iv.

[2] Defoe, vol. ii. p. 37.   [3] *Ibid.*, vol. ii. p. 17.

[4] *Annals of Agriculture*, chap. iv. p. 157.

took the form of a division of labour according to season. Where the weaving was not concentrated in towns it furnished a winter occupation to many men who gave the bulk of their summer time to agriculture. Generally speaking, we may take as fairly representative of the manufacturing parts of England the picture which Defoe gave of the condition of affairs in the neighbourhood of Halifax. He found "the land divided into small enclosures from two acres to six or seven acres each, seldom more; every three or four pieces of land had a house belonging to it—one continued village, hardly a house standing out of speaking distance from another—at every house a tenter, and on almost every tenter a piece of cloth or kersie or shalloon—every clothier keeps a horse—so every one generally keeps a cow or two for his family."[1]

Not only were agriculture and many forms of manufacture conjoined, but the division of labour and differentiation of processes within the several industries was not very far advanced. The primitive tillage of the common-fields which still prevailed in the early eighteenth century, though the rapid enclosure of commons was effecting a considerable, and from the wealth-producing point of view, a very salutary change, did not favour the specialisation of land for pasture or for some particular grain crops. Each little hamlet was engaged in providing crops of hay, wheat, barley, oats, beans, and had to fulfil the other purposes required by a self-subsisting community. This partly arose from the necessity of the system of land tenure, partly from ignorance of how to take advantage of special qualities and positions of soil, and partly from the self-sufficiency improved by difficulties of conveyance. As the century advanced, the enclosure of commons, the increase of large farms, the application of new science and new capital led to a rapid differentiation in the use of land for agricultural purposes. But in the earlier part of the century there was little specialisation of land except in the West Riding and round the chief centres of the woollen trade, and to a less extent in the portions of the counties round London whose position forced them to specialise for some particular market of the metropolis.

[1] Defoe, vol. iii. pp. 78, 79.

§ 10. As the small agriculturist on a self-sufficing farm must perform many different processes, so the manufacturer was not narrowed down to a single process of manufacture. A large part of the ruder manufactures were home productions for home consumption, and the same hands tended the sheep which furnished the wool, and spun and wove the wool for family use. The smith was in a far fuller sense the maker of the horse-shoe or the nail or bolt than he is to-day; the wheelwright, the carpenter, and other handicraftsmen performed a far larger number of different processes than they do now. Moreover, each household, in addition to its principal employments of agriculture and manufacture, carried on many minor productive occupations, such as baking, brewing, butter-making, dressmaking, washing, which are now for the most part special and independent branches of employment.

In the more highly-developed branches of the textile and metal trades the division of processes appears at first sight more sharply marked than to-day. The carder, spinner, weaver, fuller in the cloth trade worked in the several processes of converting raw wool into finished cloth, related to one another only by a series of middlemen who supplied them with the material required for their work and received it back with the impress of their labour attached, to hand it out once more to undergo the next process.[1] But though modern machine-production will show us these various processes drawn together into close local proximity, sometimes performed under the same roof and often making use of the same steam power, we shall find that a chief object and effect of this closer local co-ordination of the several processes is to define and narrow more precisely the labour of each worker and to make the spinner and the weaver confine himself to the performance of a fractional part of the full process of spinning or weaving. Thus we find that English industry in the early eighteenth century is marked on the one hand by a lack of clear differentiation as regards industries, and on the other hand by a lack of minute differentiation of processes within the industry. —

§ 11. We must now descend from the consideration of the Industry and the Market, or group of related businesses, to

---

[1] Cf. Burnley, *Wool and Wool-combing*, p. 417.

examine the character and structure of the unit of industry —the Business.

In a study of the composition or co-operation of labour and capital in a Business before the era of machine-production there are five points of dominant importance—(1) The ownership of the material; (2) the ownership of the tools; (3) the ownership of the productive power; (4) the relations subsisting between the individual units of labour; (5) the work-place.

English manufacturing industry in the first half of the eighteenth century furnishes a variety of different forms of business of widely different nature and complexity. The simplest form of manufacturing industry is that in which an industrial family owning the raw material and the requisite tools, and working with the power of their own bodies in their own homes, produce commodities for their own consumption. This private production for private consumption survived largely in the eighteenth century, not merely in the case of agriculturists who produced the more necessary articles of food for themselves as well as for the market, but also in the case of farmers and cottagers in the remotest parts of the country who produced their own wool and flax, and spun and wove it for their own use.[1]

From this primitive form which required no commerce and no industrial organisation we may trace the growth of various forms of higher industrial development, many of which co-existed in eighteenth century England.

The simplest structure of "domestic" manufacture is that in which the farmer-manufacturer is found purchasing his own material, the raw wool or flax if he is a spinner, the warp and weft if he is a weaver, and, working with his family, produces yarn or cloth which he sells himself, either in the local market or to regular master-clothiers or merchants. The mixed cotton weaving trade was in this condition in the earlier years of the eighteenth century. "The workshop of the weaver was a rural cottage, from which, when he was tired of sedentary labour, he could sally forth into his little garden, and with the spade or the hoe tend its culinary productions. The cotton-wool which was to form his weft was picked clean by the fingers of his

---

[1] Smith, *Memoirs of Wool*, vol. ii. p. 297.

younger children, and was carded and spun by the older girls assisted by his wife, and the yarn was woven by him-self assisted by his sons." [1]

Following as the central point the ownership of the requisites of production, we find in the next stage that the ownership of the material has passed from the workman into the hands of the organising merchant or middleman, who usurps the title "manufacturer." The workman, how-ever, still retains the ownership of the implements of his craft and works in his own house. The condition of the worsted trade later in the century, about 1770, well illus-trates this industrial form.

"The work was entirely domestic, and its different branches widely scattered over the country. First, the manufacturer had to travel on horseback to purchase his raw material among the farmers, or at the great fairs held in those old towns that had formerly been the exclusive markets, or, as they were called, 'staples' of wool. The wool, safely received, was handed over to the sorters, who rigorously applied their gauge of required length of staple and mercilessly chopped off by shears or hatchet what did not reach the standard as wool fit for the clothing trade. The long wool thus passed into the hands of the combers, and, having been brought back to them into the combed state, was again carefully packed and strapped on the back of the sturdy horse, to be taken into the country to be spun. . . . Here, at each village, he had his agents, who received the wool, distributed it amongst the peasantry and received it back as yarn. The machine employed was still the old one-thread wheel, and in summer weather on many a village green might be seen the housewives plying their busy trade, and furnishing to the poet the vision of contentment spinning at the cottage door. Returning in safety with his yarn, the manufacturer had now to seek out his weavers, who ultimately delivered to him his camblets or russels, or tammies or calimancoes (such were the leading names of the fibres) ready for sale to the merchant or delivery to the dyer." [2]

The condition of the cotton-trade in Lancashire about

---

[1] Ure, *History of the Cotton Manufacture*, vol. i. p. 224.

[2] James, *History of the Worsted Manufacture*, p. 323 (quoted Taylor, *The Modern Factory System*, p. 61).

1750 illustrates most clearly the transition from the independent weaver to the dependent weaver. So far as the linen warp of his fabric was concerned he had long been in the habit of receiving it from the larger "manufacturer" in Bolton or in Manchester, but the cotton yarn he had hitherto supplied himself, using the yarn spun by his own family or purchased by himself in the neighbourhood. The difficulty of obtaining a steady, adequate supply, and the waste of time involved in trudging about in search of this necessary material, operated more strongly as the market for cotton goods expanded and the pressure of work made itself felt.[1] It was this pressure which we shall see acting as chief stimulus to the application of new inventions in the spinning[2] trade. In the interim, however, the habit grew of receiving not only linen warp but cotton weft from the merchant or middleman. Thus the ownership of the raw material entirely passed out of the weaver's hands, though he continued to ply his domestic craft as formerly.[3] This had grown into the normal condition of the trade by 1750. The stocking-trade illustrates one further encroachment of the capitalist system upon domestic industry. In this trade not only was the material given out by merchants, but the "frames" used for weaving were likewise owned by them, and were rented out to the workers, who continued, however, to work in their own homes.[4]

§ 12. Two further steps remained to be taken in the transition from the "domestic" to the "factory" system, the one relating to the ownership of "power," the other to the workplace. (a) The substitution of extra-human power owned by the employer for the physical power of the worker; (b) the withdrawal of the workers from their homes, and the concentration of them in factories and work-places owned by the capitalists.

Although these steps were not completely taken until the age of steam had well set in, before the middle of the eighteenth century there were found examples of the factory, complete in its essential character, side by side and in

---

[1] Baines, *History of the County Palatine of Lancashire*, vol. ii. p. 413.
[2] Ure, *History of Cotton Manufacture*, vol. i. p. 224, etc.
[3] Dr. Aikin, *History of Manchester* (quoted Baines, p. 406).
[4] Taylor, *The Modern Factory System*, p. 69.

actual competition with the earlier shapes of domestic industry.

Capitalist ownership of extra-human industrial "power" was of course narrowly restricted before the age of steam. Water-power, horse-power, and to a much smaller extent, wind-power, were utilised. But the most important services water rendered to industry prior to the great inventions were in facilitating the transport of goods, and in certain subsidiary processes of manufacture such as dyeing. Though a considerable number of water-mills existed early in the century, they played no large part in manufacture A natural force so strictly confined in quantity and in local application, and subject to such great waste from the backward condition of mechanical art, was not able to serve to any great extent as a substitute for or aid to the muscular activity of man.

But although the economy of mechanical power was not yet operative to any appreciable extent in concentrating labour, certain other notable economics of large-scale production were beginning to assert themselves in all the leading manufactures. Indeed so powerful are some of the economies of division of labour and co-operation even in a primitive condition of the industrial arts, that Professor Ashley considers it not improbable that the great manufactory might have become an important or even a dominant feature of the woollen trade as early as the sixteenth century, if legislative enactments had not stood in the way.[1] As it was, these earlier centralising forces, while they drove the workers to work and live in closer and compacter masses, did not at first dispose them in factories to any great extent. They continued for the most part to work in their own houses, though for material and sometimes for the implements of their craft they were dependent upon some merchant or large master-manufacturer. This was the condition of industry in the neighbourhood of Leeds in 1725. "The houses are not scattered and dispersed as in the vicarage of Halifax, one by one, but in villages, and those houses thronged with people and the whole country infinitely populous."[2] In the more highly-developed branches

---

[1] *Economic History*, vol. ii. p. 237.
[2] Defoe, *Tour*, vol. iii. p. 89.

of the cloth trade, however, where the best looms were a relatively costly form of capital, the foundation of the factory system was clearly laid. In Norwich, Frome, Taunton, Devizes, Stourbridge, and other clothing centres, Defoe found the weaving industry highly concentrated, and rich employers owning considerable numbers of looms. Some of this work was put out by the master-manufacturers, but other work was done in large sheds or other premises owned by the master. This large organised "business," half factory, half domestic, continued to prevail in the important West of England clothing industry up to the close of the eighteenth century. "The master clothier of the West of England buys his wool from the importer, if it be foreign, or in the fleece if it be of domestic growth ; after which, in all the different processes through which it passes, he is under the necessity of employing as many distinct classes of persons ; sometimes working in their own houses, sometimes in that of the master clothier, but none of them going out of their proper line. Each class of workman, however, acquires great skill in performing its particular operation, and hence may have arisen the acknowledged excellence, and, till of late, the superiority of the cloths of the West of England." [1]

So again, in the cotton industry of Lancashire, the hold which the merchants had got over the weavers by supplying them with warp and weft led in some cases, before the middle of the century, to the establishment of small factories containing a score or two of looms, in which hired men were employed to weave. A little later, though long before steam power, Arthur Young finds a factory at Darlington with over fifty looms, a factory at Boynton with 150 workers, and a silk mill at Sheffield with 152 workers. Even where the final step of substituting the factory for the home had not been taken the subordination of the handicraftsman to the master who provided the materials and paid the wages was tolerably complete. By the middle of the century the free artisan was gradually passing into the condition of a hired "hand." Improved means of communication were beginning to expand the area of the

---

[1] *Report from the Committee on the Woollen Manufacture of England* (1806).

market, enlarged businesses enabled labour to be profitably divided, and required a more effective control over the workers than could be obtained over a scattered population of agricultural manufacturers.

§ 13. Regarding the Business as a combination of Labour and Capital, we perceive that one strongly distinctive characteristic of the pre-machinery age is the small proportion which capital bears to labour in the industrial unit. It is this fact that enabled the "domestic" worker to hold his own so long in so many industries as the owner of a separate business. So long as the mechanical arts are slightly developed and tools are simple, the proportion of "fixed capital" to the business is small and falls within the means of the artisan who plies his craft in his home. So long as tools are simple, the processes of manufacture are slow, therefore the quantity of raw material and other "circulating capital" is small and can also be owned by the worker. The growing divorcement in the ownership of capital and labour in the industrial unit will be found to be a direct and most important result of those improvements in mechanical arts which, by continually increasing the proportion of capital to labour in a business, placed capital more and more beyond the possession of those who supplied the labour power required to co-operate in production.

In the middle of last century there were very few instances of a manufacturing business in which a large capital was engaged, or in which the capital stood to the labour in anything like modern proportion. It was indeed the merchant and not the manufacturer who represented the most advanced form of Capitalism in the eighteenth century. Long before Dr. Johnson's discovery that "an English merchant is a new species of gentleman," Defoe had noted the rise of merchant-princes in the Western clothing trades, observing that "many of the great families who now pass for gentry in these counties have been originally raised from and built out of this truly noble manufacture."[1] These wealthy *entrepreneurs* were sometimes spoken of as "manufacturers," though they had no claim either upon the old or the new signification of that

---

[1] *Tour*, vol. ii. p. 35.

name. They neither wrought with their hands nor did they own machinery and supervise the labour which worked with it. They were, as has been shown above, merchant-middlemen. The clothing trade being the most highly developed, evolved several species of middlemen, including under that term all collectors and distributors of the raw material or finished goods.

(*a*) One important class of "factors" engaged themselves in buying wool from farmers and selling it to clothiers, and appear to have sometimes exercised an undue and tyrannous control over the latter by an unscrupulous manipulation of the credit system which was growing up in trade.[1]

(*b*) The "clothiers" themselves must be regarded in large measure as middleman-collectors, analogous in function to the distributors, who still rank as one of the grades of middlemen in the cheap clothing trade of London to-day.[2]

(*c*) After the cloth was made three classes of middlemen were engaged in forwarding it to the retailer—(1) travelling merchants or wholesale dealers who attended the big fairs or the markets at Leeds, Halifax, Exeter, etc., and made large purchases, conveying the goods on pack-horses over the country to the retail trader; (2) middlemen who sold on commission through London factors and ware-housemen, who in their turn disposed of the goods to shopkeepers or to exporters; (3) merchants directly engaged in the export trade.

With the exception of shipping and canal transport (which became important after the middle of the century) there were no considerable industries related to manufacture where large capitals were laid down in fixed plant. Even the capital sunk in permanent improvements of land, which played so important a part in the development of agriculture, belonged chiefly to the latter years of the eighteenth century. Almost the only persons who wielded large capitals within the country were those merchants, dealers, or middlemen, whose capital at any given time consisted of a large stock of raw material or finished

---

[1] For an interesting account of the cunning devices of "factors" see Smith's *Memoirs of Wool*, vol. ii. p. 311, etc.
[2] Cf. Booth, *Labour and Life of the People*, vol. i. p. 486, etc.

goods. Even the latter were considerably restricted in the magnitude of their transactions by the imperfect develop- ment of the machinery of finance and the credit system. In 1750 there were not more than twelve bankers' shops out of London.[1] Until 1759 the Bank of England issued no notes of less value than £20.

Joint-ownership of capital and effective combination of the labour units in a business were only beginning to make progress. The Funded Debt, the Bank of England, the East India Company were the only examples of really large and safe investments at the opening of the eighteenth century. Joint-ownership of large capitals for business purposes made no great progress before the middle of the eighteenth century, except in the case of chartered com- panies for foreign trade, such as the East India Company, the Hudson's Bay Company, the Turkish, Russian, East- land, and African companies. Insurance business became a favourite form of joint-stock speculation in the reign of George I. The extraordinary burst of joint-stock enterprise culminating in the downfall of the South Sea Company shows clearly the narrow limitations for sound capitalist co-operation. Even foreign trade on joint-stock lines could only be maintained successfully on condition that the competition of private adventurers was precluded.

Joint-capital had yet made no inroad into manufacture, one of the earliest instances being a company formed in 1764 with a capital of £100,000 for manufacturing fine cambrics.[2]

The limits of co-operative capitalism at the opening of the period of Industrial Revolution are indicated by Adam Smith in a passage of striking significance :—"The only trades which it seems possible for a joint-stock company to carry on successfully, without an exclusive privilege, are those of which all the operations are capable of being reduced to what is called a routine, or to such a uniformity of method as admits of little or no variation. Of this kind is, first, the banking trade; secondly, the trade of insurance from fire and from sea risk and capture in time of war; thirdly, the trade of making and maintaining a navigable

[1] Toynbee, *Industrial Revolution*, p. 55.
[2] Cunningham, vol. ii. p. 350.

cut or canal; and fourthly, the similar trade of bringing water for the supply of a great city."[1]

In other words, the businesses amenable to joint-stock enterprise are those where skilled management can be reduced to a minimum, and where the scale of the business or the possession of a natural monopoly limits or prohibits competition from outside.

[1] *Wealth of Nations*, Bk. V., chap. i., part 3.

CHAPTER III.

THE ORDER OF DEVELOPMENT OF MACHINE INDUSTRY.

§ 1. *A Machine differentiated from a Tool.*
§ 2. *Machinery in Relation to the Character of Human Labour.*
§ 3. *Contributions of Machinery to Productive Power.*
§ 4. *Main Factors in Development of Machine Industry.*
§ 5. *Importance of Cotton-trade in Machine Development.*
§ 6. *History refutes the "Heroic" Theory of Invention.*
§ 7. *Application of Machinery to other Textile Work.*
§ 8. *Reverse order of Development in Iron Trades.*
§ 9. *Leading Determinants in the General Application of Machinery and Steam-Motor.*
§ 10. *Order of Development of modern Industrial Methods in the several Countries—Natural, Racial, Political, Economic.*

§ 1. It appears that in the earlier eighteenth century, while there existed examples of various types of industrial structure, the domestic system in its several phases may be regarded as the representative industrial form.   The object of this chapter is to examine the nature of those changes in the mechanical arts which brought about the substitution of machine-industry conducted in factories or large workshops for the handicrafts conducted within the home or in small workshops, with the view of discovering the economic bearing of these changes.

A full inductive treatment would perhaps require this inquiry to be prefaced by a full history of the inventions which in the several industries mark the rise of the factory system and the adoption of capitalist methods.   This, however, is beyond the scope of the present work, nor does it strictly belong to our scientific purpose, which is not to write the narrative of the industrial revolution, but to bring such analysis to bear upon the records of industrial changes as shall enable us to clearly discern the laws of those changes.

The central position occupied by machinery as the chief material factor in the modern evolution of industry requires that a distinct answer should be given to the question, What is machinery?

In distinguishing a machine from a mere tool or handicraft implement it is desirable to pay special attention to two points, complexity of structure and the activity of man in relation to the machine. Modern machinery in its most developed shape consists, as Karl Marx points out, of three parts, which, though mechanically connected, are essentially distinct, the motor mechanism, the transmitting mechanism, and the tool or working machine.

"The motor mechanism is that which puts the whole in motion. It either generates its own motive power, like the steam-engine, the caloric engine, the electro-magnetic machine, etc., or it receives its impulse from some already existing natural force, like the water-wheel from a head of water, the windmill from wind, etc. The transmitting mechanism, composed of fly-wheels, shafting, toothed wheels, pullies, straps, ropes, bands, pinions, and gearing of the most varied kind, regulates the motion, changes its form where necessary, as, for instance, from linear to circular, and divides and distributes it among the working machines. These two first parts of the whole mechanism are there solely for putting the working machines in motion, by means of which motion the subject of labour is seized upon and modified as desired."[1]

Although the development of modern machinery is largely concerned with motor and transmitting mechanisms, it is to the working machine we must look in order to get a clear idea of the differences between machines and tools. A tool may be quite simple in form and action as a knife, a needle, a saw, a roller, a hammer, or it may embody more complex thought in its construction, more variety in its movement, and call for the play of higher human

[1] Karl Marx, *Capital*, p. 367.

skill. Such tools or implements are the hand-loom, the lathe, the potter's-wheel. To these tools man stands in a double relation. He is handicraftsman in that he guides and directs them by his skill within the scope of activity to which they are designed. (He also furnishes by his muscular activity the motive force with which the tool is worked.) It is the former of these two relations which differentiates the tool from the machine. When the tool is removed from the direct and individual guidance of the handicraftsman and placed in a mechanism which governs its action by the prearranged motion of some other tool or mechanical implement, it ceases to be a tool and becomes part of a machine. The economic advantage of the early machines consisted chiefly in the economy of working in combined action a number of similar tools by the agency of a single motor. (In the early machine the former tool takes its place as a central part, but its movements are no longer regulated by the human touch.[1]) The more highly evolved modern machinery generally represents an orderly sequence of processes by which mechanical unity is given to the labour once performed by a number of separate individuals, or groups of individuals with different sorts of tools. But the economy of the earlier machines was generally of a different character. For the most part it consisted not in the harmonious relation of a number of different processes, but rather in a multiplication of the same process raised sometimes to a higher size and speed by mechanical contrivances. So the chief economic value of the earlier machinery applied to spinning consisted in the fact that it enabled each spinner to work an increased number of spindles, performing with each the same simple process as that which he formerly performed with one. In other cases, however, the element of multiplication was not present, and the prime economy of the machine consisted in the superior skill, regularity, pace, or economy of power obtained by substituting mechanical direction of the tool for close and constant human direction. In modern machinery the sewing-machine illustrates the latter, as the knife-cleaning machine illustrates the former.

---

[1] Marx points out how in many of the most highly evolved machines the original tool survives, illustrating this from the original power-loom. (*Capital*, p. 368.)

The machine is inherently a more complex structure than the tool, because it must contain within itself the mechanical means for working a tool, or even for the combined working of many tools, which formerly received their direction from man. In using a tool man is the direct agent, in using a working machine the transmitting mechanism is the direct agent, so far as the character of the several acts of production is not stamped upon the form of the working machine itself. The man placed in charge of a machine determines whether it shall act, but only within very narrow limits how it shall act. The two characteristics here brought out in the machine, complexity of action and self-direction or automatic character, are in reality the objective and subjective expression of the same factor—namely, the changed relation of man towards the work in which he co-operates.

Some of the directing or mental effort, skill, art, thought, must be taken over, that is to say, some of the processes must be guided not directly by man but by other processes, in order to constitute a machine. A machine thus becomes a complex tool in which some of the processes are relatively fixed, and are not the direct expression of human activity. A machinist who feeds a machine with material may be considered to have some control over the pace and character of the first process, but only indirectly over the later processes, which are regulated by fixed laws of their construction which make them absolutely dependent on the earlier processes. A machine is in the nature of its work largely independent of the individual control of the "tender," because it is in its construction the expression of the individual control and skill of the inventor. A machine, then, may be described as a complex tool with a fixed relation of processes performed by its parts. Even here we cannot profess to have reached a definition which enables us in all cases to nicely discriminate machine from tool. It is easy to admit that a spade is a tool and not a machine, but if a pair of scissors, a lever, or a crane are tools, and are considered as performing single simple processes, and not a number of organically relative processes, we may by a skilfully arranged gradation be led on to include the whole of machinery under tools. This difficulty is of course one which besets all work of definition.

But while it is not easy by attention to complexity of structure always to distinguish a tool from a machine, nothing is gained by making the differentia of a machine to consist in the use of a steam or other non-human motor.

A vast amount of modern machinery is of course directed not to combining tools or series of productive processes upon which the productive skill of man is closely engaged, but to substituting other motors for the muscular power of man. But though certain tools as well as certain forms of human effort are here replaced by machines, these tools are not commonly embodied in the machinery for generating and transmitting the new force, so that the mere consideration of the different part played by the worker in generating productive force does not assist us to distinguish a machine from a tool. A type-writer, a piano, which receive their impulse from the human muscles, must evidently be included among machines. It is indeed true that these, like others of the same order, are exceptional machines, not merely in that the motive power is derived more essentially from human muscles, but in that the *raison d'être* of the mechanism has been to provide scope for human skill and not to destroy it. But though it is true that a high degree of skill may be imparted to the first process of the working of a piano or type-writer, it is none the less true that the "tool," the implement which strikes the sound or makes the written mark, is not under immediate control of human touch. The skill is confined to an early process, and the mechanism as a whole must be classed under machinery. Nothing would indeed be gained in logical distinctness if we were to abandon our earlier differentia of the machine and confine that term to such mechanical appliances as derived their power from non-human sources—the fact which commonly marks off modern from earlier forms of machine production. For we should find that this substitution of non-human for human power was also a matter of degree, and that the most complex steam-driven machinery of to-day cannot entirely dispense with some directing impulse of human muscular activity, such as the shovelling of coal into a furnace, though the tendency is ever to reduce the human effort to a minimum in the attainment of a given output.

This consideration of the difficulties attending exact definitions of machinery is not idle, for it leads to a clearer recognition of the nicely graded evolution which has changed the character of modern industry, not by a catastrophic substitution of radically different methods, but by the continuous steady development of certain elements, common to all sorts of industrial activity, and a corresponding continuous degeneration of certain other elements.

§ 2. The growth of machine-industry then may be measured by the increased number and complexity of the processes related to one another in the mechanical unit or machine, and by a corresponding shrinkage of the dependence of the product upon the skill and volition of the human being who tends or co-operates with the machine. Every product made by tool or machine is *quâ* industrial product or commodity the expression of the thought and will of man; but as machine-production becomes more highly developed, more and more of the thought and will of the inventor, less and less of that of the immediate human agent or machine-tender is expressed in the product. But it is evidently not enough to say that the labour-saving machine has merely substituted the stored and concentrated effort of the inventor for that labour of the handicraftsman which is saved. This would be to ignore the saving of muscular power due to the substitution of forces of nature—water, steam, electricity, etc., for the painful effort of man. It is the thought of the inventor, plus the action of various mechanical and other physical forces, which has saved the labour of man in the production of a commodity The further question—how far this saving of labour in respect of a given commodity is compensated by the increased number of commodities to which human labour is applied—is a consideration which belongs to a later chapter.

In tracing the effect of the application of modern machinery to English industry there appear two prominent factors, which for certain purposes require separate treatment—the growth of improved mechanical apparatus, and the evolution of extra-human motor power.

We speak of the industry which has prevailed since the middle of the eighteenth century as machine-production, not because there were no machines before that time, but firstly, because a vast acceleration in the invention of complex machinery applied to almost all industrial arts dates from that period, and secondly, because the application upon an extensive scale of non-human motor powers manifested itself then for the first time.

One important external effect and indication of the momentous character of these changes is to be found in the quickening of that operation, the beginning of which was observable before the great inventions, the substitution of the Factory System for the Domestic System.

The peculiar relation of Machinery to the Factory System consists in the fact that the size, expensiveness, and complexity of machinery on the one hand, and the use of non-human power on the other hand, were forces which united to drive labour from the home workshop to the large specialised workshop—the Factory.

"The water frame, the carding engine, and the other machines which Arkwright brought out in a finished state, required both more space than could be found in a cottage, and more power than could be applied by the human arm. Their weight also rendered it necessary to place them in strongly-built walls, and they also could not be advantageously turned by any power then known but that of water. Further, the use of machinery was accompanied by a greater division of labour, and therefore a greater co-operation was requisite to bring all the processes of production into harmony and under a central superintendence."[1] Hence the growth of machine-production is to a large extent synonymous with the growth of the modern Factory System.

§ 3. Man does his work by moving matter. Hence machinery can only aid him by increasing the motive power at his disposal.

(1) Machinery enables forces of man or nature to be more effectively applied by various mechanical contrivances composed of levers, pulleys, wedges, screws, etc.

(2) Machinery enables man to obtain the use of various motor forces outside his body—wind, water, steam, electricity, chemical action, etc.[2]

Thus by the provision of new productive forces, and by the more economical application of all productive forces, machinery improves the industrial arts.

[1] Cooke Taylor, *History of the Factory System*, p. 422.
[2] Cf. Babbage, p. 15.

Machinery can increase the scope of man's productive ability in two ways. The difficulty of concentrating a large mass of human force upon a given point at the same time provides certain quantitative limits to the productive efficiency of the human body. The steam-hammer can perform certain work which is quantitatively outside the limit of the physical power of any number of men working with simple tools and drawing their motor power from their own bodies. The other limit to the productive power of man arises from the imperfect continuity of human effort and the imperfect command of its direction. The difficulty of maintaining a small, even, accurate pressure, or a precise repetition of the same movement, is rather a qualitative than a purely quantitative limit. The superior certainty and regularity of machinery enables certain work to be done which man alone could not do or could do less perfectly. The work of the printing machine could not be achieved by man. Machinery has improved the texture and quality of certain woollen goods;[1] recent improvements in milling result in improved quality of flour and so on. Machinery can also do work which is too fine or delicate for human fingers, or which would require abnormal skill if executed by hand. Economy of time, which Babbage[2] accounts a separate economy, is rightly included in the economies just named. The greater rapidity with which certain manufacturing processes—e.g., dyeing—can be achieved arises from the superior concentration and continuity of force possible under machinery. All advantages arising from rapid transport are assignable to the same causes.

The continuity and regularity of machine work are also reflected in certain economies of measurement. The faculty of self-registering, which belongs potentially to all machinery, and which is more utilised every day, performs several services which may be summed up by saying that they enable us to know exactly what is going on. When to self-registration is applied the faculty of self-regulation, within certain limits a new economy of force and knowledge is added. But machinery can also register and regulate the expenditure of human power. Babbage well says :—" One of the most singular advantages we derive from machinery

---

[1] Burnley, *Wool and Wool-combing*, p. 417.
[2] *Economy of Machinery*, p. 6.

is in the check which it affords against the inattention, the idleness, or the knavery of human agents."[1] This control of the machine over man has certain results which belong to another aspect of machine economy.[2]

These are the sources of all the improvements of economies imputed to machine-production. All improvements in machinery, as applied to industrial arts, take therefore one of the following forms:—

(1) Re-arrangement or improvement of machinery so as to utilise more fully the productive power of nature or man. Improvements enabling one man to tend more spindles, or enabling the same engine at the same boiler-pressure to turn more wheels, belong to this order of improvement.

(2) Economies in the source of power. These will fall under four heads—

1. Substitution of cheaper for dearer kinds of human power. Displacement of men's labour by women's or children's.

2. Substitution of mechanical power for human power. Most great improvements in the "labour-saving" character of machinery properly come under this head.

3. Economies in fuel or in steam. The most momentous illustration is the adoption of the hot blast and the substitution of raw coal for coke in the iron trade.[3]

4. The substitution of a new mechanical motor for an old one derived from the same or from different stores of energy—e.g., steam for water power, natural gas for steam.

(3) Extended application of machinery. New industrial arts owing their origin to scientific inventions and their practice to machinery arise for utilising waste products. Under "waste products" we may include (a) natural materials, the services of which were not recognised or could not be utilised without machinery—e.g., nitrates and other "waste" products of the soil; (b) the refuse of manufacturing processes which figured as "waste" until some unsuspected use was found for it. Conspicuous examples of this economy are found in many trades. During the interval between great

---

[1] *Economy of Machinery*, p. 39.
[2] *Vide infra*, p. 249.
[3] Scrivener, *History of the Iron Trade*, pp. 296, 297.

new inventions in machinery or in the application of power many of the principal improvements are of this order. Gas tar, formerly thrown into rivers so as to pollute them, or mixed with coal and burnt as fuel, is now "raw material for producing beautiful dyes, some of our most valued medicines, a saccharine substance three hundred times sweeter than sugar, and the best disinfectants for the destruction of germs of disease." "The whole of the great industries of dyeing and calico-printing have been revolutionised by the new colouring matters obtained from the old waste material gas tar."[1] These economies both in fuel and in the utilisation of waste material are largely due to the increased scale of production which comes with the development of machine industry. Many waste products can only be utilised where they exist in large quantities.

§ 4. If we trace historically the growth of modern capitalist economies in the several industries we shall find that they fall generally into three periods—

   1. The period of earlier mechanical inventions, marking the displacement of domestic by factory industry.
   2. The evolution of the new motor in manufacture. The application of steam to the manufacturing processes.
   3. The evolution of steam locomotion, with its bearing on industry.

As these periods are not materially exclusive, so also there are close economic relations subsisting between the development of machinery and motor, and between the improvements in manufacture and in the transport industry. But in order to understand the nature of the irregularity which is discernible in the history of the development of machinery, it is essential to consider these factors both separately and in the historical and economic relation they stand to each other. For this purpose we will examine two large staple industries, the textile and the iron industries of England, in order that we may trace in the chief steps of their progress the laws of the evolution of modern machinery.

The textile industry offers special facilities to such a study. The strongest and most widespread of English manufactures, it furnishes in the early eighteenth century the

---

[1] Sir Lyon Playfair, *North American Review*, Nov. 1892.

clearest examples of the several forms of industry. To the
several branches of this industry the earliest among the
great inventions were applied.   This start in industrial
development has been maintained, so that the most advanced
forms of the modern factory are found in textile industry.
Moreover, the close attention which has been given to,
and the careful records which have been kept of certain
branches of this work, in particular the Lancashire cotton
industry, enable us to trace the operation of the new
industrial forces here with greater precision than is the
case with any other industry.   As Schulze-Gaevernitz,
in his masterly study, says of the cotton industry—
"The English cotton industry is not only the oldest, but
is in many respects that modern industry which manifests
most clearly the characteristics of modern industrial methods,
both in their economic and their social relations."[1]

The iron industry has been selected on the ground of
its close connection with the application of steam-driven
machinery to the several industries.   It is in a sense the
most fundamental industry of modern times, inasmuch
as it furnishes the material environment of the great
modern economic forces.   Moreover, we have the advantage of tracing the growth of the iron manufacture *ab ovo*,
for, as we have seen, before the industrial revolution it
played a most insignificant part in English commerce.

Lastly, a study of the relations between the growth of the
iron and the textile industries will be of special service in
assisting us to realise the character of the interaction of the
several manufactures under the growing integration of
modern industry.[2]

§ 5. In observing the order of inventions applied to
textile industries, the first point of significance is that
cotton, a small industry confined to a part of Lancashire,
and up to 1768 dependent upon linen in order to furnish
a complete cloth, should take the lead.

The woollen trades, in the first half of the eighteenth

[1] *Der Grossbetrieb*, p. 85.
[2] The important part which the cotton and iron industries play in
the export trade of England entitles them to special consideration as
representatives of world-industry.   Out of £263,530,585 value of
English exports in 1890, cotton comprised £74,430,749; iron and
steel, £31,565,337.

century, as we saw, engaged the attention of a vastly larger number of persons, and played a much more important part in our commerce. The silk trade had received new life from the flow of intelligent French workers, and the first modern factory with elaborate machinery was that set up for silk throwing by Lombe. Yet by far the larger number of the important textile inventions of the eighteenth century were either applied in the first instance to the cotton manufacture and transferred, sometimes after a lapse of many years, to the woollen, worsted, and other textile trades, or being invented for woollen trades, proved unsuccessful until applied to cotton.[1]

Although the origin and application of inventive genius is largely independent of known laws, and may provisionally be relegated to the domain of "accident," there are certain reasons which favoured the cotton industry in the industrial race. Its concentration in South Lancashire and Staffordshire, as compared with the wide diffusion of the woollen industries, facilitated the rapid acceptance of new methods and discoveries. Moreover, the cotton industry being of later origin, and settling itself in unimportant villages and towns, had escaped the influence of official regulations and customs which prevailed in the woollen centres and proved serious obstacles to the introduction of new industrial methods.[2] Even in Lancashire itself official inspectors regulated the woollen trade at Manchester, Rochdale, Blackburn, and Bury.[3]

The cotton industry had from the beginning been free from all these fetters. The shrewd, practical business character which marks Lancashire to-day is probably a cause as well as a result of the great industrial development of the last hundred years.

Moreover, it was recognised, even before the birth of the great inventions, that cotton goods, when brought into free competition with woollen goods, could easily undersell them and supplant them in popular consumption. This knowledge held out a prospect of untold fortune to inventors who should, by the application of machinery, break through the limitations imposed upon production

---

[1] Cunningham, chap. ii. p. 450.
[2] Schulze-Gaevernitz, *Der Grossbetrieb*, p. 34.
[3] Ure, *The Cotton Manufacture*, p. 187.

by the restricted number of efficient workers in some of the processes through which the cotton yarn must pass.

But the stimulus which one invention afforded to another gave an accumulative power to the application of new methods. This is especially seen in the alternation of inventions in the two chief processes of spinning and weaving.

Even before the invention of John Kay's Fly Shuttle, which doubled the quantity of work a weaver could do in a day, we found that spinners had great difficulties in supplying sufficient yarn to the weavers. This seems to have applied both to the Lancashire cotton and to the Yorkshire woollen manufactures. After the fly-shuttle had come into common use this pressure of demand upon the spinners was obviously increased, and the most skilful organisation of middleman-clothiers was unable to supply sufficient quantities of yarn. This economic consideration directed more and more attention to experiments in spinning machinery, and so we find that, long before the invention of the jenny and the water-frame, ingenious men like John Kay of Bury, Wyatt, Paul, and others had tried many patents for improved spinning. The great inventions of Hargreaves and Arkwright and Crompton enabled spinning to overtake and outstrip weaving and when, about 1790, steam began to be applied to considerable numbers of spinning mills, it was no longer spinning but weaving that was the limiting process in the manufacture of woollen and cotton cloths.

This strain upon weaving, which had been tightening through the period of the great spinning improvements, acted as a special incentive to Cartwright, Horrocks, and others to perfect the power-loom in its application, first to woollen, then to cotton industries. Not until well into the nineteenth century, when steam power had been fully applied by many minor improvements, were the arts of spinning and weaving brought fully into line. The complete factory, where the several processes of carding, spinning, weaving (and even dyeing and finishing), are conducted under the same roof and worked in correspondence with one another, marks the full transition from the earlier form of domestic industry, where the family performed with simple tools their several processes under the domestic roof.[1]

§ 6. The history of these textile inventions does a good deal to dispel the " heroic " theory of invention—that of an idea flashing suddenly from the brain of a single genius and effecting a rapid revolution in a trade. No one of the inventions which were greatest in their effect, the jenny, the water-frame, the mule, the power-loom, was in the main attributable to the effort or ability of a single man; each represented in its successful shape the addition of many successive increments of discovery; in most cases the successful invention was the slightly superior survivor of many similar attempts. " The present spinning machinery which we now use is supposed to be a compound of about eight hundred inventions. The present carding machinery is a compound of about sixty patents."[2] This is the history of most inventions. The pressure of industrial circumstances direct the intelligence of many minds towards the comprehension of some single central point of difficulty, the common knowledge of the age induces many to reach similar solutions: that solution which is slightly better adapted to the facts or "grasps the skirts of happy chance " comes out victorious, and the inventor, purveyor, or, in some cases, the robber is crowned as a great inventive genius. It is the neglect of these considerations which gives a false interpretation to the annals of industrial invention by giving an irregular and catastrophic appearance to the working of a force which is in its inner pressure much more regular than in its outward expression. The earlier increments of a great industrial invention make no figure in

[1] Modern economy now favours the specialisation of a factory and often of a business in a single group of processes—*e.g.*, spinning or weaving or dyeing, both in the cotton and woollen industries. This, however, is applicable chiefly to the main branches of textile work. In minor branches, such as cotton thread, the tendency is still towards an aggregation of all the different processes under a single roof, both in England and in the United States.

[2] P. R. Hodge, civil engineer—evidence before House of Lords Committee in 1857.

In Germany a spinning-wheel had been long in use for flax-spinning, which in effect was an anticipation of the throstle (cf. Karmarch, *Technologie*, vol. ii. p. 844, quoted Schulze-Gaevernitz, p. 30), and machine-weaving is said to have been discovered in Danzig as early as 1579.

the annals of history because they do not pay, and the final increment which reaches the paying-point gets all the credit, though the inherent importance and the inventive genius of the earlier attempts may have been as great or greater.

There is nothing fortuitous or mysterious in inventive energy. Necessity is its mother, which simply means that it moves along the line of least resistance. Men like Kay, Hargreaves, Arkwright, Cartwright, set their intelligence and industry to meet the several difficulties as they arose. Nearly all the great textile inventors were practical men, most of them operatives immersed in the details of their craft, brought face to face continually with some definite difficulty to be overcome, some particular economy desirable to make. Brooding upon these concrete facts, trying first one thing then another, learning from the attempts and failures made by other practical men, and improving upon these attempts, they have at length hit upon some contrivance that will get over the definite difficulty and secure the particular economy. If we take any definite invention and closely investigate it, we shall find in nearly every case it has thus grown by small increments towards feasibility. Scientific men, strictly so-called, have had very little to do with these great discoveries. Among the great textile inventors, Cartwright alone was a man leading a life of thought.[1] When the spinning machinery was crippled in its efficiency by the crude methods of carding, Lees and Arkwright set themselves to apply improvements suggested by common-sense and experience; when Cartwright's power-loom had been successfully applied to wool, Horrocks and his friends thought out precisely those improvements which would render it remunerative in the cotton trade.

Thus in a given trade where there are several important processes, an improvement in one process which places it in front of the others stimulates invention in the latter, and each in its turn draws such inventive intelligence as is required to bring it into line with the most highly-developed process. Since the later inventions, with new knowledge and new power behind them, often overshoot the earlier ones, we have a certain law of oscillation in the several

[1] Cf. Brentano, *Uber die Ursachen der heutigen socialen Not; Der Grossbetrieb*, p. 30.

processes which maintains progress by means of the stimulus constantly applied by the most advanced process which "makes the pace." There is nothing mysterious in this. If one process remains behind in development each increment of inventive effort successfully applied there brings a higher remuneration than if applied to any of the more forward processes. So the movement is amenable to the ordinary law of "Supply and Demand" enforced by the usual economic motives. As the invention of the fly-shuttle gave weaving the advantage, more and more attention was concentrated upon the spinning processes and the jenny was evolved ; the deficiency of the jenny in spinning warp evolved the water-frame, which for the first time liberated the cotton industry from dependence upon linen warp : the demand for finer and more uniform yarns stimulated the invention of the mule. These notable improvements in spinning machinery, with their minor appendages, placed spinning ahead of weaving, and stimulated the series of inventions embodied in the power-loom. The power-loom was found to be of comparatively little service until the earlier processes of dressing and sizing had been placed on a level of machine development by the efforts of Horrocks and others. Not until after 1841 was an equilibrium reached in the development of the leading processes. So likewise each notable advance in the machinery for the main processes has had the effect of bringing an increase of inventive energy to bear upon the minor and the subsidiary processes —bleaching, dyeing, printing, etc. Even now the early process of "ginning" has not been brought fully into line in spite of the prodigious efforts, made especially in the United States, to overcome the difficulties involved in this preparatory stage of the cotton industry.

The following schedule will serve to show the relation of the growth of the cotton industry as measured by consumption of raw cotton to the leading improvements of machinery.

Cotton Imported. lbs.		Inventions &c.
1730	1,545,472	1730 Wyatt's roller-spinning (patented 1738).
		1738 Kay's fly-shuttle.
1741	1,645,031	1748 Paul's carding-machine (useless until improved by Lees, Arkwright, Wood, 1772-74).

Cotton Imported. lbs.		Inventions, &c.	
1764	3,870,392	1764	Hargreave's spinning-jenny (patented 1770), for weft only.
		1764	Calico-printing introduced into Lancashire.
		1768	Arkwright perfects Wyatt's spinning-frame (patented 1769), liberating cotton from dependence on linen warp.
1771 to 1775	4,764,589	1771	Arkwright's mill built at Cromford.
		1775	Arkwright takes patents for carding, drawing, roving, spinning.
		1779	Crompton's mule completed (combining jenny and water-frame, producing finer and more even yarn).
1781	5,198,775		
1785	18,400,384	1785	Cartwright's power-loom. Watt and Boulton's first engine for cotton-mills.
1792	34,907,497	1792	Whitney's saw-gin.
1813	51,000,000	1813	Horrocks' dressing-machine.
1830	261,200,000	1830	The "Throstle" (almost exclusively used in England for spinning warp).
1832	287,800,000	1832	Roberts' self-acting mule perfected.
1841	489,900,000	1841	Bullough's improved power-loom. Ring spinning (largely used in U.S.A., recently introduced into Lancashire).

From this schedule it is evident that the history of this trade may be divided with tolerable accuracy into four periods.

(1) The preparatory period of experimental inventions of Wyatt, Paul, etc., to the year 1770.

(2) 1770 to 1792 (*circa*), the age of the great mechanical inventions.

(3) 1792 to 1830, the application of steam-power to manufacture and improvements of the great inventions.

(4) 1830 onward, the effect of steam locomotion upon the industry (1830, the opening of the Liverpool and Manchester railway).

If we measure the operation of these several industrial forces within these several periods, as they are reflected on the growing size of the cotton industry, we shall realise the accumulative character of the great industrial movement, and form some approximately accurate conception of the relative importance of the development of mechanical inventions and of the new motor-power.

§ 7. The history of the cotton industry is in its main outlines also the history of other textile industries. We do not possess the same means of measuring statistically the growth of the woollen industries in the period of revolution; but since, on the one hand, many of the spinning and weaving inventions were speedily adapted into the woollen from the cotton industry, while the application of steam to manufacture and the effects of steam locomotion were shared by the older manufacture, the growth of the trade in the main conforms to the same divisions of time. The figures of imported wool are not so valuable a register as in the case of cotton, because no account is taken of home-produce, but the following statistics of foreign and colonial wool imported into England serve to throw light upon the growth of our woollen manufactures.

STATISTICS OF WOOL IMPORTED INTO ENGLAND.

	lbs.		lbs.
1766	1,926,000	1830	32,305,000
1771	1,829,000	1840	49,436,000
1780	323,000	1850	74,326,000
1790	2,582,000	1860	151,218,000
1800	8,609,000	1870	263,250,000
1810	10,914,000	1880	463,309,000
1820	9,775,000	1892	743,046,104

In the silk industry the influence of machinery is complicated by several considerations especially affecting this manufacture. Although the ingenuity and enterprise of the Lombes had introduced complex machinery into silk throwing many years before it was successfully applied to any other branch of textile industry, the trade did not grow as might have been expected, and the successive increments of great mechanical invention were slowly and slightly applied to the silk industry. There are special reasons for this, some of them connected with the intrinsic value of the commodity, others with the social regulation of the trade.

The inherent delicacy of many of the processes, the capricious character of the market for the commodities, the expensive production of which renders them a luxury and especially amenable to the shifts of taste and fashion, have preserved for artistic handicraft the production of many of the finer silk fabrics, or have permitted the application of machinery in a far less degree than in the cotton and woollen industries.

Moreover, the heavy duties imposed upon raw and thrown silk, which accompanied the strict prohibition of the importation of manufactured silk goods in 1765, by aggravating the expenses of production and limiting the market at the very epoch of the great mechanical inventions, prevented any notable expansion of consumption of silk goods, and rendered them quite unable to resist the competition of the younger and more enterprising cotton industry, which, after the introduction of colour-printing early in the nineteenth century, was enabled to out-compete silk in many markets.

Even in the coarser silk fabrics where weaving machinery was successfully applied at an early date, the slow progress in "throwing" greatly retarded the expansion of the trade, and after the repeal of the duty on imported silk in 1826 the number of throwing mills was still quite inadequate to keep pace with the demands of the weavers.[1] Subsequent improvements in throwing mills, and the application of the ingenious weaving machinery of Jacquard and later improvers, have given a great expansion to many branches of the trade in the last fifty years.

But the following statistics of the consumption of raw and thrown silk from 1765 to 1844 indicate how slight and irregular was the expansion of the trade in England during the era of the great inventions and the application of the steam-motor, and how disastrously the duties upon raw and thrown silks weighed upon this branch of manufacture.

---

[1] Porter, *Progress of the Nation*, p. 219.

AVERAGE IMPORTATION.[1]

lbs.			lbs.
1765		1823	2,468,121
1766 }	715,000	1824	4,011,048[2]
1767		1825	3,604,058
1785		1826	2,253,513
1786 }	881,000	1827	4,213,153
1787		1828	4,547,812
1801		1829	2,892,201
to }	1,110,000	1830	4,693,517
1812		1831	4,312,330
1814	2,119,974	1832	4,373,247
1815	1,475,389	1833	4,761,543
1816	1,088,334	1834	4,522,451
1817	1,686,659	1835	5,788,458
1818	1,922,987	1836	6,058,423
1819	1,848,553	1837	4,598,859
1820	2,027,635	1838	4,790,256
1821	2,329,808	1839	4,665,944
1822	2,441,563	1840	4,819,262

In the linen industry the artificial encouragement given to the Irish trade, which, bounty-fed and endowed with a monopoly of the British markets, was naturally slow to adopt new methods of production, and the uncertain condition of the English trade, owing to the strong rivalry of cotton, prevented the early adoption of the new machine methods. Although Adam Smith regarded linen as a promising industry, it was still in a primitive condition. Not until the very end of the eighteenth century were flax spinning mills established in England and Scotland, and not until after 1830 was power-loom weaving introduced, while the introduction of spinning machinery into Ireland upon a scale adequate to supply the looms of that country took place a good deal later.

We see that the early experimental period in the cotton industry produced no very palpable effect upon the volume of the trade. Between 1700 and 1750 the manufacture was

---

[1] Selected from Porter, p. 218.

[2] In 1824 Mr. Huskisson introduced the principle of free trade, securing a reduction of the duties on raw and thrown silks, and in 1825, 1826, considerable further reductions were made. (Cf. Ure, *Philosophy of Manufacture*, p. 454, etc.) But protection of English silk manufactured goods was maintained until the French Treaty of 1860.

stagnant.[1]   The woollen manufacture, owing largely to
the stimulus of the fly-shuttle, showed considerable expansion.   The great increase of cotton production in 1770-90
measures the force of the mechanical inventions without the
aid of the new motor.   The full effects of the introduction
of steam power were retarded by the strain of the French
war.   Though 1800 marks the beginning of a large continuous expansion in both cotton and woollen manufactures,
it was not until about 1817, when the new motor had established itself generally in the large centres of industry and
the energy of the nation was called back to the arts of
peace, that the new forces began to fully manifest their
power.   The period 1840 onwards marks the effect of the
revolution in commerce due to the application of the new
motor to transport purposes, the consequent cheapening of
raw material, especially of cotton, the opening up of new
markets for the purchase of raw material and for the sale of
manufactured goods.   The effect of this diminished cost of
production and increased demand for manufactured goods
upon the textile trades is measured by the rapid pace of the
expansion which followed the opening of the early English
railways and the first establishment of steam-ship traffic.

§ 8.   The development of the textile trades, and that of
cotton   in   particular,   arose   from   the   invention   of   new
machinery.   This machinery was quickened and rendered
effective by the new motor.   The iron trade in its development presents the reverse order.   The discovery of a new
motor was the force which first gave it importance.   The
mechanical   inventions   applied   to   producing   iron   were
stimulated by the requirements of the new motor.

In 1740 the difficulty of obtaining adequate supplies of
timber, and the failure of attempts to utilise pit-coal, had
brought the iron trade to a very low condition.   According
to Scrivener, at this time "the iron trade seemed dwindling
into insignificance and contempt."[2]

The earlier steps in its rise from this degradation are
measured by the increased application of pit-coal and the
diminished use of charcoal.

The progress may be marked as follows :—

---

[1] Cf. Ure, *History of the Cotton Manufacture*, vol. i. p 223.
[2] Scrivener *History of the Iron Trade*, p. 56.

(1) The application of Watt's earlier improvements upon Newcomen's engines, patented 1769, was followed by a rise in the average output for furnaces worked with charcoal. The average output of 294 tons in 1750 was increased to 545 tons in 1788.

(2) The substitution of coke for charcoal proceeding *pari passu* with improved methods of smelting yielded an average output for coke-fed furnaces of 903 tons in 1788. To this epoch belong also Cort's inventions for puddling and rolling (patented 1783-84), which revolutionised the production of bar-iron.

(3) The introduction of Watt's double-power engine in 1788-90. In 1796 the production of pig-iron was double that of 1788, and the average output per furnace raised to 1048 tons.

(4) The substitution of hot for cold blast in 1829, effecting an economy of coal to the extent of 2 tons 18 cwt. per ton of cast-iron.

(5) The adoption of raw coal instead of coke in 1833, effecting a further reduction of expenditure of coal from 5 tons 3½ cwt. to 2 tons 5¼ cwt. in producing a ton of cast-iron.

These were the leading events in the establishment of the iron industry of this country. The following table indicates the growth of the production of English iron from 1740 to 1840:—

Year.	No. of Furnaces.	Average Output. Tons.	Total Produce. Tons.
1740	59	294	17,350
1788	77	909 coke 545 charcoal }	61,300
1796	121	1048	125,079
1806	133	1546	258,206
1825	364 (261 in blast)	2228	703,184
1828	365 (277 in blast)	2530	
1839	378	3592	1,347,790

Here we see that economy of power rather than improved machinery is the efficient cause of the development of industry, or more properly, that economy of power precedes and stimulates the several steps in improvement of machinery.

5

The substitution of coke for charcoal and the application of steam power not merely increased enormously the volume of the trade, but materially affected its localisation. Sussex and Gloucester, two of the chief iron-producing counties when timber was the source of power, had shrunk into insignificance by 1796, when facilities of obtaining coal were a chief determinant. By 1796, it is noteworthy that the four districts of Stafford, Yorkshire, South Wales, and Salop were to the front.

The discovery of the hot blast and substitution of raw coal for coke occurring contemporaneously with the opening of railway enterprise mark the new interdependence of industries in the age of machinery.

Iron has become a foundation upon which every machine-industry alike is built. The metal manufactures, so small in the eighteenth century, attained an unprecedented growth and a paramount importance in the nineteenth.

The application of machinery to the metal industries has led to an output of inventive genius not less remarkable in this century than the textile inventions of the eighteenth century.

"In textile manufacture it was improved machinery that first called for a new motor; in metal manufacture it was the new motor which rendered necessary improved machinery. . . . For all modern purposes the old handicraft implements were clearly obsolete. The immediate result of this requirement was the bringing to the front a number of remarkable men, Brindley, Smeaton, Maudsley, Clements, Bramah, Nasmyth, etc., to supply mechanism of a proportionate capacity and nicety for the new motive-power to act upon and with, and the ultimate result was the adoption of the modern factory system in the larger tool-making and engineering workshops, as well as in metal manufactories proper. Thus there gradually grew up," says Jevons, "a system of machine-tool labour, the substitution of iron hands for human hands, without which the execution of engines and machines in their present perfection would be impossible."[1]

In the later era of machine development an accumulative

---

[1] Cooke Taylor, *Modern Factory System*, p. 164; cf. also Karl Marx, *Capital*, p. 381.

importance is attached to the improvements in the machine-making industries. The great inventions associated with the names of Maudsley and Nasmyth, the cheapening of steel by the Bessemer process, and the various steps by which machines are substituted for hands in the making of machinery, have indirect but rapid and important effects upon each and every machine-industry engaged in producing commodities directly adapted to human use. The economy of effort for industrial purposes requires that a larger and larger proportion of inventive genius and enterprise shall be directed to an interminable displacement of handicraft by machinery in the construction of machinery, and a smaller proportion to the relatively unimportant work of perfecting manufacturing machinery in the detailed processes of each manufacture engaged in the direct satisfaction of some human want.

A general survey of the growth of new industrial methods in the textile and iron industries marks out three periods of abnormal activity in the evolution of modern industry. The first is 1780 to 1795, when the fruits of early inventions are ripened by the effective application of steam to the machine-industries. The second is 1830 to 1845, when industry, reviving after the European strife, utilised more widely the new inventions, and expanded under the new stimulus of steam locomotion. The third is 1856 to 1866 (*circa*), when the construction of machinery by machinery became the settled rule of industry.

§ 9. Bearing in mind how the invention of new specific forms of machinery in the several processes of manufacture proceeds simultaneously with the application of the new motor-power, we find ourselves quite unable to measure the amount of industrial progress due to each respectively. But seeing that the whole of modern industry has thus been set upon a new foundation of coal and iron, it is obvious that the bonds connecting such industries as the textile and the iron must be continually growing closer and stronger. In earlier times the interdependency of trades was slight and indirect, and the progress in any given trade was almost wholly derived from improvements in specific skill or in the application of specific mechanical invention. The earlier eighteenth century did indeed display an abnormal activity in these specific forms of invention. For examples

of these it is only necessary to allude to Lombe's silk
mill at Derby, the pin factory made famous by Adam
Smith, Boulton's hardware factory at Soho, and the
renowned discoveries of Wedgwood. But all increased
productivity due to these specific improvements was but
slight compared with that which followed the discovery of
steam as a motor and the mechanical inventions rendering
it generally applicable, which marked the period 1790 to
1840. By this means the several specific industries were
drawn into closer unity, and found a common basis or
foundation in the arts of mining, iron-working, and engineering which they lacked before.

From these considerations it will follow that the order in
which the several industries has fallen under the sway of
modern industrial methods will largely depend upon the
facility they afford to the application of steam-driven
machinery. The following are some of the principal characteristics of an industry which determine the order, extent,
and pace of its progress as a machine industry:—

(a) *Size and complexity of Structure.*—The importance of
the several leading textile manufactures, the fact that some
of them were highly centralised and already falling under
a factory system, the control of wealthy and intelligent
employers, were among the chief causes which enabled the
new machinery and the new motor to be more quickly and
successfully applied than in smaller, more scattered, and
less developed industries.

(b) *Fixity in quantity and character of demand.*—Perfection of routine-work is the special faculty of machine-
production. Where there is a steady demand for the same
class of goods, machinery can be profitably applied. Where
fashion fluctuates, or the individual taste of the consumer is
a potent factor, machinery cannot so readily undertake the
work. In the textile industries there are many departments
which machinery has not successfully invaded. Much lace-
making, embroidery, certain finer weaving is still done
by human power, with or without the aid of complex
machinery. In the more skilled branches of tailoring,
shoe-making, and other clothing trades, the individual
character of the demand—*i.e.*, the element of irregularity—
has limited the use of machinery. A similar cause retains
human motor-power in certain cases to co-operate with

and control complex machinery, as in the use of the sewing-machine.

(c) *Uniformity of material and of the processes of production.*—Inherent irregularity in the material of labour is adverse to machinery. For this reason the agricultural processes have been slow to pass under steam-power, especially those directly concerned with work on the soil, and even where steam-driven machines are applied their economy, as compared with hand labour, is less marked than in manufacturing processes. To the getting of coal and other minerals steam and other extra-human power has been more slowly and less effectively applied than in dealing with the matter when it is detached from the earth.

(d) *Durability of valuable properties.*—The production of quickly perishable articles being of necessity local and immediate demands a large amount of human service which cannot economically be replaced or largely aided by machinery. The work of the butcher and the baker have been slow to pass under machinery. Where butchering has become a machine-industry to some extent, the direct cause has been the discovery of preservative processes which have diminished the perishability of meat. So with other food industries, the facility of modern means of transport has alone enabled them gradually to pass under the control of machinery. Until quite recently cakes and the finer forms of bakery were a purely local and handicraft product.

(e) *Ease or simplicity of labour involved.*—Where abundance of cheap labour adequate to the work can be obtained, and particularly in trades where women and children are largely engaged, the development of machinery has been generally slower. This condition often unites with (b) or (c) to retain an industry in the "domestic" class. A large mass of essentially "irregular" work requiring a certain delicacy of manipulation, which by reason of its narrowness of scope is yet easily attained, and which makes but slight demands upon muscular force or intelligence, has remained outside machine-production. Important industries containing several processes of this nature have been slower to fall into the complete form of the factory system. The slow progress of the power-loom in cotton and wool until after 1830 is explained by these considerations. The stocking-frame held out against machinery still longer, and hand work still plays an important part in several processes of silk manufacture. Even now, in the very centre of the factory system, Bolton, the old hand-weaving is represented by a few belated survivors.[1]

(*f*) *Skilled Workmanship.*—High skill in manipulation or treatment of material, the element of art infused into handicraft, gives the latter an advantage over the most skilful machinery, or over such machinery as can economically be brought into competition with it. In some of the metal trades, in pottery and glass-making there are many processes which have not been able to dispense with human skill. In these manufactures, moreover, more progress is attributable to specific inventions than to the adoption of the common machinery and motor-power which are not largely available in the most important processes.

From these considerations it will appear that where an industry is large and regular in character, it falls more readily and completely under the control of machinery, where it is small and irregular it conforms more slowly and partially to the new methods. Most of the extractive industries of agriculture, stock-raising, fishing, mining, hunting, are irregular by reason of the nature of their material and its subjection to influences, geological, chemical, climatic, and others which are but slightly under calculation or human control. The final processes by which commodities are adapted to the use of individual consumers necessarily partake of the irregularity or variety of human tastes and desires. We shall therefore find most regularity in the intermediate processes where the raw materials, having been extracted from nature, are being endowed with those qualities of shape, position, etc., which are required to enable them to satisfy human wants. The manufacturing stages where machinery finds fullest application are in nearly all cases intermediate stages of production. Even where machine-production seems directly to satisfy some human want, there are commonly some final processes required which involve individual skill. Almost all products which satisfy the desires of man pass through a large number of productive processes which may be classed as extractive, transport, manufacturing, and distributive. These are, of course, not in all cases clearly distinguishable. Mixed with

[1] Schulze-Gaevernitz, p. 140.

the extractive processes of mining and wheat-raising are several processes of transport and manufacture : the various stages of manufacture may be broken by stages of transport: a final process of manipulation or manufacture may precede the final act of distribution, as in the sale of drugs to the consumer. But, generally speaking, these four kinds of productive processes mark four historic stages in the passage from raw material to finished commodity.

The two middle stages of transport and manufacture have fallen far more fully under the control of steam-driven machinery than the others, and it is in the elaboration of older manufacturing and transport processes and the addition of new processes that we trace the largest effects of the evolution of modern industrial methods.

The following list of the divisions under which workers engaged in the production of material wealth are classified for purposes of the census may serve to bring out more clearly this proportionate development of machinery. The figures appended give the numbers engaged in the several occupations in 1891, and serve to approximately indicate the relative importance of the several principal branches of industry :—

Agriculture	...	1,311,720
Fishing ...	...	25,225
Mining ...	...	561,637
Stone, clay, road-making ...	...	209,972
Transport—		
(a) Railways	...	186,774
(b) Roads	...	366,605
(c) Canals, rivers, seas	...	208,443
(d) Messages and porterage	...	194,044
Houses, furniture, and decorations		820,582
Food and lodgings		797,989
Iron and steel	...	380,193
Other metals	...	146,550
Ships and boats	...	170,517
Carriages and harness	...	108,780
Machines and implements	...	342,231
Textiles ...	...	1,128,589
Dress ...	...	1,099,833
Earthenware and glass ...	...	90,007
Chemicals and compounds ...	...	56,047
Books ...	...	135,616
Animal substances (manufacture) ...		76,566
Vegetable substances (paper, etc.) ...		196,889
General mechanics and labourers ...		805,105
Commercial—		
(a) Merchants and agents...		363,037
(b) Dealers in money ...		21,891
(c) Insurance ...		31,437
Engineers and surveyors ...	...	15,441

In glancing down this list of the chief industries engaged in the production of commercial wealth, it will be recognised at once that the manufacturing and transport industries are those to which steam-power and the economies of large pro- duction have been especially applied. Though, historically, the first industrial use of steam-power was in coal-mining, it remains true that the extensive application of modern machinery to agriculture and the other extractive industries is of comparatively recent growth, while the work of retail distribution has hitherto made but trifling use of machinery and steam-power. Only within the last few years have a few gigantic retail distributive businesses shown a tendency to apply steam and electricity to mechanical contrivances for purposes of distribution.

§ 10. The new industrial forces first applied to the cotton spinning of South Lancashire, and rapidly forcing their way into other branches of the textile manufactures, then more gradually transforming the industrial methods of the machinery, hardware, and other staple English manu- factures, passed into the Western Continent of Europe and America, destroying the old domestic industry and establishing in every civilised country the reign of steam- driven machinery. The factors determining the order and pace of the new movement in the several countries are numerous and complex. In considering the order of machine-development, it must be remembered that the different nations did not start from an equal footing at the opening of the age of great inventions. By the begin- ning of the eighteenth century England had established a certain supremacy in commerce. The growth of her colonial possessions since the Revolution and the drastic and successful character of her maritime policy had enabled her to outstrip Holland. In 1729 by far the greater part of the Swedish iron exported from Gothenburg went to England for shipbuilding purposes.[1] At the close of the seventeenth century Gregory King placed England, Hol- land, and France at the head of the industrial nations with regard to the productivity of their labour.[2] Italy and

---

[1] Yeats, *The Growth and Vicissitudes of Commerce*, p. 284.
[2] The average income for England in 1688 he puts at £7 18s. ; for Holland, £8 1s. 4d. ; France, £6—p. 47. Such an estimate, however, has little value.

Germany were little behind in the exercise of manufacturing arts, though the naval superiority and foreign possessions of the above-named nations gave them the commercial superiority. By 1760 England had strengthened her position as regards foreign commerce, and her woollen industry was the largest and most highly-developed industry in the world. But so far as the arts of manufacture themselves were concerned there was no such superiority in England as to justify the expectation of the position she held at the opening of the nineteenth century. In many branches of the textile arts, especially in silk spinning and in dyeing, in pottery, printing, and other manufactures, more inventive genius and more skill were shown on the Continent, and there seemed *à priori* no reason why England should outstrip so signally her competitors.

The chief factors in determining the order of the development of modern industrial methods in the several countries may be classified as natural, political, economic.

NATURAL. (1) *The structure and position of the several countries.*—The insular character of Great Britain, her natural facilities for procuring raw materials of manufacture and supplies of foreign food to enable her population to specialise in manufacture, the number and variety of easily accessible markets for her manufactures, gave her an immense advantage. Add to this a temperate climate, excellent internal communication by river (or canal), and an absence of mountain barriers between the several districts. These advantages were of greater relative importance before steam transport, but they played a large part in facilitating the establishment of effective steam transport in England. Extent of sea-board and good harbourage have in no small measure directed the course of modern industry, giving to England, Holland, France, Italy an advantage which the levelling tendency of modern machinery has not yet been able to counteract. The slow progress of Germany until recent years, and the still slow progress of Russia, is attributable more to these physical barriers of free communication, internal and external, than to any other single cause that can be adduced. Inherent resources of the soil, quality of land for agriculture, the proximity of large supplies of coal and iron and other requisites of the production of machinery and power rank as important determinants

of progress.   The machine development of France in
particular has been retarded by the slow discovery of her
natural areas of manufacture, the districts where coal and
iron lie near to one another in easily accessible supply.
The same remark applies to Germany and to the United
States.   At the close of last century, when the iron trade of
England was rapidly advancing, the iron trade of France
were quite insignificant, and during the earlier years of the
nineteenth century the progress was extremely slight.[1]

(2) *Race and National Character.*—Closely related to
climate and soil, these qualities of race are a powerful
directing influence in industry.   Muscular strength and
endurance, yielding in a temperate climate an even continuity of vigorous effort; keen zest of material comfort
stimulating invention and enterprise; acquisitiveness, and
the love of external display; the moral capacities of industry,
truth, orderly co-operation; all these are leading factors determining the ability and inclination of the several nations
to adopt new industrial methods.   Moral qualities in
English workmanship have indisputably played a large
part in securing her supremacy.   "A British trade-mark
was accepted as a guarantee of excellence, while the products of other countries were viewed with a suspicion
justified by experience of their comparative inferiority."[2]
The more highly civilised nations have thus gained by this
civilisation, and have widened the distance which separates
them from the less civilised.   England, France, Germany,
Holland, and the United States are in wealth and in
industrial methods far more widely removed from Spain and
Russia than was the case a hundred years ago.

(b) POLITICAL.—Statecraft has played an important part
in determining the order and pace of industrial progress.
The possession of numerous colonies and other political
attachments in different parts of the world, comprising a large
variety of material resources, gave to England, and in a less
measure to France, Holland, Spain, a great advantage.
The tyrannical use these nations made of their colonies for

---

[1] In 1810 the total produce was 140,000 tons.
     ,, 1818   ,,   ,,   ,, 114,000 ,,
     ,, 1824   ,,   ,,   ,, 164,000 ,,
     (Scrivener, *History of the Iron Trade*, p. 153.)
[2] Yeats, *Growth and Vicissitudes of Commerce*, p. 285.

the purpose of building up home manufactures enabled them to specialise more widely and safely in those industries to which the new methods of production were first applied. Even after the North American colonies broke loose, the policy of repression England had applied to their budding manufactures enabled her to retain to a large extent the markets thus created for her manufactured goods.

The large annexations England made during the eighteenth and early nineteenth centuries gave her a monopoly of many of the finest markets for the purchase of raw materials and for the sale of manufactured goods. The large demand thus established for her textile and metal wares served not only to stimulate fresh inventions, but enabled her to utilise many improvements which could only be profitably applied in the case of large industries with secure and expanding markets.

But the most important factor determining the priority of England was the political condition of continental Europe at the very period when the new machinery and motor-power were beginning to establish confidence in the new industrial order. When Crompton's mule, Cartwright's power-loom, Watt's engines were transforming the industry of England, her continental rivals had all their energies absorbed in wars and political revolutions. The United States and Sweden were the only commercial nations of any significance who, being neutral, obtained a large direct gain from the European strife. Yet England, in spite of the immense drain of blood and money she sustained, under the momentum of the new motor-power far outstripped the rivalry of such states. Though she had to pay a heavy price for her immunity from invasion, she thereby secured an immense start in the race of modern machine-production. Until 1820 she had the game in her own hands. In European trade she had a practical monopoly of the rapidly advancing cotton industry. It was this monopoly which, ruthlessly applied to maintain prices at a highly remunerative rate, and to keep down wages to starvation point, built up, in an age of supreme and almost universal misery for the masses, the rapid and colossal fortunes of the cotton kings. Not until peace was established did the textile and other factories begin to take shape upon the Continent, and many years elapsed before they were able to compete effectively with England. Switzerland was the first continental country to actively adopt the new methods. The large supply of water-power stood her in good stead, and the people took more willingly to the factory system than in other countries.[1] France was slower in her development, in spite of the strong protective system by which she strove, though not very successfully, to exclude English cotton goods. The fall of English prices and profits in the cotton trade between 1820 and 1830 marks clearly the breakdown of the English monopoly before the cheap labour of Alsace and the cheap raw material of the United States, now organised in the factory system with the new machinery.[2] In this, the most advanced trade, the world-competition which now is operative in a thousand different industries, measuring and levelling economic advantages, first clearly shows itself, and in 1836 Ure finds the continental nations and America competing successfully with England in markets which had hitherto been entirely her own.

(c) ECONOMIC CONDITIONS.—The transformation of English agriculture, the growth of large farms, drove great numbers of English peasants into the towns, and furnished a large supply of cheap labour for the new machinery.

This movement was accelerated by the vices of our land tenure. In France and Germany, where the agricultural workers had a stronger interest and property in their land, they were less easily detached for factory purposes. But in England, where the labourer had no property in the land, reformed methods of agriculture and the operation of the Poor Law combined to incite the large proprietors and farmers to rid themselves of all superfluous population in the rural parts and accelerated the migration into the towns.

---

[1] Schulze-Gaevernitz, *Der Grossbetrieb*, p. 48.

[2] Ellison, *History of the Cotton Trade*, presents the following interesting table (yarn, 40 hanks to the lb.) :—

	1779.	1784.	1799	1812.	1830.	1882.
	s. d.	s. d.	s. d.	s. d.	s. d.	s. d.
Selling price	16 0	10 11	7 6	2 6	1 2½	0 10½
Cost of Cotton (18 oz.)	2 0	2 0	3 4	1 6	0 7¾	0 7⅛
Labour & Capital	14 0	8 11	4 2	1 0	0 6¾	0 3⅞

Here the population bred with a rapidity hitherto unknown. The increase of population in England and Wales during the thirty years from 1770 to 1800 is placed at 1,959,590, or 27$\frac{1}{10}$ per cent., while during the next thirty years, 1800 to 1830, it amounted to 5,024,207, or 56$\frac{2}{3}$ per cent.[1] This large supply of cheap labour in the towns enabled the Lancashire and Yorkshire factories to grow with startling rapidity. The exhaustion left by the Napoleonic wars, the political disorder and insecurity which prevailed on the Continent, retarded until much later the effective competition of other European nations who were behind England in skill, knowledge, and the possession of markets. The American manufactures which had sprung up after the revolution had made considerable strides, but the conquest and settlement of vast new areas of land, and the immense facilities afforded for the production of raw material, retarded their rate of growth until long after the opening of this century. It was, indeed, not until about 1845 that the cotton manufacture made rapid strides in the United States. During the twenty years previous the progress had been very slight, but between 1845 and 1859 a very substantial and, making allowance for fluctuations in the cotton crops, a very steady growth took place.[2]

Another great economic advantage which assisted England was the fact that she, more than any other European nation, had broken down the old industrial order, with its guilds, its elaborate restrictions, and conservative methods. Personal freedom, security of property, liberty to work and live where and how one liked, existed in England to an extent unknown on the Continent before the French Revolution. The following account of the condition of the cotton manufacture in Germany in the eighteenth century will serve to indicate the obstacles to the reformed methods of industry:—"Everything was done by rule. Spinning came under public inspection, and the yarn was collected by officials. The privilege of weaving was confined to the confraternity of the guild. Methods of production were strictly prescribed; public inspectors exercised control. Defects in weaving were visited with punishment. Moreover,

---

[1] Porter, *Progress of the Nation*, p. 13. Eighteenth century figures are, however, not trustworthy. The first census was in 1801.

[2] Ure, *Philosophy of Manufactures*, p. 531.

the right of dealing in cotton goods was confined to the
confraternity of the merchant guild: to be a master-weaver
had almost the significance of a public office. Besides
other qualifications, there was the condition of a formal
examination. The sale also was under strict supervision; for a long time a fixed price prevailed, and a
maximum sale was officially prescribed for each dealer.
The dealer had to dispose of his wares to the weaver,
because the latter had guaranteed to him a monopoly of
the export trade."[1]

Under such conditions the new machine-industry could
make little advance. Excepting in the case of the woollen
industries, England had for the most part already shaken
off the old regulations before 1770. In particular, the
cotton trade, which was in the vanguard of the movement,
being of recent growth and settling outside the guild towns,
had never known such restrictions, and therefore lent itself
to the new order with a far greater facility than the older
trades. Moreover, England was free from the innumerable
and vexatious local taxes and restrictions prevalent in
France and in the petty governments of Germany.
Although the major part of these foolish and pernicious
regulations has been long swept away from Germany and
other continental nations, the retarding influence they
exercised, in common with the wider national system of
protection which still survives, kept back the cotton
industry, so that in Germany it still stands half a century
behind its place in England.[2]

The following figures show how substantial was the lead
held by England in the cotton manufacture a little before
the middle of the century.

[1] Schulze-Gaevernitz, *Der Grossbetrieb*, p. 34.
[2] In 1882 42 per cent. of the German textile industry was still conducted in the home or domestic workshop, while only 38 per cent. was
carried on in factories employing more than 50 persons. More weavers
were still engaged with hand-looms than with power-looms, and the
latter was so little developed that the hand-loom could still hold its own
in many articles. Knitting, lace-making, and other minor textile industries are still in the main home industries.—(*Social Peace*, p. 113.)
"While in England in 1885 each spinning or weaving mill had an
average of 191 operatives, each spinning mill in Germany in 1882
employed an average of 10 persons only."—(Brentano, *Hours, Wages,
and Production*, p. 64.)

NUMBER OF SPINDLES WORKING IN COTTON MILLS IN 1846.[1]

	Spindles.
England and Wales	15,554,619
Scotland	1,727,871
Ireland	215,503
Austria and Italy	1,500,000
France	3,500,000
Belgium	420,000
Switzerland	650,000
Russia	7,585,000
United States	3,500,000
States of the Zollverein	815,000
	35,467,993

The development of the cotton industry in 1888 in the chief industrial countries, as indicated by the consumption of raw cotton, is expressed in the accompanying diagram.

Lastly, the national trade policy of England was of signal advantage in her machine development. Her early protective system had, by the enlargement of her carrying trade and the increase of her colonial possessions, laid the foundation of a large complex trade with the more distant parts of the world, though for a time it crippled our European commerce. While we doubtless sacrificed other interests by this course of policy, it must be generally admitted that " English industries would not have advanced so rapidly without Protection."[2] But as we built up our manufacturing industries by Protection, so we undoubtedly conserved and strengthened them by Free Trade—first, by the remission of tariffs upon the raw materials of manufacture and machine-making, and later on by the free admission of food stuffs, which were a prime essential to a nation destined to specialise in manufacture. France, our chief national competitor, weakened her position by a double protective policy, not merely refusing admittance to foreign manufactures in her markets, but retaining heavy duties upon the importation of foreign coal and iron, the foundational constituents of machine-production. This protective policy, adopted by nations whose skill, industry, and natural resources would have rendered them formidable competitors

[1] Ure, *Philosophy of Manufactures*, p. 515.
[2] Toynbee, *Industrial Revolution*, p. 79.

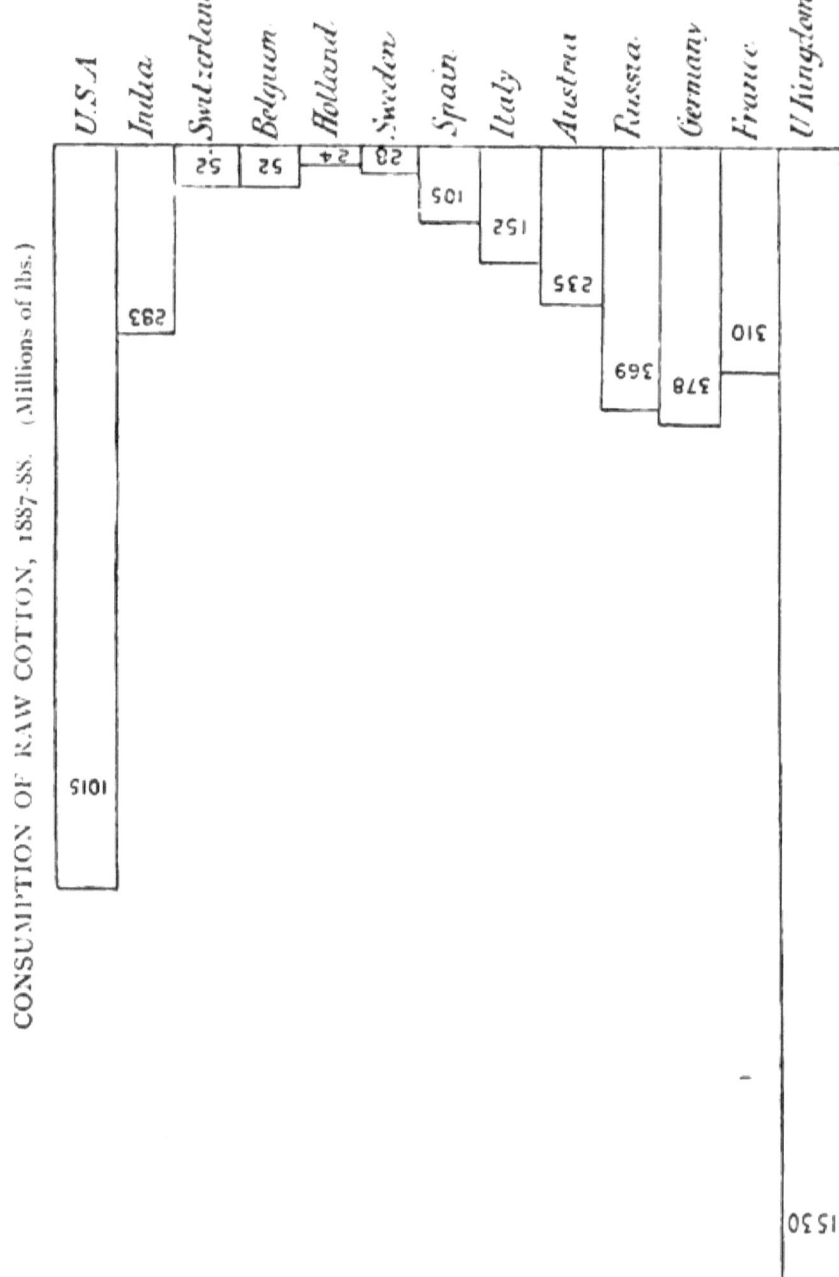

CONSUMPTION OF RAW COTTON, 1887-88. (Millions of lbs.)

U.S.A	India	Switzerland	Belgium	Holland	Sweden	Spain	Italy	Austria	Russia	Germany	France	U.Kingdom
1015	293	25	25	24	28	105	152	235	369	378	310	1550

to English manufacturers, has hindered considerably the operation of those economic forces which impel old and thickly-peopled countries to specialise in manufacture and trade, and so has retarded the general development of modern machine-production. But while protective tariffs indisputably operate in this way, it is not possible to determine the extent of their influence. In a large country of rich resources a high degree of specialisation in manufacture is possible in spite of a protective policy. The pressure of high wages is an economic force more powerfully operative than any other in stimulating the adoption of elaborate machinery.[1] Both in the textile and the iron industries the United States present examples of factory development more advanced even than those of England. Certain processes of warping and winding are done by machinery in America which are still done by hand labour in England.[2] The chain and nail-making trades, which employ large numbers of women in South Staffordshire and Worcestershire, are made more cheaply by machinery in America.[3] Moreover, the high standard of living and the greater skill of the American operatives enables them to tend more machines. In German factories a weaver tends two, or rarely three looms; in Lancashire women weavers undertake four, and in Massachusetts often six looms, and sometimes eight.[4]

Thus we see how the new industrial forces were determined in the order of their operation by the character and conditions of the several countries, their geographical position and physical resources, the elements of racial character, political and industrial institutions, deliberate economic policies, and, above all, by the absorbing nature of the military and political events contemporary with the outburst of inventive ingenuity. The composition of these forces determined the several lines of less resistance along which the new industry moved.

The exact measurement of so multiform a force is

[1] The highly elaborate American machine industry of watch-making is a striking example of this influence of high wages. Cf. Schulze-Gaevernitz, *Social Peace*, p. 125.

[2] Schoenhof, *Economy of High Wages*, p. 279.

[3] *Ibid.*, pp. 225, 226.

[4] Schulze-Gaevernitz, p. 66 (note). This six and eight-loom weaving is, however, at a lower speed.

impossible. The appended tables and diagrams may, however, serve to indicate the progress of the several industrial nations as measured by (i.) development of railway and merchant shipping; (ii.) consumption of coal and iron; (iii.) application of steam-power; (iv.) estimated annual value of manufactures :—

I. COMPARATIVE MILEAGE OF RAILWAYS, 1840 TO 1890.

	1840.	1850.	1860.	1870.	1880.	1890.
United Kingdom	800	6,600	10,400	15,500	17,900	19,800
Continent of Europe	800	7,800	21,400	47,800	83,800	110,200
United States	2,800	9,000	30,600	53,400	93,600	156,000
India	—	—	800	4,800	9,300	16,000
Australia	—	—	200	1,200	5,400	10,100
Rest of the World	—	—	2,800	5,500	18,400	42,300

RAILWAY MILEAGE IN RELATION TO AREA AND POPULATION.

Area.	Square Miles.	Density of Population per Square Mile (1890).	Railway Mileage (1888).
United Kingdom	120,849	... 320 ...	19,810
France	204,092	... 184 ...	20,900
Germany	208,738	... 233 ...	24,270
Russia	1,902,227	... 42 ...	17,700
Austria	240,942	... 166 ...	15,610
Italy	110,623	... 260 ...	7,830
Spain	197,670	... 86 ...	5,930
Portugal	34,038	... 136 ...	1,190
Sweden	170,979	... 28 ...	4,670
Norway	124,495	... 16 ...	970
Denmark	15,289	... 133 ...	1,220
Holland	12,648	... 350 ...	1,700
Belgium	11,373	... 530 ...	2,760
Switzerland	15,976	... 190 ...	1,870
Greece	25,041	... 88 ...	370
Turkey	65,909	... 73 ...	900
U.S.A. (excluding Alaska and Indian territory)	1,175,550	... 21 ...	156,080
Japan	145,655	... 274 ...	910
India	964,992	... 229 ...	15,250
Australia	3,030,771	... 1.20 ...	10,140
Canada	3,315,647	... 1.45 ...	12,700
Egypt (cultiv. area)	12,976	... 638 ...	1,260

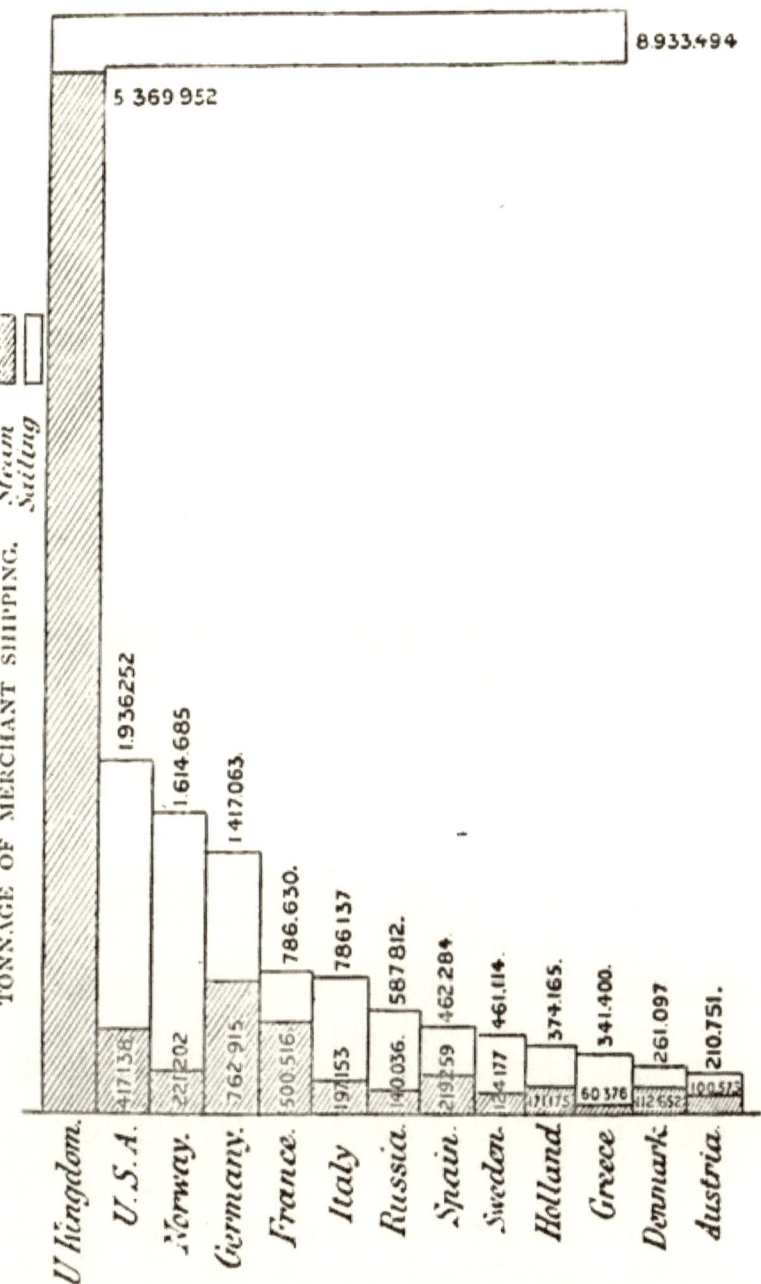

TONNAGE OF MERCHANT SHIPPING. Steam Sailing

8.933.494

5 369 952

1.936.252

1.614.685

1.417.063

786.630.

786.137

587.812.

462.284

461.014

374.165.

341.400.

261.097

210.751.

417.136

221.202

762.915

500.516

197.153

40.036.

219.159

124.177

171.175

60.376

112.652

100.515

U. Kingdom. U. S. A. Norway. Germany. France. Italy. Russia. Spain. Sweden. Holland. Greece. Denmark. Austria.

COMPARATIVE TABLE OF CONSUMPTION OF COAL AND IRON
PER INHABITANT IN DIFFERENT COUNTRIES

Coal (cwts.)

Iron (lbs.)

Country	Iron (lbs.)	Coal (cwts.)
U.Kingdom	400	73
Belgium	310	48
U.S.A	290	40
Germany	204	28
Sweden	170	6
France	112	16
Austria	45	11
Spain	37	2
Italy	22	2
Russia	19	2

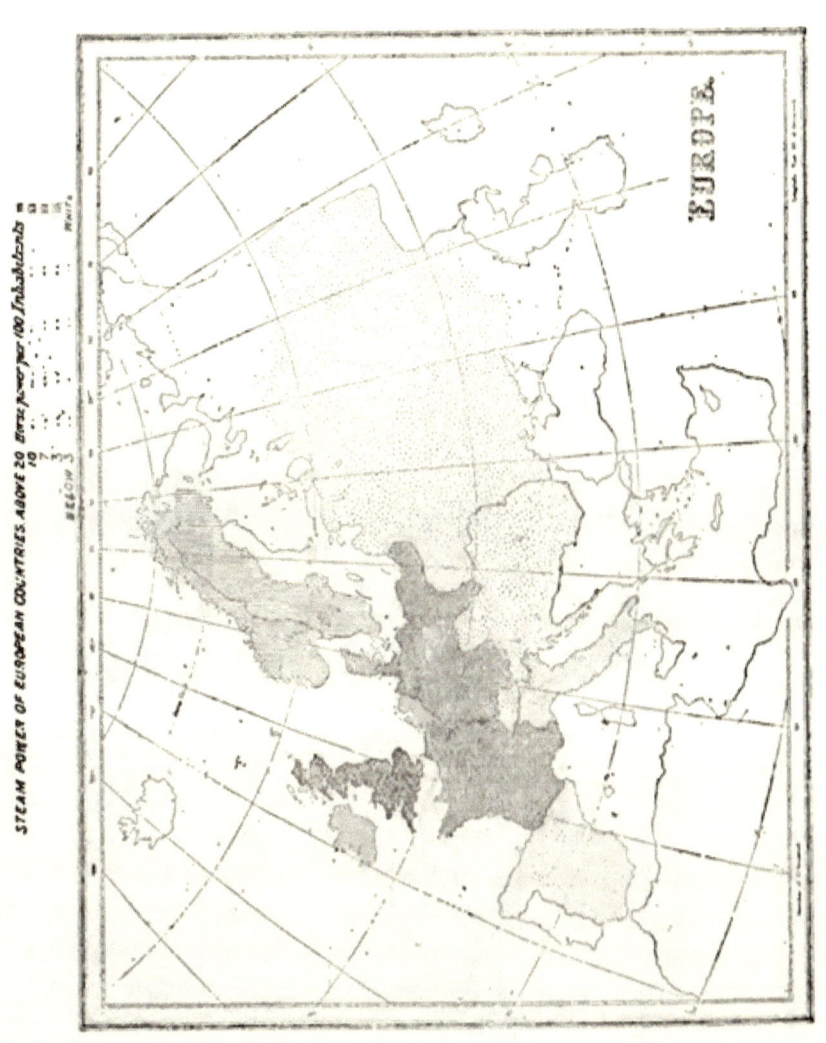

STEAM POWER OF EUROPEAN COUNTRIES ABOVE 20 Horse power per 100 Inhabitants

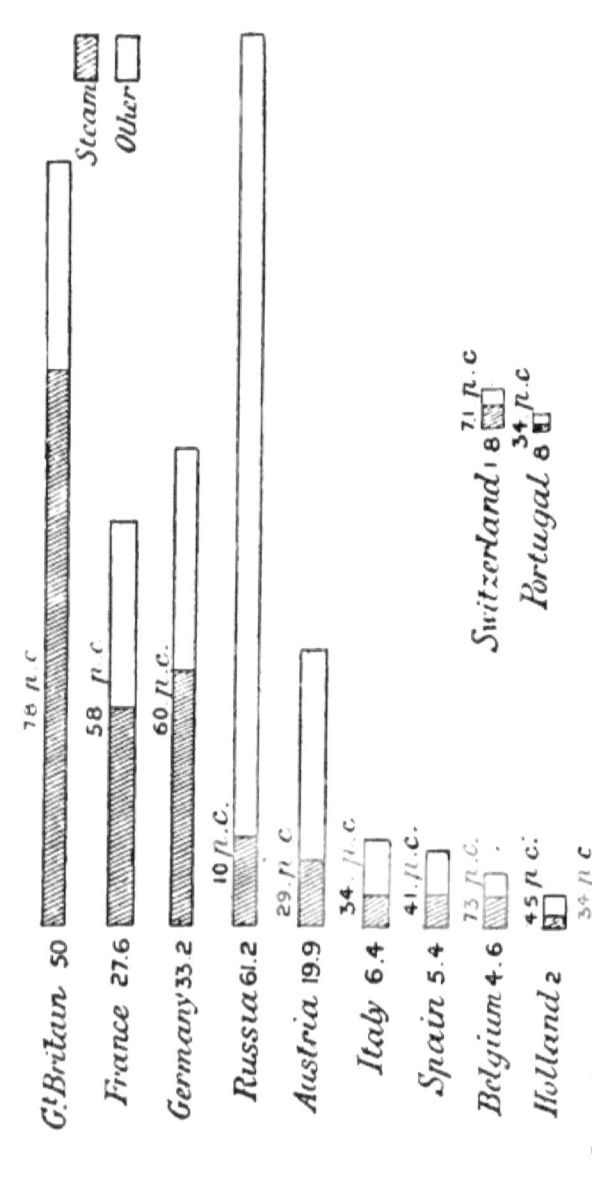

STEAM AND OTHER POWER IN DIFFERENT COUNTRIES.

ESTIMATED ANNUAL VALUE OF MANUFACTURES.

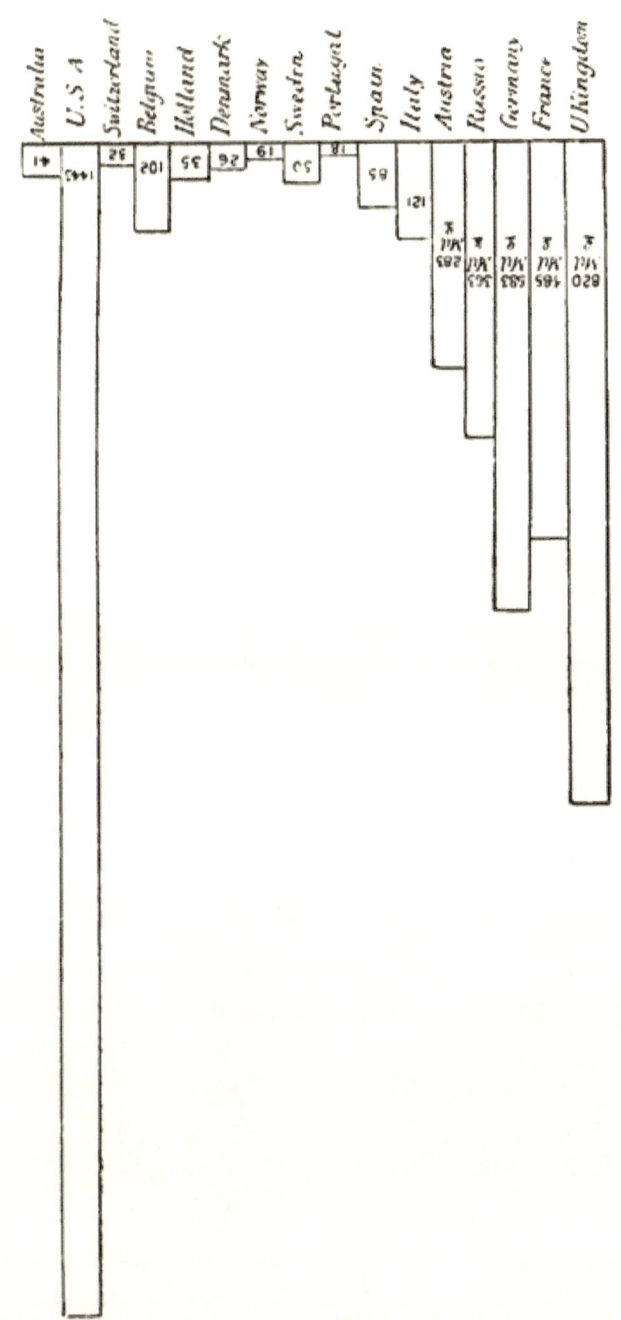

88

CHAPTER IV.

THE STRUCTURE OF MODERN INDUSTRY.

§ 1. *Growing Size of the Business-Unit.*
§ 2. *Relative Increase of Capital and Labour in the Business.*
§ 3. *Increased Complexity and Integration of Business Structure.*
§ 4. *Structure and Size of the Market for different Commodities.*
§ 5. *Machinery a direct Agent in expanding Market Areas.*
§ 6. *Expanded Time-area of the Market.*
§ 7. *Interdependency of Markets.*
§ 8. *Sympathetic and Antagonistic Relations between Trades.*
§ 9. *National and Local Specialisation in Industry.*
§ 10. *Influences determining Localisation of Industry under World-Competition.*
§ 11. *Impossibility of Final Settlement of Industry.*
§ 12. *Specialisation in Districts and Towns.*
§ 13. *Specialisation within the Town.*

§ 1. Turning once more to the unit of industry, the Business, and thence to the Trade and the Market, or area of competition, it is necessary to examine the structural and functional changes brought about by the action of the new industrial forces.

In considering the effect of modern machine-production upon the Business, the most obvious external change is a great increase in size. The typical unit of production is no longer a single family or a small group of persons working with a few cheap simple tools upon small quantities of material, but a compact and closely organised mass of labour composed of hundreds or thousands of individuals, co-operating with large quantities of expensive and intricate machinery, through which passes a continuous and mighty volume of raw material on its journey to the hands of the consuming public.

The expansion in mass of labour and capital composing the industrial unit does not, however, proceed at the same pace in the different industries.

The largest growths are found in two classes of industry. First, those which close dependence on monopoly of land, or other privilege conferred by state or municipal government, has placed outside competition. The size here is determined by that amount of capital required to achieve the most profitable equation of supply and demand prices under terms of monopoly.[1] In this class are placed such large businesses as railways, gas, or water companies. Second, those industries where the net advantages of large-scale production over small scale in competitive industry are greatest. Generally speaking, those industries where the most expensive machinery is employed come under this head, or where, as in banking and financial business, a large capital is managed more economically, and enjoys a monopoly of certain profitable kinds of work.

In retail trade, where neither of these forces is so powerfully operative, the increase in mass of capital and labour is not so great, though here too the economies of large-scale production are giving more and more prominence to the Universal Provider, and a large number of local shops are falling into the hands of companies. Large syndicates of capital at Smithfield are owning butchers' shops in most large towns, the drapery, jewellery, shoe trade are more and more passing into the hands of large companies, while an increased proportion of tobacconists, publicans, grocers, and other retailers are practically but agents of large capitalist firms. In such branches of agriculture as have lent themselves most effectively to new machinery the same movement is visible in the prevalence of large farming. This is seen everywhere where land is placed on the same property footing as other forms of capital. Though small farms are for some purposes still capable of yielding a large net as well as gross product, it is for the most part the legal,

---

[1] Cf. Chap. VI. for a discussion of this equation of maximum profit.

customary, and sentimental restrictions on free transfer of land that impede the tendency towards large farming.

It is, however, in the manufacturing and transport industries that we trace the most general and rapid growth of the unit of production. And here machinery is the chief external cause. Gigantic railways and steamship companies are the successors of stage coach businesses and small shippers. The size and value of the modern cotton factory, iron works, sugar refinery, or brewery are incomparably greater than the units of which these industries were composed a century and a half ago. In certain highly-machined industries the size of the unit is so enlarged that the number of businesses engaged in turning out the ever-growing output is actually diminishing. Among textile industries the spinning mills of England and Wales show a marked diminution in numbers between 1870 and 1890, while a similar movement in weaving mills is only retarded by the capacity of small sweating masters to compete with the more developed factories in certain minor branches, such as tape manufacture, and by the survival of the home worker owning his loom and hiring his power in such trades as the ribbon weaving of Coventry.[1]

The following statistics[2] of the cotton and woollen industries in Great Britain serve to illustrate the growing size of the unit of production in the representative branches of textile work:—

COTTON.

	NO. OF MILLS.					NO. OF SPINDLES.		
	Spinning.	Weaving.	Spinning and Weaving.	Others.	Total.	Spinning.	Doubling.	Power-Looms.
1870 ..	1108	693	532	150	2483	33,995,221	3,723,537	440,676
1890 ..	935	990	438	175	2538	40,511,934	3,992,885	615,714

WOOLLEN.

| 1870 .. | 648 | 100 | 860 | 212 | 1829 | 2,531,768 | 160,903 | 48,140 |
| 1890 .. | 494 | 124 | 895 | 280 | 1793 | 2,107,209 | 299,793 | 61,831 |

This increase of the number of spindles and looms in the average textile mill is more significant when the "speeding

---

[1] *Report to Labour Commission on Employment of Women* (1893), p. 125.

[2] *Statistical Abstract*, 1878-92, p. 182.

up" of modern machinery is taken into account. The increased size of the unit of industry as measured by productivity is even greater than appears from the statistics above quoted.

Schulze-Gaevernitz points out that in the thirty years between 1856 and 1885, while the factories in cotton spinning and weaving only increased from 2210 to 2633, the number of spindles increased from 28,010,217 to 44,348,921, the number of looms from 298,847 to 560,955, and that since both spindles and looms worked much faster in 1885 than in 1856, the output has increased in still greater proportion.[1]

Turning to another highly-developed machine industry, that of milling, we find a similar movement. Flour mills are diminishing in number both in England and in the United States. The period 1884-86 showed a diminution in the number of flour mills in the United States from 25,079 to 18,267, though the total productive power of the smaller number was greatly increased. Mr. Wells finds a similar tendency in the general manufacturing industry of the United States:—"Between 1850 and 1860 the number of manufacturing firms and corporations in the United States increased from 123,025 to 140,433, and the value of manufactured products increased from $1,019,106,616 to $1,885,861,876, so that in that decade there was an increase of 17,408 establishments, to an increase of $866,755,060 in the value of products. In 1870 there were 252,148 firms and corporations so employed, producing $4,232,325,442 in manufactured products; or an increase of 111,715 establishments in the decade of 1860 to 1870 gave an increase of $2,346,463,766 in the value of products. In 1880 the number of manufacturing establishments was returned at 253,852, producing articles valued at $5,365,579,191, or an addition of only 1704 firms and corporations was accompanied with an increase of product of $1,133,537,749. Here then is a demonstration that the average product of a manufacturing establishment in the United States in 1880 was just 60 per cent. greater than it was in 1860."[2]

---

[1] *Social Peace*, p. 126; cf. also Brentano, *Hours, Labour, and Production*, p. 60.

[2] *Contemporary Review*, 1889, p. 394.

§ 2. While the mass of capital and labour which constitutes a business is growing, the latter grows less rapidly than
the former. That is to say, capital is in point of size becoming more and more the dominant factor in the business.
With the effect of this upon the economic character and conditions of labour we are not here concerned. The subject
requires a separate treatment. Here it suffices to recognise
the quantitative change that has taken place. Under
domestic industry the value of the implements used was, as
a rule, equivalent only to a few months' wages. In 1845
McCulloch estimated that the fixed capital in well-appointed
cotton mills amounted to about two years' wages of an
operative.[1] In 1890 Professor Marshall assigns a capital in
plant amounting to about £200 or five years' wages for
every man, woman, and child in a fully-equipped spinning
mill.[2] In the typical modern industry, that of cotton-spinning and weaving, the increasing size is both continuous
and rapid. The average number of spindles and looms to
the single factory in 1850 and 1885 are as follows :—

	Spindles.	Power-Looms.
1850 ...	... 10,858	... 155
1885 ...	... 15,227	... 213

Even these figures do not fully represent the facts, for
they include considerable numbers of mills of the older sort,
where spinning and weaving are carried on together.
Taking the more highly specialised spinning mills in the
Oldham district, the average is stated at 65,000, while the
largest mills have as many as 185,000 spindles. So also
the average number of power-looms in the North Lancashire
district is placed at 600, the largest number in a single
business amounting to 4500.[3]

"Again, the cost of a steamship is perhaps equivalent to
the labour of ten years or more of those who work her,
while a capital of about £900,000,000 invested in railways
in England and Wales is equivalent to the work for about
twenty years of the 400,000 people employed on them."[4]

This growth in the unit of capital is, as we perceive,

[1] Porter, *Progress of the Nation*, p. 216.
[2] *Principles of Economics*, 2nd edit., p. 282.
[3] Schulze-Gaevernitz, *Der Grossbetrieb*, p. 90.
[4] Marshall, *Principles of Economics*, 2nd edit., p. 283.

largely due to the establishment of large and expensive machinery and other plant as a leading feature in modern production. The fact that modern methods are largely instrumental in increasing the quantity of products might lead us to suppose that the growth of the raw material or circulating part of the capital of a business would correspond with the growth of fixed forms of capital. This, however, is not the case. In the most highly organised machine industry an increasing proportion of the economy goes into the improved methods of manipulating material so as to prevent waste, and by improved quality of work and elaboration of manufacture to get a larger net amount of product out of a given quantity of raw material.

In cotton-spinning, for example, since 1834 the waste of raw material has been reduced from $\frac{1}{4}$ to about $\frac{1}{10}$; inferior material, once useless, is now mixed with better stuff; and more important still, modern machinery has, by adapting itself to the spinning of finer yarn, effected great saving in the quantity consumed by each spindle. In many other industries we shall find this same process going on, whereby the proportion of capital which consists of raw material is reduced, and the proportion which consists in machinery and other fixed capital enhanced.

The growth of the unit of capital in the developed modern manufacturing business entails also a growth in the unit of labour, though not a corresponding growth. The number of employees in a business is larger in proportion as the business passes into the stage of highest industrial organisation. In the United States in 1880 it was estimated that the average number of employees in a manufacturing business for the whole country was a little less than 11, but in the chief manufacturing states of Massachusetts, Connecticut, and Rhode Island it was about 25, while in Pittsburg, the great centre of iron industry, it was more than 33.

§ 3. In addition to increased size we find increased and ever-increasing complexity of structure in the business-unit. This has proceeded in two directions, horizontally and laterally—that is to say, by subdivision and accession of processes on the one hand, and by an increased variety of products, and therefore of processes, upon the other hand. The constantly growing specialisation of fixed capital and of

labour in our factories and workshops is a commonplace.
Adam Smith's famous pin manufactory, with its ten separate
processes, has been left far behind. In a modern shoe
factory in the United States there are sixty-four distinct
processes. Grain, in the elaborate machinery of a steam
flour mill, passes through a score of different stages,
cleaning, winnowing, grinding, etc. The American machine-
made watch is the product of 370 separate processes.
The organisation of a modern textile factory provides
a dozen different processes contributing to the spinning
or weaving of cotton or silk. New processes of cleaning,
finishing, and ornamenting are continually being added.
The subsidiary process of packing, the manufacture of
packing cases, the printing of labels, etc., are taken on
in many factories.[1] Many branches of production which
were formerly carried on in separate places and as
separate business-units are grouped together under the
factory roof, or if still separated locally, and executed
by separate machinery and power, are related as forming
part of the same business, and are under the same management. So in the woollen manufactures the preliminary
processes of sorting and cleansing, carding or combing,
as well as the main processes of spinning and weaving,
fulling, dyeing, and finishing, each of which was once
committed to a separate and independent group of workers,
are now frequently found going on simultaneously in a single
factory.[2] Thus a number of small simple business-units
representing the various stages in the production of a
commodity, come to group themselves into a large complex
unit.

This complexity is further increased by constant demand
for variety in size, quality, and character of goods to meet
the growing variety of demand in a market of increasing
area. Special classes of goods must be manufactured for
Australia, for Egypt, for Burmah. Less civilised customers,

[1] The works of Messrs. Colman, at Norwich, comprise among others
the following subsidiary departments:—Coopery, engineering shop,
saw mills, box-making, packing, paper-making, printing, laboratory.
To the most highly developed businesses of pottery and machine-
making schools of art and design are not uncommonly attached.

[2] A good deal of the cleansing and combing in the cloth and worsted
trades is, however, done separately on commission by large firms such
as Lister's. Cf. Burnley, p. 417.

including such countries as China and Persia, insist upon
their imported goods being made up and packed in some
familiar form long after the use or convenience of this
form has passed away. The exigencies of close competition require constant experiment in new lines of goods to
benefit the fancy of a newly-opened market, or to get away
the trade of some competitor. Moreover, the increasingly
important part which is played by advertising in the trades
where competition is keenest is followed by a very singular
result, which seems at first sight to contravene the growing
specialism or differentiation of function that marks modern
trade. Finding that goods advertise one another, manufacturers are frequently induced to add new departments to
their business, expanding the scope and variety of their
productions. In retail trade this tendency is widely operative. The modern grocer sells tinned meats, cakes, wine,
tea-pots, and Christmas cards, the draper sells every sort of
ornamental ware, the stationer, the oil shop, the china shop
set out an increasing and miscellaneous number of differing
wares, moving towards the position of a general dealer.
The Stores and the Universal Providers represent the
culmination of this movement in the retail business, returning to an enlarged and more complex form of the
primitive little "general shop" of the village. But this
same economy is strong enough in certain classes of manufacture to overpower the advantages of an expansion of
business in the older form. Up to a certain point the
economies of production upon a large scale will make it
advantageous to a manufacturer to employ all the capital at
his command in producing increased quantities of the same
class of goods. But after the market for these goods is
fairly supplied it may pay better to appeal to a variety of
wants by new species of goods of the same generic character, than by attempting to force new markets, or to effect
an increased sale in the old markets at such reduced prices
as the increased scale of production may permit. The
business of Messrs. Huntley & Palmer is a striking example
of this enterprise, issuing in a large variety of products and
of processes which, though generically related, cover a
widening range of food luxuries. The new products which
are taken on will of course not only reap the advantage of
being effectively advertised by the earlier products, but con-

sisting largely of new adaptations of the same kind of raw material, the economies of purchase and transport will be almost as great as attend an increased production of the same goods, while much of the machinery of management, and even of manufacture, can be utilised for the new processes. This tendency not merely to multiply processes in the manufacture of a single commodity, but to increase the variety of commodities turned out by analogous processes in a single business, is also operative in certain textile and metal industries, where an increasing proportion of the expensive machinery and skilled labour is engaged, not in narrowly specific processes of manufacture, but in generating power and in transmitting it for a number of later uses to be governed by specific machinery. There is in many factories an increasing facility to take on new processes, and to transfer a large portion of the plant from the manufacture of one class of goods to another class.

"Most of the operatives in a watch factory would find machines very similar to those with which they were familiar if they strayed into a gun-making factory or sewing-machine factory, or a factory for making textile machinery. A watch factory, with those who worked in it, could be converted without any overwhelming loss into a sewing-machine factory."[1] Thus in the evolution of the modern business we see not only a number of processes in the production of a commodity, each of which constituted a separate business-unit in the earlier division of labour, growing together into a large complex whole, but a growing together of analogous processes in the production of different commodities, a lateral aggregation of processes. So we recognise that the growing complexity of the business-unit, whether we regard it from the point of view of capital or of labour, arises in large measure from an increased integration of productive processes. The business-unit is larger, more heterogeneous, and more highly integrated.

§ 4. Ascending from the business-unit to the larger unit in the structure of industry, the Market, or groups of directly competing businesses, we find similar changes have taken place. In considering these changes the relation

---

[1] Marshall, *Principles of Economics*, 2nd edit., p. 517.

between Market and Trade should be clearly grasped. The mere fact that two persons or groups of persons in different places are engaged in similar processes of production, that is to say, belong to the same trade, has no significance for us. The trade or aggregate of productive units of a particular sort receives industrial unity only in so far as there is competition of the units in buying the raw materials, tools, and labour for carrying on their trade, and in selling the results of their activity. Weavers of cotton goods in Central China belong to the same trade as weavers in Lancashire, and conduct their craft with similar implements to those which still prevail in the cottage industries of France and Germany, but such competition as may exist between them is so indirect and slight that it may be neglected in considering industrial structure. It is in the competition of a market that businesses meet and are vitally related. In a trade there may be several markets whose connection is distant and indirect. Market is the name given to a number of directly competing businesses. "Economists understand by the term market not any particular market-place in which things are bought and sold, but the whole of any region in which buyers and sellers are in such free intercourse with one another that the prices of the same goods tend to equalise easily and quickly."[1]

A single competitive price is then the essential feature and the test of a market. Businesses in such close relation with one another that the prices at which they buy and sell are the same, or differ only by reason of and in correspondence with certain local advantages or disadvantages, are members of a single market. The money market is a single market throughout the world. The price of money in London, Rome, Rio de Janeiro, may differ, but this difference will correspond to certain differences of risk. There will be a tendency towards a single price, or, putting the case in other words, wherever in the world £100 of money represents the same commodity the same price will be paid for its use, while any difference in its value as a commodity will be accurately reflected in the difference of price.

---

[1] Cournot, *Recherches sur les Principes Mathématiques de la Theorie des Richesses* (quoted Marshall, *Principles of Economics*, p. 384).

Absolute freedom of intercourse is not essential to the establishment of a common market. Market tariffs and other advantages and disadvantages may place the competitors on an unequal footing. Moreover, in order to form part of a market as helping to determine the price, a business need not actively enter the field of competition. Fear of the potential competition of outsiders often keeps down prices to a level above which they would rise were it not for the belief that such a rise would bring into active, effective competition the outsider. England had until recently a monopoly of the market for cotton goods in certain Eastern countries, but the price at which she sold was determined by the possibility of rival French or German merchants, as well as by the direct competition of the several English firms. In certain commodities the market is conterminous with the trade, that is, we have a world-market. This is the case with many of the forms of money, the most abstract form of wealth, and the most highly competitive.

Dealers in Stock Exchange securities, in the precious metals, are in active, constant competition at all the great commercial centres of the world. Other staple commodities, whose value is great, durable, and portable, such as jewels, wheat, cotton, wool, have to all intents and purposes a single market.

This world-market represents the fullest expansion due to modern machinery of transport and exchange, the railway, steamship, newspaper, telegraph, and the system of credit built up and maintained by the assistance of these material agents.

The market-area for various commodities varies with the character of these commodities, from the world-market for stock exchange securities down to the minimum market consisting of a few neighbouring farmers competing to sell their over-ripe plums or their skim-milk. The chief qualities which determine the market-area are—

(a) *Extent of demand.* — Things in universal or very wide demand, which are at the same time durable, such as money, wool, wheat, compete over very wide areas. Things specially accommodated to the taste or use of a particular locality or a small class of individuals will have a narrow market. This is the case with clothes of a particular cut, and with many kinds of fabrics out of which clothes are made. The market for certain classes of topographical books will be confined to the limits of a county, though the book market for many books is a world-market.

(b) *Portability.*—Even where the demand is far from a general one, the market-area may be very wide where high value is stored in small bulk. Smoking tobacco and more highly valued wines and liqueurs are examples of this order. The market for common bricks is local, though Portland marble finds a national market.

(c) *Durability.*—Durable objects and objects which can easily be brought within reach of modern means of rapid transport have a wide market. Perishable goods, as, for example, many fruits and vegetables, have for these reasons a narrow market.

§ 5. Modern machinery has in almost all cases raised the size of the market. The space-area of competition has been immensely widened, especially for the more durable classes of goods. It is machinery of transport—the transport of goods and news—that is chiefly responsible for this expansion. Cheaper, quicker, safer, and more calculable journeys have shrunk space for competing purposes. Improved means of rapid and reliable information about methods of production, markets, changes in price and trade have practically annihilated the element of distance.

Machinery of manufacture as well as of transport has a levelling tendency which makes directly for expansion of the area of competition. As the spread of knowledge places each part of the industrial world more closely *en rapport* with the rest, the newest and best methods of manufacture are more rapidly and effectively adopted. Thus in all production where less and less depends on the skill of the workers, and more and more upon the character of the machinery, every change which gives more prominence to the latter tends to equalise the cost of production in different countries, and thus to facilitate effective competition.

§ 6. Modern methods of production have also brought about a great expansion in the time-area of the market. Competition covers a wider range of time as well as of space. Production is no longer directed by the quantity and quality of present needs alone, but is more and more dependent

upon calculation of future consumption. A larger proportion of the brain power of the business man is devoted to
forecasting future conditions of the market, and a larger
proportion of the mechanical and human labour to providing future goods to meet calculated demands. This
expansion of the time-market, or growth of speculative
production, is partly cause, partly effect of the improved
mechanical appliances in manufacture and in transport.
The multiplication of productive power under the new
machinery has in many branches of industry far outstripped
the requirements of present known consumption at remunerative prices, while increased knowledge of the widening
market has given a basis of calculation which leads manufacturers to utilise their spare productive power in providing
against future wants. So long as industry was limited by
the labour of the human body, assisted but slightly by
natural forces and working with simple tools, the output of
productive energy could seldom outstrip the present demand
for consumable goods.

But machinery has changed all this. Modern industrial
nations are able to produce consumables far faster than
those who have the power to consume them are willing to
exercise it. Hence there is an ever-increasing margin of
productive power redundant so far as the production of
present consumptive goods is concerned. This excess of
productive power is saved. It can only be saved by being
stored up in some material forms which are required not for
direct consumption but for assisting to increase the rate at
which consumables may be produced in the future. In
order to make a place for these new forms of saving it is
necessary to interpose a constantly increasing number of
mechanical processes between the earliest extractive process
which removes the raw material from the earth and the final
or retailing process which places it in the consumer's hands.
New machinery, more elaborate and costly, is applied;
special workshops, with machines to make this machinery—
other machinery to make these machines; there is an
expansion of the mechanism of credit, the system of agents
and representatives is expanded, new modes of advertising
are adopted. Thus an ever-widening field of investment is
provided for the spare energy of machine-production. The
change is commonly described by saying that production is

more "roundabout."[1] A larger number of steps are inserted in the ladder of production. This increased complexity in the mechanism of production is not, however, the central point of importance. We must realise that the change is one which is essentially an increase in the "speculative" character of commerce. The "roundabout" method of production signifies a continual increase in the proportion of productive forces devoted to making "future goods" as compared with those devoted to making "present goods." Now future goods, plant, machinery, raw material of commodities, are essentially "contingent goods": their worth or waste depends largely upon conditions yet unborn: their social utility and the value based upon it depend entirely upon the future powers and desires of those unknown persons who are expected to purchase and consume the commodities which shall come into existence as results of the existence and activity of these future goods.

The actual time which elapses between the extractive stage and the final retail stage of a commodity may not be greater and is in many cases far less under the new methods of industry. The raw cotton of South Carolina gets on the wearer's back more quickly than it did a century and a half ago. But when we add in the time-elements involved in the provision of the various forms of intricate plant and machinery whose utility entirely consists in forwarding these cotton goods, and whose existence in the industrial mechanism depends upon them, we shall perceive that the "roundabout" method signifies a great extension of the speculative or time-element in the market.[2]

§ 7. The growing interdependency of trades and markets, the ever closer sympathy which exists between them, the increased rapidity with which a movement affecting one communicates itself to others, is another striking characteristic of modern trade. This interdependency is in large measure one of growing structural attachment between trades

---

[1] It ought, however, to be kept in mind that the application of the "roundabout" method is only economically justified by a continual increase in consumption. So far as a given quantity of consumption is concerned the result of the "roundabout" method is to diminish the quantity of capital which assists to produce it.

[2] Professor Böhm Bawerk shows this increased time of production to be the essential characteristic of capitalist production. Cf. *Positive Theory of Capital.*

and markets formerly in faint and distant sympathetic relationship.   Formerly, agriculture was the one important
foundational industry, and from the feebleness of the
transport system the vital connections and the unity it
supplied was local rather than national or international.
Now the agricultural industries no longer occupy this
position of prominence.   The coal and iron industries
engaged in furnishing the raw material of machinery and
steam-motor, the machine manufacture, and the transport
services, are the common feeders and regulators of all
industries, including that of agriculture.   They form a
system corresponding to the alimentary system of the
human body, any quickening or slackening of whose functional activities is directly and speedily communicated
to the several parts.   Any disturbance of price, of efficiency,
or regularity of production in these foundational industries
is reflected at once and automatically in the several
industries which are engaged in the production and distribution of the several commodities.   The mining and
metal industries, shipbuilding, and the railway services are
recognised more and more as furnishing the true measure
and test of modern trade ; their labour enters in ever
larger proportion into the production of all the consumptive
goods.

Besides the general integration or unification of industry
implied by the common dependency of the specific
trades upon these great industries, there are other forces
engaged in integrating groups of trades.   Foremost is the
"roundabout" method of production, to which our attention has been already directed.   Not merely does this
capitalist system bring a number of trades and processes
under the control of a single capital, as a single complex
business, but it establishes close identity of trade-life and
interests among businesses, trades, and markets which
remain distinct so far as ownership and management are
concerned.

§ 8. If we take the mass of capital and labour composing
one of our staple productive industries, we shall find that it
is related in four different ways to a number of other
industries.

(1) It has a number of trades which are directly co-
ordinate—*i.e.*, engaged in the earlier or later processes of

producing the same consumptive goods. Thus the manufacture of shoes is related co-ordinately to the import
trades of hides and bark, to tanning, to the export trade
in shoes, and to the retail shoe trade. A common stream
of produce is flowing through these several processes, and
though from the point of view of ownership and management there may be no connection, there is a close identity
of trade interest and a quick sympathy of commercial life
at these several points.

(2) Each important manufacturing industry has a number
of industries which in their relation to it are secondary,
although in some cases, having similar relations to a number
of other trades, they may in themselves be large and important. In the large textile centres are found a number of
minor industries, planers, sawyers, turners, fitters, smiths,
engaged in irregular work of alteration and repairs upon the
plant and machinery of the textile factories. The same
holds of all important manufactures, especially those which
are closely localised.

A somewhat similar relation appertains between those
manufactures engaged in producing the main body of any
product and the minor industries, which supply some slighter
and essentially subsidiary part. In relation to the main
textile and clothing industries, the manufacture of buttons,
of tape, feathers, and other elements of ornament or
trimmings may be regarded as subsidiary. In the same
way the manufacture of wall-papers or house paint may be
considered subsidiary to the building trades, that of black-
ing to the shoe manufacture. These subsidiary trades are
related to the primary one more or less closely, and are
affected by the condition of the latter more or less powerfully in proportion as the subsidiary elements they furnish are
more or less indispensable in character. The fur and feather
trades are far more dependent upon direct forces of fashion
than upon any changes of price or character in the main
branches of the clothing trade. On the other hand, any
cause which affected considerably the price of sugar would
have a great and direct influence on the jam manufacture,
while the rise in price of tin due to the M'Kinley tariff
caused serious apprehension to the Chicago manufacturers
and exporters of preserved meats.

(3) The relations between one of the great arterial

industries, such as coal-mining, railway transport, or machine-
making, and a specific manufacture may be regarded as
auxiliary. The extent to which the price of coal, railway
rates, etc., enters into the price of the goods and affects the
condition of profits in the trade measures the closeness of
this auxiliary connection. In the case of the smelting
industries or in the steam transport trades, even in the
pottery trades, the part played by coal is so important that
the relation is rather that of a primary than an auxiliary
connection—*i.e.*, coal-mining must be ranked as co-ordinate
to smelting. But where heat is not the direct agent of
manufacture, but is required to furnish steam-motor alone,
as in the textile factories, the connection may be termed
auxiliary.

(4) The relationship between some industries is "sympathetic" in the sense that the commodities they produce
appeal to closely related tastes, or are members of a group
whose consumption is related harmoniously. In foods we
have the relations between bread, butter, and cheese ; the
relation in which sugar and salt stand to a large number of
consumables. Some of these are natural relations in the
sense that one supplies a corrective to some defect of the
other, or that the combination enhances the satisfaction or
advantage which would accrue from the consumption of
each severally. In other cases the connection is more
conventional, as that between alcohol and tobacco. The
sporting tastes of man supply a strong sympathetic bond
between many trades. The same is true of literary, artistic,
or other tastes, which by the simultaneous demand which
they make upon several industries, in some proportion
determined by the harmonious satisfaction of their desires,
throw these industries into sympathetic groups.[1] These four
bonds mark an identity of interest between different
industries.

The relationship is sometimes one of divergency or competition of trades. Where the same service may be supplied
by two or more different commodities the trades are related
by direct competition. Oil, gas, electricity, as illuminants, are
a familiar example of this relationship. Many trades which

[1] For a full and valuable treatment of these harmonious relations,
from the point of view of consumption and production, see Patten's
Economics of a Dynamic Society.

produce commodities that are similar, but far from identical in character, feel this relationship very closely. The
competition between various kinds of food, which with
different kinds and degrees of satisfaction may produce
the same substantial effects, between fish and meat,
between various kinds of vegetables and drinks, enables
us to realise something of the intricacy of the relations
of this kind. In clothing we have antagonism of interests
between the various fabrics which has led to great industrial
changes. The most signal example is the rise of cotton,
its triumph over woollen clothes by the earlier application
of the new machinery, and over silk by the early superiority
of its dyeing and printing processes.[1] So in recent years
in the conflict among beverages, tea, and in a less measure
cocoa, have materially damaged the growth of the coffee
industry so far as English consumption is concerned.
Where such rivalry exists, an industry may be as powerfully and immediately affected by a force which raises or
depresses its competitor as by a force which directly affects
itself.

§ 9. The growth of numerous and strongly-built structural
attachments between different trades and markets related to
different localities implies the existence of a large system
of channels of communication throughout our industrial
society. By the increased number and complexity of these
channels connecting different markets and businesses, and
relating the most distant classes of consumers, we can
measure the evolution of the industrial organism. Through
these channels flow the currents of modern industrial life,
whose pace, length, and regularity contrast with the feeble,
short, and spasmodic flow of commerce in earlier times.
This advance in functional activity of distribution is thus
expressed by Mr. Spencer:—"In early English times the
great fairs, annual and other, formed the chief means of distribution, and remained important down to the seventeenth
century, when not only villages, but even small towns, devoid
of shops, were irregularly supplied by hawkers who had
obtained their stocks at these gatherings. Along with
increased population, larger industrial centres, and improved
channels of communication, local supply became easier;

---

[1] Cf. Porter, *Progress of the Nation*, pp. 177-206.

and so frequent markets more and more fulfilled the purpose
of infrequent fairs. Afterwards, in chief places and for chief
commodities, markets themselves multiplied, becoming in
some cases daily. Finally came a constant distribution,
such that of some foods there is to each town an influx
every morning; and of milk even more than once in the
day. The transition from times when the movements of
people and goods between places were private, slow, and
infrequent, to times when there began to run at intervals
of several days public vehicles moving at four miles an
hour, and then to times when these shortened their intervals
and increased their speed, while their lines of movement
multiplied, ending in our own times, when along each line
of rails there go at full speed a dozen waves daily that are
relatively vast, sufficiently show us how the social circulation progresses from feeble, slow, irregular movements to a
rapid, regular, and powerful pulse."[1]

   The differentiation of function in the several parts of the
industrial organism finds a partial expression in the localisation of certain industries. As there is growing division of
labour among individuals and groups of individuals, so the
expansion of the area of competition has brought about a
larger and larger amount of local specialisation.

   Roughly speaking, the West of Europe and of America
has specialised in manufacture, drawing an ever larger
proportion of their food supplies from the North-West States
of America, from Russia, the Baltic Provinces, Australia,
Egypt, India, etc., and their raw materials of manufacture
from the southern United States, South America, India, etc.,
while these latter countries are subjected to a correspondent
specialisation in agriculture and other extractive arts. If we
take Europe alone, we find certain large characteristics
which mark out the Baltic trade, the Black Sea trade, the
Danube trade, the Norwegian and White Sea trade. So the
Asiatic trade falls into certain tolerably defined divisions of
area, as the Levant trade, the Red Sea trade, the Indian, the
Straits, and East Indian, the China trade, etc. The whole
trade of the world is thus divided for commercial purposes.[2]
Though these trade divisions are primarily suggested by

---

[1] *Principles of Sociology*, vol. i. p. 500 (3rd edit.).
[2] For a detailed account of the national trade divisions, cf. Dr. Yeats,
The Golden Gates of Trade.

considerations of transport rather than of the character of production, the geographical, climatic, and other natural factors which determine convenient lines of transport are found to have an important bearing on the character of the production, and convenience of transport itself assists largely to determine the kind of work which each part of the world sets itself to do.

The establishment of a world-market for a larger and larger number of commodities is transforming with marvellous rapidity the industrial face of the globe. This does not now appear so plainly in the more highly-developed countries of Europe, which, under the influence of half a century's moderately free competition for a European market, have already established themselves in tolerably settled conditions of specialised industry. But in the new world, and in those older countries which are now fast yielding to the incursions of manufacturing and transport machinery, the specialising process is making rapid strides.

Improved knowledge of the world, facile communication, an immense increase in the fluidity of capital, and a considerable increase in that of labour, are busily engaged in distributing the productions of the world in accordance with certain dominant natural conditions. Those industrial forces which have during the last century and a half been operative in England, draining the population and industry from the Southern and Eastern counties, and concentrating it in larger proportions in Lancashire, the West Riding, Staffordshire, and round the Northumbrian and South Wales coal-fields, specialising each town or locality upon some single branch of the textile, metal, or other industries for which its soil, position, or other natural advantages made it suitable, are now beginning to extend the area of their control over the whole surface of the known and inhabited globe.

As large areas of Asia, South and Central Africa, Australia, and South America fall under the control of European commercial nations, are opened up by steamships, railways, telegraphs, and are made free receptacles for the increased quantity of capital which is unable to find a safe remunerative investment nearer home, we are brought nearer to a condition in which the whole surface of the world will be disposed for industrial purposes by these same forces which have long been confined in their direct and potent influence to a small portion of Western Europe and America. This vast expansion of the area of effective competition is beginning to specialise industry on the basis of a world-market, which was formerly specialised on the more confined basis of a national or provincial market. So in England, where the early specialisation of machine-industry was but slightly affected by outside competition, great changes are taking place. Portions of our textile and metal industries, which naturally settled in districts of Lancashire, Yorkshire, and Staffordshire, while the area of competition was a national one,[1] seem likely to pass to India, to Germany, or elsewhere, now that a tolerably free competition on the basis of world-industry has set in. It is inevitable that with every expansion of the area of competition under which a locality falls the character of its specialisation will change. A piece of English ground which was devoted to corn-growing when the market was a district one centred in the county town, becomes the little factory town when competition is established on a national basis; it may become the pleasure-ground of a retired millionaire speculator if under the pressure of world-competition it has been found that the manufacture which now thrives there can be carried on more economically in Bombay or Nankin, where each unit of labour power can be bought at the cheapest rate, or where some slight saving in the transport of raw material may be effected.

§ 10. The question how industry would be located, assuming the whole surface of the globe was brought into a single market or area of competition, with an equal development of transport facilities in all its parts; or in other words, "What is the ideal disposition of industry in a world-society making its chief end the attainment of industrial wealth estimated at present values?" is one to which of course no very exact answer can be given. But since this ideal represents the goal of modern industrial pro-

---

[1] Foreign competition with English textiles, though comparatively modern so far as the more highly developed machine-made fabrics is concerned, was keenly felt early in the century in hand-made goods. Schulze-Gaevernitz points out that the depression in work and wages of the hand-loom workers in 1820 was due more to foreign competition than to the new machinery. (*Der Grossbetrieb*, p. 41.)

gress, it is worth while to call attention to the chief determinants of the localisation of industries under free world-
competition. The influences may be placed in three
groups, which are, however, interrelated at many points.

(1) The first group may be called Climatic, the chief
influences of which are astronomical position, surface con-
tour, prevalent winds, ocean currents, etc. Climatic zones
have their own flora and fauna, and so far as these enter
into industry as agricultural and pastoral produce, as raw
materials of manufacture, as sustenance of labour, they are
natural determinants of the localisation of industry. In
vegetable products the climatic zones are very clearly
marked. "The boreal zone has its special vegetation of
mosses, lichens, saxifrages, berries, oats, barley, and rye;
the temperate zone its peas, beans, roots, hops, oats, barley,
rye, and wheat; this zone, characterised by its extent of
pastures, hop gardens, and barley fields, has also a distinctive title in the 'beer and butter region.' The warm
temperate zone, or region of 'wine and oil,' is characterised
by the growth of the vine, olive, orange, lemon, citron,
pomegranate, tea, wheat, maize, and rice; the sub-tropical
zone, by dates, figs, the vine, sugar-cane, wheat, and maize;
the tropical zone is characterised by coffee, cocoa-nut,
cocoa, sago, palm, figs, arrowroot, and spices; and the
equatorial by bananas, plantains, cocoa-nut, etc."[1]

(2) The second group is geographical and geological.
The shape and position of a country, its relation in space
to other countries, the character of the soil and sub-soil, its
water-supply, though closely related to climatic influences,
have independent bearings. The character of the soil, which
provides for crops their mineral food, has an important bearing upon the raw materials of industry. The shape and
position of the land, especially the configuration of its coast,
have a social as well as climatic significance, directing the
intercourse with other lands and the migrations of people and
civilisations which play so large a part in industrial history.

(3) Largely determined by the two groups of influences
named above are the forces which represent the national
character at any given time, the outcome of primitive race
characteristics, food supply, speed and direction of industrial

---

[1] Yeats, *The Golden Gates of Trade*, p. 12. (Philip & Son.)

development, density of population, and the various other causes which enter in to determine efficiency of labour. The play of these natural and human forces in world-competition leads to such a settlement of different industries in different localities as yields the greatest net productiveness of labour in each part.

§ 11. But this world-competition, however free it may become, can lead to no finality, no settled appointment of industrial activity to the several parts of the earth. Setting aside all political and other non-economic motives, there are three reasons which render such local stability of industry impossible.

There is first the disturbance and actual loss sustained by nature in working up the mineral wealth of the soil, and the flora and fauna sustained by it, into commodities which are consumed, and an exact equivalent of which cannot be replaced. The working out of a coal-field, the destruction of forests which reacts upon the elementary climatic influences, are examples of this disturbance.

Secondly, there is the progress of industrial arts, new scientific discoveries applicable to industry. There is no reason to believe that human knowledge can reach any final goal : there is infinity alike in the resources of nature and in the capacity of the development of human skill.

Lastly, as human life continues, the art of living must continually change, and each change alters the value attached to the several forms of consumption, and so to the industrial processes engaged in the supply of different utilities. New wants stimulate new arts, new arts alter the disposition of productive industry, giving value to new portions of the earth. Ignoring those new material wants which require new kinds of raw material to be worked up for their satisfaction, the growing appreciation of certain kinds of sport, the love of fine scenery, a rising value set upon healthy atmosphere, are beginning to exercise a more and more perceptible influence upon the localisation of certain classes of population and industry in the more progressive nations of the world.

§ 12. The same laws and the same limitations which are operative in determining the character and degree of specialisation of countries or large areas are also seen to apply to smaller districts, towns, and streets. Industries engaged

in producing valuable, durable material objects in wide
demand are locally specialised ; those engaged in providing
bulky perishable non-material goods, or goods in narrow
demand, are unspecialised. England, where internal intercourse has been most highly developed, and where internal
competition has been freest and keenest, shows the most
advanced specialisation in several of its staple industries.
The concentration of cotton spinning in South Lancashire
is an example, the full significance of which often escapes
notice. From the beginning South Lancashire was the
chief seat of the industry, but it is now far more concentrated than was the case a century ago. Several of the
most valuable inventions in spinning were first applied in
Derbyshire, in Nottingham, at Birmingham, and in Scotland.
Scotland then competed closely in weaving with Lancashire.
Now the Scotch industry is confined to certain specialities.
In spite of the enormous growth of the manufacture, the
local area it covers is even narrower than last century.
Within Lancashire itself the actual area of production has
shrunk to some 25 square miles in the extreme south, while
the two great cities are further specialised—Liverpool as the
market for cotton, Manchester for yarn and cotton cloths.

Moreover, the localisation of various departments of the
trade within Lancashire is still more remarkable. Not only
have the old mills in which spinning and weaving were
carried on together given way before division of labour, but
the two processes are mostly conducted in different districts,
the former in the towns immediately around Manchester,
the latter in the more distant northern circuit. Nor is the
specialisation confined to this. Spinning is again divided
according to the coarser and finer qualities of yarn. The
Oldham district, with Ashton, Middleton, and other towns
south of Manchester are chiefly confined to the medium
numbers. Bolton, Chorley, Preston, and other northern
towns undertake the finer numbers. In weaving there
is even more intricate division of labour, each town or
district specialising upon some particular line of goods.[1]
Moreover, it must be borne in mind that the substitution of the factory for the domestic system and the

[1] Cf. Schulze-Gaevernitz's minute investigation of this whole subject,
Der Grossbetrieb, pp. 98, 99, etc.

continual enlargement of the average factory indicates an important progressive concentration. So the cotton industry does not in fact cover nearly so large a local area as when it was one-hundredth the size. The same is true of the other chief branches of the textile and metal industries. Nor is it only in the manufactures that towns and districts are closely specialised. The enormous increase of commerce due to machinery of manufacture and of transport requires the specialisation of certain towns for purely commercial purposes. London, Liverpool, Glasgow, and Hull are more and more devoted to the functions of storage and conveyance. Manchester itself is rapidly losing its manufacturing character and devoting itself almost exclusively to import and export trade. The railway service has made for itself large towns, such as Crewe, Derby, Normanton, and Swindon. Cardiff is a portentous example of a new mining centre created when the machine development of England was already ripe.

The specialisation of function in a large town is, however, qualified in two ways. The strong local organisation of a staple trade requires the grouping round it of a number of secondary or auxiliary trades. In large textile towns the manufactures of textile machinery, and of subsidiary materials, are found. The machine-making of Manchester is one of its most important industries, furnishing the neighbouring textile towns. Leeds is similarly equipped for the woollen trade. This is one of the respects in which the superior development of the English cotton industry over the continental ones is indicated. In Alsace alone of the continental centres has the concentration of industry advanced so far as to furnish a local machine industry specially devoted to cotton machinery. Germany is still mainly dependent upon England for her machines.[1] So likewise with regard to co-ordinate trades, there is an advantage in the leading processes being grouped in local proximity, though they are not united in the same business. Thus we find dye-works and the various branches of the clothing trade largely settled in the large textile towns, such as Leeds, Bradford, Manchester, Bolton. The unit of local specialisation is thus seen to be not a single

[1] Schulze-Gaevernitz, p. 110.

trade, but a group of closely allied trades, co-ordinate, dependent, and derivative.

Round some large industries in which men find employment minor parasitic industries spring up stimulated by the supply of cheap abundant labour of women and children. In metal and machine towns such as Birmingham, Dudley, Walsall, in Newcastle-on-Tyne, and other shipbuilding towns, where the staple industries are a masculine monopoly, textile factories have been planted. The same holds of various mining villages and of agricultural villages in the neighbourhood of large textile centres. There is in the midland counties a growing disposition to place textile factories in rural villages where cheap female labour can be got, and where the independence of workers is qualified by stronger local attachments and inferior capacity of effective trade union organisation. As textile work passes more and more into the hands of women,[1] this tendency to make it a parasitic trade thriving upon the low wages for which women's labour can be got where strong and well-paid male work is established, will probably be more strongly operative.

§ 13. The specialisation of certain districts within the town, though far less rigid than in the mediæval town, is very noticeable in the larger centres of industry. Natural causes often determine this division of localities, as in the case of the riverside industries, brick-making and market-gardening in the outer suburbs. Round the central station in every large town, for convenience of work and life, settle a number of industries related to the carrying trade. Every trade, market, or exchange is a centre of attraction. So the broking, banking, and the general financing businesses are grouped closely round the Royal Exchange. Mark Lane and Mincing Lane are centres of the corn and tea trades. In all town industries not directly engaged in retail distribution there are certain obvious economies and conveniences in this gregariousness. Agents, travellers, collectors, and others who have relations of sale or purchase with a number of businesses in a trade find a number of disadvantages in dealing with a firm locally detached from the main body, so

---

[1] For the gain of female over male employment in textile factories, cf. Chap. xi.

that when a district is once recognised as a trade centre, it becomes increasingly important to each new competitor to settle there. The larger the city the stronger this force of trade centralisation. Hence in London, untrammelled by guild or city regulations, we find a strong localisation of most wholesale and some retail businesses. In retail trade, however, the economic gain is less universal. Since retail commodities are chiefly for use in the home, and homes are widely distributed, the convenience of being near one's customers and away from trade competitors is often a predominating motive. Shops which sell bread, meat, fish, fruit, groceries, articles which are bought frequently and mostly in small quantities, shops selling cheaper articles of ordinary consumption, such as tobacco, millinery, stationery, and generally shops selling articles for domestic use, the purchase of which falls to women, are widely dispersed. On the other hand, where the articles are of a rarer and more expensive order, when it is likely that the purchaser will seek to compare price and character of wares, and will presumably be willing to make a special journey for the purpose, the centralising tendency prevails in retail trade. So we find the vendors of carriages, pianos, bicycles, the heavier articles of furniture, jewellery, second-hand books, furs, and the more expensive tailors and milliners clustering together in a special street or neighbourhood.

Effective competition in retail trade sometimes requires concentration, sometimes dispersion of business. But the most characteristic modern movement in retail trade is a combination of the centralising and dispersive tendencies, and is related to the enlargement of the business-unit which we found proceeding everywhere in industry. The large distributing company with a number of local branch agents, who call regularly at the house of the consumer for orders, is the most highly organised form of retail trade. In all the departments of regular and general consumption the movement is towards this constant house-to-house supply. The wealthier classes in towns have already learned to purchase all the more perishable forms of food and many other articles of house consumption in this way, while the growing facilities of postage and conveyance of goods enable them to purchase from a large central store by means of a price-list all other consumables into which the element of individual taste or caprice does not largely enter. This habit is spreading in the smaller towns among the middle classes, so that the small dispersed retail businesses are becoming more and more dependent upon the supply of the needs of the working classes, and of such articles of comfort and luxury as may appeal to the less regular and calculable tastes of the moneyed classes. Just as in towns we have a constant automatic supply of water and gas instead of an intermittent supply dependent on a number of individual acts of purchase, so it seems likely that all the routine wants of the consumer will be supplied.

How far mechanical inventions may be applied to increase the facility and cheapen the cost of this distribution it is difficult to say. The automatic machine for distributing matches and sweetmeats is adaptable to most forms of routine consumption. In the larger stores many kinds of labour-saving machinery are already applied. As steam or electric power is adopted more widely in the local transport services the retail distribution of goods from a large single centre is likely to proceed apace, and a displacement of human labour by machinery similar to that which is taking place in manufacture will take place in distribution. So far as the wants of large classes of the public become regular and their consumption measurable in quantity, machinery will unquestionably take over the labour of distribution, especially in the large towns which are absorbing in a way convenient for mechanical distribution a larger proportion of the consuming public. With each new encroachment of machinery into the domain of the distributing trades the characteristics of machine-industry, enlarged mass of the business, increased area of the market, increased complexity of relations to other trades, increased specialisation of local activity will be clearly discernible.

We thus see in the several departments of industry, under the pressure of the same economic forces, an expansion of size, a growing complexity of structure and functional activity, and an increased cohesion of highly differentiated parts in the business, the market, and in that aggregation of related trades and markets which forms the world-industry. The physical instrument by which these economic forces, making for increased size, heterogeneity, and cohesiveness,[1] have been able to operate is machinery applied to manufacture and transport. Moreover, each new encroachment of machinery upon the extractive and the distributing

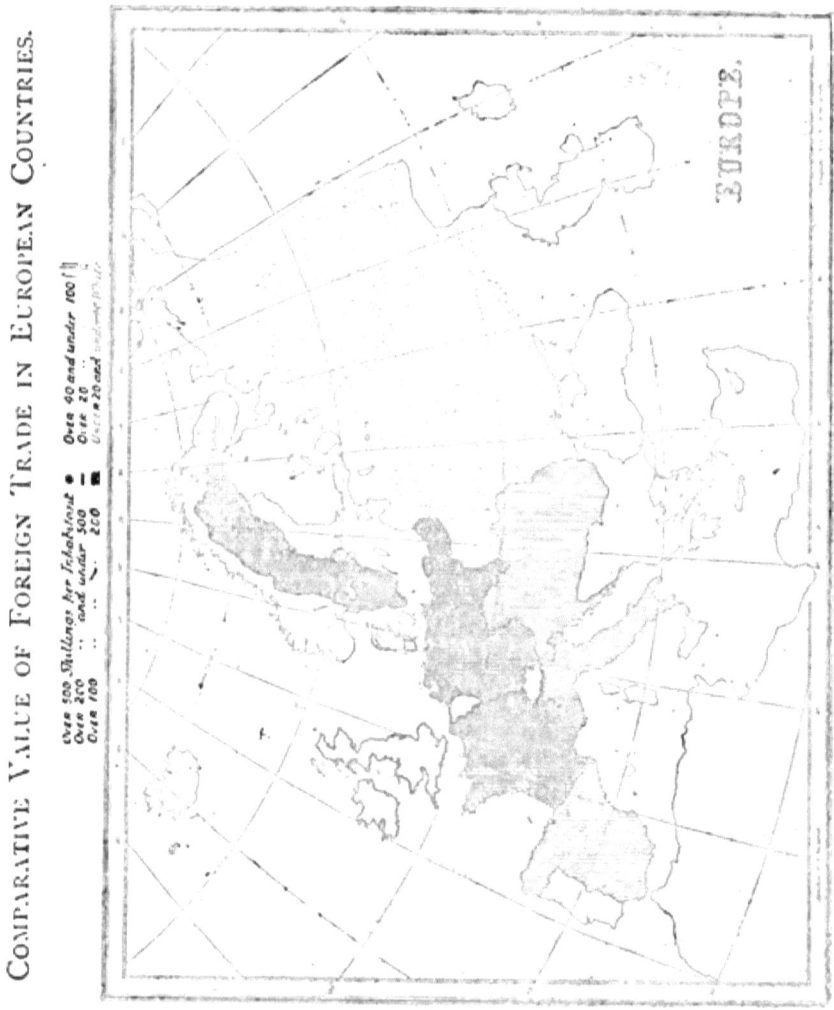

COMPARATIVE VALUE OF FOREIGN TRADE IN EUROPEAN COUNTRIES.

industries brings into prominence within these processes the same structural and functional characteristics.

[1] In a free application of Spencer's formula of evolution to modern industry I have not included the quality of "definiteness," which close reflection shows to possess no property which is not included under heterogeneity and cohesiveness.

CHAPTER V.

THE FORMATION OF MONOPOLIES IN CAPITAL.

§ 1. *Productive Economies of the Large Business.*
§ 2. *Competitive Economies of the Large Business.*
§ 3. *Intenser Competition of the few Large Businesses.*
§ 4. *Restraint of Competition and Limited Monopoly.*
§ 5. *Facilities for maintaining Price-Lists in different Industries.*
§ 6. *Logical Outcome of Large-Scale Competition.*
§ 7. *Different Species of "Combines."*
§ 8. *Legal and Economic Nature of the "Trust."*
§ 9. *Origin and "Modus Operandi" of the Standard Oil Trust.*
§ 10. *The Economic Strength of other Trusts.*
§ 11. *Industrial Conditions favourable to "Monopoly."*

§ 1. The forces which are operating to drive capital to group itself in larger and larger masses, and the consequent growth of the business-unit, require special study in relation to changes effected in the character of competition in the market and the establishment of monopolies. The economies which give to the large business an advantage over the small business may be divided into two classes—economies of productive power, and economies of competitive power.

In the first class will be placed those economies which arise from increased sub-division of labour and increased efficiency of productive energy, and which represent a net saving in the output of human energy in the production of a given quantity of commodities, from the standpoint of the whole productive community. These include—

(*a*) The effort saved in the purchase and transport of

raw materials in large quantities as compared with small quantities, and a corresponding saving in the sale and transport of the goods, manufactured or other. Under this head would come the discovery and opening up of new markets for purchase of raw materials and sale of finished goods, and everything which increases the area of effective competition and co-operation in industry.

(*b*) The adoption of the best modern machinery. Much expensive machinery will only "save labour" when it is used to assist in producing a large output which can find a tolerably steady market. The number of known or discoverable inventions for saving labour which are waiting either for an increase in the scale of production or for a rise in the wages of the labour they might supersede, in order to become economically available, may be considered infinite. With every rise in the scale of production some of these pass from the "unpaying" into the "paying" class, and represent a net productive gain in saved labour of the community.

(*c*) The performance of minor or subsidiary processes upon the same premisses or in close organic connection with the main process, the establishment of a special workshop for repairs, various economies in storage, which attend large-scale production.

(*d*) Economies consisting in saved labour and increased efficiency of management, superintendence, clerical and other non-manual work, which follow each increase of size in a normally constructed business. These are often closely related to (*b*), as where clerical work is economised by the introduction of type-writers or telephonic communication, and to (*c*), as by the establishment of more numerous and convenient centres of distribution.

(*e*) The utilisation of waste-products, one of the most important practical economies in large-scale production.

(*f*) The capacity to make trial of new experiments in machinery and in industrial organisation.

§ 2. To the class Economies in Competitive Power belong those advantages which a large business enjoys in competing with smaller businesses, which enable it either to take trade away from the latter, or to obtain a higher rate of profits without in any way increasing the net productiveness of the community. This includes—

(1) A large portion of the economy in advertising, travel-ling, local agents, and the superiority of display and touting which a large business is able to afford. In most cases by far the greater part of this publicity and self-recommenda-tion is no economy from the standpoint of the trade or the community, but simply represents a gain to one firm compensated by a loss to others. In not a few cases the "trade" may be advantaged to the damage of other trades or of the consumer, as when a class of useless or deleterious drugs is forced into consumption by persistent methods of self-appraisal which deceive the public.

(2) The power of a large business to secure and maintain the sole use of some patent or trade secret in machinery or method of manufacture which would otherwise have gone to another firm, or would have become public property in the trade, represents no public economy, and sometimes a public loss. Where such improvement is due solely to the skill and enterprise of a business man, and would not have passed into use unless the sole right were secured to his business, this economy belongs to the productive class.

(3) The superior ability of a large business to depress wages by the possession of a total or partial monopoly of local employment, the corresponding power to obtain raw material at low prices, or to extort higher prices from con-sumers than would obtain under the pressure of free competition, represent individual business economies which may enable a large business to obtain higher profits.

§ 3. Now all these forces operative in trades which are said to be subject to the law of increasing returns tend to increase the size and to diminish the number of businesses competing within a given area. In some industries the expanding size of the market or area of competition keeps pace with this movement, so that the total number of the larger competitors within the market may be as great as before. But in most of the markets the growing scale of the business is attended by an absolute diminution in the number of effective competitors, or at any rate by an increase which is very much smaller than the increase in the amount of trade that is done.

So long as we have merely the substitution of a smaller number of large competing businesses for a larger number of small ones, no radical change is effected in the nature of industry. So long as every purchaser is able to buy from two or more equally developed and effectively competing firms he can make them bid against one another until he obtains the full advantage of the economies of large-scale production which are common to them. So long as there remains effective competition, all the productive economies pass into the hands of the consumer in reduction of price. Nay, more than this, a competing firm cannot keep to itself the advantages of a private individual economy if its competitor has another private economy of equal importance. If A and B are two closely competing firms, A owning a special machine capable of earning for him 2 per cent. above the normal trade profit, and B owning a similar advantage by possession of "cheaper labour," these private economies will be cancelled by competition, and pass into the pocket of the consuming public.

There is every reason to believe that with a diminution in the number of competitors and an increase of their size, competition grows keener and keener. Under old business conditions custom held considerable sway; the personal element played a larger part alike in determining quality of goods and good faith; purchasers did not so closely compare prices; they were not guided exclusively by figures, they did not systematically beat down prices, nor did they devote so large a proportion of their time, thought, and money to devices for taking away one another's customers.[1] From the new business this personal element and these customary scruples have almost entirely vanished, and as the net advantages of large-scale production grow, more and more attention is devoted to the direct work of competition. Hence we find that it is precisely in those trades which are most highly organised, provided with the most advanced machinery, and composed of the largest units of capital, that the fiercest and most unscrupulous competition has shown itself. The precise part which machinery, with its incalculable tendency to over-production, has played in this competition remains for later consideration. Here it is enough to place in evidence the acknowledged fact that

---

[1] There still survive in certain old-fashioned trades firms which do business without formal written contracts, and which would be ashamed to take a lower price than they had at first asked, or to seek to beat down another's price.

the growing scale of the business has intensified and not
diminished competition. In the great machine industries
trade fluctuations are most severely felt; the smaller
businesses are unable to stand before the tide of depression
and collapse, or are driven in self-defence to coalesce. The
borrowing of capital, the formation of joint-stock enterprise
and every form of co-operation in capital has proceeded most
rapidly in the textile, metal, transport, shipping, and machine-
making industries, and in those minor manufactures, such as
brewing and chemicals, which require large quantities of expensive plant. This joining together of small capitals to
make a single large capital, this swallowing up of small by
large businesses, means nothing else than the endeavour to
escape the risks and dangers attending small-scale production
in the tide of modern industrial changes. But since all are
moving in the same direction, no one gains upon the other.
Certain common economies are shared by the monster competitors, but more and more energy must be given to the
work of competition, and the productive economies are
partly squandered in the friction of fierce competition, and
partly pass over to the body of consumers in lowered prices.
Thus the endeavour to secure safety and high profits by the
economies of large-scale production is rendered futile by
the growing severity of the competitive process. Each
big firm finds itself competent to undertake more business than it already possesses, and underbids its neigh-
bour until the cutting of prices has sunk the weaker and
driven profits to a bare subsistence point for the stronger
competitors.

So long as the increased size of business brings with it
a net economic advantage, the competition of ever larger
competitors, whose total power of production is far ahead
of sales at remunerative prices, and who are therefore
constrained to devote an increased proportion of energy
to taking one another's trade, must intensify this cut-throat
warfare. The diminishing number of competitors in a
market does not ease matters in the least, for the intensity
of the strife reaches its maximum when two competing
businesses are fighting a life or death struggle. As the
effective competitors grow fewer, not only is the proportion
of attention each devotes to the other more continuous and
more highly concentrated, but the results of success are

more intrinsically valuable, for the reward of victory over the last competitor is the attainment of monopoly.

§ 4. To keen-eyed business men engaged in the thick of large-scale competition it becomes increasingly clear that good profits can only be obtained in one of two ways. A successful firm must either be in possession of some trade secret, patent, special market, or such other private economy as places it in a position of monopoly in certain places or in certain lines of goods, or else it must make some arrangement with competing firms whereby they shall consent to abate the intensity or limit the scope of their competition. It will commonly be found that both these conditions are present where a modern firm of manu-facturers or merchants succeeds in maintaining during a long period of time a prosperous or paying business. The firm, though in close competition over part of the field of industry, will have a speciality of a certain class of wares, at any rate in certain markets, and it will be fortified by a more or less firmly fixed rate of prices extending over the whole class of commodities. Both of these forces signify a restriction upon competition.

To the older economists, who regarded free competition as the only safe guarantee of industrial security and pro-gress, it appeared natural that capitalists continually engaged in the maximum competition would yet secure a living rate of profit, for if this were not the case, they ingenuously urged, capital would cease to remain in such a trade. With the fallacy involved in this theory we shall deal in a later chapter. It is sufficient here to observe that where keen competition is operative in modern machine industries the average rate of profits obtained for capital is generally below that which would suffice to induce new capital invested with full knowledge to come into the trade.

In highly organised trades, where the natural effects of free competition have been fully manifested, we find that the hope of a profitable business is entirely based upon the possibility that a trade agreement will so mitigate competition as to allow a rate of selling prices to obtain which remains considerably higher than that which free competition would allow.

As the field of competition is narrowed to a compara-

tively few large competitors, there arises a double
inducement to suspend or mitigate hostilities; as the
competition is fiercer more is gained by a truce; as the
number of combatants is smaller, a truce can be more
easily formed and maintained. In most machine-using
countries each branch of a staple industry endeavours to
protect itself from free competition by a combination of
masters to fix a scale of prices. This is the normal condition of trade in England to-day. These combinations to
fix and maintain prices are not equally successful in all
trades, but they are always operative to a more or less
extent in modifying or retarding the effects of competition.
Where trade unions of operatives are strong, well-informed,
and resolute, or where outsiders have large facilities for investing capital and dividing the trade, the endeavours to maintain prices and to secure a higher than the competitive
rate of profits are unsuccessful. The joint operation of both
these conditions in the cotton-spinning trade explains
why the Lancashire spinners have been unable to check
the effects of cut-throat competition. But throughout
all branches of textile, metal, pottery, engineering, and
machine-making trades strong and persistent endeavours
are made by co-operative action of capitalists to limit
competition by fixing a scale of prices which should not
be underbid.

Where competing railways fix a tariff of rates for carriage,
or competing manufacturers fix a scale of prices for their
goods, their object is to secure to themselves in higher
profits a portion or the whole of the productive and competitive economies attending large-scale production, instead
of allowing them by unrestricted competition to pass into
the hands of their customers. Suppose that a number of
steel rail manufacturers freely competing would drive down
the selling price to £1 a ton, but that by a trade agreement
they maintain £1 10s. as the minimum price, 10s. per
ton represents the economies of production which they
divert from their customers into their own possession by
a limitation of the competition. Part of the 10s. may
represent the actual saving of the labour which would have
been spent in competition as prices fell from £1 10s. to
£1. Part may represent a taking in higher profits of some
of the economies of new machinery or improved methods

of production common to the competing firms, and which would inevitably have led to a fall of price if the competitive process had been allowed free play.

The prices thus fixed are monopoly prices—that is to say, they are determined by the action of a number of competing capitals which at a certain point agree to suspend their conflict and act as a single capital; when the bidding is above a certain figure they are many, when it is below that figure they are one. The condition in such a trade is one of limited monopoly. The prices fixed by such trade agreements will generally be different from those of a single firm with the absolute monopoly of a market, whose prices are arranged to yield the maximum net profit on the capital engaged. For since the economies of competition and some of the economies of production would be far greater for a single producing firm with a monopoly, the schedule of supply prices measuring the expenses of producing the different quantities of goods will be different, and this difference will be reflected in a different scale of non-competitive market prices from that which would issue from a trade agreement. Moreover, a loose voluntary compact between trade rivals yields a monopoly of a far feebler order than does the unity of a single capital. If a scale of prices were fixed which would yield a considerably higher profit than the market rate, the temptation to secure a larger share of trade by secret underbidding through commissions, drawbacks, or otherwise, or even by an open cutting of rates, is very powerful. Moreover, the ability of a number of firms with conflicting interests to secure this monopoly by quick and vigorous repression of the attempts of outside capital to come in either for the purpose of sharing the higher profits, or of being bought out, is far less than in the case of a single monopolist firm. So the scale of prices fixed by a number of competing firms will generally be nearer to the competition prices than would be the case with the prices of a single monopolist.

§ 5. The recognition of the advantages of limiting competition by price tariffs, and the experience of the difficulty of maintaining such tariffs, lead competing businesses to take further steps in the curtailment of competition. Where a powerful trade opinion can be focussed on an offender against the scale, where he can be boycotted or otherwise

subjected to punishment, and where outsiders can be prevented from intruding into the trade, a common scale of
profitable prices can often be maintained with the verbal or
even the tacit consent of those concerned. This is the
case in many manufactures where the fixed and well-known
character of the goods makes a close price-list possible.
Retail dealers in local markets are often able to keep a close
adherence to a rigid scale by the pure force of *esprit de
corps.* The price of bread, meat, milk, coals, and other
articles sold locally by well-known measures, is seldom, if
ever, regulated by free competition among the vendors. In
articles where more depends upon the individual quality of
wares, and where a rigid tariff is less easily fixed and less
easily maintained, as in the case of vegetables, fruit, fish, and
groceries, trade agreements are less easy to maintain. Still
more difficult is it to maintain a tariff for articles of dress
or adornment of the person or the house, and in other
articles where the consumer is less confined to a narrow
local market.

The general experience of manufacturing and mercantile
businesses, where each firm is closely confronted by other
firms of similar capacity and equipment at every point in
the market, indicates an increasing difficulty in maintaining
prices at a profitable level. Everywhere complaints are
heard of a reckless use of the productive power of
machinery, of over-stocked markets, of a cutting of prices in
order to get business, and of a growing inability to make
a living rate of profit.

§ 6. The endeavour of a number of individual businesses
in a trade to fix and maintain a certain profitable scale of
prices is constantly frustrated. The introduction of new
machinery enabling certain firms to make a profit at prices
below the tariff induces them to utilise their full productivity, cut prices, and still sell at a profitable price;
others involved in the meshes of speculative production
are compelled to cut prices and effect sales even at a
loss; the difficulty of finding safe investments drives new
capital into the hands of company-promoters, who fling it
with criminal negligence into this or that branch of production, underbidding the tariff to win a footing in the
market. All these forces render loose agreements to limit
competition more and more inadequate to secure their

purpose. Frequent experience of the impotence of these partial forms of co-operation drives trade competitors to seek ever closer forms of combination. An issue of this necessity is the Syndicate and the Trust. By raising the co-operative action so as to cover the whole, and by thus reducing the competition to zero, it is hoped that a union may be formed strong enough to maintain monopoly prices. Thus the Trust is seen as the logical culmination of the operation of economic forces which have been continually engaged in diminishing the number of effective competitors, while increasing their size and the proportion of their energy devoted to the competition.

At each stage in the process the smaller competitors are eliminated, and the larger driven to increase their size so that the whole may be illustrated by a pyramid, the base or first stage of which consists of a larger number of small units, and each higher stage of a smaller number of larger units, with a Trust or Monopoly Syndicate for its apex.

§ 7. The motive which induces a number of businesses hitherto separate, or associated merely for certain specific actions, such as the fixing of prices or wages, to amalgamate so that they form a single capital on which a single rate of interest is paid, is a double-edged one. There is, on the one hand, the desire to protect themselves against excessive competition and cutting of rates, and on the other hand a desire to secure the advantages which arise from monopoly. The way in which Syndicates and Trusts are regarded depends very much from which of these two aspects they are regarded. Those who consider these business "combines" as arbitrary and high-handed interferences with freedom of commerce, undertaken in order to place in the hands of a few persons a power to rob and oppress the consuming public by legalised extortion, regard the motive of combination to be monopoly. On the other hand, the combining firms represent themselves as the victims of circumstances, bound in self-protection to combine. Our analysis of the operations of commercial competition enables us to see that these two forces are not really separate, but are only two ways of looking at the same action. Every avoidance of so-called "excessive" competition is *ipso facto* an establishment of a monopoly. The tariff of prices established a weak and partial monopoly.

The "combine," whether it takes the name of "ring," "syndicate," or "trust," succeeds, in so far as it establishes a stronger and more absolute monopoly.

In their economic aspect these terms are somewhat vague, the vagueness arising in some degree from the changing and secret shapes these combinations often find it convenient to adopt in order to preserve the appearance of competition, or to avoid public obloquy or legal interference. "Combine" is probably the generic term which covers all these operations. A syndicate of capitalists are said to form a "combine" with the view of controlling prices so as to pay a profitable interest. If they apply their capital not to the acquisition of the plant and machinery of manufacture with the view of regulating production, but directly and mainly to the planning of some speculative stroke or series of strokes in the produce market, obtaining temporary control of sufficient goods of a particular kind to enable them to manipulate prices, they are said to form a "corner" or "ring." Such forms of combined action are generally of short duration. Technically they consist in an artificial diversion[1] of a particular class of goods from the ordinary channel of a number of competing owners into a single ownership, so that they may be held and placed upon the supply market at such times and in such ways as to enable the owner to obtain a famine price. The following description of a wheat "corner" will serve to exemplify this method of "combine" :—

"The man who forms a corner in wheat, first purchases or secures the control of the whole available supply of wheat, or as near the whole supply as he can. In addition to this he purchases more than is really within reach of the market by buying 'futures,' or making contracts with others who agree to deliver him wheat at some future time. Of course he aims to secure the greater part of his wheat quietly, at low figures; but after he deems that the whole supply is nearly in his control, he spreads the news that there is a 'corner' in the market, and buys openly all the wheat he can, offering higher and higher prices, until he raises the price sufficiently high to suit him. Now the men

---

[1] There need, of course, be no actual diversion of goods into the possession of the Ring : the essence of the monopoly consists in the control, not in the possession of goods.

who have contracted to deliver wheat to him at this date
are at his mercy. They must buy their wheat of him at whatever price he chooses to ask, and deliver it as soon as
purchased, in order to fulfil their contracts. Meanwhile
mills must be kept in operation, and the millers have to pay
an increased price for wheat ; they charge the bakers higher
prices for flour, and the bakers raise the price of bread.
Thus is told by the hungry mouths in the poor man's home
the last act in the tragedy of the corner."[1]

These "corners," of which in various forms and degrees the
speculative business on the stock and produce markets largely
consists, are attempts to substitute for a time a high monopoly price for a competitive price by "rigging the market."
Since the calculations upon which these "corners" are
based are essentially hazardous, attempted corners frequently break down. One of the most special examples of
the collapse of a powerful corner in recent years is that of
"La Société Industrielle Commerciale des Métaux," commonly known as the "Copper Syndicate." A body of
French capitalists, for the most part not owners of mines or
metal merchandise, but speculators pure and simple, placed
a sum of money with the intention of cornering the supply
of "tin." Before completing this design they were induced
to undertake a larger speculation in the "copper market."
In 1887 they entered into contracts with the largest
copper-producing companies in various countries, agreeing
to buy all the copper produced for the next three years at
a fixed price of 13 cents per pound, with an added bonus
equivalent to half the profit from their sale of the same.
In 1888 the Syndicate sought to extend its contracts with
chief mining companies to cover a period of twelve years,
arranging with them also to limit the output of copper. For
some time they held the market in their grip, and prices
advanced considerably. But partly owing to a failure to
complete their contracts securing a restriction in production,
and partly from inability to meet their current liabilities, the
"corner" was broken down in 1889, and the artificially inflated prices fell. Not only are the makers of "corners"
liable to these miscalculations, but they are liable to be
overthrown by counter combinations of capitalists or of

[1] Baker, *Monopolies and the People*, p. 81.

operatives. The breakdown of a formidable attempt to "corner" cotton in Lancashire in 1889 was due to the prompt action of the Trades Unions, who undertook to unite with their employers in a stoppage of work for such length of time as was requisite to force the collapse of the "ring."

In the same year a formidable flour syndicate broke down before the firm attitude of the co-operative flour mills.[1]

But though the speculative character of modern commerce, assisted by the abundant use of credit, has lent special facilities to the formation of "corners" and "rings," it is hardly necessary to say that commerce has never been free from them. The celebrated "corner" in grain which Joseph organised on behalf of the King of Egypt was one of the largest and most successful. The commercial law of the Middle Ages is full of provisions against engrossers, forestallers, and regrators, all of whom were engaged in artificially raising prices to the consumer by obtaining some sort of monopoly. Organised rings to secure a monopoly of the food supply of some great city have been frequent throughout history. Cicero informs us of the celebrated ring of capitalists under Crassus to raise food prices at Rome. A closely-formed combination of northern coalowners continued to restrict output and impose monopoly prices upon London consumers for a considerable time in the middle of the eighteenth century.[2]

In modern times these "corners" are essentially of brief duration so far as they consist in narrowing the stream of commerce at a particular point so as to check its free flow. Most of them are confined to goods which are dealt with upon commercial exchanges, and are amenable to the operations of skilled speculators. The "deal" must be upon a scale large enough to enable a big net profit to be secured in a short time. The stimulation which artificially inflated prices apply to the early productive processes, the activity of other speculators, and the check given to consumption by high prices, generally preclude the possibility of a "corner" lasting long. The strength of the copper "corner," had it succeeded, would have lain in the hold it would have obtained over

[1] Cf. Miss Potter, *The Co-operative Movement*, p. 199.
[2] Porter, *Progress of the Nation*, pp. 283-285.

the early extractive stage, preventing the operation of the natural stimulus of high prices to increase production. If the Copper Syndicate had established its hold upon the mining companies, it would have been able to hold the market for an indefinite period, passing from the state of a "corner" into the more durable and established position of the Trust.

§ 8. A Trust may be regarded from an economic aspect, or from a legal aspect. Economically, the term Trust is applied to a class of syndicates which have established a partial or total monopoly in certain productive industries by securing the ownership of a sufficient proportion of the instruments of production to enable them to control prices. Legally, a Trust is a form of business association—"a trust of corporate stocks by means of which a body of men united in interest are enabled to carry on business through separate corporate agencies."[1] It is a company of companies, under which, while the formal structure of the original companies is maintained, they are incorporated as single cells in the larger organism which directs their activity. The constitution of the Trust is best explained by a description of its origin in the industry of the United States. The owners of a majority of the shares in a number of corporations hitherto separate in their constitution (though they may have been acting in agreement with one another, or have been largely owned by the same persons) agree to place their shares of stock in the full control of a body of persons called trustees. These trustees may or may not be shareholders or directors of the several corporations. They "act under an agreement that they will cast the votes represented by the stock so held for the perpetuation of the trust during the time agreed upon, and in furtherance of its purposes : will elect the officers provided for by law in each of the corporations, and in behalf of all of them manage the business of all, except, it may be, in small matters of detail." "Each shareholder, upon surrendering his corporate stock to the board of trustees, receives a certificate entitling him to an interest in all the property and earnings of all the corporations of the trust."[2]

[1] C. S. T. Dodd, "Ten Years of the Standard Oil Trust," *Forum*, May 1892.

[2] "The Standard Oil Trust," Roger Sherman, *Forum*, July 1892.

These certificates are believed in many cases to certify a money value far in excess of the real value of the stock surrendered at the time when the Trust was formed. The Report of the New York Chamber of Commerce for 1887-88 estimates the "certificates" given by the Sugar Trust to the shareholders of its constituent corporations as bearing "water" to the amount of 200 per cent., so that the nominal dividend of $10\frac{1}{2}$ per cent. paid during the year represented a real net profit of $31\frac{1}{2}$ per cent. Such statements cannot, however, be verified, since it is the interest of the only persons who actually know to keep secret such an arrangement.

It is asserted by many, and several State courts have sustained the position, that a Trust is in America an illegal association, because it implies on the part of its constituent corporations a violation of the conditions under which they received the powers and privileges conferred in their charters by the government of the several States. Their illegality consists, it is held—

(1) In surrendering the power to manage and control their business to some persons other than those legally authorised.

(2) In engaging, through the Trust, in kinds of business not authorised by the charter.

§ 9. It is, however, the economic character and powers of the Trust, and not its legal position, which concern us here.

The following short history of the origin and *modus operandi* of the Standard Oil Trust, the largest and in some respects the strongest of these organisations, will serve to give distinctiveness to the idea of the Trust:—

Petroleum began to be an article of extensive commerce about the year 1862. The wells from which the crude petroleum oil was drawn were in Pennsylvania, and the work of boring the wells with machinery and extracting the oil grew to be a considerable business. The crude oil was sold to various refiners, who set up factories in Cleveland (Ohio), in Pittsburg, and in several other cities. By 1865 these factories had become pretty numerous, and in that year a private refinery at Cleveland, owned by a few partners, obtained a charter forming it into a corporation entitled the Standard Oil Company, with a capital of

$100,000. Until 1870 the progress of the company was comparatively slow. In order to increase their hold upon the sources of production in Pennsylvania, and to expand their trade, they began to purchase stock in corporations already existing in that State, and succeeded in establishing others, with which they worked in close alliance. A Standard Oil Company was organised at Pittsburg, the stock of which passed into the hands of the owners of the Cleveland Company. They then proceeded to establish agencies in other States, primarily for the sale of their goods, but when these businesses were firmly planted they obtained for them from the several States charters incorporating them as companies for refining oil. In 1872 the shareholders of the Standard Oil Companies at Cleveland, Pittsburg, and Philadelphia organised another corporation called the South Improvement Company, obtaining a charter from the State of Pennsylvania. This corporation, which was in fact though not in legal form the "Standard Oil Companies," then entered into contracts with the New York Central and Hudson River Railroad Company, the Erie Railway Company, and several other lines which traversed the oil-producing country, for the shipment of petroleum. The South Improvement Company agreed to ship over these railways all the petroleum products. In return the railway companies agreed to carry their goods, not upon the terms open to other customers, but with a system of rebates, paid not only upon the oil shipped by the company, but upon that shipped by any other competing companies. "In one locality the railroad companies were to charge oil shippers as freight not exceeding $1.50 per barrel, and pay a rebate to the South Improvement Company of $1.06 per barrel, whether it was the shipper of the oil or not, so that under these contracts the Standard Oil Company members would pay no more than 44 cents per barrel as freight to the carrier, while their competitors would pay $1.50, and of this last sum the railways were to pay back to the combination $1.06 per barrel."[1]

Though this monstrous conspiracy was quickly unmasked, and the South Improvement Company lost its charter,

[1] Roger Sherman, "The Standard Oil Trust," *The Forum*, July 1892.

secret negotiations with the railway companies enabled the Standard Oil Companies to strengthen themselves by this system of rebates paid out of the pockets of their business rivals. Chiefly by means of these and other discriminating contracts they were enabled to enlarge their sphere of activity, and making full use of their growing capital, succeeded in destroying or absorbing their competitors, until, as early as 1875, they held a practical monopoly of the refineries of the interior. No fewer than seventy-four refineries are stated to have been bought up, leased, or bankrupted by the Standard Oil Company in Pennsylvania alone in the course of its career.

Until about 1878 the chief source of power of the company seems to have been the alliance with the railroads and the local monopolies obtained by buying up or crushing rival businesses. But the president, Mr. Rockefeller, and his associates were men of keen business ability, who understood how to make use of the inventive genius of the abler employees who passed into their service, and of the improvements in method of production and distribution of oil which were suggested. In the next few years the company were enabled to effect enormous economies in the storage and conveyance of oil. Pipe lines were laid down connecting New York, Philadelphia, Baltimore, Buffalo, Pittsburg, Cleveland, and Chicago, and a network of feeding lines joining the sources of supply. Thousands of huge tanks were erected for holding surplus stores; a large number of agencies were established along the sea-shore with storage attached. Further considerable economies were effected by the undertaking of the manufacture of barrels and cans and other subsidiary articles required in the trade. At the close of 1881 the owners of the entire capital of fifteen corporations and parts of the stock of a number of others, the latter chiefly trading companies, established the Trust. The number of shareholders thus associated was forty, and they placed their stocks in the hands of nine of their number as trustees, who continued to administer the whole business, paying interest upon the certificates which represented the stock of the several shareholders until March 1892, when the Trust was legally dissolved. The legal dissolution of the Trust has not, however, materially impaired its economic unity and power; on the contrary, it has extended in the

United States its monopolic control of the market, and has already established a strong control over several European markets for the sale of oil, and over the chief natural sources of supply. Although a practical monopoly in many parts of the interior had been acquired at a tolerably early date, there continued to be active competition in all branches of the petroleum business until 1884, when the war of rates, which had been waged for some time with a formidable Canadian competitor, the Tidewater Company, ceased, an alliance being formed between the rivals. From that time the Standard Oil Trust has held a practical monopoly over the greater part of the country. It has introduced new economies in the machinery of refining, has found profitable uses for naphtha and other waste products, and has vastly increased its output and the machinery of distribution. Not content with controlling the market for crude oil, it has during the last few years obtained the possession of larger and larger portions of the oil-producing country, forming companies to acquire mining rights, sink wells, and oust the private producers from whom it had previously been content to purchase the raw material at their own prices.

Bearing in mind the fact that the actual unification of businesses took place a good many years before the formation of the Trust, there is nothing in the account given above inherently inconsistent with the following explanation afforded by the Standard Oil Trust of their proceedings :—

"The Standard Oil Trust offers to prove by various witnesses that the disastrous condition of the refining business, and the numerous failures of refiners prior to 1875, arose from imperfect methods of refining, want of co-operation among refiners, the prevalence of speculative methods in the purchase and sale of both crude and refined petroleum, sudden and great reductions in price of crude, and excessive rates of freight ; that these disasters led to co-operation and association among the refiners, and that such association and co-operation, resulting eventually in the Standard Oil Trust, has enabled the refiners so co-operating to reduce the price of petroleum products, and thus benefit the public to a very marked degree."[1]

[1] Argument of Standard Oil Trust before the House Committee on Manufactures, 1888 (quoted Baker, *Monopolies and the People*, p. 21).

So far as this furnishes an explanation of the motives leading to the earlier growth of the Company, the consolidation of rival companies, no doubt it contains a considerable element of truth. The Standard Oil Trust, however, differs from most others in that it was not directly formed by the union of a number of leading rival businesses, but was merely a reorganisation upon a firmer basis of a single complex business. The motive of self-protection, though it might be operative in the early history of the Company, cannot be adduced as the true motive of the formation of the Trust.

Since the claim of the Standard Oil Trust to be a public benefit rests upon the fall of price to the customer, resulting from the various economies and improvements adopted by the Trust, it may be well to append a diagram showing the actual fall of prices during the twenty years 1870 to 1890.

In this diagram we note that from 1870 to 1875 there was a rapid reduction of price in consequence of the fact that these were years of keen competition with other Pennsylvanian businesses. 1875, which marks the establishment of a monopoly of the interior trade in the hands of the Standard Oil Trust, also marks a sharp rise of prices. The expansion of their business brought them into contact with new and more distant competitors, and a fall of price continued until 1879, while prices continued to oscillate until 1881, the year of the formation of the Trust. From the time of the formation of the Trust the fall of price has been only half a cent. The moral is obvious. So long as there is competition, in spite of the expense of conducting the strife, prices fall; when the competition is suspended, and there is a saving of friction, the public gains no further reduction.

The reason why, even after the complete monopoly had been attained, the price of oil was not put up again will be apparent when we come to examine the economic limits of the power of a Trust.

§ 10. A large number of these Trusts, similar in their constitution to the Standard Oil Trust, and with the same object of maintaining a scale of prices based upon monopoly, have been founded in the United States. Some have undoubtedly owed their establishment to the prevalence of

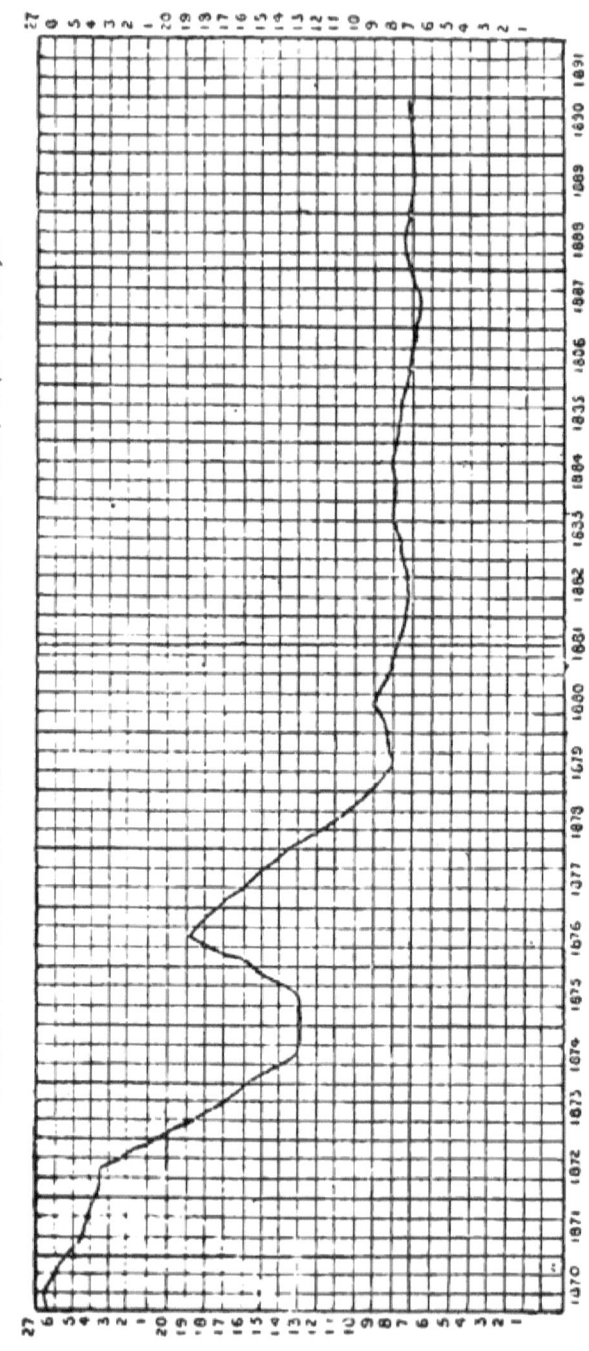

FLUCTUATIONS OF PRICES OF STANDARD OIL, 1870 TO 1890.

low profits in a trade where close competition has led to a
constant cutting of prices, and their foundation has been
leniently regarded as an act of self-defence. To this order
belong the Whisky Trust, the Cotton Oil Trust, the Cotton
Bagging Trust, and others. Indeed, one well-informed
writer upon the subject holds that this is the normal origin
of the Trust. "With the exception of the Standard Oil
Trust, and perhaps one or two others that rose somewhat
earlier, it may be fairly said, I think, that not merely competition, but competition that was proving ruinous to many
establishments, was the cause of the combinations."[1]

This condition of ruinous competition must be recognised
as the normal condition of all highly-organised businesses
where modern machinery is applied, and which are not
sheltered by some private economy in the shape of special
facilities in producing or in disposing of their goods. Even
the Standard Oil Company, as we saw, claimed that a policy
of consolidation was forced upon it by the conditions of
the market. But this claim is not a refutation, but an
admission of the statement that the object of a Trust is to
obtain monopoly prices ; for these ruinously low prices
and profits are the result of free competition, and the only
alternative to this free competition is monopoly. Hence it
is a legitimate conclusion that the economic object of a
Trust is to substitute monopoly for competitive prices, and
to do this more effectively than can be done by the mere
acceptance of a common price-list by the separate firms
engaged in a branch of production. In order to attain this
object it is not necessary that the Trust shall comprise all the
capital engaged in an industry. Even when the Standard Oil
Trust was firmly established, and was, according to its own
admission, paying 12½ or 13 per cent. on its highly-watered
stock, there appears to have existed no fewer than 111
smaller independent companies competing with it directly
or indirectly at some point within the area of its market.[2]
But the Standard Oil Trust was able to control prices, as
the producer of some 75 per cent. of the total product, and
the practical monopolist over the main area of its market.
Similarly the Sugar Refineries Trust in 1888 had a firm grip

[1] J. W. Jenks, Economic Journal, vol. ii. p. 73.
[2] Report to the Commission of the Senate of New York State, p. 440.

over prices by its possession of 80 per cent. of the sugar refining capacity of the Atlantic Coast, or 65 per cent. of the sugar consumed in the United States.[1]   There are other cases where a formally constructed Trust is for a time engaged in close effective competition, either with another Trust, as was the position of the Standard Oil Trust over a portion of its markets in the period 1881 to 1884, or with powerful companies not organised as Trusts.   This is what Mr. Gunton appears to consider the normal condition of a Trust, one in which competition takes place between a few large bodies of capital instead of between many smaller bodies.[2]   Certain Trusts have certainly been compelled to struggle for the retention of their monopoly power over the market.   A notorious example is that of the Sugar Trust, which, after a most successful start in 1888, found itself in 1890 face to face with a new and formidable competitor in the shape of the Claus Spreckles refineries of Philadelphia and San Francisco, and was compelled to forego the high profits it had been making and fight for its existence under terms of keenest competition.

But in so far as a Trust stands in this position it has failed to achieve its industrial end of checking "ruinous competition" and the "cutting of prices."   It is not in the possession of the chief economies of a Trust so long as it remains at warfare, for it is compelled to expend all that it gains from the enlarged scale of business and from the cessation of competition among its constituent companies upon the strife with its single antagonist.   A Trust in this inchoate condition has no special economic character distinguishing it from other large aggregates of competing capital.   It is with fully-formed trusts which are able to control prices and regulate to some degree production and profits that we are concerned.   An economic Trust has its *raison d'être* in monopoly.   It may not have eliminated all actual competitors, and is generally limited in its power by the possibility of outside opposition, but so far as its power extends it must be able to regulate prices upon non-competitive lines.

§ 11. A large number of different articles have at some

---

[1] *Economic Journal*, vol. ii. p. 83.
[2] "The Economic and Social Aspect of Trusts," *Political Science Quarterly*, Sept. 1888.

stage in their production fallen under the monopoly of a Trust.[1]

As is the case with "corners" and "rings" in the produce market, certain classes of commodities lend themselves more readily than others to the monopoly of Trusts.

There are three classes of industry which more easily than others permit the formation of effective trusts.

(1) Industries connected with, or closely dependent on, the nature and properties of land. When the whole or a large proportion of the raw material required for producing any class of goods is confined within a restricted area, the possession of that land by a single body of owners will give a strong monopoly. It was not essential to the Standard Oil Trust in its earlier years to own the sources of the oil provided they could possess themselves of the stream after it had left the source. But they have strengthened this monopoly lately by securing the ownership of the oil lands in Pennsylvania. The most striking example, however, is the monopoly of the anthracite coal region in Pennsylvania by the shareholders of the Pennsylvania and Reading Railway. The tendency of a Trust to strengthen its industrial position and at the same time to find a profitable investment for its surplus profits by fastening upon an earlier process of production or a contiguous industry, and drawing it under the control of its monopoly, is one of the most important evidences of the rapid growth of the system in America. The rapidity with which the whole railway system is passing into the hands of the two great monopolist syndicates with the necessary result of stifling competition is in some respects the most momentous economic movement in the United States at the present time. The magnificent distances which separate the great mass of the producers of agricultural and other raw products from their market makes the railway their only high-road, and the fact that except between a few large centres of population there is no competition of rival railways, places the producer entirely at the mercy of a single carrier, who regulates his rates so as to secure his maximum profit. Indeed, so fast is the amalgamation of railway capital proceeding

[1] Baker, writing 1890, names fifty-nine articles which have at various times formed the material of Trusts, ranging in importance from sugar and iron rails to castor-oil, school slates, coffins, and lead pencils.

that even between large cities there is little genuine competition. The same is true of the telegraph and the supply
of such things as water and gas, which, by reason of their
relation to land, and the power thus conferred upon the
owner of the first and most convenient means of supply,
are "natural" monopolies. Where such industries are
left, as in most cities of America, to private enterprise, they
form the objects of a monopoly which is commonly so
strong as to crush with ease attempts at competition where
such are legally permissible. Jay Gould's Western Union
Telegraph Company is an example of an absolute monopoly maintained for many years without the possibility
of effective competition. The purchase of Western lands
in order to hold them for monopoly prices has been a
favoured form of syndicate investment during the last forty
years.

(2) Articles which for economy of transport and distribution require to be massed together in large quantities are
specially amenable to monopoly. Grains produced over a
wide area have often to be collected in large quantities to
be re-assorted according to quality, and to be warehoused
before being placed in the market. So the produce of
thousands of competing farmers passes into the hands of
a syndicate of owners of grain elevators at Chicago or elsewhere. The same is true of meat, fish, fruit, vegetables,
dairy produce. All these things, raised under circumstances which render effective co-operation for purposes of
sale well-nigh impossible, flow from innumerable diverse
places into a common centre, where they fall into the hands
of a small group of middlemen, merchants, and exporters.
Even the retail merchants, as we have seen, are able to
make effective combinations to maintain prices in the case
of more perishable goods.

In England the combination of retail merchants commonly takes the form of a trade regulation of prices restricting competition. But in the United States regular
Trusts have been in some cases established in retail trade.
The Legislative Committee of New York State, in its
investigations, discovered a milk trust which had control of
the retail distribution in New York City, fixing a price of
three cents per quart to be paid to the farmer, and a selling
price of seven or eight cents for the consuming public.

Hence it arises that the prices paid by the consumer for farm produce are picked pretty clean by various groups of monopolists or restricted competitors before any of them get back to the farmers or first producers.

The farmer, from his position in the industrial machine, is more at the mercy of Trusts and other combinations than any other body of producers. In the United States he is helpless under the double sway of the railway and the syndicate of grain elevators and of slaughterers in Chicago, Kansas City, and elsewhere. In England, in France, and in all countries where the farmer is at a long distance from his market, farm produce is subject to this natural process of concentration, and we hear the same complaints of the oppressive rates of the railway and the monopoly of the groups of middlemen who form close combinations where the stream of produce narrows to a neck on its flow to the consumer. The position of the American farmer, crushed between the upper and the nether mill-stone of monopoly, is one of pathetic impotence.

(3) In those industries to which the most elaborate and expensive machinery is applied, and where, in consequence, the proportion of fixed capital to labour is largest, the economies of large-scale production are greatest. Here, as we have seen, the growing strain of the fiercer competition of ever larger and ever fewer capitals drives towards the culminating concentration of the Trust. Where, owing either to natural advantages, as in the case of oil and coal, or to other social and industrial reasons, a manufacture is confined within a certain district, and is in the hands of a limited number of firms in fairly close commercial touch with one another, we have conditions favouring the formation of a Trust. In most of the successful manufacturing Trusts some natural economy of easy access to the best raw material, special facilities of transport, the possession of some state or municipal monopoly of market, are added to the normal advantages of large-scale production. The artificial barriers in the shape of tariff, by which foreign competition has been eliminated from many leading manufactures in the United States, have greatly facilitated the successful operation of Trusts. Where the political, natural, and industrial forces are strongly combined, we have the most favourable soil for the Trust. Where a

manufacture can be carried on in any part of the country, and in any country with equal facility, it is difficult to maintain a Trust, even though machinery is largely used and the individual units of capital are big.

Each kind of commodity, as it passes through the many processes from the earth to the consumer, may be looked upon as a stream whose channel is broader at some points and narrower at others. Different streams of commodities narrow at different places. Some are narrowest and in fewest hands at the transport stage, when the raw material is being concentrated for production, others in one of the processes of manufacture, others in the hands of export merchants. Just as a number of German barons planted their castles along the banks of the Rhine, in order to tax the commerce between East and West which was obliged to make use of this highway, so it is with these economic "narrows." Wherever they are found, monopolies plant themselves in the shape of " rings," "corners," "pools," " syndicates," or " trusts."

CHAPTER VI.

ECONOMIC POWERS OF THE TRUST.

§ 1. *Power of a Monopoly over earlier or later Processes in Production of a Commodity.*
§ 2. *Power over Actual or Potential Competitors.*
§ 3. *Power over Employees of a Trust.*
§ 4. *Power over Consumers.*
§ 5. *Determinants of a Monopoly Price.*
§ 6. *The Possibility of low Monopoly Prices.*
§ 7. *Considerations of Elasticity of Demand limiting Prices.*
§ 8. *Final Summary of Monopoly Prices.*

§ 1. It remains to investigate the actual economic power which a "monopoly" possesses over the several departments of an industrial society. Although the "trust" may be taken as the representative form of monopoly of capital, the economic powers it possesses are common in different degrees to all the other weaker or more temporary forms of combination, and to the private business which, by the possession of some patent, trade secret, or other economic advantage, is in control of a market. These powers of monopoly may be placed under four heads in relation to the classes upon whose interests they operate—(*a*) business firms engaged in an earlier or later process of production; (*b*) actual and potential competitors or business rivals; (*c*) employees of the Trust or other monopoly; (*d*) the consuming public.

(*a*) The power possessed by a monopoly placed in the transport stage, or in one of the manufacturing or merchant stages, to "squeeze" the earlier or less organised producers, has been illustrated by the treatment of farmers by the railways and by the Elevator Companies and the Slaughtering Companies of the United States. The Standard Oil Trust, as we saw, preferred, until quite recently, to leave the oil lands and the machinery for extracting crude oil in the hands of unattached individuals or companies, trusting to their position as the largest purchasers of crude oil to enable them to dictate prices. The fall in the price paid by the company for crude oil from 9.19 cents in 1870 to 2.30 in 1881, when the Trust was formed, and the maintenance of an almost uniform lower level from 1881 to 1890, testifies to the closeness of the grip in which the company held the oil producers; for although improvements in the machinery for sinking wells and for extracting oil took place during the period, these economies in production do not at all suffice to explain the fall. Indeed, the method of the company's transactions with the oil producers, as described by their own solicitor in his defence of the Trust, is convincing testimony of their control of the situation:— " When the producer of oil puts down a well, he notifies the pipe line company (a branch of the Trust), and immediately a pipe line is laid to connect with his well. The oil is taken from the tank at the well, whenever requested, into the large storage tanks of the company, and is held for the owner as long as he desires it. A certificate is given for it, which can be turned into cash at any time; and when sold it is delivered to the purchaser at any station on the delivery lines."[1] In similar fashion the Sugar Trust, before the competition of the Spreckles refineries arose, controlled the market for raw sugar. Nor was this power exercised alone over the producers of raw sugar. It extended to dictating the price at which the wholesale grocers who took from them the refined sugar should sell to their customers.[2] This power of a monopoly is not merely extended to the control of prices in the earlier and later processes of production and distribution of the commodity. One of the most potent forms it assumes in manufactures where machinery is much used is a control over the patentees and even the manufacturers of machinery. Where a strong Trust exists, the patentee of a new in-

---

[1] S. C. T. Dodd, *The Forum*, May 1892.
[2] " Trusts in the United States," *Economic Journal*, p. 86.

vention can only sell to the Trust and at the Trust's price.
Charges are even made against the Standard Oil Trust
and other powerful monopolies to the effect that they are
in the habit of appropriating any new invention, whether
patented or not, without paying for it, trusting to their
influence to avoid the legal consequences of such conduct.
There is indeed strong reason to believe that the irrespon-
sible position in which some of these corporations are
placed induces them to an unscrupulous use of their great
wealth for such purposes.

§ 2. (*b*) Since the prime object of a Trust is to effect
sales at profitable prices, and prices are directly determined
by the quantitative relation between supply and demand, it
is clearly advantageous for a Trust to obtain as full a power
in the regulation of the quantity of supply as is possible.
In order to effect this object the Trust will pursue a double
policy. It will buy up such rival businesses as it deems can
be worked advantageously for the purposes of the Trust.
The price at which it will compel the owners of such
businesses to sell will have no precise relation to the value
of the business, but will depend upon the amount of trouble
which such a business can cause by refusing to come into
the Trust. If the outstanding firm is in a strong position
the Trust can only compel it to sell, by a prolonged
process of cutting prices, which involves considerable
loss. For such a business a high price will be paid. By
this means a strongly-established Trust or Syndicate will
bring under its control the whole of the larger and better-
equipped businesses which would otherwise by their competition weaken the Trust's control of the market. A smaller
business, or an important rival who persistently stands out
of the Trust, is assailed by the various weapons in the hands
of the Trust, and is crushed by the brute force of its stronger
rival. The most common method of crushing a smaller
business is by driving down prices below the margin of
profit, and by the use of the superior staying power which
belongs to a larger capital starving out a competitor. This
mode of exterminating warfare is used not merely against
actually existing rivals, as where a railway company is known
to bring down rates for traffic below cost price in order to
take the traffic of a rival line, but is equally effective against
the potential competition of outside capital. After two or

three attempts to compete with Jay Gould's telegraph line
from New York to Philadelphia had been frustrated by a
lowering of rates to a merely nominal price, the notoriety of
this terrible weapon sufficed to check further attempts at competition.   In this way each strongly-formed Trust is able to
fence off securely a certain field of investment, thus narrowing the scope of use for any outside capital. This employment
of brute force is sometimes spoken of as "unfair" competition,
and treated as something distinct from ordinary trade competition.   But the difference drawn is a purely fallacious
one.   In thus breaking down a competitor the Trust simply
makes use of those economies which we have found to
attach to large-scale businesses as compared with small.
Its action, however oppressive it may seem from the point
of view of a weaker rival, is merely an application of those
same forces which are always operating in the evolution of
modern capital.   In a competitive industrial society there
is nothing to distinguish this conduct of a Trust in the use
of its size and staying power from the conduct of any
ordinary manufacturer or shopkeeper who tries to do a
bigger and more paying business than his rivals.   Each
uses to the full, and without scruple, all the economic
advantages of size, skill in production, knowledge of
markets, attractive price-lists, and methods of advertisement
which he possesses.   It is quite true that so long as there
is competition among a number of fairly equal businesses
the consuming public may gain to some extent by this
competition, whereas the normal result of the successful
establishment of a Trust is simply to enable its owners to
take higher profits by raising prices to the consumer.   But
this does not constitute a difference in the mode of competition, so that in this case it deserves to be called " fair,"
in the other "unfair."

It is even doubtful whether such bargains as that above
described between the Standard Oil Company and the
Railways, whereby a discriminative rate was maintained in
favour of the Company, is "unfair," though it was under-
hand and illegal.   In the ordinary sense of the term it was
a "free" contract between the Railways and the Oil Company, and in spite of its discriminative character might have
been publicly maintained had the law not interfered on a
technical point.   The same is even true of the flagrant act

of discrimination described by Mr. Baker:—"A combination among manufacturers of railway car-springs, which wished to ruin an independent competitor, not only agreed with the American Steel Association that the independent company should be charged $10 per ton more for steel than the members of the combine, but raised a fund to be used as follows: when the independent company made a bid on a contract for springs, one of the members of the Trust was authorised to under-bid at a price which would incur a loss, which was to be paid out of the fund. In this way the competing company was to be driven out of business."[1] These cases differ only in their complexity from the simpler modes of underselling a business rival. Mean, underhand, and perhaps illegal many of these tactics are, but after all they differ rather in degree than in kind from the tactics commonly practised by most businesses engaged in close commercial warfare. If they are "unfair," it is only in the sense that all coercion of the weak by the strong is "unfair," a verdict which doubtless condemns from any moral standpoint the whole of trade competition, so far as it is not confined to competing excellence of production.

The only exercise of power by a Trust or Monopoly in its dealings with competing capital which deserves to be placed in a separate category of infamy, is the use of money to debauch the legislature into the granting of protective tariffs, special charters or concessions, or other privileges which enable a monopoly company to get the better of their rivals, to secure contracts, to check outside competition, and to tax the consuming public for the benefit of the trust-maker's pocket. Under this head we may also reckon the tampering with the administration of justice which is attributed, apparently not without good reason, to certain of the Trusts, the use of the Trust's money to purchase immunity from legal interference, or, in the last resort, to buy a judgment in the Courts.

How far the more or less definite allegations upon this subject are capable of substantiation it is beyond our scope to inquire, but certain disclosures in connection with the Tweed Ring, the Standard Oil Company, the Anthracite Coal Trust, and other syndicates induce the belief that

[1] Baker, *Monopolies and the People*, p. 85.

the more unscrupulous capitalists seek to influence the
Courts of Justice as well as the Houses of Legislature in
the pursuance of their business interests.

§ 3. (c) The more or less complete control of the capital
engaged in an industry, and of the market, involves an
enormous power over the labour engaged in that industry.
So long as competition survives, the employee or group of
employees are able to obtain wages and other terms of
employment determined in some measure by the conflicting
interests of different employers. But when there is only
one employer, the Trust, the workman who seeks employment has no option but to accept the terms offered by the
Trust. His only alternative is to abandon the use of the
special skill of his trade and to enter the ever-swollen
unskilled labour market. This applies with special force to
factory employees who have acquired great skill by incessant practice in some narrow routine of machine-tending.
The average employee in a highly-elaborated modern
factory is on the whole less competent than any other
worker to transfer his labour-power without loss to another
kind of work.[1] Now, as we have seen, it is precisely in
these manufactures that many of the strongest Trusts spring
up. The Standard Oil Company or the Linseed Oil Trust
are the owners of their employees almost to the same extent
as they are owners of their mills and machinery, so subservient has modern labour become to the fixed capital
under which it works. It has been claimed as one of the
advantages of a Trust that the economies attending its
working enable it to pay wages higher than the market
rate. There can be no question as to the ability of the
stronger Trusts to pay high wages. But there is no power
to compel them to do so, and it would be pure hypocrisy
to pretend that the interests of the labourers formed any
part of the motive which led a body of keen business men
to acquire a monopoly. One of the special economies
which a large capital possesses over a small, and which a
Trust possesses *par excellence*, is the power of making
advantageous bargains with its employees.

It is possible that a firm like the Standard Oil Trust may
to some limited extent practise a cheap philanthropy of

---

[1] Cf. Chapter ix.

profit-sharing in order to deceive the public into supposing that its huge profits enrich many instead of few. But there is no evidence that the employees of a Trust have gained in any way from the economies of industrial monopoly, nor, as we see, is there any *à priori* likelihood they should so gain.[1]

But the practical ownership of its employees involved in the position of a monopoly is by no means the full measure of the oppressive power exercised by the Trust over labour. Since the means by which Trust prices are maintained is the regulation of production, the interests of the Trust often require that a large part of the fixed capital of the companies entering the Trust shall stand idle. "When competition has become so fierce that there is frequently in the market a supply of goods so great that all cannot be sold at remunerative prices, it is necessary that the competing establishments, in order to continue business at all (of course, under perfectly free competition many will fail), check their production. Now an ordinary pool makes provision for each establishment to run in one of the two ways suggested. Manifestly a stronger organisation like the Trust, by selecting the best establishments, and running them continuously at their full capacity, while closing the others, or selling them, and making other use of the capital thus set free, will make a great saving. The most striking example of this kind in the recent history of the Trusts is furnished by the Whisky Trust. More than eighty distilleries joined the Trust. Formerly, when organised as a pool, as has been said, each establishment ran at part capacity, one year at 40 per cent., one year at only 28 per cent. A year after the organisation of the Trust only twelve were running; but these were producing at about their full capacity, and the total output of alcohol was not at all lessened. The saving is to be reckoned by the labour and running capital which had formerly been employed in nearly sixty distilleries. It must be borne in mind that on

---

[1] Mr. George Gunton, in writing upon "The Economic Aspect of Trusts" (*Political Science Quarterly*, Sept. 1888), claims a rise in wages as one of the advantages of Trusts, but Mr. Gunton throughout his argument assumes that a Trust is a large competing capital and not a monopoly. If a Trust were a competing capital its formation would be an economic and social advantage, tending, as he says, "to increase production, to lower prices, and to raise wages." But as a Trust is not a competing capital it does none of these things.

the product of these twelve distilleries good profits were made on the capital represented in more than eighty plants. All the greater Trusts, such as the Standard Oil, the Cotton Oil, the Cotton Bagging, and the Sugar Trust, have followed this plan of closing entirely the weaker establishments and running only the stronger, thereby effecting a saving in capital and labour."[1]

Here we see a Trust exercising its economic power of regulating production. That power, as we shall see below, is not merely confined to closing the inferior mills in order that the same aggregate output may be obtained by a full working of the more efficient plant. Where over-production ✔ has occurred it is to the interest of the Trust to lessen production. With this end in view it will suddenly close half the mills, or works, or elevators in a district. The owners of these closed plants get their interest from the Trust just as if they were working. But the labour of these works suddenly, and without any compensation for disturb-ance, is "saved"—that is to say, the employees are deprived of the services of the only kind of plant and material to which their skilled efforts are applicable. It is probable that one result of the formation of each of these larger trusts has been to throw out of employment several thousands of workers, and to place them either in the ranks of the unemployed or in some other branch of industry where their previously acquired skill is of little service, and where their wages are correspondingly depressed. From the account given above of the changes in organisation of production under the Trust it might appear that the effect upon labour was not to reduce the net employment, but to give full, regular employment to a smaller number instead of partial and irregular employment to many, and that thus labour, considered as a whole, might be the gainer. An industrial movement which substitutes the regular employment of a few for the irregular employment of many is so far a progressive movement. But it must be borne in mind first that there is usually a net reduction of employment, a substitution not of 50 workers at full-time for 100 at half-time, but of 30 only. For not only will there be a net

[1] J. W. Jenks, "Trusts in the United States," *Economic Journal*, vol. ii. p. 80.

saving of labour in relation to the same output, the result of using exclusively the best equipped and best situated factories, but since the Trust came into existence in order to restrict production and so raise prices, the aggregate output of the business will be either reduced or its rate of increase will be less than under open competition. The chief economy of the Trust will in fact arise from the net diminution of employment of labour. As the Trust grows stronger and absorbs a larger and larger proportion of the total supply for the market, the reduction of employment will as a rule continue. Of course, if the scale of prices which the Trust finds most profitable happens to be such as induce a large increase of consumption, and therefore to permit an expansion of the machinery of production, the aggregate of employment may be maintained or even increased. But, as we shall see below, there is nothing in the nature of a Trust to guarantee such a result. The normal result of placing the ordering of an industry in the hands of a monopoly company is to give them a power which it is their interest to exercise, to narrow the scope of industry, to change its *locale*, to abandon certain branches and take up others, to substitute machinery for hand labour, without any regard to the welfare of the employees who have been associated with the fixed capital formerly in use. When to this we add the reflection that the ability to choose its workmen out of an artificially made over-supply of labour, rid of the competition of other employers, gives the Trust a well-nigh absolute power to fix wages, hours of work, to pay in truck, and generally to dictate terms of employment and conditions of life, we understand the feeling of distrust and antagonism with which the working classes regard the growth of these great monopolies on both sides of the Atlantic.

The following is a short summary of the findings of a Committee of Congress with reference to the relations existing between the railroad and coal companies which control the anthracite coal-fields in Pennsylvania and the coal-miners:—"Congress has found (Document No. 4) that the coal companies in the anthracite regions keep thousands of surplus labourers in hand to underbid each other for employment and for submission to all exactions; hold them purposely ignorant when the mines are to be

worked and when closed, so that they cannot seek employment elsewhere; bind them as tenants by compulsion in
the companies' houses, so that the rent shall run against
them whether wages run or not, and under leases by which
they can be turned out with their wives and children on
the mountain-side in mid-winter if they strike; compel
them to fill cars of larger capacity than agreed upon; make
them buy their powder and other working outfit of the
companies at an enormous advance on the cost; compel
them to buy coal of the company at the company's price,
and in many cases to buy a fixed quantity more than they
need; compel them to employ the doctor named by the
company and to pay him whether sick or well; 'pluck'
them at the company's store, so that when pay-day comes
round the company owes the men nothing, there being
authentic cases where ' sober, hard-working miners toiled for
years, or even a lifetime, without having been able to draw a
single dollar, or but few dollars in actual cash,' in 'debt until
the day they died;' refuse to fix the wages in advance,
but pay them upon some hocus-pocus sliding-scale, varying
with the selling price in New York, which the railway slides
to suit itself; and most extraordinary of all, refuse to let the
miners know the prices on which their living slides, a
'fraud,'" says the report of Congress, " on its face" (pp. 71
and 72). The companies dock the miners' output arbitrarily
for slate and other impurities, and so can take from their
men 5 to 50 tons more in every 100 than they pay for
(p. 76). In order to keep the miners disciplined and the
coal market under supplied, the railroads restrict work, so
that the miners often have to live for a month on what they
can earn in six or eight days, and these restrictions are enforced upon their miners by holding cars from them to fill,
as upon competitors by withholding cars to go to market.
(Document No. 4, p. 77.)

Labour organisations are forbidden, and the men inten-
tionally provoked to strike to affect the coal market. The
labouring population of the local regions, finally, is kept
"down" by special policemen, enrolled under special laws,
and often in violation of law, by the railroads and coal and
iron companies, practically when and in what number they
choose, and practically without responsibility to any one but
their employers, armed as the Corporation see fit with army

revolvers or Winchester rifles, or both ; made detectives by statute, and not required to wear their shields, provoking the public to riot (pp. 9 and 93-98), and then shooting them legally. "By the percentage of wages," says the report of Congress, "by false measurements, by rents, stores, and other methods the workman is virtually a chattel of the operator."[1]

§ 4. (d) Those who admit that a Trust is in its essence a monopoly, and that it is able, by virtue of its position, to sell commodities at high prices, sometimes affirm that it is not to the interest of a Trust to maintain high prices, and that in fact Trusts have generally lowered prices. We have here a question of fact and a question of theory. Of these the former presents the greater difficulty. It seems a simple matter to compare prices before and after the formation of the Trust, and to observe the tendencies to rise or fall. This comparison has been made in a good many cases, with the result that some Trusts seem to lower prices, others to raise them. The growth of the Standard Oil Company and the strengthening of its power was attended, as we saw, by a considerable fall of price. So also we are told respecting the Cotton Seed Oil Trust, formed in 1883, that "during these four years the price of cotton seed oil fell more than eight times as much as it did during the five years before the Trust was formed."[2] The rates of the most absolute monopoly, the Western Union Telegraph Company, are very little higher than those which prevail in England, where the Government works the telegraph system at a considerable loss each year. The Sugar Trust, on the other hand, directly it was formed, raised prices considerably. The same is true of several of the other most conspicuous combinations.

Now, it is argued, if it be admitted that prices have in fact fallen under the administration of some of the strongest Trusts, it cannot be maintained that Trusts have a tendency to raise prices. In reply, it is pointed out that in almost all

---

[1] H. D. Lloyd, Essay on "Trusts," reprinted in *Boston Daily Traveller* (June 16, 1893).

[2] G. Gunton, *Political Science Quarterly*, Sept. 1888. This statement, however, appears in contradiction to the "Report of the Committee on Investigations relative to Trusts in the State of New York," p. 12.

highly-organised modern industries improved methods of production are rapidly lowering the expenses of production and prices, and that therefore the statement that Trusts tend to maintain high prices is quite consistent with the fact of an absolute fall, the question at issue being whether the fall of prices under the Trust was as great as it would have been under free competition. Moreover, a comparison of dates appears to indicate that the Trust's prices, as we saw in the Standard Oil Company, fluctuate with the degree of their monopoly, falling rapidly under the pressure of actual or threatened competition, rising when the danger is past. Finally, opponents of the Trust allude to certain Trusts which, in spite of the greater economies of production they possess, have raised prices.

Excepting by the inverse and questionable method of arguing that the high profits distributed by a Trust are themselves proof that prices have not fallen as they would have fallen under free competition, it is not possible to build a very convincing condemnation of the Trust from statistics of price. And even when profits are high it is open to the defenders of the Trust to maintain that they only represent the saving of the cost of competition, and that if competition were introduced the profits would be squandered in the struggle instead of passing into the consumer's pocket.

It is only from a deductive treatment of the subject that we are able to clearly convict the Trust of possessing a power over prices antagonistic to the interests of the consuming public.

A Trust, or other company, or a single individual who has a complete monopoly of a class of goods for which there is a demand, will strive to fix that price which shall give him the largest net profit on his capital. The question with him will be simply this, "How many articles shall I offer for sale?" If he offers only a small number the competition of more urgent wants among the consumers will enable him to sell the small number at a high price. Assuming, for the moment, that the production of these articles was subject to the law of constant returns—*i.e.*, that a few things were produced relatively as cheaply as many, this small sale would give the highest rate of profit on each sale, for the "marginal utility" of the supply would be high and would enable a high price to be obtained for the whole supply. But if he possesses large facilities of production it may pay him better to sell a larger number of articles at a lower price with a lower rate of profit on each sale, because the aggregate of a larger number of small profits may yield a larger net profit on his whole capital. How far it will pay him to go on increasing the supply and selling a larger number of articles at a lower price will entirely depend upon the effect each increment of supply exercises upon demand, and so upon prices and profits. Everything will hinge upon the "elasticity of demand" in the particular case. If the object of the monopoly satisfies a keen, widely-felt want, or stimulates a craving for increased consumption among those who take off the earlier supply, a large increase in supply may be attended by a comparatively small fall in prices. Sometimes a large increase of supply at a lowered price will, by reaching a new social stratum, or by forcing the substitution of this article for another in consumption, so enlarge the sale that though the margin of profit on each sale is small, the net profit on the whole capital is very large. In all such cases of great elasticity it may pay a monopolist to sell a large number of articles at a low price.

Where the article belongs to that class in which the law of increasing returns is strongly operative — i.e., where great economies in expenses of production attend a larger scale of production, this increase of supply and fall of prices may continue with no assignable limit. On the other hand, where there is little elasticity of demand, where an increase of supply can be taken off only at a considerable fall of price, it will probably. pay a monopolist to restrict production and sell a small number of articles at a high price. It is this motive which often induces the destruction of tons of fish and fruit in the London markets for fear of spoiling the market. These goods could be sold at a sufficiently low price, but it pays the companies owning them to destroy them, and to sell a smaller number which satisfies the wants of a limited class of people who "can afford to pay." Now, when free competition exists among sellers, as among buyers, this can never happen. It will always be to the interest of a competing producer or dealer to lower his price below that which would yield him the largest net profit on his capital were he a monopolist.   If he is a monopolist he will only lower his prices provided the elasticity of demand in the commodity in question is so great that the increased consumption will be so considerable as to yield him a larger net profit.   But if he is a competing dealer he does not look chiefly to the consumption of the community, but to the proportion of that consumption which he himself shall supply.   The elasticity of demand, so far as his individual business is concerned, is not limited to the amount of the increased consumption of the community stimulated by a lowering of prices, but includes that portion of the custom of his rivals which he may be able to divert to himself.   Hence it arises that under free competition it will be the tendency of the several competitors to drive down the prices to the point at which the most advantageously placed competitors make the minimum profit on their capital.

§ 5.   It is all important to an understanding of the subject to recognise that a monopoly price and a competitive price are determined by the operation of an entirely different set of economic forces.   The loose opinion that it must be to the interest of a Trust or other monopoly to sell at the same price as would be fixed by competition is quite groundless.

Let us look more closely at the determinants of a monopoly price.   Suppose we are dealing with a Trust owning a large amount of fixed capital, some of it more and some less favourably ordered for production, and having an absolute monopoly in the market for steel rails, cotton bagging, or other manufactured articles.   First look at expenses of production.   A very small output, though produced by the exclusive use of the very best machinery and labour, would not be produced very cheaply, because the economies attending large-scale production would be sacrificed.   Each successive increment in output would involve a decreased expense per unit of production so long as the most favourably situated plant was employed.   If the output grew so large that worse material or works fitted with inferior plant, or less favourably placed, were called into requisition, the economies of an increased scale of production would be encroached upon by this lowering of the margin of production.   Taking the Trust's capital at a fixed amount, there would necessarily come an increment of output which it would not pay to produce even if sold at the price fetched

by the previous increment. The ton of steel or of cotton
bagging which would only yield a bare margin of profit,
if sold at the price fetched by the last ton, limits the maximum output of the business. Under the pressure of free
competition this marginal ton will be actually produced.
But though, considered by itself, it yields a margin of profit,
it will rarely if ever be produced as part of the actual output
of a Trust. The actual output of a Trust, we shall find,
will be determined at any point between the first unit of
output and this marginal increment. The expenses of production will not increase in any close correspondence with

CURVE OF PROFIT IN TRUST.

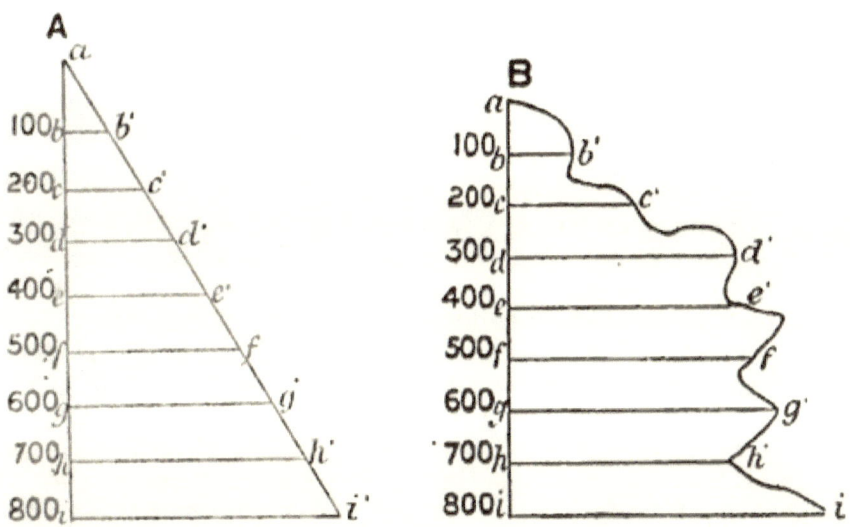

the growth of the output, but will represent the fluctuating
resultant of the several economies of production at the
several points.

In the figúres A and B the perpendicular line ai
represents a number of increments of production. The
expense of producing a supply of 100 will be measured by
the line bb', that of producing 200 by cc', and so on. But
never in actual industry will the lines of growing expense
be regular in their relation to the increase of production, as
would be the case in the figure A; they will always be
irregular, as in the figure B. The curve of expense ai'' in

the figure B will be determined by the resultant of the various forces which make for increasing and diminishing returns for each new increment of the requisites of production required to produce the new portion of output. When the increased scale of production makes some new application of machinery economically possible, or where recourse must be had to some decidedly inferior land for the raw material, a large sudden irregularity may show itself in the curve of expense.

When we turn from expenses of production to the aggregate takings from the sale of the several quantities of supply, we shall find a similar irregularity of increase. Elasticity in demand, as tested by the stimulus given to consumption by a fall of price, differs not merely in different commodities, but at different points in a falling scale of prices. A number of equal decrements in price, according as they stimulate the satisfaction of weaker wants of earlier consumers, or strike into new classes of consumers, or supply new kinds of wants, will have widely different effects in increasing the aggregate takings.

We have then two widely fluctuating and highly irregular gradations of money terms, representing expenses of production and the aggregate price of the various quantities of supply, each determined by a wholly different class of considerations. But the interest of a Trust, as we see, lies in fixing supply at the highest net profits. Now the net profits of producing and selling any specified quantity of supply are ascertained by deducting the expenses of production from the aggregate takings. The relation between the growth of expenses of production and of aggregate takings will yield a different net amount of profit at each increment of supply. The diagram opposite will illustrate the nature of these relations.

AL is the line indicating at the several points, B, C, D, etc., proportional increments in supply. If the monopoly be a steel rail trust, B marks the millionth ton, C the two millionth ton of output, and so on. A'L' is a curve indicating, by its diminishing distance from AL, the diminishing expense of producing each unit of the increased output, so that the expense of producing the first ton, if only one is produced, is AA', that of the millionth ton, if one million are produced, BB', and so on. The expenses of producing one million tons will thus be represented by the figure ABB'A', those of two millions by the figure ACC'A'. Further, let the curve *al* represent, by its diminishing distance from AL, the diminishing price at which the several additions to supply can be sold, so that the first ton sells at A*a*, the millionth at B*o*, and so on, the aggre-

DIAGRAM OF TRUST PRICES.

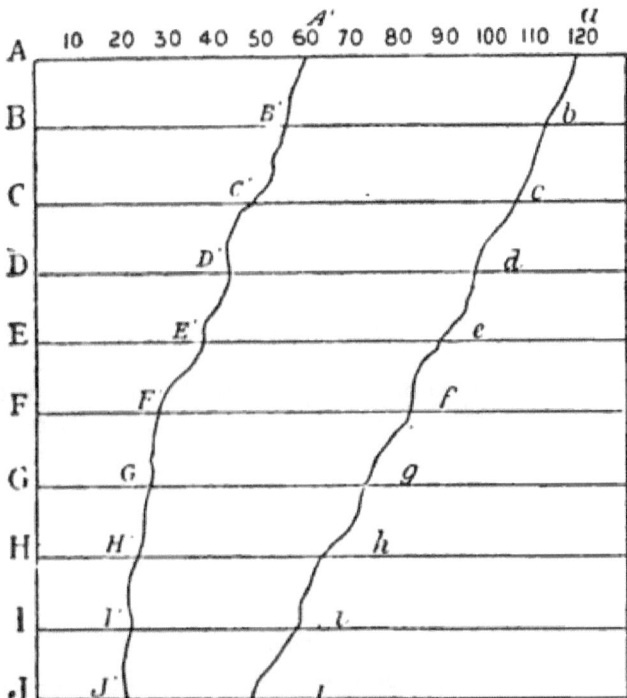

gate price of the first million tons being AB*ba*, that of the first two millions being AC*ca*.

Assuming that the Trust is planning a new business and determining the most profitable output, it will limit that output not necessarily at the point where the selling price gives the widest margin of profit upon the expenses of production, as might be the case at the point B in the diagram, but at the point F, where the margin of profit bears the largest proportion to the expenses of production, or in other words, where the area of absolute takings shows the largest surplus over the area of aggregate expenses. Thus it will here be to the interest of the Trust to produce and sell six millions (limiting production at F) with an aggregate expense AFF'A' and an aggregate takings AFfa, yielding an aggregate net profit A'F'fa. They will not pro-duce five millions because the figure AEea bears a smaller proportion to AEE'A' than does AFfa' to AFF'A'. For a similar reason they will not produce seven millions.

Since the fluctuations in the curve of expenses and in that of selling price or "demand" are determined by an entirely different set of forces, it will be evident that there may be several points in AL where the proportions between the area of expenses and that of profits may be the same. So there may be several maxima at which Trust prices may be indifferently fixed. The figure upon F'f may have the same quantitative relation to the figure upon FF', as that upon H'h to that upon HH'. In such a case it will be a matter of indifference to the Trust whether it sells five million tons at a price 100s. per ton, or seven millions at 90s.

We have seen that the causes which determine expenses at the several points in A'L' have no relation to the causes which determine the selling price at the various points, except to furnish a minimum below which the price cannot fall. Above this limit expenses of production in no sense help to determine monopoly prices; the true determinants are entirely in the region of demand, and are measured by the marginal utility or satisfaction afforded to consumers by the several quantities which constitute supply at any given time.

Since expenses of production always enter into the de-termination of competition-prices, which are fixed by the interaction of expenses and money estimates of utility—*i.e.*, by supply and demand, it is evident that the curve of monopoly prices has no assignable relation whatever to the curve of competition prices, and that the most profitable output and prices of Trust-made goods are in no way identi-fied with the most profitable output and prices in a com-

petitive trade. In competition the curve of selling prices
tends to follow closely the curve of expenses, and consequently the areas of profits and expenses tend to bear
the same proportion to each other at different points of
increment in the trade. For if at any point great increases
in economy of production are achieved, while the large
elasticity of demand maintains a price nearly the same as
before, the wide margin of profit which might fix the actual
price at that point for a monopolist only serves to stimulate
such increased output on the part of trade competitors as
will continue until the flexibility of demand weakens, and
prices are lowered to such a point as will yield the normal
margin or market rate of profit.

There is, therefore, nothing in common between competition prices and monopoly prices for different quantities of
supply, nor anything to secure that the actual quantity of
supply and the price shall be the same in the two cases.

§ 6. It is, however, conceivable that in a certain commodity where a genuine monopoly holds the market, the
price should be as low as under free competition. This
may be illustrated by the following curves of expense and
price :—

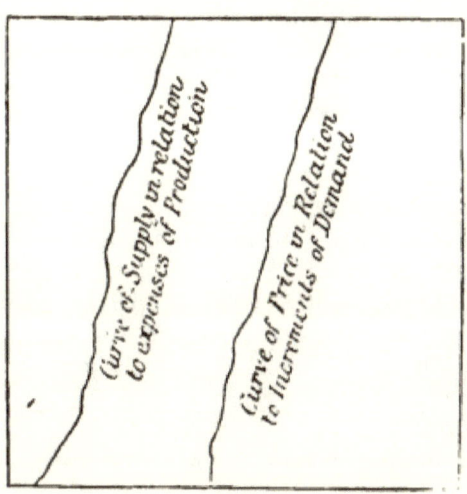

where the economics of increased production continue to
be very great, while the flexibility of demand is also high.
In other words, it may pay the Trust better to make very
large sales at a low price when the expenses of production

are low, than to sell a smaller quantity at a higher price and with a higher expense of production. In this case the con- sumer may get a part of the advantage of large-scale pro- duction along with the saving of expense of competition. There is, however, no guarantee to society that low prices will be fixed. In the vast majority of cases it will probably pay the Trust better to limit production and sell at higher prices.

In the illustration above we have assumed that a monopoly was starting *de novo*. Where a Trust is formed, as is commonly the case, by an amalgamation of existing capitals largely embodied in plant and machinery of production, it will probably not pay to limit production to a very small output, even though the largest proportionate margin of profit might seem to stand there. For the interest upon the closed mills and other idle capital should be reckoned among the ex- penses of production for the purposes of determining the profitable price. Thus where large means of production are owned by a monopoly it will seldom pay to sell a very small supply at a very high price.

So far we have treated of absolute monopolies, eliminating all consideration of competition. We have found that the supply and the price of an article of absolute monopoly is determined by the relation between expenses of production and flexibility of demand. Although a new invention or a wide expansion of market may alter so considerably the expenses of production of the several quantities of supply as to materially affect monopoly-supply and prices, it is the latter influence, that of flexibility of demand, that directly in each specific case determines whether a Trust's prices shall be high or low. When we find the Standard Oil Trust maintaining a low level of prices, or the Western Union Telegraph Company charging low rates, we shall find the explanation in the character of the public demand for oil and telegraphic messages.

§ 7. A number of considerations relating to "demand" limit the economic power of monopolies to charge high prices.

A monopoly price, as we have seen, exactly measures the marginal utility of the supply, as indicated by the quantity of money which the purchaser of the last increment of supply is just willing to pay for it. When this marginal utility sinks fast with an increase of supply the monopoly price will be high for it, and it will pay the monopolist better to restrict the output and sell the limited supply at a high price, because a large reduction of price will not stimulate a proportionably large increase of consumption. So where the marginal utility sinks slowly, it will pay to increase the supply and lower the price, for each fall of price will stimulate a large increase of consumption.

Since the marginal utility of a number of increments of supply will not be the same in the case of any two commodities, it is evident that the determination of monopoly prices is a very delicate operation.

It is not possible to present even an approximately accurate classification of commodities in relation to the powers of a Trust or Monopoly. But the following considerations will assist us to understand why in some cases a Trust appears to raise prices, in others to keep them as they were, and in others even to lower them :—

(a) The urgency of the need which a commodity satisfies enables the monopolist to charge high prices. Where a community is dependent for life upon some single commodity, as the Chinese on rice, the monopolist is able to obtain a high price for the whole of a supply which does not exceed what is necessary to keep alive the whole population. Thus a monopolist of corn or rice in a famine can get an exorbitant price for a considerable supply. But after the supply is large enough to enable every one to satisfy the most urgent need for sustenance, the urgency of the need satisfied by any further supply falls rapidly, for there is no comparison between the demand of famine and the demand induced by the pleasures of eating.

A monopoly of a necessity of life is therefore more dangerous than any other monopoly, because it not merely places the lives of the people at the mercy of private traders, but because it will generally be the interest of such monopolists to limit supply to the satisfaction of the barest necessaries of life.

Next to a necessary in this respect will come what is termed a "conventional necessary," something which by custom has been firmly implanted as an integral portion of the standard of comfort. This differs, of course, in different classes of a community. Boots may now be regarded as a "conventional necessary" of almost all grades of English society, and a monopolist could probably raise the price of boots considerably without greatly diminishing the consumption. Half a century ago, however, when boots were not firmly established as part of the standard of comfort of the great mass of the working classes, the power of a monopolist to raise prices would have been far smaller.

As we descend in the urgency of wants supplied we find that the comforts and luxuries form a part of the standard of life of a smaller and smaller number of persons, and satisfying intrinsically weaker needs, are more liable to be affected by a rise of price.

(b) Closely related to this consideration, and working in with it at every point, is the question of the possibility of substituting another commodity for the one monopolised. This everywhere tempers the urgency of the need attaching to a commodity. There are few, if any, even among the commodities on which we habitually rely for food, shelter, clothing, which we could not and would not dispense with if prices rose very high. The incessant competition which is going on between different commodities which claim to satisfy some particular class of need cannot be got rid of by the monopoly of one of them. This is probably the chief explanation of the low prices of the Standard Oil. As an illuminant, oil is competing with gas, candles, electricity, and unless the monopoly were extended laterally so as to include these and any other possible illuminants, the Trust's prices cannot be determined merely by the pressure of the need for artificial light. Though to a modern society artificial light is probably even more important than sugar, a Sugar Trust may have a stronger monopoly and be able to raise prices higher than an Oil Trust, because the substitutes for sugar, such as molasses and beetroot, are less effective competitors than gas, candles, and electricity with oil.

The power of railway monopolies largely depends upon the degree in which their services are indispensable, and no alternative mode of transport is open. Sometimes, however, they miscalculate the extent of their power. The high railway rates in England have recently led in several quarters to a substitution of road and canal traffic in the case of goods where rapidity of conveyance was not essential. So also in other cases sea-transport has been substituted.

The stronger monopoly of American railways consists partly in the fact that distances are so great, and the sea-board or other water conveyance so remote, that over a large part of the Continent the monopoly is untempered by alternative possibilities of transport.

The reverse consideration, the possibility of substituting the article of monopoly for other articles of consumption, and so securing a wider market, has quite as important an influence on prices. The possibility of substituting oil for coal in cooking and certain other operations has probably a good deal to do with the low price of oil. A Trust will often keep prices low for a season in order to enable their article to undersell and drive out a rival article, a competition closely akin to the competition with a rival producer of the same article. When natural gas was discovered in the neighbourhood of Pittsburg, the price was lowered sufficiently to induce a large number of factories and private houses to give up coal and to burn gas. After expensive fittings had been put in, and the habit of using gas established, the Gas Company, without any warning, proceeded to raise the rates to the tune of 100 per cent. When we ascend to the higher luxuries, the competition between different commodities to satisfy the same generic taste, or even to divert taste or fashion from one class of consumption to another class, is highly complicated, and tempers considerably the control of a Trust over prices.

The power of a company which holds the patent for a particular kind of corkscrew is qualified very largely not only by competition of other corkscrews, but by screw-stoppers and various other devices for securing the contents of bottles. The ability to dispense with the object of a monopoly, though it does not prevent the monopolist from charging prices so much higher than competition prices as to extract all the "consumer's rent," of the marginal consumer, forms a practical limit to monopoly prices.

(c) Lastly, there is the influence of existing or potential competition of other producers upon monopoly prices. Where prices and profits are very high a Trust is liable to more effective competition on the part of any surviving independent firms, and likewise to the establishment of new competitors. This ability of outside capital to enter into competition will of course differ in different trades.

Where the monopoly is protected by a tariff the possibility of new competition from outside is lessened. When the monopoly is connected with some natural advantage or the exclusive possession of some special convenience, as in mining or railways, direct competition of outsiders on equal terms is prohibited. Where the combination of large capital and capable administration is indispensable to the possibility of success in a rival producer, the power of a monopoly is stronger than where a small capital can produce upon fairly equal terms and compete. If the monopoly is linked with close personal qualities and with special opportunities of knowledge, as in banking, it is most difficult for outside capital to effectively compete.

§ 8. These considerations show that the power of a Trust or other monopoly over prices is determined by a number of intricate forces which react upon one another with varying degrees of pressure, according as the quantity of supply is increased or diminished. But a Trust is always able to charge prices in excess of competitive prices, and it is generally its interest to do so. It will commonly be to the interest of a Trust or other monopoly to maintain a lower scale of prices in those commodities which are luxuries or satisfy some less urgent and more capricious taste, and to maintain high prices where the article of monopoly is a common comfort or a prime necessary of life for which there is no easily available substitute.

CHAPTER VII.

MACHINERY AND INDUSTRIAL DEPRESSION.

§ 1. *The external phenomena of Trade Depression.*

§ 2. *Correctly described as Under-production and Over-production.*

§ 3. *Testimony to a general excess of Productive Power over the requirement for Consumption.*

§ 4. *The connection of modern Machine-production and Depression shown by statistics of price.*

§ 5. *Changing forms in which Over-supply of Capital is embodied.*

§ 6. *Summary of economic relation of Machinery to Depression.*

§ 7. *Under-consumption as the root-evil.*

§ 8. *Economic analysis of "Saving."*

§ 9. *Saving requires increased Consumption in the future.*

§ 10. *Quantitative relation of parts in the organism of Industry.*

§ 11. *Quantitative relation of Capital and Consumption.*

§ 12. *Economic limits of Saving for a Community.*

§ 13. *No limits to the possibility of individual Saving—Clash of individual and social interests in Saving.*

§ 14. *Objection that excess in forms of Capital would drive interest to zero not valid.*

§ 15. *Excess is in embodiments of Capital, not in real Capital.*

§ 16. *Uncontrolled Machinery a source of fluctuation.*

§ 1. The leading symptom of the disease called Depression of Trade is a general fall of wholesale prices, accompanied by a less than corresponding fall of retail prices. Whatever may be the ultimate causes of a trade depression, the direct and immediate cause of every fall of price must be a failure of demand to keep pace with supply at the earlier price. So long as those who have goods to sell can sell all these goods at the price they have been getting, they will not lower the price. The efficient cause then of any fall of price is an actual condition of over-supply at earlier prices. A very small quantity of over-supply will bring down prices in a business, or in a whole market, provided the competition between the businesses is keen. Where such a fall of prices quickly stimulates demand so that the over-supply is carried off and the rate of demand is equated to the rate of supply at the lower price level, the condition is commonly described as a "tendency to over-supply." But it is important to bear in mind that in strictness it was not a "tendency" but an actually existing quantity of over-supply which brought down the price.

Where any fall of price thus brought about quickly stimulates a corresponding increase of demand, stability of prices follows, and there will be a full, healthy production at the lower prices.

The mere fact then that prices are generally lower than they were five or ten years ago is no evidence of depressed trade. Depressed trade signifies not merely low prices but relaxed production: more has been produced than can be sold at the lowest profitable prices, and markets are congested with stock, but less is being produced than could be produced with existing means of production. The fact which faces us in a period of depression is an apparent excess of productive power. If this excess were of labour alone it might be explained with some plausibility as due to the displacement of labour by machinery. For it has been admitted that the first and immediate effect of introducing labour-saving or labour-aiding machines may be a diminution in the demand for labour, even when the labour of making and repairing the machines and of distributing the increased product which finds a sale is taken into consideration. The simultaneous application of a number of new forms of machinery attended by other general economies in the organisation of industry might seem to explain why for a time there should be a general redundancy of labour in all or most of the chief industries of a country. Such an over-supply of labour would result from the accumulated action of "first effects."

When the cheapening influences of machinery had time to exercise their full natural influence in stimulating consumption the labour temporarily displaced would be again fully utilised ; for the moment, past labour saved and stored in forms of fixed capital would do a great deal of the work which would otherwise be done by present living labour. But such an explanation is wholly negatived by the fact that in a depressed condition of trade there is an excess of forms of capital as well as of labour. There exists simultaneously a redundancy of both factors in production. Labourers are out of work or are in irregular employment, mills and factories are closed or working short time, the output of coal and metals is reduced, and yet with this relaxed production the markets are glutted with unsold goods unable to find purchasers at a price which will yield a minimum profit to their owners. To this must be added, in the case of the extractive industries, agriculture, mining, etc., the exclusion from productive use of land which had formerly found a profitable employment.

§ 2. To this condition of industry the antithetical terms, over-production and under-production, may be both correctly applied, according as one regards production as a state or as a process. The state of trade in a depression is one of over-production—the industrial body is congested with goods which are not drawn out for consumption fast enough. This plethora debilitates the industrial body, its functional activities are weakened. The slackness of trade thus induced is rightly described as under-production.

It is commonly said by English writers upon economics that the state of over-production, the redundancy of capital and labour, though found in one or two or several trades at the same time, cannot be of general application. If too much capital and labour is engaged in one industry there is, they argue, too little in another, there cannot be at the same time a general state of over-production. Now if by general over-production is meant not that every single industry is supplied with an excess of capital, but that there exists a net over-supply, taking into account the plethora in some trades and the deficiency in others, this assertion of English economists is not in accordance with ascertained facts or with the authority of economists outside of England.

§ 3. If a depression of trade signified a misapplication of

capital and labour, so that too much was applied in some
industries, too little in others, there would be a rise of
prices in as many cases as there was a fall of prices, and the
admitted symptom of depression, the simultaneous fall of
price in all or nearly all the staple industries, would not
occur. The most careful students of the phenomena of
depressed trade agree in describing the condition as one of
general or net excess of the forms of capital. They are
also agreed in regarding the enormous growth of modern
machinery as the embodiment of a general excess of producing power over that required to maintain current consumption.

Lord Playfair, writing on this subject in 1888, says, "It
matters not whether the countries were devastated by war
or remained in the enjoyment of peace ; whether they were
isolated by barriers of Protection or conducted these
industries under Free Trade ; whether they abounded in
the raw materials of industry or had to import them from
other lands ; under all these varying conditions the machine-
using countries of the world have felt the fifteen years of
depression in the same way, though with varying degrees of
intensity." His conclusion is "that the improvements of
machinery used in production have increased the supply of
commodities beyond the immediate demands of the world."[1]
In support of this position he adduces the authority of continental writers such as Dr. A. von Studnitz, Piermez, Jules
Duckerts, Laveleye, Trasenster, Annecke, and Engel. In
the United States, Carroll Wright, David Wells, and Atkinson
are foremost in upholding this to be the explanation of
depression of trade. Mr. Carroll D. Wright, Commissioner
of Labour at Washington, is emphatic in his assertion of
the fact. "So far as the factories and the operatives of the
countries concerned are to be taken into consideration
(England, the United States, France, Belgium, Germany),
there does exist a positive and emphatic over-production,
and this over-production could not exist without the introduction of power-machinery at a rate greater than the
consuming power of the nations involved, and of those
dependent upon them, demand ; in other words, the over-
production of power-machinery logically results in the over-

[1] *Contemporary Review*, March 1888.

production of goods made with the aid of such machinery, and this represents the condition of those countries depending largely upon mechanical industries for their prosperity."[1] The Reports of the English "Commission on the Depression of Trade and Industry" make similar admissions of an excess of producing power as distinct from a mere miscalculation in the application of capital and labour. The Majority Report, defining "over-production" as "the production of commodities, or even the existence of a capacity for production at a time when the demand is not sufficiently brisk to maintain a remunerative price to the producer," affirms "that such an over-production has been one of the prominent features of the course of trade during recent years, and that the depression under which we are now suffering may be partially explained by this fact. . . ."[2] The Minority Report lays still stronger stress upon "systematic over-production," alleging "that the demand for commodities does not increase at the same rate as formerly, and that our capacity for production is consequently in excess of our home and export demand, and could, moreover, be considerably increased at short notice by the fuller employment of labour and appliances now partially idle."[3]

The most abundant information regarding the excess of the machinery of production in the several branches of industry has been given by Mr. D. A. Wells, who regards machinery as the direct cause of depressed trade, operating in three ways—(1) increased capacity of production, (2) improved methods of distribution, (3) the opening up of new abundant supplies of raw material. Thus production grows faster than consumption. "In this way only is it possible to account for the circumstances that the supply of the great articles and instrumentalities of the world's use and commerce have increased during the last twelve or fifteen years in a far greater ratio than the contemporaneous increase of the world's population or of its immediate consuming capacity."[4]

The earlier inventions in the textile industries, and the general application of steam to manufacture and to the trans-

---

. [1] *Report on Industrial Depressions*, Washington, 1886.
[2] Report, pars. 61-66.   [3] Report, par. 106.
[4] *Contemporary Review*, July 1887.

port services, have played the most dramatic part in the industrial revolution of the last hundred years. But it should be borne in mind that it is far from being true that the great forces of invention have spent themselves, and that we have come to an era of small increments in the growth of productive power. On the contrary, within this last generation a number of discoveries have taken place in almost all the chief industrial arts, in the opening up of new supplies of raw material, and in the improvement of industrial organisation, which have registered enormous advances of productive power. In the United States, where the advance has been most marked, it is estimated that in the fifteen or twenty years preceding 1886 the gain of machinery, as measured by "displacement of the muscular labour," amounts to more than one-third, taking the aggregate of manufactures into account. In many manufactures the introduction of steam-driven machinery and the factory system belongs to this generation. The substitution of machinery for hand labour in boot-making signifies a gain of 80 per cent. for some classes of goods, 50 per cent. for others. In the silk manufacture there has been a gain of 50 per cent., in furniture some 30 per cent., while in many minor processes, such as wood-planing, tin cans, wall-papers, soap, patent leather, etc., the improvement of mechanical productiveness per labourer is measured as a rise of from 50 to 300 per cent. or more. The gain is, however, by no means confined to an extension of "power" into processes formerly performed by human muscle and skill. Still more significant is the increased mechanical efficiency in the foundational industries. In the manufacture of agricultural implements the increase is put down at from 50 to 70 per cent., in the manufacture of machines and machinery from 25 to 40 per cent., while "in the production of metals and metallic goods long-established firms testify that machinery has decreased manual labour 33⅓ per cent." The increase in the productive power of cotton mills is far greater than this. From 1870 to 1884 the make of pig-iron rose 131 per cent. in Great Britain and 237 per cent. in the rest of the world.[1] "In building vessels an approximate idea of the relative labour

---

[1] *Contemporary Review*, March 1888.

displacement is given as 4 or 5 to 1—that is, four or five times the amount of labour can be performed to-day by the use of machinery in a given time that could be done under old hand methods."[1]

In England the rise in productiveness of machinery is roughly estimated at 40 per cent. in the period 1850 to 1885, and there is no reason to suppose this is an excessive estimate. In the shipping industry, where more exact statistics are available, the advance is even greater. The diminution of manual labour required to do a given quantity of work in 1884 as compared with 1870 is put down at no less than 70 per cent., owing in large measure to the introduction and increased application of steam-hoisting machines and grain elevators, and the employment of steam power in steering, raising the sails and anchors, pumping, and discharging cargoes.[2] In the construction of ships enormous economies have taken place. A ship which in 1883 cost £24,000 can now be built for £14,000. In the working of vessels the economy of fuel, due to the introduction of compound-engines, has been very large. A ton of wheat can now be hauled by sea at less than a farthing per mile. Similarly with land haulage the economy of fuel has made immense reductions in cost. "In an experiment lately made on the London and North Western Railway, a compound locomotive dragged a ton of goods for one mile by the combustion of two ounces of coal."[3] The quickening of voyages by steam motor, and by the abandonment of the old Cape route in favour of the Suez Canal, enormously facilitated commerce. The last arrangement is calculated to have practically destroyed a tonnage of two millions. The still greater facilitation of intelligence by electricity did away with the vast system of warehousing required by the conditions of former commerce. These economies of the foundational transport industries have deeply affected the whole commerce and manufacture of the country, and have played no inconsiderable part in

---

[1] *Report of the Commissioner of Labour*, Washington, 1886, pp. 80 to 88.

[2] D. A. Wells, *Contemporary Review*, August 1887.

[3] Lord Playfair, in the *Contemporary Review*, March 1888, gives a number of interesting illustrations of recent economies in transport and manufacture.

bringing about the general fall of prices by lowering the expenses of production and stimulating an increased output.

Excessive production of transport-machinery, especially of railways, has played an important part as an immediate cause of modern trade depression. The depression beginning in 1873 and culminating in 1878 is described as having its origin "in the excessive lock-up of capital in the construction of railways, especially in America and Germany, many of which, when built, had neither population to use them nor traffic to carry; in the wild speculation that followed the German assertion of supremacy on the Continent; in the exaggerated armaments, which withdrew an inordinate amount of labour from productive industry, and over-weighed the taxpayers of the great European nations; and in over-production in the principal trades in all European countries."[1]

Mr. Bowley points out that "after each of the great railway booms of the century, for instance in England about 1847, in America before 1857 and 1873, in India in 1878, and on the Continent in 1873, the collapse has been very violent; for the materials are bought at exaggerated prices; the weekly wage during construction is enormous; no return is obtained till the whole scheme, whose carrying out probably lasts many years, is complete."

A great deal of this railway enterprise meant over-production of forms of transport-capital and a corresponding withholding of current consumption. In other words, a large part of the "savings" of England, Germany, America, etc., invested in these new railways, were sterilised; they were not economically needed to assist in the work of transport, and many of them remain almost useless, as the quoted value of the shares testifies. It is not true, as is sometimes suggested, that after a great effort in setting on foot such gigantic enterprises, a collapse is economically necessary. If the large incomes and high wages earned in the period prior to 1873, when capital and labour found full employment in these great enterprises, had been fully applied in increased demand for commodities and an elevated standard of consumption, much of the new

---

[1] *Statist*, 1879, quoted Bowley, *England's Foreign Trade in the Nineteenth Century*, p. 80.

machinery of transport, which long stood useless, would
have been required to assist in forwarding goods to maintain
the raised standard of consumption. This argument, of
course, assumes that ignorance or fraud have not caused
a misdirection of investment. There is no evidence to
indicate that the vast sums invested in 1869-72 in railway
enterprise could have found any safer or more remunerative
investment. It is the overflow of "savings," after all capital
economically needed to carry on the work of production
to supply steady current wants has been secured, that flows
into the hands of speculative company-promoters. Such
savings are not diverted from safe and useful forms of
investment, they are "savings" which ought never to have
been attempted, for they have no economic justification in
the needs of commerce, as is proved by results.

§ 4. The direct causal connection between the increased
productive power of modern machinery and trade depression clearly emerges from a comparison of the fluctuations
in the several departments of industry in different industrial
countries. As modern machinery and modern methods of
commerce are more highly developed and are applied more
generally, trade fluctuations are deeper and more lasting. A
comparison between more backward countries largely engaged in raising food and raw materials of manufacture for
the great manufacturing countries is sometimes adduced in
support of the contention that highly-evolved industry is
steadier. But though Mr. Giffen is undoubtedly correct in
holding that depressions are often worse in countries producing raw materials than in manufacturing countries,[1] this
is only true of raw-material producing countries which
produce for export, and which are therefore dependent for
their trade upon fluctuations in demand for commodities in
distant markets whose movements they are least able to
calculate or control. Irregularity of climate, disease, and
other natural causes must be a constant source of fluctuation in the productivity of agriculture. But those non-
manufacturing countries which are little dependent upon
commerce with manufacturing nations, and which are chiefly
self-supporting, will of necessity retain a larger variety of
agriculture and of other primitive industries, and will there-

[1] *Essays in Finance*, vol. i. p. 137, etc.

fore be less at the mercy of some climatic or other injury than a country more specialised in some single crop or other industry. The specialisation impressed upon a backward country by commerce with advanced industrial countries, confining it to growing cotton or wheat or sheep or wine, exaggerates the irregularity imposed by nature upon its productivity, by making it subservient to the fluctuating demands of distant and wholly incalculable markets. The fluctuations brought about by irregular consumption and uncontrolled production in highly-evolved industrial countries are thus reflected with terrible force upon the more primitively-ordered parts of the industrial world. Thus does the character of modern machine-industry impress itself on the countries which feed it with raw materials.

If we turn to investigate the several departments of industry in the more highly-evolved communities, where statistics yield more accurate information, we have most distinct evidence that so far as the world-market is concerned, the fluctuations are far more extreme in the industries to which machine-production and high organisation have been applied. An investigation of changes of wholesale prices indicates that the most rapid and extreme fluctuations are found in the prices of textile and mineral materials which form the foundation of our leading manufactures. A comparison of the price changes of food as a whole, and of corn prices with textiles and minerals, shows that especially during the last thirty years the fluctuations of the latter have been much more rapid and pronounced. (See following diagrams.)

§ 5. It ought to be clearly understood that the real congestion with which we are concerned, the over-supply, does not chiefly consist of goods in their raw or finished state passing through the machine on their way to the consumer. The economic diagnosis is sometimes confused upon this point, speaking of the increased productive power of machinery as if it continued to pour forth an unchecked flood of goods in excess of possible consumption. This shows a deep misunderstanding of the malady. Only in its early stages does it take this form. When in any trade the producing power of machinery is in excess of the demand at a remunerative price, the series of processes through

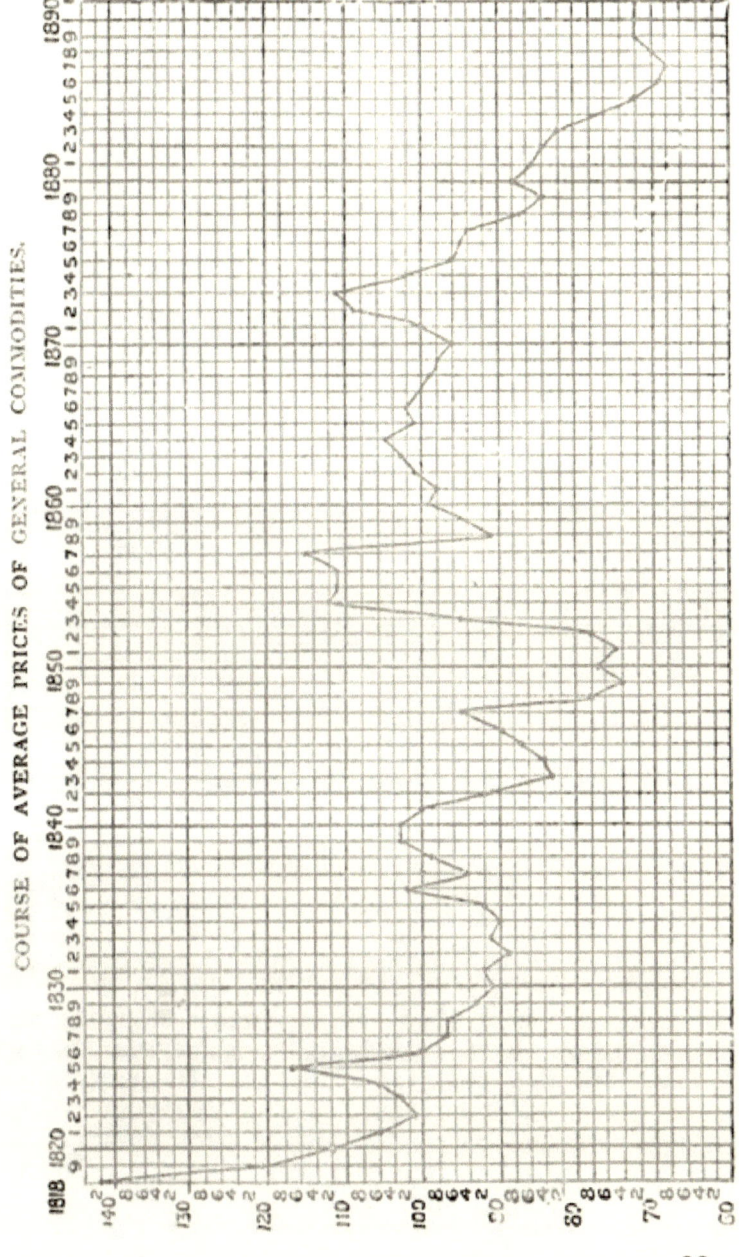

which the raw material passes on its way to the consumer
soon become congested with an over-supply.   This, however, need not be very large, nor does it long continue to
grow.   So long as the production of these excessive wares
continues, though we have a growing glut of them, the
worst features of industrial disease do not appear ; profits
are low, perhaps business is carried on at a loss, but
factories, workshops, mines, railways, etc., are in active

CORN PRICES.

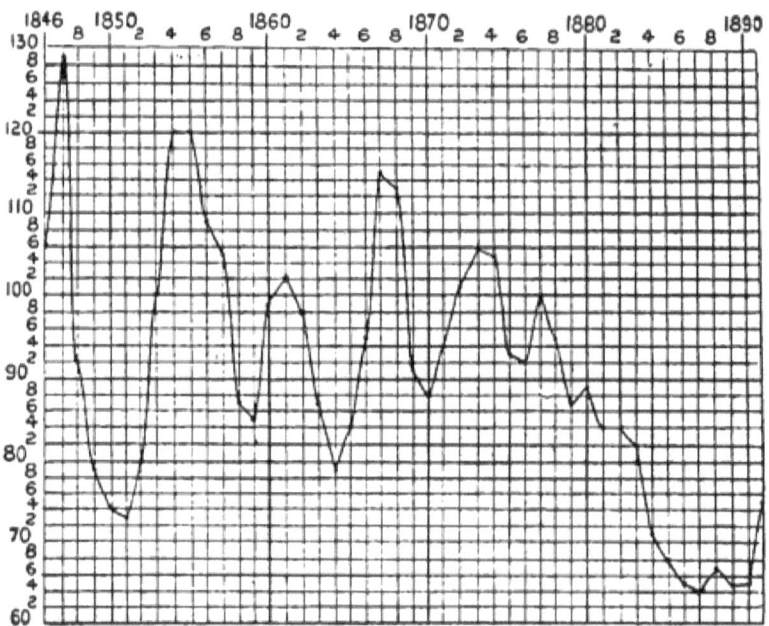

operation ; wages may be reduced, but there is plenty of
employment.   It is when this congestion of goods has
clogged the wheels of the industrial machine, retarded the
rate of production, when the weaker manufacturers can no
longer get credit at the bank, can no longer meet their
engagements, and collapse, when the stronger firms are
forced to close some of their mills, to shut down the less
productive mines, to work short hours, to economise in
every form of labour, that depression of trade assumes its

more enduring and injurious shape. The condition now is
not that of an increasing glut of goods; the existing glut
continues to block the avenues of commerce and to check
further production, but it does not represent the real
burden of over-supply. The true excess now shows itself
in the shape of idle machinery, closed factories, unworked
mines, unused ships and railway trucks. It is the auxiliary
capital that represents the bulk of over-supply, and whose
idleness signifies the enforced unemployment of large
masses of labour. It is machinery, made and designed to
increase the flow of productive goods, that has multiplied
too fast for the growth of consumption. This machinery
does not continue in full use, a large proportion of it is not

GENERAL, FOOD PRICES.

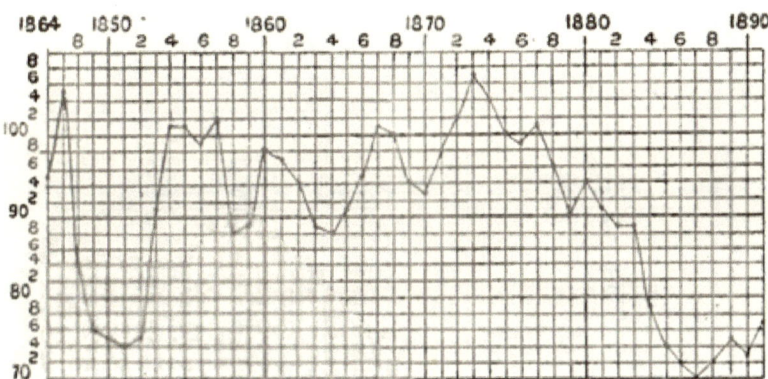

required to assist in producing the quantity of consumptive
goods which can find a market, and must of necessity stand
idle; it represents a quantity of useless forms of capital,
over-supply, and its unused productive power represents
an incomparably larger amount of potential over-supply of
goods. Economic forces are at work preventing the con-
tinuation of the use of this excessive machinery; if it were
used in defiance of these forces, if its owners could afford to
keep it working, there would be no market for the goods
it would turn out, and these too would swell the mass of
over-supply.

§ 6. The general relation of modern Machinery to Commercial Depression is found to be as follows :—Improved

machinery of manufacture and transport enables larger and
larger quantities of raw material to pass more quickly and
more cheaply through the several processes of production.
Consumers do not, in fact, increase their consumption as
quickly and to an equal extent. Hence the onward flow of
productive goods is checked in one or more of the manu-

MINERAL PRICES.

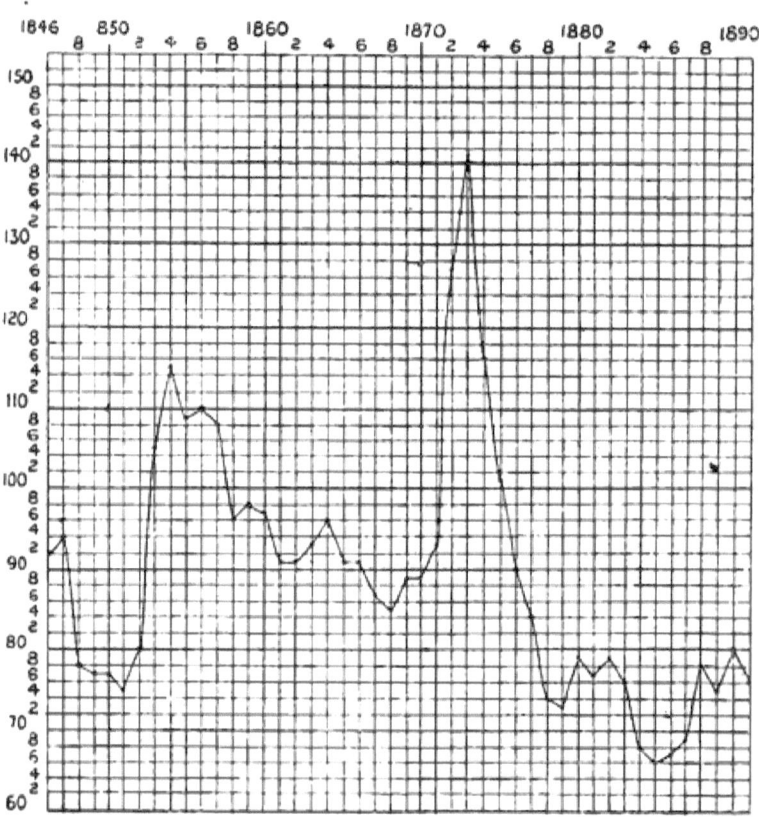

facturing stages, or in the hands of the merchant, or even in
the retail shop. This congestion of the channels of production automatically checks production, depriving of all use
a large quantity of the machinery, and a large quantity of
labour. The general fall of money income which has
necessarily followed from a fall of prices, uncompensated by

a corresponding expansion of sales, induces a shrinkage of consumption. Under depressed trade, while the markets

TEXTILE PRICES.

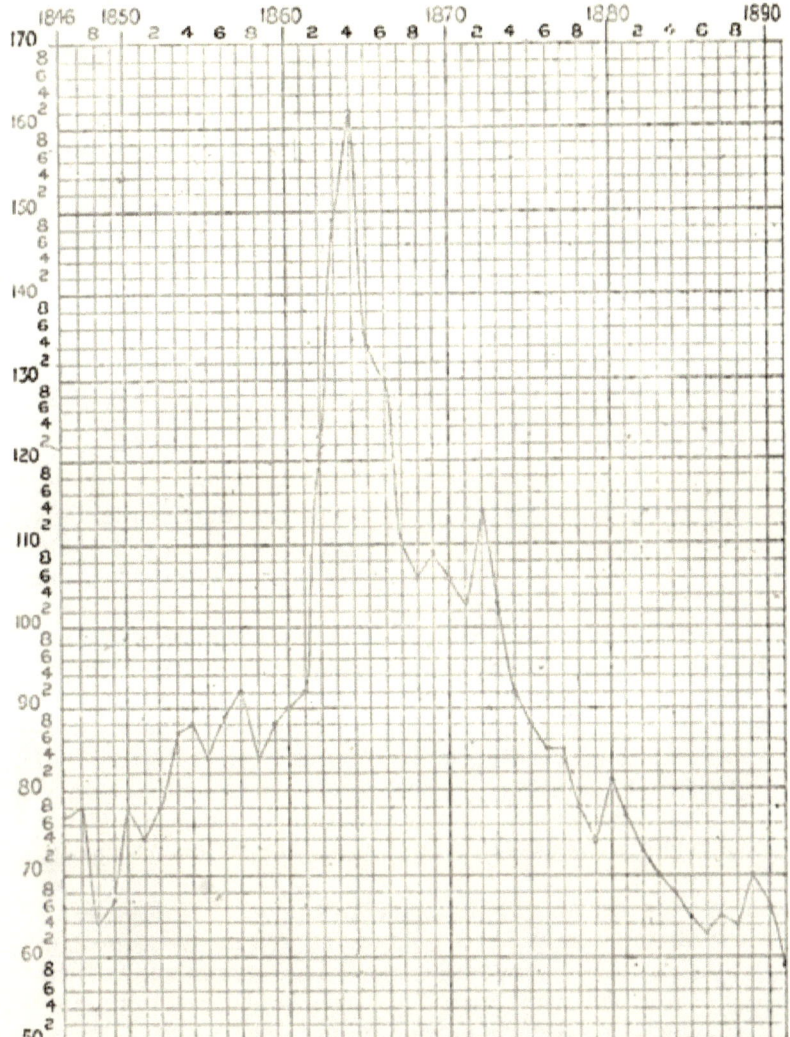

continue to be glutted with unsold goods, only so much current production is maintained as will correspond to the

shrunk consumption of the depressed community. Before
the turn in the commercial tide, current production even
falls below the level of current consumption, thus allowing
for the gradual passage into consumption of the glut of
goods which had congested the machine. After the congestion which had kept prices low is removed, prices begin
to rise, demand is more active at each point of industry,
and we see the usual symptoms of reviving trade.

This is an accurate account of the larger phenomena
visible in the commercial world in a period of disturbance.
When the disease is at its worst, the activity of producer and
consumer at its lowest, we have the functional condition of
under-production due to the pressure of a quantity of over-
supply, and we have a corresponding state of under-consumption.

§ 7. Machinery thus figures as the efficient cause of
industrial disease, but the real responsibility does not rest
on the shoulders of the inventor of new machinery, or of
the manufacturer, but of the consumer.

The root-evil of depressed trade is under-consumption.[1]
If a quantity of capital and labour is standing idle at the
same time, in all or in the generality of trades, the only
possible reason why they remain unemployed is that there
is no present demand for the goods which by co-operation
they are able to produce.

English economists, most of whom, ever since the time
of J. B. Say, have denied the possibility of the condition of
general over-supply which is seen to exist in depressed trade,
are contented to assume that there can be no general over-
supply because every one who produces creates a corresponding power to consume. There cannot, it is maintained, be
too much machinery or too much of any form of capital
provided there exists labour to act with it ; if this machinery,
described as excessive, is set working, some one will have
the power to consume whatever is produced, and since we
know that human wants are insatiable, too much cannot be
produced. This crude and superficial treatment, which
found wide currency from the pages of Adam Smith and
McCulloch, has been swallowed by later English economists,
unfortunately without inquiring whether it was consistent

---

[1] For the view that over-consumption is cause, see Appendix II.

with industrial facts. Since all commerce is ultimately resolvable into exchange of commodities for commodities, it is obvious that every increase of production signifies a corresponding increase of power to consume. Since there exists in every society a host of unsatisfied wants, it is equally certain that there exists a desire to consume everything that can be produced. But the fallacy involved in the supposition that over-supply is impossible consists in assuming that the power to consume and the desire to consume necessarily co-exist in the same persons.

In the case of a glut of cotton goods due to an increased application of machinery, the spinners and manufacturers have the power to consume what is produced, while a mass of starving, ill-clad beings in Russia, East London —even in Manchester—may have the desire to consume these goods. But since these latter are not owners of anything which the spinners and manufacturers wish to consume or to possess, the exchange of commodities for commodities cannot take place. But, it will be said, if the Lancashire producers desire to consume anything at all, those who produce such articles of desire will have the power, and possibly the desire, to consume more cotton goods, or at any rate the desire to consume something produced by other people who will have both power and desire to consume cotton goods. Thus, it will be said, the roundabout exchange of commodities for commodities must be brought about. And this answer is valid, on the assumption that the Lancashire producers desire to consume an equivalent of the goods they produce. But let us suppose they do not desire to do so. The reply that since human wants are insatiable every one with power to consume must have desire to consume, is inadequate. In order to be operative in the steady maintenance of industry the desire to consume must be a desire to consume *now*, to consume continuously, and to consume to an extent corresponding with the power to consume.

Let us take the Lancashire trade as a test case. Evidently, there could be no superfluous capital and labour in Lancashire trade if the cotton-spinners, manufacturers and their operatives, increased their own consumption of cotton goods to correspond with every increase of output.

But if they do not do this, they can only make good

and maintain their capital and labour in employment by
persuading others to increase their consumption of cotton
goods. How can they do this? If, instead of desiring
to consume more cotton goods, the Lancashire employers
and operatives desire to consume, and do actually consume,
more hardware, houses, wine, etc., then the increased
consumption of these things, raising their prices and so
stimulating their production, and distributing a larger
purchasing-power among the capitalists and operatives
engaged in producing the said hardware, houses, wine, etc.,
will enable the latter to consume more cotton goods, and
if these desire to do so, their effective demand will maintain
the new capital and labour employed in Lancashire trade.

But if, instead of taking this course, the Lancashire
capitalists and operatives want not to consume either cotton
or anything else, but simply to *save* and put up more mills
and prepare more yarn and cloth, they will soon find they
are attempting the impossible. Their new capital, and the
fresh labour conjoined with it, can only be employed on
condition that they or others shall increase their consumption of cotton goods. They themselves *ex hypothesi*
will not do so, and if the capitalists and operatives engaged
in setting up the new cotton-mills, etc., will consent to do
so, this only postpones the difficulty, unless we suppose a continuous erection of new mills, and a continuous application
on the part of those who construct these mills of the whole of
their profits and wages in demanding more cotton goods—
a *reductio ad absurdum*. In short, cotton capitalists and
operatives can only effect this saving and provide this
increased employment of capital and labour on condition
that either those engaged in erecting and working the new
mills shall spend all their income in demanding cotton
goods, or that other persons shall diminish the proportion
of their incomes which hitherto they have saved, and shall
apply this income in increased demand for cotton goods.

Now if the same motives which induce Lancashire
capitalists and workers to refuse to increase their present
consumption *pari passu* with the rate of production are
generally operative, it will appear that capital and labour
lie idle because those who are able to consume what they
could produce are not willing to consume, but desire to
postpone consumption—*i.e.*, to save.

§ 8. The process of "Saving" has received but scant attention from economic writers. Jevons appears to have held that superfluous food and other necessary consumptive goods, in whosoever hands they were, constituted the only true fund of capital in a community at any given time. Sidgwick also holds that all "Savings" are in the first instance "food." That this is not the case will appear from the following example:—A self-sufficing man produces daily for his daily consumption a quantity of food, etc., denoted by the figure 10. 5 of this is necessary and 5 superfluous consumption. This man, working with primitive tools, discovers an implement which will greatly facilitate his production, but will cost 4 days' labour to make. Three alternatives are open to him. He may spend half his working day in producing the strictly necessary part of his previous consumption, 5, and devote the other half to making the new implement, which will be finished in 8 days. Or he may increase the duration of his working day by one quarter, giving the extra time to the making of his new implement, which will be finished in 16 days. Or lastly, he may continue to produce consumptive goods as before, but only consume half of them, preserving the other half for 8 days, until he has a fund which will suffice to keep him for 4 continuous days, which he will devote to making the new implement. If he adopts the first alternative, he simply changes the character of his production, producing in part of his working day future goods instead of present consumptive goods. In the second he creates future goods by extra labour. In the third case only does the "saving" or new "capital" take as its first shape food. In the same way a community seeking to introduce a more "roundabout" method of production requiring new plant, or seeking to place in the field of industry a new series of productive processes to satisfy some new want, may achieve their object by "saving" food, etc., or by changing for awhile the character of their production, or by extra labour. Thus new capital, whether from the individual or the community point of view, may take either "food" or any other material form as its first shape.

Since "savings" need not take the shape of food or any article capable of immediate consumption, Adam Smith and J. S. Mill are clearly wrong when they urge in terms almost identical[1] that what is saved is necessarily consumed, and consumed as quickly as that which is spent. The antithesis of saving and spending shows these writers, and the bulk of English economists who follow them, are misled, because they regard "saving" as doing something with money, and do not sufficiently go behind the financial aspect of putting money into a bank.

A closer analysis of saving yields the result that, except in one of the simple cases taken in our example above, where "saving" implied withholding consumable goods from present consumption, every act of saving in a complex industrial society signifies making, or causing to be made, forms of capital which are essentially incapable of present consumption—*i.e.*, future or productive goods.

Each member of an industrial community receives his money income as the market equivalent of value created in goods or services by the requisites of production, land, capital, labour which he owns. For every £1 paid as income an equivalent quantity of material or non-material wealth has been already created.

Let A be the owner of a requisite of production, receiving £500 a year as income in weekly payments of £10. Before receiving each £10 he has caused to come into existence an amount of wealth which, if material goods, may or may not be still in existence ; if services, has already been consumed. It is evident that A may each week consume £10 worth of goods and services without affecting the general condition of public wealth. A, however, determines to consume only £5 worth of goods and services each week, and puts the other £5 into the bank. Now what becomes of the £5 worth of goods and services which A might have consumed, but refused to consume? Do they necessarily continue to exist so long as A is credited with the money which represents their "saving"; if so, in what form? In other words, what actually takes place in the world of commerce when money income is said to be saved, what other

[1] "What is annually saved is as regularly consumed as what is annually spent, and nearly in the same time too ; but it is consumed by a different set of people." (*Wealth of Nations*, p. 149 *b*, McCulloch.) "Everything which is produced is consumed ; both what is saved and what is said to be spent, and the former quite as quickly as the latter." (*Principles of Political Economy*, Book I., chap. v., sec. 6.)

industrial facts stand behind the financial fact of A depositing part of his income in the bank as "savings"?

To this question several answers are possible.

(1) B, a spendthrift owner of land or capital, wishing to live beyond his income, may borrow from the bank each £5 which A puts in, mortgaging his property. In this case B spends what A might have spent; B's property (former savings perhaps?) falls into A's hands. A has individually effected a "saving" represented by tangible property, but as regards the community there is no saving at all, real or apparent.

(2) C, a fraudulent promoter of companies, may by misrepresentation get hold of A's saved money, and may spend it for his own enjoyment, consuming the goods and services which A might have consumed, and giving to A "paper" stock which figures as A's "savings." Here A has individually effected no saving.

From the point of view of the community there is no real saving (C has consumed instead of A), but so long as the "stock" has a market value there is an apparent saving. To this category belongs the "savings" effected if A lends his money to a government to be spent on war. From the standpoint of the community there is no saving (unless the war be supposed to yield an asset of wealth or security), but A's paper stock represents his individual saving. A's "saving" is exactly balanced by the spending of the community in its corporate capacity, A receiving a mortgage upon the property of the community.[1]

(3) D and E, manufacturers or traders, engaged in producing luxuries which A used to buy with his £5 before he took to saving, finding their weekly "takings" diminished and being reduced to financial straits, borrow A's "savings" in order to continue their business operations, mortgaging their plant and stock to A. So long as, with the assistance of A's money, they are enabled to continue producing, what they produce is over-supply, not needed to supply current consumption, assuming the relation between spending and saving in the other members of the community remains unaltered. This over-supply is the material

---

[1] An able analysis of the nature of "paper savings" is found in Mr. J. M. Robertson's *Fallacy of Saving*. (Sonnenschein.)

representative of A's "savings." So far as real capital is
concerned there is no increase by A's act of saving, rather
a decrease, for along with the net reduction in the consumption of luxuries on the part of the community due to A's
action, there must be a fall in the "value" of the capital
engaged in the various processes of producing luxuries,
uncompensated by any other growth of values. But by
A's "saving" new forms of capital exist which bear the
appearance of capital, though in reality they are "over-
supply." These empty forms represent A's saving. Of
course A, with full knowledge of the facts, would only
lend to D and E up to the real value of their mortgaged
capital. When this point was reached D and E could get
no further advances, and their stock and plant would pass
into A's hands. From the point of view of the community
A's action has resulted in the creation of a number of
material forms of capital which, so long as the existing
relations between the community's production and consumption continue, stand as over-supply.

(4) A may hand over his weekly £5 to F on security.
F by purchase obtains the goods which A refused to consume, and may use them (or their equivalent in other
material forms) as capital for further production. If F can
with this capital help to produce articles for which there is
an increasing consumption, or articles which evoke and
satisfy some new want, then A's action will have resulted in
"saving" from the point of view of the community—i.e.,
there will be an increase of real capital; forms of capital
which would otherwise have figured as over-supply have the
breath of economic life put into them by an increase in
general consumption. No real difficulty arises from a doubt
whether the goods and services which A renounced were
capable of becoming effective capital. The things he
renounced were luxurious consumptive goods and services.
But he could change them into effective capital in the
following way:—Designing henceforth to consume only half
his income, he would deliberately employ half the requisites
of production which furnished his income in putting extra
plant, machinery, etc., into some trade. Whether he does
this himself, or incites F to do it, makes no difference; it
will be done. In this way, by establishing new forms of
useful capital, A can make good his saving, assuming an

increase of general consumption. These are the four possible effects of A's saving from the point of view of the community—

(1) Nil.
(2) Bogus or "paper" saving.
(3) Over-supply of forms of capital.
(4) Increase of real capital.

It appears then that every act which in a modern industrial society is "saving," from the standpoint of the community, and not a mere transfer of "spending" from one person to another, consists in the production of a form of goods in its nature or position incapable of present consumption.

This analysis of "saving" convicts J. S. Mill of a double error in saying, "Everything which is produced is consumed; both what is saved and what is said to be spent; and the former quite as rapidly as the latter." In the first place, by showing that "saving," from the point of view of the community, generally means producing something incapable of present consumption, it proves that even if what is "saved" is consumed, it is not consumed as quickly as what is spent. Mill seemed to think that what was "saved" was necessarily food, clothing, and so-called finished goods, because "saving" to him was not a process, but a single negative act of refusing to buy. Because a man who has "saved" has command of an extra stock of food, etc., which he may hand over to labourers as real wages, he seems to think that a community which saves will have its savings in this form. We see this is not the case. Even where in a primitive society extra food is the first form savings may take, it belongs to the act of saving that this food shall not be consumed so soon as it was available for consumption. In short, Mill's notion was that savings must necessarily mean a storing up of more food, clothing, etc., which, after all, is not stored, but is handed over to others to consume. He fails to perceive that a person who saves from the social as opposed to the individual point of view necessarily produces something which neither he nor any one else consumes at once—*i.e.*, steam engines, pieces of leather, shop goods. A "saving" which is merely a transfer of spending from A to B is obviously no saving from the point of view of the com-

munity to which both A and B belong. If A, who is said
to save, pays wages to B, who makes a machine which
would otherwise not have been made, when this machine is
made something is saved, not before.

Though Mill does not seem, in Bk. I. chap. v., to regard
increased plant, machinery, etc., as "savings," but rather as
something for which "savings" may be exchanged,[1] the
more usual economic view of "savings" embodies part of
them in plant and raw material, etc., and considers the
working up of these into finished goods as a "consumption."
But though industrial usage speaks of cotton yarn, etc.,
being consumed when it is worked up, the same language is
not held regarding machinery, nor would any business man
admit that his "capital" was consumed by the wear and
tear of machinery, and was periodically replaced by
"saving." The wearing away of particular material embodiments of capital is automatically repaired by a process
which is not saving in the industrial or the economic
sense. No manufacturer regards the expenditure on maintenance of existing plant as "saving"; what he puts into
additional plant alone does he reckon "savings." It would
be well for economists to clearly recognise that this business aspect of capital and saving is also the consistent
scientific aspect. "Saving" will then be seen to apply
exclusively to such increased production of plant and
productive goods as will afterwards yield an increased crop
of consumptive goods, provided the community is willing to
consume them. "Saving" is postponed consumption—*i.e.*,
the production of "future goods," plant, machinery, raw
materials in their several stages, instead of commodities
suitable for immediate consumption.

§ 9. There are, in fact, two distinct motives which
induce individuals to continue to produce, one is the
desire to consume, the other the desire to save—*i.e.*, to
postpone consumption. It is true that the latter may be
said also to involve a desire to consume the results of the
savings at some indefinitely future time, but the motive of
their production at present is a desire to reduce the quantity
of the present consumption of the community, and to
increase the quantity of postponed consumption.

---

[1] Chap. v. § 5.

It is this consideration which gives the answer to the
single sentence of J. S. Mill, which has been sometimes
held to offer a complete refutation of the notion of an
existing state of over-supply. "The error is in not per-
ceiving that, though all who have an equivalent to give
might be fully provided with every conceivable article which
they desire, the fact that they go on adding to the production proves that this is not actually the case."[1]   Here the
present desire to consume either what is produced or its
equivalent is assumed to be the only motive which can lead
an individual to produce.   The fact that people go on producing is regarded as proof that they are not "fully provided
with every conceivable article they desire."   If this were
true it would be a final and conclusive refutation of the
idea of over-supply.   But if saving means postponed consumption, and the desire to save, as well as the desire to
consume, is a *vera causa* in production, then the fact of
continued production affords no proof that such production
must be required to supply articles which are desired for
consumption.   Ultimately a belief that some one will
consent to consume what is produced underlies the continued production of "a saving person," but, as we shall
see presently, the belief of a competing producer that he
can get a market for his goods, even when justified by
events, is no guarantee against excessive production in the
whole trade.

If, then, those who have the power to consume in the ✓
present desire to postpone their consumption they will
refuse to demand consumptive goods, and will instead
bring into existence an excess of productive goods.

§ 10. The diagram on next page may serve more clearly
to indicate the quantitative maladjustment of Consuming
and Saving which constitutes under-consumption, and
exhibits itself in a plethora of machinery and productive
goods.

A, B, C, D, E represent the several stages through which
the raw material obtained from Nature passes on its way to
the position of a consumer's utility. The five stages represent the five leading processes in production—the
extractive process, transport, manufacture, wholesale and

[1] Bk. III., chap. xiv. § 3.

retail trade. The raw materials extracted at A, the wheat,
skins, iron, timber, cotton, etc., obtained from various
quarters of the globe, are gathered together in large quantities into places where they undergo various transformations
of shape and character; they are then distributed by
wholesale and retail merchants, who hand them over to
persons who consume them as bread, boots, kettles,
chairs, shirts. The extractive, transport, manufacturing,
and merchant stages may of course be subdivided into many

MECHANISM OF PRODUCTION.

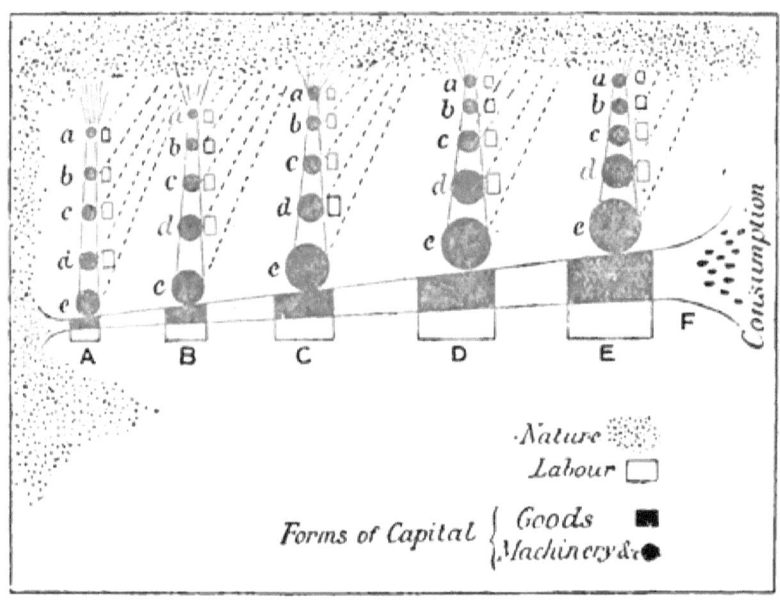

complex processes, as applied to the history of the more
elaborately-produced commodities. But at each point in
the process of production there must stand a quantity of
plant and machinery designed to assist in moving the
productive goods a single step further on the road towards
consumption. This fixed capital is denoted by the black
circles placed at the points A, B, C, D, E. But each
machine, or factory building, or warehouse is itself the
ultimate product of a series of steps which constitute a
process similar to that denoted by the main channel of

production. Consisting in raw material extracted from nature, the machinery and plant are built up by a number of productive stages, which correspond to A, B, C, D, E, into the completed shapes of fixed capital, adjusted to the positions where they can give the proper impulse to the main tide of production. Each productive stage in the production of plant or machinery requires the presence of other plant and machinery to assist its progress. Each of these secondary forms of fixed capital situate at a, b, c, d, e, has of course a similar history of its own. To represent the full complexity of the mechanism of industry thus suggested would be confusing and would serve no purpose here. It is sufficient that we recognise that at each point A, B, C, D, E, and at each of the points a, b, c, d, e, upon the perpendicular lines, stands a quantity of forms of fixed capital which are gradually worn out in the work of forwarding quantities of A to B, and quantities of B to C, and so on. Now if we turn to the point F, where goods pass out of the productive machine into the hands of consumers, who destroy them by extracting their "utility or convenience," we shall find in this flow of goods out of the industrial machine the motive-force and regulator of the activity of the whole machine.

Let us take an illustration from a single trade, the shoe trade. The number of boots and shoes purchased by consumers at retail shops and drawn out from the mechanism at the point F, determines the rate at which retailers demand and withdraw shoes from wholesale merchants, assuming for the sake of simplicity that all shopkeepers deal with manufacturers through the medium of merchant middlemen. If the number of sales effected in a given time by retailers increases, they increase their demand from the merchants, if it falls off they lower their demand. The quantity of goods which retailers will in normal conditions keep in stock will be regulated by the demand of consumers.[1] Thus the flow of shoes from D to E, and the

[1] The stock of a small retailer will not, however, in all cases vary proportionately with the aggregate sales of all classes of goods. A small shopkeeper, to retain his custom and credit, is often required to keep a small stock of a large variety of goods not often in request. If he sells them rather more quickly, he does not necessarily increase his stock in hand at any particular time.

quantity of shoes which at any given time are at the point
E, are determined by the demand of consumers—that is to
say, by the quantity or pace of consumption. If, owing to
miscalculation, a larger number of shoes stands in the retail
shops than is required to satisfy current consumption, or if
the flow from D to E is faster than the outflow from E,
this excess ranks as an over-supply of these forms of capital.
Now just as the demand of consumers determines the
number of shoes which stand at E and flow from D to E, so
the demand of the retailer determines the number of shoes
which at any time constitutes the stock of the merchants at
D, and the size and number of the orders they give to the
manufacturers at C.   Similarly with the earlier processes of
production ; the flow of leather from the "tanners" and
the quantity of leather kept in stock are likewise determined by the demand of the manufacturers ; and the
transport of hides and bark, and the demand for these
materials of tanning, will be regulated by the demands of the
tanners.   So the quantity of stock at each of the points
A, B, C, D, E, and the rate of their progress from one point
to the next, are dependent in each case upon the quantity
demanded at the next stage.   Hence it follows that the
quantity of productive goods at any time in stock at each of
the points in the production of shoes, and the quantity
of productive work done and employment given at each
point, is determined by the amount of consumption of
shoes.   If we knew the number of purchases of shoes
made in any community by consumers in a given time,
and also knew the condition of the industrial arts at
the different points of production, we should be able to
ascertain exactly how much stock and how much auxiliary
capital was required at each point in the production
of shoes.   At any given time the flow of consumption
indicated by F determines the quantity of stock and
plant of every kind economically required at each point
A, B, C, D, E.   What applies to the shoe trade applies
to trade in general.   Given the rate or quantity of consumption in the community, it is possible to determine exactly
the quantity of stock and plant required under existing industrial conditions to maintain this outflow of consumptive
goods, and any stock or plant in excess of this amount
figures as waste forms of capital or over-supply.   F then is

the quantitative regulator of A, B, C, D, E.[1] Nor is the accuracy of this statement impaired by the speculative character of modern trade. Speculative merchants or manufacturers may set up business at D or C and provide themselves with stock and machinery to start with, but unless they meet or create a growing demand of consumers their capital is waste, or else if they succeed in getting trade it is at the expense of other members of the trade, and their capital is made productive by negativing the capital of other traders.

§ 11. The truth here insisted on, that an exact quantitative relation exists between the amount of stock and plant, severally and collectively, required at the different points A, B, C, D, E, and that the amount economically serviceable at each point is determined by the quantity of current consumption, would seem self-evident. But though this has never been explicitly denied, the important results following from its recognition have been obscured and befogged by several conceptions and phrases relating to capital which have found acceptance among English economists.

Chief and foremost among these errors is the framing of a definition of capital so as to exclude the clear separation of productive goods and machinery, the economic means, from consumptive goods, the economic end. So long as a definition of capital is taken which includes any consumptive goods whatsoever, two results follow. One is a hopeless confusion in the commercial mind, for in commerce everything is capital which forms the stock or plant of a commercial firm, and nothing is capital which does not form part of such stock or plant. Secondly, to include under capital the food in the possession of productive

---

[1] It likewise determines the quantity of plant and stock at a, b, c, d down each of the perpendicular lines, for the demand at each of these points in the production of plant and machinery is derived from the requirements at the points A, B, C, D, E. The flow of goods therefore up these channels, though slower in its movement (since in the main channel only goods flow, while fixed capital is subject to the slower "wear and tear"), is equally determined by and derived from the consumption at F. The whole motive-power of the mechanism is engendered at F, and the flow of money paid over the retail counter as it passes in a reverse current from F towards A, supplies the necessary stimulus at each point, driving the goods another stage in their journey.

labourers or any other consumptive goods is an abandonment of the idea of consumption as the economic end and a
substitution of production.

If we follow Böhm-Bawerk and the Austrian economists
in definitely refusing to include the consumptive goods of
labourers as capital,[1] we get a conception of capital which
is at once in accordance with the universal conception of
commercial men, and which enables us to realise the vital
relation between capital and consumption. We now see
Capital in the form of stock and plant at each point in the
industrial machine deriving its use and value from its contribution to the end, Consumption, and dependent for its
quantity upon the quantity of Consumption. We have
seen that a demand for commodities is the true and exact
determinant of the quantity of capital at each industrial
stage. It is therefore the determinant of the aggregate of
wealth which can function as useful forms of capital in
the industrial community at any given time. The aggregate
of plant and stock which constitute the material forms of
capital at the points A, B, C, D, E must in a properly adjusted
state of industry have an exact quantitative relation to the
consumption indicated by F. If F increases, the quantity of
forms of capital at A, B, C, D, E may severally and collectively
increase; if F declines, the useful forms of capital at each
point are diminished. Since we have seen that the sole
object of saving from the social point of view is to place
new forms of capital at one of the points A, B, C, D, E, it is
evident that the amount of useful saving is limited by the
rate of consumption, or financially, by the amount of "spending." Where there is an improvement in the general productive power of a community, only a certain proportion
of that increased power can be economically applied to
"saving"—i.e., to the increase of forms of capital; a due
proportion must go to increased spending and a general
rise in consumption.

§ 12. This will hardly be disputed, except by those who
still follow Mill in maintaining that the whole of the current
production could be "saved," with the exception of what
was required to support the efficiency of labour, a doctrine

---

[1] Böhm-Bawerk, *Positive Theory of Capital*, p. 67. See Appendix
I. for conflict of opinion among English economists.

to which even he could only give passing plausibility by
admitting that the increased savings which resulted from an
attempt to do this would take the shape of luxuries consumed by the said labourers—that is to say, would not be
"savings" at all, but a transfer of "spending" from one
class to another.[1] If capital be confined to commercial
capital, and "saving" to the establishment of the forms of
such capital, no one will deny that the quantity of "saving"
which can be effectually done by a community at any time
depends upon the current rate of consumption, or that any
temporary increase of such saving must be justified by a
corresponding future increase in the proportion of spending.[2]

This will be generally admitted. But there are those
who will still object that production just as much limits
and determines consumption as consumption does production, and who appear to hold that any increase in present
saving, and the consequent increase of amount of plant and
stock, has an economic power to force a corresponding rise
of future consumption which shall justify the saving. This
they urge in the teeth of the fact that in a normal state
of industry in machine-using countries there exists more
machinery and more labour than can find employment, and
that only for a brief time in each decennial period can the
whole productive power of modern machinery be fully used,
notwithstanding the increasing blood-letting to which superfluous saving is exposed by the machinations of bogus
companies, in which the "saving" done by the dupes is
balanced by the "spending" of the sharps. Ignoring the
fact that the alleged power of increased saving to stimulate
increased consumption is not operative, they still maintain
that there cannot be too much "saving," because the
tendency of modern industry is to make production more
and more "roundabout" in its methods, and thus to provide scope for an ever-increasing quantity of forms of
capital.

Under modern machinery we see a constant increase in

---

[1] *Principles of Political Economy*, Bk. I., chap. v. § 3; see also
Bk. III., chap. xiv. § 3.

[2] It should be noted that an increased amount of consumption in the
future does not necessarily compensate for a disturbance of the current
balance of saving and spending, for an *increased proportion of future
income* will have to be spent in order to compensate.

the number of direct and subordinate processes connected
with the forwarding of any class of commodities to its completion.   A larger proportion of the productive labour and
capital is employed, not upon the direct horizontal line, but
upon the perpendicular lines which represent the making of
subsidiary machinery.   More and more saving may be ✓
stored up in the shape of machines to make machines, and
machines to make these machines, and thus the period at
which the "saving" shall fructify in consumption may be
indefinitely extended.

Some of the labour stored and the capital established in
the construction of harbours, the drainage of land, the
construction of scientific instruments, and other works of
durable nature and indirect service, may not be represented
in consumptive goods for centuries.   Admitting this, it may
be urged, can any limits be set to present "saving" and
its storage in forms of capital, provided those forms be
selected with a due regard to a sufficiently distant future?
The answer is that only under two conditions could an
indefinitely large amount of present "saving" be justified.
The first condition is that an unlimited proportion of this
"saving" can be stored in forms which are practically
imperishable; the second condition is that our present
foresight shall enable us to forecast the methods of produc- ✓°
tion and consumption which shall prevail in the distant
future.   In fact neither of these conditions exists.   However much present "saving" we stored in the most enduring
forms of capital with which we are acquainted—*e.g.*, in the
permanent way of railroads, in docks, in drainage and
improvement of land, a large proportion of this "saving"
would be wasted if the consumption it was destined to
subserve was postponed for long.[1]   Neither can we predict
with any assurance that the whole value of such "savings"

---

[1] It must be borne in mind that many articles of utility and enjoyment must in their final processes be produced for immediate consumption.   The "saving" of perishable goods is confined to a saving of
the more enduring forms of machinery engaged in their production,
or in some few cases to a storing up of the raw material.   So likewise that large portion of productive work termed "personal services" cannot be antedated.   These limits to the possibility of
"saving" are important.   No amount of present sacrifice in the
interest of the next generation could enable them to live a life of
luxurious idleness.

will not have disappeared before a generation has elapsed by reason of changes in industrial methods.

The amount of present "saving" which is justified from the point of view of the community is strictly limited. We cannot forecast the demand of our twentieth generation of descendants, or the industrial methods which will then prevail; we do not even know whether there will be a twentieth generation ; there are certain large inevitable wastes in postponed consumption by reason of the perishability of all material forms of wealth, or the abstraction of them by others than those for whose use they were intended. Moreover, we do not believe it would be good for our descendants to have the enjoyment of excessive wealth without a corresponding personal effort of producing, nor would it be good for us to exert effort without some proximate and corresponding enjoyment. The limits of individual life rightly demand that a large proportion of individual effort shall fructify in the individual life.

Thus there are practical limits set upon the quantity of "saving" which can be usefully effected by extending the interval between effort and enjoyment. If the right period be exceeded the risk and waste is too great. The analogy of gardening adduced by Ruskin is a sound one.[1] By due care and the sacrifice of bud after bud the gardener may increase the length of the stem and the size of the flower that may be produced. He may be said to be able to do this indefinitely, but if he is wise he knows that the increased risks of such extension, not to mention the sacrifice of earlier units of satisfaction, impose a reasonable limit upon the procrastination. The proportion of "saving" which may be and is applied to establish late-fructifying forms of wealth, differs not only with the different developments of the industrial arts, but with the foresight and moral character of the race and generation. As our species of civilisation advances, and the demand for complex luxuries and the arts of supplying them advance, a larger amount of "roundabout" production becomes possible, and as regard for the future generations advances, more capital will be put into forms which fructify for them. But at the present in any given community there is a rational and a necessary

---

[1] Ruskin, *Unto this Last*, p. 145.

limit to the quantity of "saving" which can be applied to such purposes.

Secondly, we find that in fact the surplus "saving" over and above what is needed to provide the necessary forms of capital to assist in satisfying current consumption is not absorbed in making provision for distant future consumption by more "roundabout methods." Much of it goes into a mere increase of the number of existing forms of capital whose *raison d'être* lies in the satisfaction of present or immediately future wants. The multiplication of cotton-spinning-mills, of paper-mills, of breweries, ironworks, has gone on far faster than the growth of current consumption. This increase of productive machinery has not in fact been able to force such an increase of consumption as gives adequate employment to these new forms of machinery and to the labour which is at hand to work them.

§ 13. It is not therefore correct to say that the rate of production determines the rate of consumption just as much as the rate of consumption determines the rate of production. The current productive power of capital and labour places a maximum limit upon current consumption, but an increase of productive power exercises no sufficient force to bring about a corresponding rise in consumption. Just as in a particular trade—*e.g.*, the Lancashire cotton trade, an excess of "saving" may be applied to the establishment of mills and machinery which cannot be kept working because there is no market for their output, so it is with trade in general. It is not true that the inflation of capital in the Lancashire trade is due to a misdirection which implies a lack of capital in some other branch of industry. In a period of depression like the present every other important branch of industry displays the same symptoms of excessive plant, over-supply of stock, irregular and deficient employ-ment of labour, though not to the same extent. Nor is there any *à priori* reason why there should not be from time to time such general maladjustment. If ignorance and miscalculation leads to the investment of too much capital in, say, the cotton and iron industries, it is not unreason-able to suppose that in a complex industrial society there should be such general miscalculation of the right pro-portion between saving and spending that too much should be saved at certain periods. That is to say, turning again

to the diagram of industry, just as it is admitted that
miscalculation may induce too much capital to be placed
at A or B or C, and too little at one of the other points
of production, disturbing the harmonious ordering of the
parts of capital, so likewise there may be a maladjustment
of the proportion between A, B, C, D, E, the aggregate of
forms of capital, and F, the aggregate of consumption,
between "saving" and "spending." Now if it be admitted that such maladjustment is possible, the balance
can only lean one way. There cannot be too little saving
to furnish current consumption, taking the industrial community as a whole, for it is impossible to increase the rate
of consumption, F, faster than the increase of the rate of
current production : any increase of the purchase of shop-
goods by raising prices and circulating more money down
the paths of production stimulates and strains the sinews
of production, and if the existing machinery of production is inadequate it supplies a motive-power to increase
"saving." In no case can a community consume faster
than it produces. An individual can do so by living on
his capital, a nation may do so for a time by living upon
its capital, giving to other nations by means of an increased
debt a lien upon its future wealth. But a whole industrial
community can never live upon its capital, can never in the
literal sense of the term "spend too much." This statement requires a single qualification. While a community
can never by "spending" deplete its capital, while it cannot increase its "spending" without at the same time
increasing its real capital,[1] it will doubtless be profitable
to a progressive community to reduce its consumption for
a while below the normal proportion in order to fully utilise
new discoveries in the industrial arts which shall justify in
the future increased consumption.

But with this necessary qualification it is true that a
community cannot exceed in the direction of spending.
But the balance may lean the other way. A community may
"save too much," that is to say, it may establish a larger

[1] This does not necessarily imply a stimulation of new saving. A
fuller vitality given to existing forms of capital will raise the quantity of
real capital as measured in money. Mills and machinery which have
no present or future use, though they embody saving, have no value
and do not increase real capital.

quantity of productive machinery and goods than is required to maintain current or prospective consumption. What is to prevent a community consisting of a vast number of individuals with no close knowledge of one another's actions, desires, and intentions, making such a miscalculation as will lead them to place at each of the points A, B, C, D, E, and in all or most branches of industry, a larger quantity of forms of capital than are required?

It is said that the harmony which subsists between the social interest and the self-interest of individuals will prevent this, or, in other words, that individuals would find that if they attempted to unduly increase the aggregate of capital beyond what was socially advantageous in view of the community's consumption, it would not pay them to do so. Is this true?

An individual working entirely for himself, whose capital lay in his tools and his raw or unfinished commodities, would never increase the latter unduly. A socialist community properly managed would never add to its stock of machinery or increase the quantity of its raw materials or unfinished goods, so as to leave any machines unused or half used, or any goods unnecessarily occupying warehouse room and deteriorating in quality. But when competition of individual interests comes in there is no such security.

It may pay individuals to build new factories and put in new machinery where it would not pay the community to do so, were it the sole owner of the means of production.

The knowledge that enough capital is already invested in an industry to fully supply all current demands at profitable prices has no power to deter the investment of fresh capital, provided the new investors have reason to believe their capital can be made to displace some existing capital owned by others. If the new-comer can, by superior business address, by successful advertising, by "sweating" his employees or otherwise, get hold of a portion of the business hitherto in the hands of other firms, it will pay him to build new factories and stock them with the requisite machinery, and to begin the process of manufacture. There may be in existence already more bicycle works than are sufficient to supply the consumption of the community.

But if a would-be manufacturer thinks he can withdraw from other makers a sufficient number of customers, he will set up works, and make new machines, though his methods of production and the goods he turns out may be no better than those of other makers. The same holds at every stage of production. In wholesale or retail distribution the fact that there are sufficient warehouses and shops in existence to adequately supply the current demand does not prevent any one from embarking new savings in more warehouses or shops, provided he believes he is able to divert into his own firm a sufficient amount of the business formerly held by others. In a district two grocers' shops may be quite sufficient to supply the needs of the neighbourhood, and to secure adequate competition. But if a third man, by an attractive shop-front or superior skill in the labelling or adulteration of his wares, can procure for himself an adequate share of the custom, it will pay him to put the requisite plant and stock into a shop, though the trade on the one hand and the community on the other is no gainer by his action.

There is indeed much evidence to show that it may be to the advantage of individuals to increase the machinery of production, even though there is no reasonable prospect of this machinery being worked at a profit. It is the unanimous testimony of business men that the Lancashire trade has been congested with mills and machinery in this way. As a result of an excessive desire to postpone consumption there are considerable sums of money which cannot find a safe remunerative investment. Here is the material for the company promoter. By means of the specious falsehoods of prospectuses he draws this money together; with him work a builder and an architect who desire the contract of putting up the factory; the various firms interested in manufacturing and supplying the machinery, the boiler-maker and fitters of various kinds, the firm of solicitors whose services are requisite to place the concern upon a sound legal footing, or to establish confidence, take up shares. It is to the interest of all these and many other classes of persons to bring into the field of production new forms of capital, quite independently of the question whether the condition of a trade or the consumption of the community have any need for them

§ 14. These operations, which imply a conflict between the interests of individuals and those of the community, pervade all modern commerce, but are more prevalent in businesses where complex machinery plays a prominent part, or where specious advertising gives the outsider a larger chance of successful entry.

In each and all of these cases it is to the interest of the individual to place new "savings" in new forms of capital in branches of industry where sufficient capital already exists to assist in supplying the current demand for consumptive goods. So far is it from being true that the self-interest of individuals provides an economic check upon over-supply, that it is possible that at each of the points of production, A, B, C, D, E, and in all or the majority of industries at the same time, there should be an excess of forms of capital as compared with that which would suffice for the output, F. The automatic growth of bubble companies and every species of rash or fraudulent investment at times of depressed trade is proof that every legitimate occupation for capital is closed, and that the current rate of saving is beyond that which is industrially sound and requisite. These bubble companies are simply tumours upon the industrial body attesting the sluggish and unwholesome circulation ; they are the morbid endeavours of "saving" which is socially unnecessary, and ought never to have taken place, to find investments. When one of these "bubble" companies collapses it is tacitly assumed by unthinking people that those who invested their money in it were foolish persons who might have sought and found some better investment. Yet a little investigation would have shown that at the time this company arose no opportunity of safe remunerative investment open to the outside public existed, every sound form of business being already fully supplied with capital.

At first sight it might appear that Consols and first-class railway and other stocks were open, and that the folly of the investors in bogus companies consisted in not preferring a safe $2\frac{1}{2}$ per cent. to a risky 5 or 10 per cent. But this argument is once more a return to the unsound individualistic view. It was doubtless open to any individual investor of new savings to purchase sound securities at $2\frac{1}{2}$ per cent., but, since the aggregate of such soundly-placed capital

would not be increased, this would simply mean the displacement of an equal quantity of some one else's capital.
A could not buy Consols unless B sold, therefore the community to which A and B belong could not invest any fresh
savings in Consols. Any widespread attempt on the part of
those who plunged into bogus companies to try first-class
investments would obviously have only had the effect of
further reducing the real interest of these investments far
below 2½ per cent. The same effect would obviously
follow any effective legal interference with company-pro-
moting of this order The fact that Consols and other
first-class investments do not rise greatly at such times is,
however, evidence that the promoters of unsound enterprises succeed in persuading individual investors that their
chance of success is not less than 2½ per cent. In many
instances the investor may be acting wisely in preferring a
smaller chance of much higher profits, because a secure 2½
per cent. may be quite inadequate to his needs. For it
must be borne in mind that a knowledge that the new bank
or new building society is unnecessary, because enough
banks and building societies already exist, does not make it
impossible or necessarily improbable that the new venture
will succeed.

The objection, then, which takes the form that over-
saving cannot exist, because the worst investments made
with open eyes must be productive of more than that which
could be obtained by investing in Consols, is not a valid one.
It would only be valid on the supposition that capital were
absolutely fluid, that the quantity of soundly-placed investments were indefinitely expansible, and that new forms of
capital had in no case the power to oust or negative the use
of old forms of capital. But this we have seen is not the
case. If there existed absolute fluidity of competition in all
forms of capital, the fact that interest for new investments
stood above zero would be a proof that there was not excess
of forms of capital. Capital appears to have this fluidity
when it is regarded from the abstract financial point of
view. A man who has "saved" appears to hold his
"savings" in the form of bank credit, or other money which
he is able to invest in any way he chooses. But, as we have
seen, the real "savings," which represent his productive
effort plus his abstinence, are of necessity embodied in

some material forms, and are therefore devoid of that fluidity which appears to attach to them when reflected in bank money.

§ 15. The evils of trade depression, or excessive growth of the forms of capital beyond the limits imposed by consumption, are traced in large measure directly, but also indirectly, to the free play of individual interests in the development of machine-production. The essential irregularities of invention, the fluctuations of public taste, the artificial restrictions of markets, all enable individual capitalists to gain at the public expense. The added interests of its individual members do not make the interest of the community. All these modes of conflict between the individual and the public interest derive force from the complexity of modern capitalist production.

In fastening upon the uncontrolled growth of machinery the chief responsibility for that depression of trade which is derived from an attempt to devote too large a proportion of the productive power of the community to forms of "saving," two points should be clearly understood.

In the first place, it is the forms of capital and not real capital which are produced in excess. If there are 500 spinning-mills in Lancashire where 300 would suffice, the destruction of 200 mills would no whit diminish the amount of real capital. If 200 mills were burnt down, though the individual owners would sustain a loss, that loss, estimated in money, would be compensated by a money rise in the value of the other mills. The quantity of real capital in cotton-spinning is dependent upon the demand for the use of such forms of capital—that is to say, upon the consumption of cotton goods. If 300 mills are sufficient to do the work of supplying yarn to meet the demand of all manufacturers, the value of 500 mills is no greater than of 300; assuming that the 500 mills equally distributed the trade, it would simply mean that the real capital was thinly spread over 500 mills, which could only work a little over half-time without producing a glut of goods, instead of being concentrated upon 300 mills fully occupied.

Turning once more to the diagram,

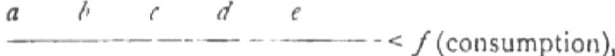

f (the current rate of consumption) determines the quantity of real productive power of capital that can be effectively employed at each point, a, b, c, d, e. The condition of the arts of industry, including the rates of wages and other conditions of the labour market, determines how many forms of capital (mills, warehouses, ironworks, raw material, etc.) at any given time are socially requisite to embody this capital. But though f has an economic power to force into existence the requisite minimum of these forms of capital, it has no power to prevent the pressure of individual interests from exceeding that minimum and planting at a, b, c, d, e more forms of capital than are required.

Secondly, over-production or a general glut is only an external phase or symptom of the real malady. The disease is under-consumption or over-saving. These two imply one another. The real income of a community in any given year is divisible into two parts, that which is produced and consumed, that which is produced and not consumed—*i.e.*, is saved. Any disturbance in the due economic proportion of these two parts means an excess of the one and a defect of the other. All under-consumption therefore implies a correspondent over-saving. This over-saving is embodied in an excess of machinery and goods over the quantity economically required to assist in maintaining current consumption. It must, however, be remembered that this over-saving is not measured by the quantity of new mills, machinery, etc., put into industry. When the mechanism of industry is once thoroughly congested, over-saving may still continue, but will be represented by a progressive under-use of existing forms of capital, that unemployment of forms of capital and labour which makes trade depression.

An increased quantity of saving is requisite to provide for an expected increase of consumption arising from a growth of population or from any other cause. Such increased saving is of course not over-saving. The proportion, as well as the absolute amount of the community's income which is saved, may at any time be legitimately increased, provided that at some not distant time an increased proportion of the then current income be consumed. If in a progressive community the proportion of "saving" to consumption, in order to maintain the current standard of living with the economic minimum of "forms" of capital, be as 2 to 10, the proportion of saving in any given year may be raised to 3 to 9, in order to provide for a future condition in which saving shall fall to 1 to 11. Such increased "saving" will not be over-saving; the forms of capital in which it is embodied will not compete with previously existing forms so as to bring down market prices. The efforts which take the form of permanent improvements of the soil, the erection of fine buildings, docks, railways, etc., for future use, may provide the opportunity to a community of increasing the proportion of its savings for a number of years. But such savings must be followed by an increased future consumption without a correspondent saving attached to it. The notion that we can indefinitely continue to increase the proportion of our savings to our consumption, bounded only by the limit of actual necessaries of life, is an illusion which places production in the position of the human goal instead of consumption.

§ 16. Machinery has intensified the malady of under-consumption or over-saving, because it has increased the opportunities of conflict between the interests of individuals and those of the community. With the quickening of competition in machine industries the opportunities to individuals of making good their new "savings" by cancelling the old "savings" of others continually grow in number, and as an ever larger proportion of the total industry falls under the dominion of machinery, more and more of this dislocation is likely to arise; the struggles of weaker firms with old machinery to hold their own, the efforts of improved machinery to find a market for its expanded product, will continue to produce gluts more frequently, and the subsequent checks to productive activity, the collapse of businesses, the sudden displacement of large masses of labour, in a word, all the symptoms of the malady of "depression" will appear with increased virulence.

It must be clearly recognised that the trouble is due to a genuine clash of individual interests in a competitive industrial society, where the frequent, large, and quite incalculable effects of improved machinery and methods of production give now to this, now to that group of competitors a temporary advantage in the struggle. It was formerly believed that this bracing competition, this free clash of individual interests, was able to strike out harmony, that the steady and intelligent pursuit by each of his own separate interest formed a sure basis of industrial order and induced the most effective and serviceable disposition of the productive powers of a community.

It now appears that this is not the case, and that the failure cannot in the main be attributed to an imperfect understanding by individuals of the means by which their several interests may be best subserved, but is due to the power vested in individuals or groups of individuals to secure for themselves advantages arising from improved methods of production without regard for the vested interests of other individuals or of society as a whole.

APPENDIX I.

ARE GOODS IN THE POSSESSION OF CONSUMERS CAPITAL?

THE question whether food, clothing, etc., which are "capital" so long as they form part of the stock of a shopkeeper, are to be regarded as ceasing to be capital when they pass into the possession of consumers has seldom been definitely faced by English economists. Jevons was perhaps the first to clearly recognise the issues involved. He writes :—" I feel quite unable to adopt the opinion that the moment goods pass into the possession of the consumer they cease altogether to have the attributes of capital. This doctrine descends to us from the time of Adam Smith, and has generally received the undoubting assent of his followers. Adam Smith, although he denied the possessions of a consumer the name of capital, took care to enumerate them as part of the stock of the community." (*The Theory of Political Economy*, 2nd edit., p. 280.)

As a historical judgment this is very misleading. Adam Smith, chiefly impressed by the necessity of separating consumptive goods from goods used as a means of making an income —*e.g.*, commercial capital, quite logically severed revenue from capital as a distinct species of the community's stock. His "followers," however, differed very widely, and usually expressed themselves obscurely. Generally speaking, the English economists of the first half of this century inclined to the inclusion of certain consumptive goods in the possession of labourers under capital. Ricardo, for example, thus expresses himself:—" In every society the capital which is employed in production is necessarily of limited durability. The food and clothing consumed by the labourer, the buildings in which he works, the implements with which his labour is assisted, are all of a perishable value. There is, however, a vast difference in the time for which all these different capitals will endure. A steam engine will last longer than a ship, a ship than the clothing of the labourer, and the clothing of the labourer than the food which he consumes." (*Principles of Political Economy*, 1817, p. 22.) The last sentence is conclusive in its inclusion under capital of goods in the possession of labourers. McCulloch again regrets Smith's exclusion of " revenue" from capital, insisting that "it is enough to entitle an article to be considered capital that it can directly contribute to the support of man or assist him in appropriating or producing commodities," and he would even go so far as to include "a horse yoked to a gentleman's coach," on the ground that it was " possessed of the capacity to assist in production." (*Principles of Political Economy*, Part I., chap. ii. § 3.)

Malthus does not, so far as I can ascertain, face the question. James Mill alone, among the earlier nineteenth century economists, definitely excludes labourers' consumptive goods from capital. (*Principles of Political Economy*, chap. i. § 2.) J. S. Mill is not equally clear in his judgment. In Bk. I., chap. iv. § 1, food "destined" for the consumption of productive labourers apparently ceases to be capital when it is already "appropriated to the consumption of productive labourers." This position, however, is not consistent with his later position regarding the unlimited character of saving, which can only be justified by regarding real wages when paid as continuing to be capital. Fawcett is vague, but he is disposed not only to include under capital food which is in the possession of consumers, but to exclude food which is in the possession of dealers. " If a man has so much wheat, it is wealth which may at any moment be employed as capital; but this wheat is not made capital by being hoarded; it becomes capital when it feeds the labourers, and it cannot feed the labourers unless it is consumed." (*Manual of Political Economy*, Bk. I., chap. iv., p. 29.) Among later English writers, Cairnes, like all holders of the "Wages fund" doctrine, does not clearly meet the question, "Does the food, etc., forming the real wage fund which is one part of capital, cease to be capital when it is actually paid out in wages?" He plays round the question in *Leading Principles*, Part II., chap. i. Bonamy Price includes consumptive goods. "It is to be remarked of all this capital, these materials, implements, and necessaries for the labourers, that they are consumed and destroyed in the process of creating wealth, some rapidly, some more slowly. Thus the very purpose of capital is to be consumed and destroyed; it is procured for that very end." (*Practical Political Economy*, pp. 103, 104.) Since, he adds a little later, "an article cannot be declared to be capital or not capital till the purpose it is applied to is determined," it would appear that flour in the dealer's hands is not capital, but that it only becomes capital when handed over to persons who productively consume it. Thorold Rogers appears to take the same view, holding the food of a country to be part of its capital irrespective of the consideration in whose hands it is. (*Political Economy*, p. 61.) Professor Sidgwick appears to regard "food" consumed by productive labourers as capital. "On this view it is only so far as the labourer's consumption is distinctly designed to increase his efficiency that it can properly be regarded as an investment of capital." (*Principles of Political Economy*, Bk. I., chap. v.)

General Walker apparently holds that stored food used to support productive work is capital in whosoever hands it lies. (*Political Economy*, 2nd edit., § 87.) He is, however, concerned with illustrations from primitive society, and possibly might hold the food ceased to be capital if paid over by one person to another as wages.

Hearn, on the contrary, definitely excludes consumptive goods. "The bullock, which when living formed part of the capital of the grazier, and when dead of the butcher, is not capital when the meat reaches the consumer." (*Plutology*, p. 135.)

Professor Marshall defers to the commercial usage so far as to apply the term Trade Capital to "those external things which a person uses in his trade, either holding them to be

sold for money, or applying them to produce things that
are to be sold for money." But turning to the individual,
he insists upon speaking of the necessaries he consumes
to enable him to work as "capital." "Some enjoyment is
indeed derived from the consumption of the necessaries of
life which are included under capital ; but they are counted
as capital because of the work for the future which they
enable people to do, and not on account of the present
pleasure which they afford." (*Principles*, 2nd edit., p. 125.)

These instances show that Jevons is wrong in attributing
to English economists a general acceptance of the belief
that goods cease to be capital when they come into the
possession of consumers. They also serve to explain the
source of the conflict of judgment and the confusion of
expression. Economists who take it to be the end of
industrial activity to place in the possession of consumers
goods which shall satisfy their desires, regard "capital"
as a convenient term to cover those forms of wealth which
are a means to this end, and are thus logically driven to
exclude all consumers' goods from capital. This view of
capital coincides with the ordinary accepted commercial
view which regards capital not from its productivity side
but from its income-yielding side. Those economists, on
the other hand, who actually, though not avowedly, take
production to be the end of industry, regard as "capital"
all forms of material wealth which are means to that end,
and therefore include food, etc., productively consumed by
labourers. If work considered as distinct from enjoyment
be regarded as the end, it is reasonable enough that some
term should be used to cover all the forms of material
wealth serviceable to that end. It is, however, unfortunate
that the term "capital" should be twisted from its fairly
consistent commercial use to this purpose.

Dr. Keynes,[1] who seems to think the sole difficulty
as regards the definition of capital arises from the difference in the point of view of the individual and of the
community, suggests the use of two terms, "revenue
capital" and "production capital." But these terms are
doubly unsatisfactory. In the first place, the "productive
consumption" economist might fairly claim that as his food,

---

[1] *Scope and Method of Political Economy*, p. 162.

etc., enabled the workman to obtain his wages or revenue, they belonged to revenue capital. On the other hand, regarding it as essential to distinct terminology to sever entirely consumptive goods from productive goods, I should insist that the " production capital" of the community was synonymous with its "revenue capital," and that although the individual view of capital is not always coincident with the community's view, that difference cannot be expressed by the distinction of " revenue capital " and " production capital."

Moreover, the consumptive-production economists, to be consistent and to preserve the continuity of the conception of economic activity, would do well to abolish labour-power as a separate factor, and to include the body of the labourer with its store of productive energy as a species of capital. For it is urged (*e.g.*, by Professor Marshall) that the fact that the food consumed by labourers enables them to earn an income entitles it to rank as capital. In that case the "wages" which form that income should rank as interest upon the capital. Again, there is no reason for breaking the continuity of the capital at the time when the "food" is actually eaten. The food is not destroyed, but built up into the frame of the labourer as a fund of productive energy. If consumptive goods are once admitted as capital, the labourer's body must be likewise capital yielding interest in the shape of wages If the other factor " natural agents " be still retained (an unnecessary proceeding, since all land, etc., which is productively serviceable is so by reason of the application of some element of stored labour, and may therefore be called "capital"), labour could be resolved into natural agents (the infant body) and capital (the food, etc., used to strengthen and support the body). Wages could then be reckoned partly as rent, partly as interest. It is difficult to understand why "productive-consumption" economists, some of whom have evidently contemplated the change of terminology, have refused to take a step which would at any rate have the merit of imparting consistency to their terminology. It is, of course, true that no " productive-consumption " economist would straightly admit production not consumption to be the economic goal, but his terminology can only approximate to consistency upon this supposition.

Mr. Cannan, in his able exposure of Adam Smith's mixed

notions upon Capital, inclines to an extended use of the term which shall include "the existing stock of houses, furniture, and clothes" on the ground that they are "just as much a part of the surplus of production over consumption, and therefore the result of saving, as the stock of warehouses, machinery, and provisions.[1] Moreover, whether in merchants' or consumers' hands they produce a real income, in the latter case consisting of the comforts and conveniences which attend their consumption. But if this view be accepted all forms of wealth must rank as capital; the distinction between those which have been saved and those which have not loses all meaning; so long as a piece of wealth which has been made exists, it has been saved, and is an "investment" which will, at any rate in the satisfaction due to its consumption, yield a real income. But this extension, though logically defensible, must be rejected on grounds of convenience. When economists can be got to recognise the necessity of measuring all "incomes," as indeed all "outputs," in terms of human satisfaction and effort, then it may be well to recognise that all forms of wealth which have figured as producers' capital continue to exist as consumers' capital, yielding an income of satisfaction until they are consumed. To place the consumptive-goods on a common level with forms of productive capital, it would of course be necessary to make the usual provision against wear and tear and depreciation before reckoning income. There would be no justification for reckoning the total use of a coat worn out and not replaced as income from capital.

As matters now stand, the only logically accurate correlation of economic activities which shall enable us to give a clear and separate meaning to capital and labour-power involves the distinct recognition of unproductive consumption —*i.e.*, consumption considered as an end and not as a means to further production of industrial wealth, as the final object of economic activity. In other words, it is the benefit or satisfaction arising from the destruction of forms of industrial wealth that constitutes the economic goal. Life not work, unproductive not productive consumption, must be regarded as the end. The consideration that a good and

---

[1] *Production and Consumption*, chap. iv. § 2.

wholesome human life is identified with work, some of
which will be industrial in character, so that many forms
of industrial wealth will be destroyed under conditions
which enable them to render direct service in creating new
forms, does not impair the validity of this conception. The
inability of most economic thinkers to clearly grasp and to
impress on others the idea of the industrial organism as a
single "going concern," has arisen chiefly from the circular
reasoning involved in making "production" at once the
means and the end, and the inconsistent definitions required
to support this fallacy.

APPENDIX II.

"OVER-CONSUMPTION" CONSIDERED AS CAUSE OF DEPRESSION.

IT is of course quite possible that a temporary over-production in one or several trades may be explained by a
correspondent under-production in others—that is to say,
there may be a misplacement of industrial enterprise. But
this can afford no explanation of the phenomenon Depression of Trade, which consists in a general or net over-
supply of capital, as evidenced by a general fall of prices.

In like manner it is possible to explain a commercial
crisis in a single country, or part of a commercial community,
as the reaction or collapse following an attempt to increase
the quantity of fixed capital out of proportion to the growth
of the current national income, by a reckless borrowing.
This attempt of a single country to enlarge its business
operations beyond the limits of the possible savings of its
own current income, Mr. Bonamy Price and M. Yves Guyot
speak of under the questionable title of Over-consumption.
Since they tender this vice of over-consumption as the true
and sufficient explanation of commercial crises, it is necessary to examine the position.

Professor Bonamy Price applied the following analysis to
the great crisis in the United States of 1877 :—

"We are now in a position to perceive the magnitude of
the blunder of which the American people were guilty in constructing this most mischievous quantity of fixed capital in

the form of railways. They acted precisely like a landowner who had an estate of £10,000 a year, and spent £20,000 on drainage. It could not be made out of savings, for they did not exist, and at the end of the very first year he must sell a portion of the estate to pay for the cost of his draining. In other words, his capital, his estate, his means of making income whereon to live was reduced. The drainage was an excellent operation, but for him it was ruinous. So it was with America. Few things in the long run enrich a nation like railways; but so gigantic an over-consumption, not out of savings, but out of capital, brought her poverty, commercial depression, and much misery. The new railways have been reckoned at some 30,000 miles, at an estimated cost of £10,000 a mile; they destroyed three hundred million of pounds worth, not of money, but of corn, clothing, coal, iron, and other substances. The connection between such over-production and commercial depression is here only too visibly that of parent and child. But the disastrous consequences were far from ending here. The over-consumption did not content itself with the wealth used up in working the railways and the materials of which they were composed. It sent other waves of destruction rolling over the land. The demand for coal, iron, engines, and materials kindled prodigious excitement in the factories and the shops; labourers were called for from every side; wages rose rapidly; profits shared the upward movement; luxurious spending overflowed; prices advanced all round; the recklessness of a prosperous time bubbled over; and this subsidiary over-consumption immensely enlarged the waste of the national capital set in motion by the expenditure on the railways themselves. Onward still pressed the gale; foreign nations were carried away by its force. They poured their goods into America, so over-powering was the attraction of high prices. They supplied materials for the railways, and luxuries for their constructors. Their own prices rose in turn; their business burst into unwonted activity; profits and wages were enlarged; and the vicious cycle repeated itself in many countries of Europe. Over-consumption advanced with greater strides; the tide of prosperity rose ever higher; and the destruction of wealth marched at greater speed."[1]

[1] *Contemporary Review*, May 1879.

Now, in the first place, our analysis of saving and the
confinement of the term consumption to direct embodiments of utility and convenience forbid us to acknowledge
that the action of the United States or the analogy of the
improving landowner is a case of over-consumption at all.
If the landowner borrowed money on his estates in order to
live in luxury for a season beyond his income, or similarly,
if a State raised loans in order to consume powder and shot,
the term over-consumption rightly applies. But where the
landowner borrows so much money to improve his land that
he is unable to hold out till the improvements bear fruit,
and must sell his land to pay the interest, he is not rightly
accused of over-consumption. His reduced consumption
later on while practising retrenchment is simply a process of "saving" which, when complete, is to take
the place of an amount of "saving" previously made
by some one else and borrowed by him. What happened was simply this. A, wishing to drain his land,
had not "saved" enough to do it; B has saved, and
A, borrowing his "saving," holds it for a time in his
shape of drainage. If he can continue to pay interest
and gradually "save" to pay off the capital, he will
do so; if not, as in the case supposed, B, the mortgagee,
will foreclose and legally enter upon his savings in the
shape of "drainage" which he really owned all along. But
even if A in this case were rightly accused of over-consumption, this over-consumption must be considered as balanced
by the under-consumption of B, so that as regards the
community of which A and B are both members there is
no over-consumption.

Now, precisely the same line of reasoning applies if for
the individual A we take the country of the United States.
If it tries to increase its factories, machinery, etc., in excess
of its ability to pay, it can only do so by borrowing from
other countries; and if it cannot pay the interest on such
loans, the "savings," in the shape of fixed capital which it
has endeavoured to secure for itself, remain the property of
the other countries which have effected the real saving
which they embody, assuming them to have a value. If
the action of the United States be called over-consumption, it is balanced by an under-consumption of England,
France, or other countries of the commercial community.

Mr. Price sought to avoid this conclusion by saying nothing about the individual from whom the landowner or the country from which the United States borrowed in order to increase the fixed capital. But as the landowner and the United States, *ex hypothesi*, did not make their improvements out of their own savings, they made them out of somebody else's savings, and that conduct which is styled over-consumption in them is balanced by an equal quantity of under-consumption in some other party. If thus we look at the individual landowner or the single country of the United States, we might say, accepting Price's view of consumption, that he and it were guilty of over-consumption, and that this was the cause of the commercial crisis. But since this over-consumption is absolutely conditioned by a correspondent under-consumption of some other member of the industrial community, it is not possible to conclude with Professor Price that over-consumption can even for a time exist in the community as a whole, or that such a condition can be the explanation of a crisis commonly felt by all or most of the members of that community.

What actually happened in the case of United States railways was that a number of people, either in America or in Europe, under-consumed or over-saved : their excessive saving could find no better form to take than American railways, which, *ex hypothesi*, were not wanted for use. A number of persons who might have made and consumed three hundred million pounds' worth more of corn, clothing, coals, etc., than they actually did consume, refused to do so, and instead of doing so made a number of railway lines, locomotives, etc., which no one could consume and which were not wanted to assist production. What occurred was a waste of saving power through an attempt to make an excessive number of forms of capital.

Even if, some years later, many of these forms obtained a use and a value, none the less they represent an excess or waste of "saving" to an extent measured by the normal rate of interest over that period of time which elapsed before they fructified into use. In a word, what had happened was not over-consumption, but under-consumption.

M. Guyot appears to think that in the community as a whole too much saving can be put into the form of "fixed" capital and too little into circulating capital, and that such a

condition of affairs will bring depression. " Fixed capital,'
he says, " cannot be utilised if there is no available circulating capital. Ships and railways are useless if there are
no commodities for them to convey; a factory cannot be
worked unless there are consumers ready to buy its products.
If, then, circulating capital has been so far exhausted as to
take a long time replacing, fixed capital must meanwhile
remain unproductive, and the crisis is so much the longer
and more severe." [1]

To this there are two sufficient answers. The prevalence
of low prices for goods of various kinds as well as for plant
in a time of depression, the general glut of goods which
forms one phase of the depression proves that the crisis
does not arise from storing too much saving in plant
and too little in goods. Where there exists simultaneously a larger quantity of plant, raw material,
finished goods, and labour than the industrial society
can find use for, no assertion of maladjustment, either
as between trade and trade, country and country, fixed
and circulating capital, will afford any explanation.
Secondly, M. Guyot gives away his entire position by
admitting "a factory cannot be worked unless there are
consumers ready to buy its products." A "consumer"
here can logically only mean one who buys finished
goods for personal use, and if this be generally applied it
amounts to a clear admission that under-consumption is the
reason why there appears to be a glut of capital, fixed or
other.

[1] *Principles of Social Economy*, p. 245.   (Sonnenschein.)

CHAPTER VIII.

MACHINERY AND DEMAND FOR LABOUR.

§ 1. *The Influence of Machinery upon the number of Employed, dependent on "elasticity of demand."*

§ 2. *Measurement of direct effects on Employment in Staple Manufactures.*

§ 3. *Effects of Machinery in other Employments—The Evidence of French Statistics.*

§ 4. *Influence of Introduction of Machinery upon Regularity of Employment.*

§ 5. *Effects of "Unorganised" Machine-industry upon Regularity.*

§ 6. *Different Ways in which modern Industry causes Unemployment.*

§ 7. *Summary of General Conclusions.*

§ 1. In discussing the direct influences of machinery upon the economic position of the labourer we must distinguish its effects upon (1) the number of workers employed; (2) the regularity of employment; (3) the skill, duration, intensity, and other qualities of labour; (4) the remuneration of labour. Though these influences are closely related in complex interaction, it is convenient to give a separate consideration to each.

(1) *Effects of Machinery upon the number of Employed.*— The motive which induces capitalist employers to introduce into an industry machinery which shall either save labour by doing work which labour did before, or assist labour by making it more efficient, is a desire to reduce the expenses of production. A new machine either displaces an old machine, or it undertakes a process of industry formerly done by hand labour without machinery.

In the former case it has been calculated that the expenses incurred in making, maintaining, and working the new machines so as to produce a given output will be less than the corresponding expenses involved in the use of the old machines. Assuming that the labour of making and working the new machines is paid at no lower rate than the labour it displaces, and that the same proportion of the price of each machine went as wages and as profits, it must follow that the reduction of expenses achieved signifies a net displacement of labour for a given quantity of production. Since the skilled labour of making new machines is likely to be paid higher than that of making more old machines, and the proportion of the price which goes as profit upon a new invention will be higher than in the case of an old one,[1] the actual displacement of labour will commonly be larger than is represented by the difference in money price of the two machines. Moreover, since in the case of an old manufacturing firm the cost of discarding a certain amount of existing machinery must be reckoned in, the substitution of new machinery for old will generally mean a considerable displacement of labour.

Similarly, when a new process is first taken over by machinery the expenses of making and working the machines, as compared with the expenses of turning out a given product by hand labour, will, other things being equal, involve a net diminution of employment. The fact that the new machinery is introduced is a proof that there is a net diminution of employment as regards a given output; for otherwise no economy would be effected.

What then is meant by the statement so generally made, that machinery gives more employment than it takes away—that its wider and ultimate effect is not to diminish the demand for labour?

The usual answer is that the economy effected by labour-saving machinery in the expenses of production will,

---

[1] Against this we may set the possibility of a fall in the rate of interest at which manufacturers may be able to borrow capital in order to set up improved machinery. Where an economy can be effected in this direction, the displacement of labour due to the introduction of machinery may not be so large—*i.e.*, it will pay a manufacturer to introduce a new machine which only "saves" a small amount of money, if he can effect the change at a cheap rate of borrowing. (Cf. Marshall, *Principles of Economics*, 2nd edit., pp. 569, 570.)

through competition of producers, be reflected in a lower scale of prices, and this fall of prices will stimulate consumption. Thus, it is urged, the output must be greatly increased. When we add together the labour spent in producing the machinery to assist the enlarged production, the labour spent in maintaining and working the same, and the labour of conveying and distributing the enlarged production, it will be found that more labour is required under the new than under the old conditions of industry. So runs the familiar argument.

The whole argument in favour of the gain which machinery brings to the working classes hinges upon the contention that it increases rather than decreases the amount of employment. Now, though we shall find reason to believe that machinery has not caused any net diminution of employment, there is nothing to support the rough-and-ready rule by which the optimism of English economists argues the case in its application to a single trade.

The following is a fair example of the argument which has passed current, drawn from the pages of a competent economic writer:—

"The first introduction of machinery may indeed displace and diminish for a while the employment of labour, may perchance take labour out of the hands of persons otherwise not able to take another employment, and create the need of another class of labourers altogether; but if it has taken labour from ten persons, it has provided labour for a thousand. How does it work? A yard of calico made by hand costs two shillings, made by machinery it may cost fourpence. At two shillings a yard few buy it; at fourpence a yard, multitudes are glad to avail themselves of it. Cheapness promotes consumption; the article which hitherto was used by the higher classes only is now to be seen in the hand of the labouring classes as well. As the demand increases, so production increases, and to such an extent that, although the number of labourers now employed in the production of calico may be immensely less in proportion to a given quantity of calico, the total number required for the millions of yards now used greatly exceeds the number engaged when the whole work was performed without any aid of machinery."[1]

[1] Leone Levi, *Work and Pay*, p. 28.

Now, turning from the consideration of the particular instance, which we shall find reason to believe is peculiarly unfortunate when we deal with the statistics of the cotton industry, it must be observed that economic theory makes dead against this *à priori* optimism. Ignoring, for the sake of convenience, the not improbable result that an economy of production may, at any rate for a time, swell profits instead of reducing prices, it will be evident that the whole value of the argument turns upon the effect of a fall of price in stimulating increased consumption. Now the problem, how far a given fall in price will force increased consumption, we have found in our discussion of monopoly prices to involve extremely intricate knowledge of the special circumstances of each case, and refined calculations of human motives. Everything depends upon "elasticity of demand," and we are certainly not justified in assuming that in a particular industry a given fall of prices due to machine-production will stimulate so large an increase of consumption that employment will be given to as many, or more persons than were formerly employed. On the contrary, if we apply a similarly graduated fall of prices to two different classes of goods, we shall observe a widely different effect in the stimulation of consumption. A reduction of fifty per cent. in the price of one class of manufactured goods may treble or quadruple the consumption, while the same reduction in another class may increase the consumption by only twenty per cent. In the former case it is probable that the ultimate effect of the machinery which has produced the fall in expenses of production and in prices will be a considerable increase in the aggregate demand for labour, while in the latter case there will be a net displacement. It is therefore impossible to argue *à priori* that the ultimate effect of a particular introduction of machinery must be an increased demand for labour, and that the labour displaced by the machinery will be directly or indirectly absorbed in forwarding the increased production caused by machinery. It is alleged that the use of steam-hammers has displaced nine of the ten men formerly required, that with modern machinery one man can make as many bottles as six men made formerly, that in the boot and shoe trade one man can do the work five used to do, that "in the manufacture of agricultural implements 600 men now do the work which fifteen or twenty years ago required 2145, thus displacing 1515," and so forth.[1] Now in some of these cases we shall find that the fall of prices following such displacements has led to so large an increase of demand that more persons are directly engaged in these industries than before; in other cases this is not the case.

The following quotation from a speech made at the Industrial Remuneration Conference in 1885 will present the most effective criticism upon Professor Leone Levi's position :—

" In carpet weaving fifty years ago the workman drove the shuttle with the hand, and produced from forty-five to fifty yards per week, for which he was paid from 9d. to 1s. per yard, while at the present day a girl attending a steam loom can produce sixty yards a day, and does not cost her employer 1½d. per yard for her labour. That girl with her loom is now doing the work of eight men. The question is, How are these men employed now? In a clothier's establishment, seeing a girl at work at a sewing machine, he asked the employer how many men's labour that machine saved him. He said it saved him twelve men's labour. Then he asked, 'What would those twelve men be doing now?' 'Oh,' he said, 'they will be much better employed than if they had been with me, perhaps at some new industry.' He asked, 'What new industry?' But the employer could not point out any except photography; at last he said they would probably have found employment in making sewing machines. Shortly afterwards he was asked to visit the American Singer Sewing Machine Factory, near Glasgow. He got this clothier to accompany him, and when going over the works they came upon the very same kind of machines as the clothier had in his establishment. Then he put the question to the manager, 'How long would it take a man to make one of these machines?' He said he could not tell, as no man made a machine; they had a more expeditious way of doing it than that—there would be upwards of thirty men employed in the making of one machine; but he said 'if they were to make this particular

[1] Statement by Mr. Shaftoe, President of the Trades Union Congress, 1888; cf. Carroll D. Wright, *Report on Industrial Depressions*, Washington, 1886, pp. 80-90.

kind of machine, they would turn out one for every four
and a half days' work of each man in their employment.'
Now, there was a machine that with a girl had done the
work of twelve men for nearly ten years, and the owner of
that machine was under the impression that these twelve
men would be employed making another machine, while
four and a half days of each of these men was sufficient to
make another machine that was capable of displacing other
twelve men."

In cases like the above we must, of course, bear in mind
that a diminution in employment in the several manufacturing processes directly and indirectly engaged in forwarding an industry, is not of itself conclusive evidence
that the machinery has brought about a net displacement of
labour.   If the output is increased the employment in the
extractive, the transport, and the various distributing processes may compensate the reduction in making goods and
machinery.

§ 2. The industrial history of a country like England can
furnish no sufficient data for a conclusive general judgment
of the case.   The enormous expansion of production induced by the application of machinery in certain branches
of textile industry during the first half of this century indisputably led to an increased demand for English labour in
trades directly or indirectly connected with textile production.   But, in the first place, this cannot be regarded as a
normal result of a fall of prices due to textile machinery,
but is largely attributable to an expansion in the area of
consumption — the acquisition of vast new markets — in
which greater efficiency and cheapness of transport played
the most considerable part.   Secondly, assuming that the
more pressing needs of the vast body of consumers are
already satisfied by machine-made textile goods, we are not
at liberty to conjecture that any further cheapening of
goods, owing to improved machinery, will have a correspondent effect on consumption and the demand for labour.
If England had been a self-contained country, manufacturing only for her own market, the result of machinery applied
to textile industries would without doubt have been a considerable net displacement of textile labour, making every
allowance for growth of population and increased home
consumption.   The expansion of English production under

15

the rapid development of machinery in the nineteenth century cannot therefore be taken as a right measure of the normal effects of the application of machinery.

What direct evidence we have of the effect of machinery upon demand for labour is very significant. Mr. Charles Booth, in his *Occupations of the People*, presents an analysis of the census returns, showing the proportion of the population engaged in various employments at decennial points from 1841 to 1881. To these may be added such statistics of the 1891 census as the present condition of their presentation allows us to relate to the former censuses.[1] If we turn to manufactures, upon which, together with transport, machinery exercises the most direct influence, we find that the aggregate of manufactures shows a considerable increase in demand for labour up to 1861—that is, in the period when English wares still kept the lead they had obtained in the world market—but that since 1861 there is a positive decline in the proportion of the English population employed in manufactures. The percentages up to 1881 run as follows :—

1841[2] .	. . 27.1	per cent.
1851 .	. . 32.7	,,
1861 .	. . 33.0	,,
1871 .	. . 31.6	,,
1881 .	. . 30.7	,,

If we take the staple manufactures, employing the largest number of workers, we shall find that for the most part they show a rising demand for labour up to 1861, a stationary or falling demand when compared with the population after that date. The foundational industries—machinery and tools, shipbuilding, metal working — whose demand for labour during the period 1841-61 increased by leaps and bounds, still show in the aggregate an increased proportion of employment, largely due to the rise since 1861 of a

[1] The merging of retail dealers with the "making" classes, the classification of merchants with those engaged in transport industries, and certain departures from precedent in the mode of classification, render a full use of the 1891 figures impossible at present.

[2] In the years 1831-41 there was an enormous increase of the factory population. Between 1835 and 1839, according to Porter, the increase amounted to 68,263, or a rise of 19.2 per cent. (*Progress of the Nation*, p. 78.)

large export trade in machinery. But while the machine-making industries continue to grow faster than the population in the employment they give, increasing from 209,353 in 1881 to 262,910 in 1891, and shipbuilding also gives a proportionate increase, it is noteworthy that the steel and iron trades, which up to 1871 grew far faster than the population, began to show signs of decline. In 1881 the number of steel and iron workers was 361,343, in 1891 it had increased to 380,193, a growth of only 5.3 per cent. as compared with a growth of population amounting to 11.7 per cent., and a growth of the number of occupied persons amounting to 15.3 per cent.

Fuel, gas, chemicals, and other general subsidiary trades show a steady advance in proportionate employment. The textile and dyeing industries, on the other hand, showing an increased proportion of employment up to 1851, by which time the weaving industry was taken over by machinery, present a continuous and startling decline in the proportion of employment since that date. A considerably smaller proportion of the employed classes are now engaged in these trades than in 1841. The dressmaking industries give the same result—a continuous decline in proportion of employment since 1851, though in this case the 1891 figures indicate a slight recovery. The following are the percentages:—

	Textile and Dyeing.	Dress.
1841	9.1	7.8
1851	11.1	10.3
1861	10.2	9.8
1871	9.3	8.5
1881	8.2	8.1
1891	7.6	8.3

The failure of demand for labour to keep pace in its growth with the growth of population in the main branches of the spinning and weaving industries is emphasised by Mr. Ellison. Comparing 1850 with 1878, he says :—"In spinning-mills there is an increase of about 189 per cent. in spindles, but only 63 per cent. in hands employed; and in weaving mills an increase of 360 per cent. in looms, but only 253 per cent. in operatives. This, of course, shows that the machinery has become more and more automatic or self-regulating, thus requiring the attendance of a relatively smaller number of workers."[1] When the subsidiary branches of textile industry are added the results point still more conclusively in the same direction.

	No. of Spindles.	No. of Looms.	No. of Operatives.
1850 ...	20,977,817 ...	249,627 ...	330,924
1878 ...	44,206,690 ...	514,911 ...	482,903

More recent statistics show that the relative diminution of employment in textile industries traceable since 1851, became a positive diminution after 1871, though the statistics of 1891 indicate a certain recovery.

1841	...	...	618,509[2]
1851	...	...	603,800
1861	...	...	934,500
1871	...	...	970,000
1881	...	...	962,000
1891	...	...	1,016,100[3]

The significance of these figures in relation to the demand for labour receives further emphasis when the large and rapid displacement of male by female labour is taken into account.   In the dress trades it may be observed that the absolute increase which every census, save that of 1871, discloses, is absorbed by the tailoring and millinery branches, where machinery plays a relatively unimportant part, and that in the boot and shoe trade, where there has been a greatly increased application of machinery, there has been not only a proportionate but an absolute fall-off of employment in the twenty years following 1861, though the 1891 census again brings up the absolute numbers of the boot and shoe trade to a little above the level of 1851.[4]

The branches of manufacture which show a large increase in the proportion of employment they give in 1891 as compared with 1861 are machinery and tools, printing and bookbinding, wood furniture and carriages, fuel, gas,

[1] T. Ellison, *Cotton Trade of Great Britain*, p. 74.

[2] Only 349,452, or 56.8 per cent. in factories. (Porter, p. 78.)

[3] This increase since 1881 is chiefly explained by the feverish expansion and over-production of the cotton industry. The census return for 1891 is reduced to correspond with the earlier estimates in Booth's *Occupations of the People.*

[4] The 1851 census gives 235,447, that of 1891 gives 240,000 (with an estimated deduction for clog and patten-makers).

chemicals, and unspecified trades (chiefly connected with machinery). Machinery and tools alone, among the larger manufactures, yield a large proportionate increase of employment, amounting, according to the Census Report, to 27.7 per cent. between 1881 and 1891, though dealers are included in this estimate as well as makers.

From these facts two conclusions may be drawn regarding the direct effects of machinery. First, so far as the aggregate of manufactures is concerned, the net result of the increased use of machinery has not been to offer an increased demand for labour in these industries commensurate with the growth of the working population. Second, an increased proportion of the manufacturing population is employed either in those branches of the large industries where machinery is least used, or in the smaller manufactures which are either subsidiary to the large industries, or are engaged in providing miscellaneous comforts and luxuries.

§ 3. When we turn from manufactures to other employments, we perceive that while mining and building employ an increasing proportion of the working classes since 1851, agriculture offers a rapidly diminishing employment, descending from 20.9 per cent. in 1851 to 11.5 per cent. in 1881, and 9.9 in 1891.[1]

It is, however, to the transport trades, to the distributing or "dealing" trades, and to industrial service that we must look for the notable increase of employment. All of these departments have grown far faster than the population since 1841.

	Transport.		Dealing.		Industrial Service.
1841 ...	... 2.1	...	5.3	...	3.4
1851 ...	... 4.1	...	6.5	...	4.5
1861 ...	... 4.6	...	7.1	...	4.0
1871 ...	... 4.9	...	7.8	...	6.0
1881 ...	... 5.6	...	7.8	...	6.7

The statistics of 1891 still further emphasise this movement. The transport services show an enormous rise upon 1881, yielding a proportionate employment of 7.4 per cent.

---

[1] The enormous fall between the census of 1861 and 1871 is partly attributable to changes in classification. (1) Female relatives of farmers, included in 1861, were excluded in later censuses; (2) certain changes were made in the treatment of "retired" persons.

The dealing classes show likewise a great increase. Merchants and agents increase from 285,138 to 363,037, dealers in money are about 30 per cent. more numerous, while insurance employs more than double the number employed in 1881, and six times the number of 1871. Taking drapers and mercers as indicative of the dealing class in a staple

DIAGRAM (COMPARISON OF ENGLISH EMPLOYMENTS).

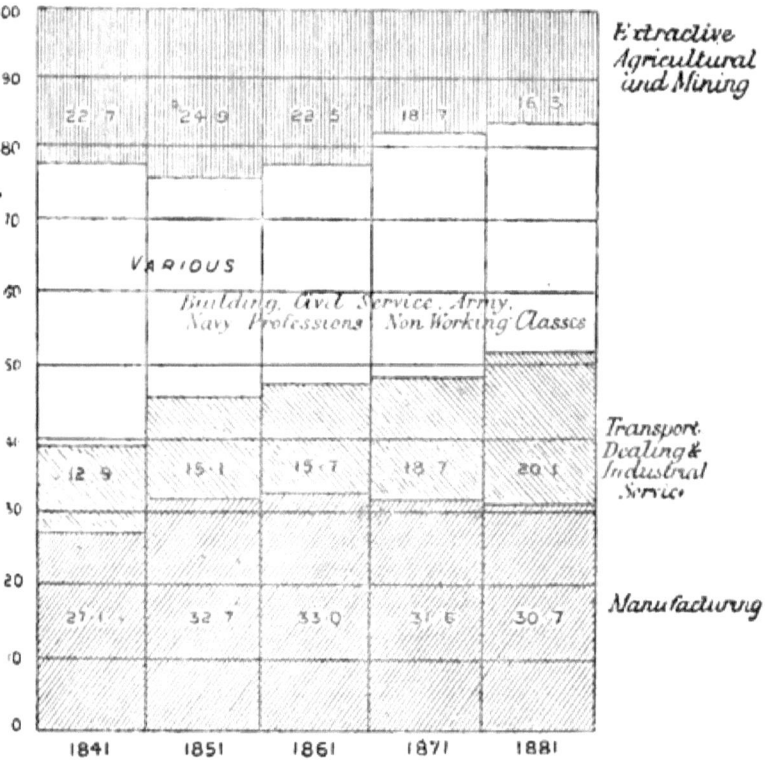

trade, we find an increase from 82,362 to 107,018, or 29.9 per cent. The numbers of those employed in thirteen representative retail trades have increased between 1881 and 1891 by not less than 27.9 per cent.

When we look at these figures there can be no doubt that one indirect result of the increased production due to the application of machinery has been increased employment in

the distributing and transport industries. This increased
employment in transport is by no means confined to the
new services of steam locomotion by land and sea. The
earlier apprehensions that railways would destroy road
traffic is not justified by experience. Though employment
on railways has of course grown very fast, road traffic has
increased almost in the same ratio.

			Railways.		Roads.
1841	...	...	.03	...	.7
1851	...	...	.3	...	.9
1861	...	...	.5	...	1.1
1871	...	...	.8	...	1.2
1881	...	...	1.2	...	1.5
1891	...	...	1.4	...	2.8

The census returns for the United States show clearly
that carts and horses have not been displaced by railways,
or, more strictly speaking, that railways have made more
cartage work than they have taken away. In 1850 the
manufacture of carriages and waggons employed 15,590 men,
in 1870 it employed 54,928. During the same period of
railway growth the number of horses in the country increased from 4,336,717 to 7,145,370. In fact, while the
population grew 66 per cent., the number of carriage and
cart makers, in spite of the increased use of labour-saving
machinery in their manufacture, grew more than 200 per
cent.

It must, however, be clearly recognised that the direct
effect of machinery upon the transport industries also is to
cause a diminished proportionate employment of labour. A
comparison of the two chief branches of steam locomotion
will bring this home.

Machinery occupies a very different place in the railway
from that which it occupies in steam transport by sea. The
engine only indirectly determines and regulates the work of
the majority of railway men. Most of them are not tenders
of machinery. Engine-driver, stoker, and guard are alone in
close direct association with the machine. To them must be
added those engaged in construction and repair within the
workshops. Pointsmen and certain station officials come
next in proximity to the machine ; shunters and porters are
also "tending" machinery, though their work is more

directly dominated by general business considerations. But
are we to say that the army of platelayers, navvies, etc.,
engaged along the line is serving machinery instead of using
tools?[1] The work of ticket clerks and collectors is only
governed by the locomotive in a very indirect way.   Though
the steam-engine is the central factor in railway work, the
bulk of the labour is skilled or unskilled work in remote
relation to the machine.   This explains why the growth of
the railway industry, after the chief work of construction has
been done, is not attended by a diminishing proportion of
employment. On the contrary, we find that railway employment increases faster than mileage and railway capital.   The
following statistics of railways in the United Kingdom
illustrate this fact:—

Year.	Mileage.	Capital (paid up).	Operatives.
1851	...	...	25,200
1861	10,865	£362,327,338	53,400
1871	15,376	£552,661,551	84,900
1881	18,175	£745,528,162	139,500
1891	20,191	£919,425,121	186,700

But when we turn to the shipping trade, where a much
larger proportion of workers is directly concerned with the
tending and direction of machinery, and trace the effect
upon employment of the application of steam, the result is
very different.

	Sailing Vessels (Tonnage).	Steamers (Tonnage).	Men on Sailing-ships.	Men on Steam-ships.
1850	3,396,359	168,474	142,730	8,700
1860	4,204,360	454,327	145,487	26,105
1870	4,577,855	1,112,934	147,207	48,755
1880	3,851,045	2,723,488	108,668	84,304
1890	2,907,405	5,037,666	84,008	129,366[2]

---

[1] The "steam-navvy" is, however, making digging a machine
industry. Thirteen men with a machine-navvy can do the work of
between 60 and 70 human navvies.

[2] The aggregate effect of the change upon employment of seamen
is traced by the following figures, in which the tonnage of sailing and
steam vessels is massed together:—

	Tonnage.		Men.
1850	3,564,833	.	151,430
1860	4,658,687	.	171,592
1870	5,690,789	.	195,962
1880	6,574,513	.	192,972
1890	7,945,071	.	213,374

If we take the period 1870-90, during which there is an absolute shrinkage of sailing tonnage, we find that this shrinkage is accompanied by a less than corresponding diminution of employment. On the other hand, the tonnage of steamships in this period increased more than fourfold, but brought with it an increase of employment which is less than threefold.

TONNAGE OF SHIPS IN RELATION TO EMPLOYMENT
OF SEAMEN.

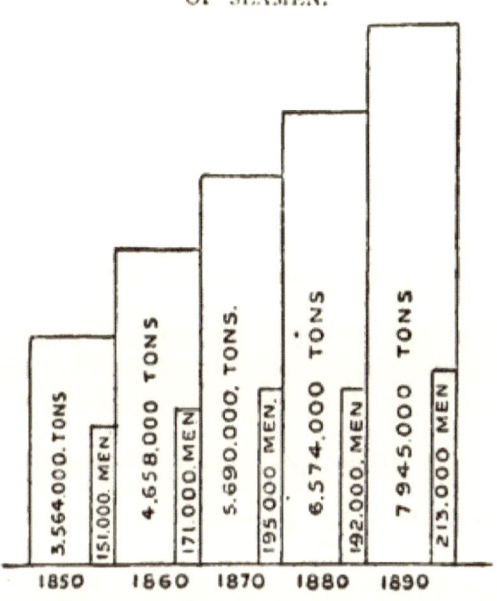

French statistics during the last half century indicate the same general movement so far as employment is concerned, though the movement is less regular.

There is the same decline in the proportion of those engaged in agriculture, though less rapid than in England, the same shrinkage of the proportion engaged in manufacture, and generally in "making" industries, and the same notable expansion of the "dealing" classes. A rapid growth of the professional and public services is common to England and France. The following percentages mark these movements in France:—[1]

[1] M. S. Levasseur, *La Population Française.* Paris, 1889.

Agricultural	1856.	1861.	1866.	1872.	1876.	1881.	1886.
classes . .	52.9	53.2	51.5	52.5	53.0	50.0	47.8
Industrial . .	29.1	27.4	28.8	24.1	25.9	25.6	25.2
Commercial .	4.5	3.9	4.0	8.4	10.7	10.5	11.5
Professional, public service, persons living on their incomes .					1	1	1
	9.1	9.2	9.5	11.1	10.3	10.2	11.1

These facts and figures seem to support the following conclusions :—

(1) That along with the increased application of machinery to the textile and other staple manufactures there has been in these industries a decrease of employment relative to the growth of the working population.

(2) That in the transport industries the increase of employment is in inverse proportion to the introduction of machinery into the several branches as a dominating factor.

(3) That the considerable diminution of agricultural employment is not compensated by any proportionate increase of manufacturing employment, but that the displaced agricultural labour finds employment in such branches of the transport and distributive trade as are less subject to machinery.

In the rough estimate of the effect of machinery upon employment, its influence upon English agriculture has been left untouched by reason of the inherent complexity of the forces which are operative. But it must not be forgotten that by far the most important factor in the decline of English agricultural employment is the transport machinery which has brought the produce of distant countries into direct competition with English agricultural produce.

So far, therefore, as the statistics of employments present a just register of the influence of machinery upon demand for labour, we are driven to conclude that the net influence of machinery is to diminish employment so far as those industries are concerned into which machinery directly

---

[1] From 1876 the transport services, which in 1886 amounted to 2.8 per cent. of the income-receiving population, were included under commercial. Taking this into consideration, a comparison of the industrial and the commercial population of 1866 and 1886 shows that while the former falls from 28.8 to 25.2, the latter rises from 4.0 to 8.7.

enters, and to increase the demand in those industries which machinery affects but slightly or indirectly. If this is true of England, which, having the start in the development of the factory system, has to a larger extent than any other country specialised in the arts of manufacture, it is probable that the net effect of machinery upon the demand for labour throughout the industrial world has been to throw a larger proportion of the population into industries where machinery does not directly enter. This general conclusion, however, for want of exact statistical inquiries conducted upon a single basis, can only be accepted as probable.

§ 4. (2) *Effects of Machinery upon the Regularity of Employment.*—The influence of machinery upon regularity of employment has a twofold significance. It has a direct bearing upon the measurement of demand for labour, which must take into account not only the number of persons employed, but the quantity of employment given to each. It has also a wider general effect upon the moral and industrial condition of the workers, and through this upon the efficiency of labour, which is attracting increased attention among students of industrial questions. The former consideration alone concerns us here. We have to distinguish—(*a*) the effects of the introduction of machinery as a disturbant of regularity of labour; (*b*) the normal effects of machine-production upon regularity of labour.

(*a*) The direct and first effect of the introduction of machinery is, as we have seen, to displace labour. The machinery causes a certain quantity of unemployment, apart from the consideration of its ultimate effect on the number of persons to whom employment is given. Professor Shield Nicholson finds two laws or tendencies which operate in reducing this disturbing influence of machinery. He holds (1) that a radical change made in the methods of production will be gradually and continuously adopted; (2) that these radical changes—these discontinuous leaps—tend to give place to advances by small increments of invention.[1]

History certainly shows that the fuller application of great inventions has been slow, though Professor Nicholson

[1] J. S. Nicholson, *Effects of Machinery on Wages*, p. 33.

somewhat over-estimates the mobility of labour and its ability to provide against impending changes. The story of the introduction of the power-loom discloses terrible sufferings among the hand-weavers of certain districts, in spite of the gradual manner in which the change was effected. The fact that along with the growth of the power-loom the number of hand-looms was long maintained, is evidence of the immobility of the hand-weavers, who kept up an irregular and ill-paid work through ignorance and incapacity to adapt themselves to changed circumstances.[1]   In most of the cases where great distress has been caused, the directly operative influence has not been introduction of machinery, but sudden change of fashion.   This was the case with the crinoline-hoop makers of Yorkshire, the straw-plaiters of Bedfordshire, Bucks, Herts, and Essex.[2]   The suddenly-executed freaks of protective tariffs seem likely to be a fruitful source of disturbance.   So far as the displacement has been due to new applications of machinery, it is no doubt generally correct to say that sufficient warning is given to enable workers to check the further flow of labour into such industries, and to divert it into other industries which are growing in accordance with the new methods of production, though much suffering is inflicted upon the labour which is already specialised in the older method of industry.

Moreover, the changes which are taking place in certain machine industries favour the increasing adaptability of labour.   Many machine processes are either common to many industries, or are so narrowly distinguished that a fairly intelligent workman accustomed to one can soon learn another.   If it is true that "the general ability, which is easily transferable from one trade to another, is every year rising in importance relatively to that manual skill and technical knowledge which are specialised in one branch of industry,"[3] we have a progressive force which tends to minimise the amount of unemployment due to new applications of specific machinery.

Professor Nicholson's second law is, however, more specu-

---

[1] Babbage, *Economy of Manufactures*, p. 230.
[2] Cf. Thorold Rogers, *Political Economy* (1869), pp. 78, 79.
[3] Marshall, *Principles of Economics*, p. 607; cf. Cunningham, *Uses and Abuses of Money*, p. 59.   See, however, *infra* Chap. ix.

lative and less reliable in its action. It seems to imply some
absolute limit to the number of great inventions. Radical
changes are no doubt generally followed by smaller increments of invention; but we can have no guarantee that
new radical changes quite as important as the earlier ones
may not occur in the future. There are no assignable limits
to the progress of mechanical invention, or to the rate at
which that progress may be effected. If certain preliminary
difficulties in the general application of electricity as a
motor can be overcome, there is every reason to believe
that, with the improved means of rapidly communicating
knowledge we possess, our factory system may be reorganised
and labour displaced far more rapidly than in the case of
steam, and at a rate which might greatly exceed the capacity
of labour to adjust itself to the new industrial conditions.
At any rate we are not at liberty to take for granted that
the mobility of labour must always keep pace with the
application of new and labour-disturbing inventions. Since
we are not able to assume that the market will be extended
pari passu with the betterment in methods of production, it
is evident that improvements in machinery must be reckoned
as a normal cause of insecurity of employment. The loss of
employment may be only "temporary," but as the life of a
working man is also temporary, such loss may as a disturbing factor in the working life have a considerable importance.

§ 5. (*b*) Whether machinery, apart from the changes due to
its introduction, favours regularity or irregularity of employment, is a question to which a tolerably definite answer can
be given. The structure of the individual factory, with its
ever-growing quantity of expensive machinery, would seem
at first sight to furnish a direct guarantee of regular employment, based upon the self-interest of the capitalist. Some
of the "sweating" trades of London are said to be maintained by the economy which can be effected by employers
who use no expensive plant or machinery, and who are
able readily to increase or diminish the number of their
employees so as to keep pace with the demands of some
"season" trade, such as fur-pulling or artificial flowers.
When the employer has charge of enormous quantities of
fixed capital, his individual interest is strongly in favour of
full and regular employment of labour. On this account,
then, machinery would seem to favour regularity of employ-

ment. On the other hand, Professor Nicholson has ample evidence in support of his statement that "great fluctuations in price occur in those commodities which require for their production a large proportion of fixed capital. These fluctuations in prices are accompanied by corresponding fluctuations in wages and irregularity of employment."[1] In a word, while it is the interest of each producer of mahcine-made goods to give regular employment, some wider industrial force compels him to irregularity. What is this force? It is uncontrolled machinery. In the several units of machine-production, the individual factories or mills, we have admirable order and accurate adjustment of parts; in the aggregate of machine-production we have no organisation, but a chaos of haphazard speculation. "Industry has not yet adapted itself to the changes in the environment produced by machinery." That is all.

Under a monetary system of commerce, though commodities still exchange for commodities, it is an essential condition of that exchange that those who possess purchasing power shall be willing to use a sufficient proportion of it to demand consumptive goods. Otherwise the production of productive goods is stimulated unduly while the demand for consumptive goods is checked,—the condition which the business man rightly regards as over-supply of the material forms of capital. When production was slower, markets[2] narrower, credit less developed, there was less danger of this big miscalculation, and the corrective forces of industry were more speedily effective. But modern machinery has enormously expanded the size of markets, the scale of competition, the complexity of demand, and production is no longer for a small, local, present demand, but for a large, world, future demand. Hence machinery is the direct material cause of these great fluctuations which bring, as their most evil consequence, irregularity of wages and employment.

[1] *Effects of Machinery on Wages.* p. 66.
[2] An increase in the space-area of a market may, however, in some cases make a trade more steady, especially in the case of an article of luxury subject to local fluctuations of fashion, etc. A narrow silk market for England meant fluctuating employment and low skill. An open market gave improved skill and stability, for though silk is still the most unsteady of the textile industries, it is far less fluctuating than was the case in the eighteenth century. (Cf. Porter, p 225.)

How far does this tend to right itself? Professor Nicholson believes that time will compel a better adjustment between machinery and its environment.

"The enormous development of steam communication and the spread of the telegraph over the whole globe have caused modern industry to develop from a gigantic star-fish, any of whose members might be destroyed without affecting the rest, into a μέγα ζῷον which is convulsed in agony by a slight injury in one part. A depression of trade is now felt as keenly in America and even in our colonies as it is here. Still, in the process of time, with the increase of organisation and decrease of unsound speculation, this extension of the market must lead to greater stability of prices; but at present the disturbing forces often outweigh altogether the supposed principal elements."[1]

The organisation of capital under the pressure of these forces is doubtless proceeding, and such organisation, when it has proceeded far enough, will indisputably lead to a decrease of unsound speculation. But these steps in organisation have been taken precisely in those industries which employ large quantities of fixed capital, and the admitted fact that severe fluctuations still take place in these industries is proof that the steadying influences of such organisation have not yet had time to assert themselves to much purpose. The competition of larger and larger masses of organised capital seems to induce heavier speculation and larger fluctuations. Not until a whole species of capital is organised into some form or degree of "combination" is the steadying influence of organisation able to predominate.

§ 6. But there is also another force which, in England at any rate, under the increased application of machinery, makes for an increase rather than a diminution of speculative production. It has been seen that the proportion of workers engaged in producing comforts and luxuries is growing, while the proportion of those producing the prime necessaries of life is declining. How far the operation of the law of diminishing returns will allow this tendency to proceed we cannot here discuss. But statistics show that this is the present tendency both in England and in the United States. Now the demand for comforts and luxuries

[1] *Op. cit.*, p. 117.

is essentially more irregular and less amenable to commercial calculation than the demand for necessaries. The
greatest economies of machine-production are found in
industries where the demand is largest, steadiest, and most
calculable. Hence the effect of machinery is to drive ever
and ever larger numbers of workers from the less to the
more unsteady employments. Moreover, there is a marked
tendency for the demand for luxuries to become more
irregular and less amenable to calculation, and a corresponding irregularity is imposed upon the trades engaged
in producing them. Twenty years ago it was possible for
Coventry ribbon-weavers to "make to stock" during the
winter months, for though silk ribbons may always be
classed as a luxury, certain patterns commanded a tolerably steady sale year after year. Now the fluctuations of
fashion are much sharper and more frequent, and a far
larger proportion of the consumers of ribbons are affected
by fashion-changes. Hence it has become more and more
difficult to forecast the market, less and less is made to
stock, more and more to order, and orders are given at
shorter and shorter notice. So looms and weavers kept
idle during a large part of the year are driven into fevered
activity of manufacture for short irregular periods. The
same applies to many other season and fashion trades.
The irregularity of demand prevents these trades from
reaping the full advantages of the economies of machinery,
though the partial application of machinery and power
facilitates the execution of orders at short notice. Hence
the increased proportion of the community's income spent
on luxuries requires an increased proportion of the labour
of the community to be expended in their production.
This signifies a drifting of labour from the more steady
forms of employment to those which are less steady and
whose unsteadiness is constantly increasing. A larger proportion of town workers is constantly passing into trades
connected with preparing and preserving animal and vegetable substances, to such industries as the hat and bonnet,
confectionery, bookbinding, trades affected by weather, holi-
day and season trades, or those in which changes in taste
and fashion are largely operative.

Thus it appears there are three modes in which modern
capitalist methods of production cause temporary unemploy-

ment. (1) Continual increments of labour-saving machinery displace a number of workers, compelling them to remain wholly or partially unemployed, until they have "adjusted" themselves to the new economic conditions. (2) Mis-calculation and temporary over-production, to which machine industries with a wide unstable market are parti-cularly prone, bring about periodic deep depressions of "trade," temporarily throwing out of work large bodies of skilled and unskilled labour. (3) Economies of machine-production in the staple industries drive an increasing proportion of labour with trades which are engaged in supplying commodities, the demand for which is more irregular, and in which therefore the fluctuations in demand for labour must be greater.

Most economists, still deeply imbued with a belief in the admirable order and economy of "the play of economic forces," appear to regard all unemployment not assignable to individual vice or incapacity as the natural and necessary effect of the process of adjustment by which industrial pro-gress is achieved, ignoring altogether the two latter classes of consideration. There is, however, reason to believe that in an average year a far larger number of the "unemployed" at any given time owe their unemployment to a temporary depression of the trade in which they are engaged, than to the fluctuations brought about by organic changes in the economic structure of the trade.

The size and importance of the "unemployment" due primarily to trade depressions is very imperfectly appreci-ated. The following statistics of the condition of the skilled labour market in the period 1886-92, based upon the reports of twenty-two trades unions, have an important bearing on this point :—

Year.	Percentage out of work.
1886	. 10.1 per cent.[1]
1887	. 8.6 "
1888	4.4 "
1889	. 1.8 "
1890	. 2.6 "
1891	. 4.45 "
1892	. 7.33 "
1893	. . . . 7.9[2] "

[1] *Board of Trade Journal*, November 1892.
[2] For twenty-six societies.

When it is remembered that these figures apply only to the well-organised trades unions, which, as a rule, comprise the best and most highly-skilled workers in the several trades, who are less likely than others to be thrown out in a "slack time," that the building and season trades are not included in the estimate, and that women's industries, notoriously more irregular than men's, are altogether ignored, it will be evident that these statistics very inadequately represent the proportion of unemployment for the aggregate of the working classes at the several periods. The *Report on Principal and Minor Textile Trades* deducts 10 per cent. from the normal wages to represent unemployment, though the year 1885, to which the figures refer, is spoken of as "fairly representative of a normal year."[1]

The injury inflicted upon the wages, working efficiency, and character of the working classes by irregular employment is, however, very inadequately represented by figures indicating the average of "unemployment" during a long period. In the first place, in such an estimate no allowance is made for the "short time," often worked for months together by large bodies of operatives. Secondly, in measuring the evil of "unemployment," we must look rather to the maximum than to the mean condition. If a man is liable to have his food supply cut off for a month at a time, no estimate showing that on the average he has more than enough to eat and drink will fairly represent the danger to which he is exposed. If once in every ten years we find that some 10 per cent. of the skilled workers, and a far larger percentage of unskilled workers, are out of employment for months together, these figures measure the economic malady of "unemployment," which is in no sense compensated by the full or excessive labour of periods of better trade.

§ 7. Our reasoning from the ascertained tendencies of machine-production points to the conclusion that, having regard to the two prime constituents in demand for labour, the number of those employed, and the regularity of employment, machinery does not, under present conditions, generally favour an increased steady demand for labour. It tends to drive an increased proportion of labour in three directions.

(1) To the invention, construction, and maintenance of

---

[1] Page xii.

machinery to make machines, the labour of machine-making being continually displaced by machines, and being thus driven to the production of machines more remote from the machines directly engaged in producing consumptive goods. The labour thus engaged must be in an ever-diminishing proportion to a given quantity of consumption. Nothing but a great increase in the quantity of consumption, or the opening of new varieties of consumption, can maintain or increase the demand for labour in these machine-making industries.

(2) To continual specialisation, subdivision, and refinement in the arts of distribution. The multiplication of merchants, agents, retailers, which, in spite of forces making for centralisation in distributive work, is so marked a feature in the English industry of the last forty years, is a natural result of the influence of machinery, in setting free from "making" processes an increased proportion of labour.

(3) To the supply of new forms of wealth, which are either (*a*) wholly non-material—*i.e.*, intellectual, artistic, or other personal services; (*b*) partly non-material—*e.g.*, works of art or skill, whose value consists chiefly in the embodiment of individual taste or spontaneous energy, or (*c*) too irregular or not sufficiently extended in demand to admit the application of machinery. The learned professions, art, science, and literature, and those branches of labour engaged in producing luxuries and luxurious services furnish a constantly increasing employment, though the supply of labour is so notoriously in excess of the demand in all such employments that a large percentage of unemployment is chronic.

So long then as a community grows in numbers, so long as individuals desire to satisfy more fully their present wants and continue to develop new wants, forming a higher or more intricate standard of consumption, there is no evidence to justify the conclusion that machinery has the effect of causing a net diminution in demand for labour, though it tends to diminish the proportion of employment in the "manufacturing" industries; but there is strong reason to believe that it tends to make employment more unstable, more precarious of tenure, and more fluctuating in market value.

CHAPTER IX.

MACHINERY AND THE QUALITY OF LABOUR.

§ 1. *Kinds of Labour which Machinery supersedes.*
§ 2. *Influence of Machine-evolution upon intensity of physical work.*
§ 3. *Machinery and the length of the working day.*
§ 4. *The Education of Working with Machinery.*
§ 5. *The levelling tendency of Machinery—The subordination of individual capacity in work.*

§ 1. In considering the influence of Machinery upon the quality of labour—*i.e.*, skill, duration, intensity, intellectuality, etc., we have first to face two questions—What are the qualities in which machinery surpasses human labour? What are the kinds of work in which machinery displaces man? Now, since the whole of industrial work consists in moving matter, the advantage of machinery must consist in the production and disposition of motive power. The general economies of machinery were found to be two[1]—(1) The increased quantity of motive force it can apply to industry; (2) greater exactitude in the regular application of motive force (*a*) in time—the exact repetition of the same acts at regulated intervals, or greater evenness in continuity, (*b*) in place—exact repetition of the same movements in space.[2] All the advantages

---

[1] Cf. *supra*, chap. iii. § 2.
[2] Karl Marx ranks the chief economies of machinery under two heads—(1) Machinery supersedes the skill of men working with tools. "The machine, which is the starting-point of the industrial revolution, supersedes the workman, who handles a single tool, by a mechanism operating with a number of similar tools, and set in motion by a single motive power, whatever the form of that power may be." (2)

imputed to machinery in the economy of human time, the utilisation of waste material, the display of concentrated force or the delicacy of manipulation, are derivable from these two general economies. Hence it follows that wherever the efficiency of labour power depends chiefly upon the output of muscular force in motive power, or precision in the regulation of muscular force, machinery will tend to displace human labour. Assuming, therefore, that displaced labour finds other employment, it will be transferred to work where machinery has not the same advantage over human labour—that is to say, to work where the muscular strain or the need for regularity of movement is less. At first sight it will thus seem to follow that every displacement of labour by machinery will bring an elevation in the quality of labour, that is, will increase the proportion of labour in employments which tax the muscles less and are less monotonous. This is in the main the conclusion towards which Professor Marshall inclines.[1]

So far as each several industry is concerned, it has been shown that the introduction of machinery signifies a net reduction of employment, unless the development of trade is largely extended by the fall of price due to the diminution in expenses of production. It cannot be assumed as a matter of course that the labour displaced by the introduction of automatic folders in printing will be employed in less automatic work connected with printing. It may be diverted from muscular monotony in printing to the less muscular monotony of providing some new species of luxury, the demand for which is not yet sufficiently large or regular to justify the application of labour-saving machinery. But even assuming that the whole or a large part of the displaced labour is engaged in work which is proved to have been less muscular or less automatic by the fact that it is not yet undertaken by machinery, it does not necessarily follow that there is a diminution in the aggregate of physical energy given out, or in the total " monotony " of labour.

Machinery supersedes the strength of man. " Increase in the size of a machine, and in the number of its working tools, calls for a more massive mechanism to drive it ; and this mechanism requires, in order to overcome its resistance, a mightier moving power than that of man." (*Capital,* vol. ii. pp. 370, 371.)

[1] *Principles of Economics,* 2nd edit., pp. 314, 322.

One direct result of the application of an increased proportion of labour power to the kinds of work which are less
"muscular" and less "automatic" in character will be a
tendency towards greater division of labour and more
specialisation in these employments. Now the economic
advantages of increased specialisation can only be obtained
by increased automatic action. Thus the routine or automatic character, which constituted the monotony of the
work in which machinery displaced these workers, will now
be imparted to the higher grades of labour in which they
are employed, and these in their turn will be advanced
towards a condition which will render them open to a new
invasion of machinery.

Since the number of productive processes falling under
machinery is thus continually increased, it will be seen that
we are not entitled to assume that every displacement of
labour by machinery will increase the proportion of labour
engaged in lighter and more interesting forms of non-
mechanical labour.

§ 2. Nor is it shown that the growth of machine-production tends to diminish the total physical strain upon the
worker, though it greatly lessens the output of purely muscular activity. As regards those workers who pass from
ordinary manual work to the tending of machinery, there
is a good deal of evidence to show that, in the typical
machine industries, their new work taxes their physical
vigour quite as severely as the old work. Professor Shield
Nicholson quotes the following striking statement from the
Cotton Factory Times:—" It is quite a common occurrence
to hear young men who are on the best side of thirty years
of age declare they are so worked up with the long mules,
coarse counts, quick speeds, and inferior material, that they
are fit for nothing at night, only going to bed and taking as
much rest as circumstances will allow. There are few
people who will credit such statements; nevertheless they
are true, and can be verified any day in the great majority
of the mills in the spinning districts."

Schulze-Gaevernitz shows that the tendency in modern
cotton-spinning and weaving, especially in England, has
been both to increase the number of spindles and looms
which an operative is called upon to tend, and to increase
the speed of spinning. "A worker tends to-day more than

twice or nearly three times as much machinery as his father did; the number of machines in use has increased more than five-fold since that time, while the workers have not quite doubled their numbers."[1] With regard to speed, "since the beginning of the seventies the speed of the spinning machines alone has increased about 15 per cent."[2]

We are not, however, at liberty to infer from Schulze-Gaevernitz's statement regarding the increased number of spindles and looms an operative tends, that an intensification of labour correspondent with this increase of machinery has taken place, nor can the increased output per operative be imputed chiefly to improved skill or energy of the operative. Much of the labour-saving character of recent improvements, especially in the carding, spinning, and intermediate processes, has reduced to an automatic state work which formerly taxed the energy of the operative, who has thereby been enabled to tend more machinery and to quicken the speed without a net increase of working energy.

In the carding, slubbing, intermediate, roving, and spinning machinery there is in every case an increase in the amount of machinery tended. But carding machinery has been revolutionised within the last few years; the drawing frame has been made to stop automatically when there is a fault, thus relieving the tender of a certain amount of supervision; in the slubbing, intermediate, and roving frames certain detailed improvements have been effected, as is also the case in the spinning mules and sizing machines.

To some extent the increased quantity of spindles, etc., and increased speed may be regarded as set off by relief due to these improvements. Moreover, though there has no doubt been some general speeding up, any exact measurement is hardly possible, for the speed of machinery is very often regulated by the amount of work each process is made to do; for example, if a roving frame makes a coarse hank, the speed of the spindles does not require to be so great as when the hank is finer; in that case the mule draws out the sliver to a greater extent than when the roving is finer, or, in other words, the mule in one case does the work of the roving frame to a certain extent.

The general opinion seems to be that in the spinning

---

[1] *Der Grossbetrieb*, p. 120.   [2] *Ibid.*, p. 117.

mills, roughly speaking, 75 per cent. of the increased output per operative may be imputed to improved machinery, 25 per cent. to increased intensity of labour in regard to quantity of spindles or "speeding up."

In the weaving processes more specific measurement is possible, though even there much depends upon the quality of yarn that is used. Here a reduction in the working day is followed by an increase in speed without any labour-saving improvements. Previous to the Factory legislation of 1878, the speed of looms was generally from 170 to 190 picks per minute during the ten hours' day. In the course of about two years after the reduction of hours (6 per cent.) the general speed had become 190 to 200 picks, without change in machinery or raw material, a growth which must have proportionately increased the intensity of the work of weaving. A deterioration in the quality of the raw material used for producing cotton cloth is also commonly assigned as a fact involving more care on the part of the weaver, and increased danger and disagreeability of work owing to the heavy sizing and steaming it has brought into vogue. It is not easy to argue much respecting increased intensity of labour from the increased average of looms attended, for, as was recently admitted in evidence before the Labour Commission, everything depends upon the class of looms and of goods they are manufacturing. "It is quite as easy to drive five looms of some classes as two of others."[1] But the prevalence of the "driving" system, by which the overlookers are paid a bonus on the product of the looms under their charge, has admittedly induced, as it was obviously designed to do, an increased intensity of labour.

Summing up the evidence, we are able to conclude that the shortening of working hours and the improvements in machinery has been attended by an increased effort per unit of labour time. In the words of an expert, "the change to those actually engaged in practical work is to lessen the amount of hard manual work of one class, but to increase their responsibility, owing to being placed in charge of more machinery, and that of a more expensive kind; while the work of the more lowly skilled will be intensified, owing to increased production, and that from

---

[1] Evidence given by Mr. T. Birtwistle.

an inferior raw material.   I mean that to the operative the improvements in machinery have been neutralised by the inferior quality of raw material used, and I think it is fair to assume that their work has been intensified at least in proportion to the increase of spindles, etc."

The direct evidence drawn from this most highly-evolved machine industry seems to justify the general opinion expressed by Professor Nicholson, "It is clear that the use of machines, though apparently labour-saving, often leads to an increase in the *quantity of labour*, negatively, by not developing the mind, positively by doing harm to the body."[1]

§ 3. When any muscular or other physical effort is required it is pretty evident that an increased duration or a greater continuity in the slighter effort may tax the body quite as severely as the less frequent or constant application of a much greater bodily force.   There can be no question but that in a competitive industrial society there exists a tendency to compensate for any saving of hard muscular, or other physical effort afforded by the intervention of machinery in two ways : first, by "forcing the pace "— *i.e.*, compelling the worker to attend more machines or to work more rapidly, thus increasing the strain, if not upon the muscles, then upon the nerves ; secondly, by extending the hours of labour.   A lighter form of labour spread over an increased period of time, or an increased number of minor muscular exertions substituted for a smaller number of heavier exertions within the same period of time, may of course amount to an increased tax upon the vital energy. It is not disputed that a general result of the factory system has been to increase the average length of the working day, if we take under our survey the whole area of machine-production in modern industrial communities.   This is only in part attributable to the fact that workers can be induced to sell the same daily output of physical energy as before, while in many cases a longer time is required for its expenditure.

---

[1] *Op. cit.*, p. 82. Babbage, in laying stress on one of the "advantages" of machinery, makes an ingenuous admission of this " forcing " power. "One of the most singular advantages we derive from machinery is the check it affords against the inattention, the idleness, or the knavery of human agents." (*Economy of Machinery*, p. 39 ; cf. also Ure, *Philo-sophy of Manufacture*, p 30.)

Another influence of equal potency is the economy of machinery effected by working longer hours. It is the combined operation of these two forces that has lengthened the average working day. Certain subsidiary influences, however, also deserve notice, especially the introduction of cheap illuminants. Before the cheap provision of gas, the working time was generally limited by daylight. Not until the first decade of this century was gas introduced into cotton-mills, and another generation elapsed before it passed in general use in manufactories and retail shops.[1] Now a portion of nature's rest has been annexed to the working day. There are, of course, powerful social forces making for a curtailment of the working day, and these forces are in many industries powerfully though indirectly aided by machinery. Perhaps it would be right to say that machinery develops two antagonistic tendencies as regards the length of the working day. Its most direct economic influence favours an extension of the working hours, for machinery untired, wasting power by idleness, favours continuous work. But when the growing pace and complexity of highly-organised machinery taxes human energy with increasing severity, and compresses an increased human effort within a given time, a certain net advantage in limiting the working day for an individual begins to emerge, and it becomes increasingly advantageous to work the machinery for shorter hours, or, where possible, to apply "shifts" of workers.[2]

But in the present stage of machine-development the economy of the shorter working day is only obtainable in a few trades and in a few countries; the general tendency is still in the direction of an extended working day.[3] The full significance of this is not confined to the fact that a larger proportion of the worker's time is consumed in the growing monotony of production. The curtailment of his time for consumption, and a consequent lessening of the subjective value of his consumables, must be set off against such increase in real wages or purchasing power as may have come to him from the increased productive power of machinery. The value of a shorter working day

[1] Porter, *Progress of the Nations*, p. 590.
[2] Cf. Schulze-Gaevernitz, p. 115.
[3] For a fuller treatment of this subject, see the next chapter.

consists not merely in the diminution of the burden of toil
it brings, but also in the fact that increased consumption
time enables the workers to get a fuller use of his purchased
consumables, and to enjoy various kinds of "free wealth"
from which he was precluded under a longer working day.[1]
So far as machinery has converted handicraftsmen into
machine-tenders, it is extremely doubtful whether it has
lessened the strain upon their energies, though we should
hesitate to give an explicit endorsement to Mill's somewhat
rhetorical verdict. "It is questionable if all the mechanical
inventions yet made have lightened the day's toil of any
human being." At any rate we have as yet no security
that machinery, owned by individuals who do not themselves tend it, shall not be used in such a way as to increase
the physical strain of those who do tend it. "There is a
temptation," as Mr. Cunningham says, "to treat the machine
as the main element in production, and to make it the
measure of what a man ought to do, instead of regarding
the man as the first consideration, and the machine as the
instrument which helps him; the machine may be made
the primary consideration, and the man may be treated as a
mere slave who tends it."[2]

§ 4. Now to come to the question of "monotony." Is the
net tendency of machinery to make labour more monotonous or less, to educate the worker or to brutalise him?
Does labour become more intellectual under the machine?
Professor Marshall, who has thoughtfully discussed this
question, inclines in favour of machinery. It takes away
manual skill, but it substitutes higher or more intellectual
forms of skill.[3] "The more delicate the machine's power
the greater is the judgment and carefulness which is called
for from those who see after it."[4] Since machinery is daily
becoming more and more delicate, it would follow that the
tending of machinery would become more and more
intellectual. The judgment of Mr. Cooke Taylor, in the
conclusion of his admirable work, *The Modern Factory
System*, is the same. "If man were merely an intellectual
animal, even only a moral and intellectual one, it could
scarcely be denied, it seems to us, that the results of the

---

[1] Cf. Patten, *The Theory of Dynamic Economics*, chap. xi.
[2] *Uses and Abuses of Money*, p. 111.
[3] *Principles*, p. 315.   [4] *Ibid.*, p. 316.

factory system have been thus far elevating." [1]   Mr. Taylor
indeed admits of the operative population that "they have
deteriorated artistically; but art is a matter of faculty, of
perception, of aptitude, rather than of intellect." This
strange severance of Art from Intellect and Morals,
especially when we bear in mind that Life itself is the finest
and most valuable of Arts, will scarcely commend itself to
deeper students of economic movements. The fuller significance of this admission will appear when the widest aspect
of the subject is discussed in our final chapter.

The question of the net intellectual effects of machinery
is not one which admits of positive answer. It would be
open to one to admit with Mr. Taylor that the operatives
were growing more intellectual, and that their contact with
machinery exercises certain educative influences, but to
deny that the direct results of machinery upon the workers
were favourable to a wide cultivation of intellectual powers,
as compared with various forms of freer and less specialised
manual labour. The intellectualisation of the town operatives (assuming the process to be taking place) may be
attributable to the thousand and one other influences of
town life rather than to machinery, save indirectly so far
as the modern industrial centre is itself the creation of
machinery.[2] It is not, I think, possible at present to offer
any clear or definite judgment. But the following dis-
tinctions seem to have some weight in forming our opinion.

The growth of machinery has acted as an enormous
stimulus to the study of natural laws. A larger and larger
proportion of human effort is absorbed in processes of invention, in the manipulation of commerce on an increasing
scale of magnitude and complexity, and in such management of machinery and men as requires and educates high
intellectual faculties of observation, judgment, and speculative imagination. Of that portion of workers who may be
said, within limits, to control machinery, there can be no

---

[1] Page 435.
[2] A similar difficulty in distinguishing town influences from specific
trade influences confronted Dr. Arlidge in his investigation into
diseases of employments. "It is a most difficult problem to solve,
especially in the case of an industrial town population, how far the
diseases met with are town-made and how far trade-made; the former
almost always predominates." (*Diseases of Occupation*, p. 33.)

question that the total effect of machinery has been highly educative.

The growing size, power, speed, complexity of machinery, undoubtedly makes the work of this class of workers " more intellectual." Some measure of these educative influences even extends to the "hand" who tends some minute portion of the machinery, so far as the proper performance of his task requires him to understand other processes than those to which his labour is directly and exclusively applied.

So likewise consideration must be taken of the skilled work of making and repairing machinery. The engineers' shop and other workshops are becoming every year a more and more important factor in the equipment of a factory or mill. But though "breakdowns" are essentially erratic and must always afford scope for ingenuity in their repair, even in the engineers' shop there is the same tendency for machinery to undertake all work of repair which can be brought under routine. So the skilled work in making and repairing machinery is continually being reduced to a minimum, and cannot be regarded, as Professor Nicholson is disposed to regard it, as a factor of growing import- ance in connection with machine-production. The more machinery is used, the more skilled work of making and repairing will be required, it might seem. But the rapidity with which machinery is invading these very functions turns the scale in the opposite direction, at any rate so far as the making of machinery is concerned. Statistics relating to the number of those engaged in making machinery and tools show that the proportion they bear to the whole working population is an increasing one ; but the rate of this increase is by no means proportionate to the rate of increase in the use of machinery. While the percentage of those engaged in making machinery and tools rises from 1.7 in 1861 to 1.8 in 1871 and 1.9 in 1881, 2.0 in 1891, the approximate increase of steam-power applied to fixed machinery and locomotives shows a much more rapid rise, —from 2,100,000 horse-power in 1860 to 3,040,000 in 1870 and 5,200,000 in 1880.[1] Moreover, an increased proportion of machinery production is for export trade, so that a large

---

[1] Mulhall, *Dictionary of Statistics*, p. 545.

quantity of the labour employed in those industries is not required to sustain the supply of machinery used in English work. In repairs of machinery, the economy effected by the system of interchangeable parts is one of growing magnitude, and tends likewise to minimise the skilled labour of repair.[1]

Finally, it should be borne in mind that in several large industries where machinery fills a prominent place, the bulk of the labour is not directly governed by the machine. This fact has already received attention in relation to railway workers. . The character of the machine certainly impresses itself upon these in different degrees, but in most cases there is a large amount of detailed freedom of action and scope for individual skill and activity.

Though the quality of intelligence and skill applied to the invention, application, and management of machinery is constantly increasing, practical authorities are almost unanimous in admitting that the proportion which this skilled work bears to the aggregate of labour in machine industry is constantly diminishing. Now, setting on one side this small proportion of intelligent labour, what are we to say of the labour of him who, under the minute subdivision enforced by machinery, is obliged to spend his working life in tending some small portion of a single machine, the whole result of which is continually to push some single commodity a single step along the journey from raw material to consumptive goods?

The factory is organised with military precision, the individual's work is definitely fixed for him; he has nothing to say as to the plan of his work or its final completion or its ultimate use. "The constant employment on one sixty-fourth part of a shoe not only offers no encouragement to mental activity, but dulls by its monotony the brains of the employee to such an extent that the power to think and reason is almost lost."[2]

The work of a machine-tender, it is urged, calls for "judgment and carefulness." So did his manual labour before the machine took it over. His "judgment and carefulness" are now confined within narrower limits

---

[1] Cf. Marshall, *Principles of Economics*, vol. i. p. 315.
[2] D. A. Wells, *Contemporary Review*, 1889, p. 392.

than before. The responsibility of the worker is greater, precisely because his work is narrowed down so as to be related to and dependent on a number of other operatives in other parts of the same machine with whom he has no direct personal concern. Such realised responsibility is an element in education, moral and intellectual. But this gain is the direct result of the minute subdivision, and must therefore be regarded as purchased by a narrowing of interest and a growing monotony of work. It is questionable whether the vast majority of machine workers get any considerable education, from the fact that the machine in conjunction with which they work represents a huge embodiment of the delicate skill and invention of many thousands of active minds, though some value may be attached to the contention that "the mere exhibition of the skill displayed and the magnitude of the operations performed in factories can scarcely fail of some educational effect."[1] The absence of any true apprenticeship in modern factories prevents the detailed worker from understanding the method and true bearing even of those processes which are closely linked to that in which he is engaged. The ordinary machine-tender, save in a very few instances, e.g., watchmaking, has no general understanding of the work of a whole department. Present conditions do not enable the "tender" to get out of machinery the educational influence he might get. Professor Nicholson expresses himself dubiously upon the educational value of the machine. "Machinery of itself does not tend to develop the mind as the sea and mountains do, but still it does not necessarily involve deterioration of general mental ability."[2] Dr. Arlidge expresses a more decided opinion. "Generally speaking, it may be asserted of machinery that it calls for little or no brain exertion on the part of those connected with its operations; it arouses no interest, and has nothing in it to quicken or brighten the intelligence, though it may sharpen the sight and stimulate muscular activity in some one limited direction."[3]

The work of machine-tending is never of course abso-

---

[1] Taylor, *Modern Factory System*, p. 435.
[2] Cf. the comparison of conditions of town and country labour in Adam Smith's *Wealth of Nations*, Bk. I., chap. x., part 2.
[3] *Diseases of Occupations*, pp. 25, 26.

lutely automatic or without spontaneity and skill. To a
certain limited extent the "tender" of machinery rules
as well as serves the machine; in seeing that his portion
of the machine works in accurate adjustment to the rest,
the qualities of care, judgment, and responsibility are
evolved. For a customary skill of wrist and eye which
speedily hardens into an instinct, is often substituted a series
of adjustments requiring accurate quantitative measurement
and conscious reference to exact standards. In such industries as those of watchmaking the factory worker, though
upon the average his work requires less manual dexterity
than the handworker in the older method, may get more
intellectual exercise in the course of his work. But though
economists have paid much attention to this industry, in
considering the character of machine-tending it is not an
average example for a comparison of machine labour and
hand labour; for the extreme delicacy of many of the
operations even under machinery, the responsibility attaching to the manipulation of expensive material, and the
minute adjustment of the numerous small parts, enable the
worker in a watch factory to get more interest and more
mental training out of his work than falls to the ordinary
worker in a textile or metal factory. Wherever the material
is of a very delicate nature and the processes involve some
close study of the individual qualities of each piece of
material, as is the case with the more valuable metals, with
some forms of pottery, with silk or lace, elements of thought
and skill survive and may be even fostered under machine
industry. A great part of modern inventiveness, however,
is engaged in devising automatic checks and indicators for
the sake of dispensing with detailed human skill and reducing the spontaneous or thoughtful elements of tending
machinery to a minimum. When this minimum is reached
the highly-paid skilled workman gives place to the low-skilled
woman or child, and eventually the process passes over
entirely into the hands of machinery. So long, however,
as human labour continues to co-operate with machinery,
certain elements of thought and spontaneity adhere to it.
These must be taken into account in any estimate of the
net educative influence of machinery. But though these
mental qualities must not be overlooked, exaggerated
importance should not be attached to them. The lay-

man is often apt to esteem too highly the nature of skilled specialist work. A locomotive superintendent of a railway was recently questioned as to the quality of engine-driving. "After twenty years' experience he declared emphatically that the very best engine-drivers were those who were most mechanical and unintelligent in their work, who cared least about the internal mechanism of the engine."[1] Yet engine-driving is far less mechanical and monotonous than ordinary tending of machinery.

So far as the man follows the machine and has his work determined for him by mechanical necessity, the educative pressure of the latter force must be predominant. Machinery, like everything else, can only teach what it practises. Order, exactitude, persistence, conformity to unbending law,—these are the lessons which must emanate from the machine. They have an important place as elements in the formation of intellectual and moral character. But of themselves they contribute a one-sided and very imperfect education. Machinery can exactly reproduce; it can, therefore, teach the lesson of exact reproduction, an education of quantitative measurements. The defect of machinery, from the educative point of view, is its absolute conservatism. The law of machinery is a law of statical order, that everything conforms to a pattern, that present actions precisely resemble past and future actions. Now the law of human life is dynamic, requiring order not as valuable in itself, but as the condition of progress. The law of human life is that no experience, no thought or feeling is an exact copy of any other. Therefore, if you confine a man to expending his energy in trying to conform exactly to the movements of a machine, you teach him to abrogate the very principle of life. Variety is of the essence of life, and machinery is the enemy of variety. This is no argument against the educative uses of machinery, but only against the exaggeration of these uses. If a workman expend a reasonable portion of his energy in following the movements of a machine, he may gain a considerable educational value; but he must also have both time and energy left to cultivate the spontaneous and progressive arts of life.

§ 5. It is often urged that the tendency of machinery is not

<hr />

[1] *The Social Horizon*, p. 22.

merely to render monotonous the activity of the individual worker, but to reduce the individual differences in workers. This criticism finds expression in the saying : " All men are equal before the machine." So far as machinery actually shifts upon natural forces work which otherwise would tax the muscular energy, it undoubtedly tends to put upon a level workers of different muscular capacity. Moreover, by taking over work which requires great precision of movement, there is a sense in which it is true that machinery tends to reduce the workers to a common level of skill, or even of un-skill.

" Whenever a process requires peculiar dexterity and steadiness of hand, it is withdrawn as soon as possible from the cunning workman, who is prone to irregularities of many kinds, and it is placed in charge of a peculiar mechanism, so self-regulating that a child can superintend it."[1]

That this is not true of the most highly-skilled or qualitative work must be conceded, but it applies with great force to the bulk of lower-skilled labour. By the aid of machinery —i.e., of the condensed embodiment of the inventor's skill, the clumsy or weak worker is rendered capable of assisting the nicest movements on a closer equality with the more skilled worker. Of course piece-work, as practised in textile and hardware industries, shows that the most complete machinery has not nearly abolished the individual differences between one worker and another. But assuming that the difference in recorded piece wages accurately represents difference in skill or capacity of work—which is not quite the case—it seems evident that there is less variation in capacity among machine-workers than among workers engaged in employments where the work is more muscular, or is conducted by human skill with simpler implements. The difference in productive capacity between an English and a Hindoo navvy is considerably greater than the difference between a Lancashire mill operative and an operative in an equally well-equipped and organised Bombay mill.

But this is by no means all that is signified by the "equality of workers before the machine." It is the adaptability of the machine to the weaker muscles and

---

[1] Ure, *Philosophy of Manufactures,* chap. i. p. 19.

intelligence of women and children that is perhaps the most important factor. The machine in its development tends to give less and less prominence to muscle and high individual skill in the mass of workers, more and more to certain qualities of body and mind which not only differ less widely in different men, but in which women and children are more nearly on a level with men. It is of course true that considerable differences of individual skill and effort survive in the typical machine industry. "Machine-weaving, for instance, simple as it seems, is divided into higher and lower grades, and most of those who work in the lower grades have not the stuff in them that is required for weaving with several colours."[1] But the general effect of machinery is to lessen rather than to increase individual differences of efficiency. The tendency of machine industry to displace male by female labour is placed beyond all question by the statistics of occupations in England, which show since 1851 a regular and considerable rise in the proportion of women to men workers in most branches of manufacture. Legal restrictions, and in the more civilised communities, the growth of a healthy public opinion, prevent the economic force from being operative to the same degree so far as children are concerned.

Those very qualities of narrowly restricted care and judgment, detailed attention, regularity and patience, which we see to be characteristic of machine work, are common human qualities in the sense that they are within the capacity of all, and that even in the degree of their development and practice there is less difference between the highly-trained adult mechanic and the raw "half-timer" than in the development and practice of such powers as machinery has superseded. It must be recognised that machinery does exercise a certain equal-ising influence by assigning a larger and larger relative importance to those faculties which are specific as com-pared with those which are individual.[2] "General ability" is coming to play a more important part in industry than specialised ability,[3] and though considerable differences may exist in the "general ability" of individuals, the differences will be smaller than in specialised abilities.[3]

[1] Marshall, *Principles of Economics*, p. 265.
[2] Cf. chap. x. [3] Cf. Marshall, p. 265.

The net influence of machinery upon the quality of labour, then, is found to differ widely according to the relation which subsists between the worker and the machine. Its educative influence, intellectual and moral, upon those concerned with the invention, management, and direction of machine industry, and upon all whose work is about machinery, but who are not detailed machine-tenders, is of a distinctly elevating character. Its effect, however, upon machine-tenders in cases where, by the duration of the working day or the intensity of the physical effort, it exhausts the productive energy of the worker, is to depress vitality and lower him in the scale of humanity by an excessive habit of conformity to the automatic movements of a non-human motor. This human injury is not adequately compensated by the education in routine and regularity which it confers, or by the slight understanding of the large co-operative purposes and methods of machine industry which his position enables him to acquire.

CHAPTER X.

THE ECONOMY OF HIGH WAGES.

§ 1. *The Economy of Low Wages.*
§ 2. *Modifications of the Early Doctrine—Sir T. Brassey's Evidence from Heavy Manual Work.*
§ 3. *Wages, Hours, and Product in Machine-industry.*
§ 4. *A General Application of the Economy of High Wages and Short Hours inadmissible.*
§ 5. *Mutual Determination of Conditions of Employment and Productivity.*
§ 6. *Compressibility of Labour and Intensification of Effort.*
§ 7. *Effective Consumption dependent upon Spare Energy of the Worker.*
§ 8. *Growth of Machinery in relation to Standard of Comfort.*
§ 9. *Economy of High Wages dependent upon Consumption.*

§ 1. The theory of a "natural" rate of wages fixed at the bare subsistence-point which was first clearly formulated in the writings of Quesnay and the so-called "physiocratic" school was little more than a rough generalisation of the facts of labour in France. But these facts, summed up in the phrase, "Il ne gagne que sa vie," and elevated to the position of a natural law, implied the general belief that a higher rate of wage would not result in a correspondent increase of the product of labour, that it would not pay an employer to give wages above the point of bare sustenance and reproduction. This dogma of the economy of cheap labour, taught in a slightly modified form by many of the leading English economists of the first half of the nineteenth century, has dominated the thought and indirectly influenced the practice of the business world. It is true that Adam Smith in a well-known passage had given

powerful utterance to a different view of the relation
between work and wages :—" The liberal reward of labour
as it encourages the propagation so it encourages the
industry of the common people.   The wages of labour are
the encouragement of industry, which, like every other
human quality, improves in proportion to the encouragement it receives."[1]   But the teaching of Ricardo, and the
writers who most closely followed him in his conception of
the industrial system, leaned heavily in favour of low wages
as the sound basis of industrial progress.

The doctrine of the economy of low wages in England
scarcely needed the formal support of the scientific economist.   It was already strongly implanted in the mind of the
eighteenth century "business man," who moralised upon
the excesses resulting from high wages much in the tone of
the business man of to-day.   It would be scarcely possible
to parody the following line of reflection :—

" The poor in the manufacturing counties will never work any
more time in general than is necessary just to live and support
their weekly debauches.   Upon the whole we may fairly aver
that a reduction of wages in the woollen manufactures would be
a national blessing and advantage and no real injury to the
poor.   By this means we might keep our trade, uphold our
rents, and reform the people into the bargain." (Smith's *Memoirs
on Wool*, vol. ii. p. 308.)

Compare with this Arthur Young's frequent suggestion that
rents should be raised in order to improve farming.[2]   So
Dr. Ure, half a century later, notwithstanding that his main
argument is for the " economy of high wages," both on the
ground that it evokes the best quality of work and because
it keeps the workman contented, is unable to avoid flatly
contradicting himself as follows :—

" High wages, instead of leading to thankfulness of temper
and improvement of mind, have, in too many cases, cherished
pride and supplied funds for supporting refractory spirits in
strikes wantonly inflicted upon one set of mill-owners after
another throughout the several districts of Lancashire for the
purpose of degrading them into a state of servitude." (*Philosophy
of Manufacture*, p. 366.)

---

[1] *Wealth of Nations*, vol. i. p. 86.
[2] Cf. *Northern Tour*, vol. ii. p. 86.

So again (p. 298):—"In fact, it was their high wages which enabled them to maintain a stipendary committee in affluence, and to pamper themselves into nervous ailments by a diet too rich and exciting for their indoor occupation."

The experiments of Robert Owen in raising wages and shortening hours in his New Lanark mills failed utterly to convince his fellow-manufacturers that a high standard of comfort among the workers would bring a correspondent rise in working efficiency.

The history of the early factory system, under which rapid fortunes were built out of the excessive toil of children and low-skilled adult workers paid at rates which were, in many instances, far below true "subsistence wages," furnished to the commercial mind a convincing argument in favour of "cheap labour," and set political economy for half a century at war with the rising sentiments of humanity.[1] Even now, the fear frequently expressed in the New World regarding the "competition of cheap labour" attests a strong survival of this theory, which held it to be the first principle of "good business" to pay as low wages as possible.

§ 2. The trend of more recent thought has been in the

---

[1] It is true that out-and-out defenders of the factories against early legislation sometimes had the audacity to assert the "economy of high wages," and to maintain that it governed the practice of early mill-owners. So Ure, "The main reason why they (*i.e.* wages) are so high is, that they form a small part of the value of the manufactured article, so that if reduced too low by a sordid master, they would render his operatives less careful, and thereby injure the quality of their work more than could be compensated by his saving in wages. The less proportion wages bear to the value of the goods, the higher, generally speaking, is the recompense of labour. The prudent master of a fine spinning-mill is most reluctant to tamper with the earnings of his spinners, and never consents to reduce them till absolutely forced to it by a want of remuneration for the capital and skill embarked in his business" (*Philosophy of Manufacture*, p. 330). This does not, however, prevent Dr. Ure from pointing out a little later the grave danger into which trade-union endeavours to raise wages drive a trade subject to the competition of " the more frugal and docile labour of the Continent and United States " (p. 363). Nor do Dr. Ure's statements regarding the high wages paid in cotton-mills, which he places at three times the agricultural wages, tally with the statistics given in the appendix of his own book (cf. p. 515). Male spinners alone received the "high wages" he names, and out of them had to pay for the labour of the assistants whom they hired to help them.

direction of a progressive modification of the doctrine of
the "economy of low wages." The common maxim that
"if you want a thing well done you must expect to pay for
it" implies some general belief in a certain correspondence
of work and wages. The clearer formulation of this idea
has been in large measure the work of economic thinkers
who have set themselves to the close study of comparative
statistics. The work in which Mr. Brassey, the great railway contractor, was engaged gave him an opportunity of
making accurate comparison of the work and wages of
workmen of various nationalities, and his son, Sir Thomas
Brassey, collected and published a number of facts bearing
upon the subject which, as regards certain kinds of work,
established a new relation between work and wages. He
found that English navvies employed upon the Grand
Trunk Railway in Canada, and receiving from 5s. to 6s. a
day, did a greater amount of work for the money than
French-Canadians paid at 3s. 6d. a day; that it was more
profitable to employ Englishmen at 3s. to 3s. 6d. upon
making Irish railways than Irishmen at 1s. 6d. to 1s. 8d.;
that "in India, although the cost of dark labour ranges
from 4½d. to 6d. a day, mile for mile the cost of railway
work is about the same as in England;" that in quarry
work, "in which Frenchmen, Irishmen, and Englishmen
were employed side by side, the Frenchman received three,
the Irishman four, and the Englishman six francs a day.
At those different rates the Englishman was found to be the
most advantageous workman of the three." Extending his
inquiries to the building trades, to mining, and to various
departments of manufactures, he found a general consensus
of opinion among employers and other men of practical
experience making for a similar conclusion. In France,
Germany, and Belgium, where wages and the standard of
living were considerably lower than in England, the cost of
turning out a given product was not less, but greater. In
the United States and in a few trades of Holland, where the
standard of comfort was as high or higher than in the
corresponding English industries, more or better work was
done. In short, the efficiency of labour was found to vary
with tolerable accuracy in accordance with the standard of
comfort or real wages.

In his introduction to his work on *Foreign Work and*

English Wages, Sir Thomas Brassey gives countenance to a theory of wages which has frequently been attributed to him, and has sometimes been accepted as a final statement of the relation of work and wages—viz., that "the cost of work, as distinguished from the daily wage of the labourer, was approximately the same in all countries." In other words, it is held that, for a given class of work, there is a fixed and uniform relation between wages and efficiency of labour for different lands and different races.

Now, to the acceptance of this judgment, considered as a foundation of a theory of comparative wages, there are certain obvious objections. In the first place, in the statement of most of the cases which are adduced to support the theory reference is made exclusively to money wages, no account being taken of differences of purchasing power in different countries. In order to establish any rational basis, the relation must be between real wages or standard of living and efficiency. Now, though it must be admitted as inherently probable that some definite relation should subsist between wages and work, or, in other words, between the standard of consumption and the standard of production, it is not *à priori* reasonable to expect this relation should be uniform as between two such countries as England and India, so that it should be a matter of economic indifference whether a piece of work is done by cheap and relatively inefficient Indian labour or by expensive and efficient English labour. Such a supposition could only stand upon one of two assumptions.

The first assumption would be that of a direct arithmetical progression in the relation of wage and work such as would require every difference in quantity of food, etc., consumed by labourers to be reflected in an exactly correspondent difference of output of productive energy—an assumption which needs no refutation, for no one would maintain that the standard of comfort furnished by wages is the sole determinant of efficiency, and that race, climate, and social environment play no part in economic production. The alternative assumption would be that of an absolute fluidity of capital and labour, which should reduce to a uniform level throughout the world the net industrial advantages, so that everywhere there was an exact quantitative relation between work and wage, production, and consumption. Though what is called a "tendency" to such uniformity may be admitted, no one acquainted with facts will be so rash as to maintain that this uniformity is even approximately reached.

§ 3. There is, then, no reason to suppose that wages, either nominal or real, bear any exact, or even a closely approximate, relation to the output of efficient work, quantity and quality being both taken into consideration. But, in truth, the evidence afforded by Sir T. Brassey does not justify a serious investigation of this theory of indifference or equivalence of work and wages. For, in the great majority of instances which he adduces, the advantage is clearly shown to rest with the labour which is most highly remunerated. The theory suggested by his evidence is, in fact, a theory of "the economy of high wages."

This theory, which has been advancing by rapid strides in recent years, and is now supported by a great quantity of carefully-collected evidence, requires more serious consideration. The evidence of Sir T. Brassey was chiefly, though by no means wholly, derived from branches of industry where muscular strength was an important element, as in road-making, railway-making, and mining; or from the building trades where machinery does not play a chief part in directing the pace and character of productive effort. It would not be unreasonable to expect that the quantitative relation between work and wages might be closer in industries where freely expended muscular labour played a more prominent part than in industries where machinery was a dominating factor, and where most of the work consisted in tending machinery. It might well be the case that it would pay to provide a high standard of physical consumption to navvies, but that it would not pay to the same extent to give high wages to factory operatives, or even to other classes of workers less subject to the strain of heavy muscular work.

In so far as the tendency of modern production is to relieve man more and more of this rough muscular work, it might happen that the true economy favoured high wages only in those kinds of work which were tending to occupy a subordinate place in the industry of the future. The earlier facts, which associated high wages with high productivity, low wages with low productivity, in textile factories and ironworks, were of a fragmentary character, and, considered as evidence of a causal connection between high wages and high productivity, were vitiated by the wide differences in the development of machinery and industrial method in the cases compared. In recent years the labours of many trained economists, some of them with close practical knowledge of the industrial arts, have collected and tabulated a vast amount of evidence upon the subject. A large number of American economists, among them General F. A. Walker, Mr. Gunton, Mr. Schoenhof, Mr. Gould, Mr. E. Atkinson, have made close researches into the relation between work and wages in America and in the chief industrial countries of Europe. A too patent advocacy of tariff reform or a shorter working day has in some cases prevented the statistics collected from receiving adequate attention, but there is no reason to doubt the substantial accuracy of the research.

The most carefully-conducted investigation has been that of Professor Schulze-Gaevernitz, who, basing his arguments upon a close study of the cotton industry, has related his conclusion most clearly to the evolution of modern machine-production. The earlier evidence merely established the fact of a co-existence between high wages and good work, low wages and bad work, without attempting scientifically to explain the connection. Dr. Schulze-Gaevernitz, by his analysis of cotton spinning and weaving, successfully formulates the observed relations between wages and product. He compares not only the present condition of the cotton industry in England and in Germany and other continental countries, but the conditions of work and wages in the English cotton industry at various times during the last seventy years, thus correcting any personal equation of national life which might to some extent vitiate conclusions based only upon international comparison. This double method of comparison yields certain definite results, which Dr. Schulze-Gaevernitz sums up in the following words:—"Where the cost of labour (*i.e.* piece wages) is lowest the conditions of labour are most favourable, the working day is shortest, and the weekly wages of the operatives are highest" (p. 133). The evolution of improved spinning and weaving machinery in

England is found to be attended by a continuous increase in the product for each worker, a fall in piece wages reflected in prices of foods, a shortening of the hours of labour, and a rise in weekly wages. The following tables, compiled by Dr. Schulze-Gaevernitz, give an accurate statement of the relations of the different movements, taking the spinning and weaving industries as wholes in England :—

SPINNING.

	Product of yarn in 1000 lbs.	Number of workers in spinning mills.	Product per worker in lbs.	Cost of labour per lb.		Average yearly wages.		
				s.	d.	£	s.	d.
1819-21	106,500	111,000	968	6	4	26	13	0
1829-31	216,500	140,000	1546	4	2	27	6	0
1844-46	523,300	190,000	2754	2	3	28	12	0
1859-61	910,000	248,000	3671	2	1	32	10	0
1880-82	1,324,000	240,000	5520	1	9	44	4	0[1]

WEAVING.

	Products in 1000 lbs.	Number of workers.	Product per worker in lbs.	Cost of labour per lb.		Average yearly income.		
				s.	d.	£	s.	d.
1819-21	80,620	250,000	322	15	5	20	18	0
1829-31	143,200	275,000	521	9	0	19	18	0[2]
1844-46	348,110	210,000	1658	3	5	24	10	0
1859-61	650,870	203,000	3206	2	9	30	15	0
1880-82	993,540	246,000	4039	2	3	39	0	0

[1] *Der Grossbetrieb*, p. 132. In regarding the advance of recent average wages it should be borne in mind that the later years contain a larger proportion of adults. In considering the net yearly wages a deduction for unemployment should be made from the sums named in the table.

[2] Account must be taken of the depressed condition of hand-loom weavers, who had not yet disappeared.

The same holds good of the growth of the cotton-weaving industry in America, as the following table shows :—

	Yearly product per worker.	Cost of labour per yard.	Yearly earnings per worker.
	Yards.	Cents.	Dollars.
1830	4,321	1.9	164
1850	12,164	1.55	190
1870	19,293	1.24	240
1884	28,032	1.07	290

Of Germany and Switzerland the same holds. Every improvement of machinery increasing the number of spindles or looms a worker can tend, or increasing the pace of the machinery and thus enlarging the output per worker, is attended by a higher weekly wage, and in general by a shortening of the hours of labour.

A detailed comparison of England, the United States, and the Continent, as regards the present condition of the cotton industry, yields the same general results. A comparison between England and the United States shows that in weaving, where wages are much higher in America, the labour is so much more efficient as to make the cost of production considerably lower than in England; in spinning, where English wages are about as highly paid, the cost of production is lower than in America (p. 156). A comparison between Switzerland and Germany, England, and America, as regards weaving, yields the following results (p. 151) :—

	Weekly product per worker	Cost per yard.	Hours of labour.	Weekly wage.
	Yards.			s. d.
Switzerland and Germany	466	0.303	12	11 8
England	706	0.275	9	16 3
America	1200	0.2	10	20 3

The low-paid, long-houred labourers of the Italian factories are easily undersold by the higher paid and more effective labour of England or America. So also a comparison between Mulhausen and the factories of the Vosges valleys shows that the more highly-paid labour of the former is the more productive.

In Russia the better-paid labour in the factories near Petersburg and in Esthland can outcompete the lower paid labour of the central governments of Vladimir and Moscow.

Schulze-Gaevernitz goes so far as to maintain that under existing conditions of low wages and long hours, the Indian factories cannot undersell their Lancashire competitors, and maintains that the stringent factory laws which are demanded for India are likely to injure Lancashire,[1] instead of giving her an advantage. The most vital points of the subject are thus summarised, after an elaborate comparison of the cotton-spinning of England and of those parts of Germany which use English machinery :—

"In England the worker tends nearly twice as much machinery as in Germany ; the machines work more quickly ; the loss as compared with the theoretic output (*i.e.*, waste of time and material) is smaller. Finally, there comes the consideration that in England the taking-off and putting-on from the spindles occupies a shorter time ; there is less breaking of threads, and the piecing of broken threads requires less time. The result is that the cost of labour per pound of yarn—especially when the work of supervision is taken into account—is decidedly smaller in England than in Germany. So the wages of the English spinners are nearly twice as high as in Germany, while the working day occupies a little over 9 hours as compared with 11 to 11½ in Germany." (P. 136.)

§ 4. From the evidence adduced by Schulze-Gaevernitz, modern industrial progress is expressed, so far as its effects on labour are concerned, in seven results : (*a*) Shorter hours of labour. (*b*) Higher weekly wage. (*c*) Lower piece-wage. (*d*) Cheaper product. (*e*) Increased product per worker.

---

[1] Here Schulze-Gaevernitz appears to strain his argument. Though official reports lay stress upon the silver question as an important factor in the rise of Bombay mills, there seems no doubt of the ability of Bombay cheap labour, independently of this, to undersell English labour for low counts of cotton in Asiatic markets. Brentano in his work, *Hours and Wages in Relation to Production*, supports Schulze-Gaevernitz.

(*f*) Increased speed of machinery. (*g*) Increased number and size of machines to the worker.

All these factors must be taken into consideration before a full judgment of the net results of machinery upon the worker can be formed. The evidence above recorded, conclusive as it is regarding the existence of some causal connection between a high standard of living and high productivity of labour, does not necessarily justify the conclusion that a business, or a federation of employers, may go ahead increasing wages and shortening hours of labour *ad libitum* in sure and certain expectation of a corresponding increase in the net productivity of labour.

Before such a conclusion is warranted, we must grasp more clearly the nature of the causal relation between high standard of living and efficiency. How far are we entitled to regard high wages and other good conditions of employment as the cause, how far as the effect of efficiency of labour? The evidence adduced simply proves that *a b c*, certain phenomena relating to efficiency—as size of product, speed of workmanship, quantity of machines tended—vary directly with *d e f*, certain other phenomena relating to wages, hours of labour, and other conditions of employment. So far as such evidence goes, we are only able to assert that the two sets of phenomena are causally related, and cannot surely determine whether variations in *a b c* are causes, or effects of concomitant variations in *d e f*, or whether both sets of phenomena are or are not governed by some third set, the variations of which affect simultaneously and proportionately the other two.

The moral which writers like Mr. Gunton and Mr. Schoenhof have sought to extract, and which has been accepted by not a few leaders in the "labour movement," is that every rise of wages and every shortening of hours will necessarily be followed by an equivalent or a more than equivalent rise in the efficiency of labour. In seeking to establish this position, special stress is laid upon the evidence of the comparative statistics of textile industries. But, in the first place, it must be pointed out that the evidence adduced does not support any such sweeping generalisation. The statistics of Mr. Gould and Mr. Schoenhof, for instance, show many cases where higher money and real wages of American operatives are not accompanied by a correspondingly larger productivity. In such cases the "cheap" labour of England is really cheap.

Again, in other cases where the higher wages of American workers are accompanied by an equivalent, or more than equivalent, increase of product, that increased product is not due entirely or chiefly to greater intensity or efficiency of labour, but to the use of more highly elaborated labour-saving machinery. The difference between the labour-cost of making and maintaining this improved machinery, and that of making and maintaining the inferior machinery it has displaced, ought clearly to be added in, where a comparison is made between the relation of net labour-cost to product in different countries, or in different stages of industrial development in the same country. The omission of this invalidates much of the reasoning of Schulze-Gaevernitz, Brentano, Rae, and other prophets of "the economy of high wages." The direct labour-cost of each commodity may be as little, or even less, than in England, but the total cost of production[1] and the selling price may be higher. Lastly, in that comparison between England and America, which is in many respects the most serviceable, because the two countries are nearest in their development of industrial methods as well as in the character of their labourers, the difference of money and of real wage is not commonly accompanied by a difference in hours of labour.

The evidence we possess does not warrant any universal or even general application of the theory of the economy of high wages. If it was generally true that by increasing wages and by shortening working hours the daily product of each labourer could be increased or even maintained, the social problem, so far as it relates to the alleviation of the poverty and misery of the lower grades of workers,

---

[1] Mr. Gould's general conclusion, from his comparison of American and European production, is "that higher daily wages in America *do not mean a correspondingly enhanced labour-cost to the manufacturers*" (*Contemporary Review*, Jan. 1893). This he holds to be partly due to superior mechanical agencies, which owe their existence to high wages, partly to superior physical force in the workers. But Mr. Gould's evidence and his conclusion here stated, taken as testimony to the "economy of high wages," are insufficient, for they only show that high wages are attended by increased output of labour, not by an increase *correspondent* to this higher wage.

would admit of an easy solution. But though it will be generally admitted that a rise of wages or of the general standard of comfort of most classes of workers will be followed by increased efficiency of labour, and that a shortening of hours will not be followed by a corresponding diminution in output, it by no means follows that it will be profitable to increase wages and shorten hours indefinitely. Just as it is admitted that the result of an equal shortening of hours will be different in every trade, so will the result of a given rise in standard of comfort be different. In some cases highly-paid labour and short hours will pay, in other cases cheaper labour and longer hours. It is not possible by dwelling upon the concomitance of high wages and good work, low wages and bad work, in many of the most highly-developed industries to appeal to the enlightened self-interest of employers for the adoption of a general rise in wages and a general shortening of hours. Because the most profitable business may often be conducted on a system which involves high wages for short intense work with highly evolved machinery, it by no means follows that other businesses may not be more profitably conducted by employing low-paid workers for long hours with simpler machinery. We are not at liberty to conclude that the early Lancashire mill-owners adopted a short-sighted policy in employing children and feeble adult labour at starvation wages.

The evidence, in particular, of Schulze-Gaevernitz certainly shows that the economy of high wages and short hours is closely linked with the development of machinery, and that when machinery is complex and capable of being worked at high pressure a net economy of high wages and short hours emerges. In this light modern machinery is seen as the direct cause of high wages and short hours. For though the object of introducing machinery is to substitute machine-tenders at low wages for skilled handicraftsmen, and though the tireless machine could be profitably worked continuously, when due regard is had to human nature it is found more profitable to work at high pressure for shorter hours and to purchase such intense work at a higher price. It must, of course, be kept in mind that high wages are often the direct cause of the introduction of improved machinery, and are an ever-present incentive to fresh mechanical inventions. This was clearly recognised half a century ago by Dr. Ure,

who names the lengthened mules, the invention of the self-
acting mule, and some of the early improvements in calico-
printing as directly attributable to this cause.[1]

But, admitting these tendencies in certain machine industries, we are not justified in relying confidently upon the
ability of a rise of wages, obtained by organisation of labour
or otherwise, to bring about such improvements of industrial
methods as will enable the higher wages to be paid without
injuring the trade, or reducing the profits below the minimum
socially required for the maintenance of a privately conducted industry.

Our evidence leads to the conclusion that, while a rise
of wages is nearly always attended by a rise of efficiency of
labour and of the product, the proportion which the increased productivity will bear to the rise of wage will differ
in every employment. Hence it is not possible to make a
general declaration in favour of a policy of high wages or of
low wages.

§ 5. The economically profitable wages and hours will vary
in accordance with many conditions, among the most
important being the development of machinery, the strain
upon muscles and nerves imposed by the work, the indoor
and sedentary character of the work, the various hygienic
conditions which attend it, the age, sex, race, and class of
the workers.

In cotton-weaving in America it pays better to employ
women at high wages to tend six, seven, or even eight
looms for short hours, than to pay lower wages to inferior
workers such as are found in Germany, Switzerland, or even
in Lancashire. But in coal-mining it appears that the
American wages are economically too high—that is to say,
the difference between American and English wages is not
compensated by an equivalent difference of output. The
gross number of tons mined by United States miners
working at wages of $326 per annum is 377, yielding a cost
of 86½ cents per ton, as compared with 79 cents per ton,

[1] Ure's *Philosophy of Manufacture*, pp. 367-369. Dr. Ure regarded
mechanical inventions as the means whereby capital should keep labour
in subjection. In describing how the "self-acting mule" came into
use he adds triumphantly: "This invention comprises the great doctrine
already propounded, that when capital enlists science in her service the
refractory hand of labour will always be taught docility " (p. 368).

the cost of North Staffordshire coal produced by miners earning $253, and turning out 322 tons per head.[1] So also a ton of Bessemer pig iron costs in labour about 50 cents more in America than in England, the American wages being about 40 per cent. higher.[2]

It is, indeed, evident from the aggregate of evidence that no determinable relation exists between cost in labour and wages for any single group of commodities.

Just as little can a general acceptance be given to the opposite contention that it is the increased efficiency of labour which causes the high wages. This is commonly the view of those business men and those economists who start from the assumption that there is some law of competition in accordance with whose operation every worker necessarily receives as much as he is worth, the full value of the product of his labour. Only by the increased efficiency of labour can wages rise, argue these people ; where wages are high the efficiency of labour is found to be high, and *vice versâ ;* therefore efficiency determines wages. Just as the advocates of the economy of high-wages theory seek by means of trade-unionism, legislation, and public opinion to raise wages and shorten hours, trusting that the increased efficiency which ensues will justify such conduct, so the others insist that technical education and an elevation of the moral and industrial character of the workers must precede and justify any rise of wages or shortening of hours, by increasing the efficiency of labour. Setting aside the assumption here involved that the share of the workers in the joint product of capital and labour is a fixed and immovable proportion, this view rests upon a mere denial of the effect which it is alleged that high wages and a rise in standard of comfort have in increasing efficiency.

The relation between wages and other conditions of employment, on the one hand, and efficiency of labour or size of product on the other, is clearly one of mutual determination. Every rise in wages, leisure, and in general standard of comfort will increase the efficiency of labour ; every increased efficiency, whether due directly to these or to other causes, will enable higher wages to be paid and shorter hours to be worked.

---

[1] " No. 64 Consular Report " (quoted Schoenhof, p. 209).
[2] Schoenhof, p. 216.

§ 6. One further point emerges from the evidence relating to efficiency and high wages. According to Schulze-Gaevernitz's formula, every fall in piece wages is attended by a rise in weekly wages. But it should be kept in mind that a rise in time wages does not necessarily mean that the price of labour measured in terms of effort has been raised. Intenser labour undergone for a shorter time may obtain a higher money wage per unit of time, but the price per unit of effort may be lower. It has been recognised that a general tendency of the later evolution of machinery has been to compress and intensify labour. In certain classes of textile labour the amount of muscular or manual labour given out in a day is larger than formerly. This is the case with the work of children employed as piecers. In Ure's day (1830) he was able to claim that during three-fourths of the time spent by children in the factory they had nothing to do. The increased quantity of spindles and the increased speed have made their labour more continuous. The same is true of the mule spinners, whose labour, even within the last few years, has been intensified by increased size of the mule. Though as a rule machinery tends to take over the heavier forms of muscular work, it also tends to multiply the minor calls upon the muscles, until the total strain is not much less than before. What relief is obtained from muscular effort is compensated by a growing strain upon the nerves and upon the attention. Moreover, as the machinery grows more complex, numerous, and costly, the responsibility of the machine-tender is increased. To some considerable extent the new effort imposed upon the worker is of a more refined order than the heavy muscular work it has replaced. But its tax upon the physique is an ever-growing one. "A hand-loom weaver can work thirteen hours a day, but to get a six-loom weaver to work thirteen hours is a physical impossibility."[1] The complexity of modern machinery and the superhuman celerity of which it is capable suggest continually an increased compression of human labour, an increased output of effort per unit of time. This has been rendered possible by acquired skill and improved physique ensuing on a higher standard of living. But it is evident that, where it appears that each

---

[1] *Der Grossbetrieb*, p. 167.

rise in the standard of living and each shortening of the
working-day has been accompanied by a severer strain
either upon muscles, nerves, or mental energy during the
shorter working day, we are not entitled to regard the
higher wages and shorter hours as clear gain for the worker.
Some limits are necessarily imposed upon this compressibility of working effort. It would clearly be impossible by a number of rapid reductions of the working
day and increases of time wages to force the effectiveness
of an hour's labour beyond a certain limit for the workers.
Human nature must place limits upon the compression.
Though it may be better for a weaver to tend four looms
during the English factory day for the moderate wage of
16s. a week than to earn 11s. 8d. by tending two looms in
Germany for twelve hours a day, it does not follow that it is
better to earn 20s. 3d. in America by tending six, seven, or
even eight looms for a ten-hours day,[1] or that the American's
condition would be improved if the eight-hours day was
purchased at the expense of adding another loom for each
worker.

The gain which accrues from high wages and a larger
amount of leisure, over which the higher consumption
shall be spread, may be more than counteracted by an
undue strain upon the nerves or muscles during the shorter
day. This difficulty, as we have seen, is not adequately met
by assigning the heavier muscular work more and more to
machinery, if the possible activity of this same machinery
is made a pretext for forcing the pace of such work as
devolves upon machine-tenders.

In many kinds of work, though by no means in all,
an increase of the amount of work packed into an hour
could be obtained by a reduction of the working-day;
but two considerations should act in determining the progressive movement in this direction: first, the objective
economic question of the quantitative relation between the
successive decrements of the working-day and the increments of labour put into each hour; second, the subjective
economic question of the effect of the more compressed
labour upon the worker considered both as worker and
as consumer.

---

[1] *Vide supra*, p. 269. These wages, however, are the average of all
the labour employed in the weaving-sheds, not of "weavers" alone.

There is not wanting evidence to show that increased leisure and higher wages can be bought too dear.

In drawing attention to this consideration it must not, however, be assumed that the increase of real wages and shortening of hours traced in progressive industries are necessarily accompanied by a corresponding increase in the compression of labour. In the textile and iron industries, for example, it is evident (*pace* Karl Marx) that the operatives had obtained some portion of the increased productivity of improved machinery in a rise of wages. Even where more machinery is tended we are not entitled to assume a correspondent increase in felt effort or strain upon the worker. A real growth of skill or efficiency will enable an increased amount of machinery to be tended with no greater subjective effort than a smaller amount formerly required. But while allowance should be made for this, the history of the factory system, both in England and in other countries, clearly indicates that factory labour is more intense than formerly, not, perhaps, in its tax upon the muscles, but in the growing strain it imposes upon the nervous system of the operatives.

The importance of this point is frequently ignored alike by advocates of a shorter working-day and by those who insist that the chief aim of workers should be to make their labour more productive. So far as the higher efficiency simply means more skill and involves no increased effort it is pure gain, but where increased effort is required the question is one requiring close and detailed consideration.

§ 7. Another effect of over-compressed labour deserves a word.

The close relation between higher wages and shorter hours is generally acknowledged. A rise of money wages which affects the standard of living by introducing such changes in consumption as require for their full yield of benefit or satisfaction an increase of consuming-time can only be made effective by a diminution in the producing time or hours of labour. When, for example, the new wants, whose satisfaction would be naturally sought from a rise of the standard living, are of an intellectual order, involving not merely the purchase of books, etc., but the time to read such books, this benefit requires that the higher wages should be supplemented by a diminution in the hours of labour in cases where the latter are unduly long. But it is not so clearly recognised that such questions cannot be determined without reference to the question of intensity of labour. Yet it is evident that an eight-hours day of more compressed labour might be of a more exhausting character than a ten-hours day of less intense labour and disqualify a worker from receiving the benefits of the opportunities of education open to him more than the longer hours of less intense labour. The advantage of the addition of two hours of leisure might be outweighed by the diminished value attached to each leisure hour. In other words, the excess of intense work might be worse in its effects than the excess of more extended work. This possibility is often overlooked in the arguments of those who support the movement towards a shorter working-day by maintaining that each unit of labour-time will be more productive. When the argument concerns itself merely with alleging the influence of higher wages, without shorter hours, upon the efficiency of labour, this neglect of the consideration of intense labour has a more urgent import- ance. It may be gravely doubted whether the benefit of the higher wages of the Massachusetts weavers is not over- balanced by the increased effort of tending so large a number of looms for hours which are longer than the English factory day. The exhausting character of such labour is likely to leave its mark in diminishing the real utility or satisfaction of the nominally higher standard of living which the high wages render possible. Where the increased productivity of labour is largely due to the improved machinery or methods of production which are stimulated by high wages without a corresponding intensi- fication of the labour itself, the gain to labour is clear. But the possibility that short hours and high wages may stimulate an injurious compression of the output of pro- ductive effort is one which must not be overlooked in considering the influence of new industrial methods upon labour.

§ 8. Duration of labour, intensity of labour, and wages, in their mutual relations, must be studied together in any attempt to estimate the tendencies of capitalist production. Nor can we expect their relations to be the same in any two industries. Where labour is thinly extended over an in-ordinately long working-day, as in the Indian mills, it is probable that such improvements of organisation as might shorten the hours to those of an ordinary English factory day, and intensify the labour, would be a benefit, and the rise of wages which might follow would bring a double gain to the workers.   But any endeavour to further shorten and intensify the working-day might injure the workers, even though their output were increased.   Such an instance, however, may serve well to bring home the relativity which is involved in all such questions.   The net benefit derived from a particular quantitative relation between hours of labour, intensity, and earnings would probably be widely different for English and for Indian textile workers.   It would, *à priori*, be unreasonable to expect that the working-day which would bring the greatest net advantage to both should be of the same duration.   So also it may well be possible that the more energetic nervous temperament of the American operative may qualify him or her for a shorter and intenser working-day than would suit the Lancashire operative.   It is the inseparable relation of the three factors —duration, intensity, and earnings—which is the important point.   But in considering earnings, not merely the money wage, nor even the purchasing power of the money, but the net advantage which can be obtained by consuming what is purchased must be understood, if we are to take a scientific view of the question.

It should be clearly recognised that in the consideration of all practical reforms affecting the conditions of labour, the "wages" question cannot be dissociated from the "hours" question, nor both from the "intensity of labour" question ; and that any endeavour to simplify discussion, or to facilitate "labour movements," by seeking a separate solution for each is futile, because it is unscientific.   When any industrial change is contemplated, it should be regarded, from the "labour" point of view, in its influence upon the net welfare of the workers, due regard being given, not merely to its effect upon wage, hours, and intensity, but to the complex and changing relations which subsist in each trade, in each country, and in each stage of industrial development between the three.

But although, when we bear in mind the effects of

machinery in imparting intensity and monotony to labour, in increasing the number of workers engaged in sedentary indoor occupations, and in compelling an ever larger proportion of the working population to live in crowded and unhealthy towns, the net benefit of machinery to the working classes may be questioned, the growth of machinery has been clearly attended by an improved standard of material comfort among the machine-workers, taking the objective measurement of comfort.

Whatever allowance may be made for the effects of increased intensity of labour, and the indirect influences of machinery, the bulk of evidence clearly indicates that machine-tenders are better fed, clothed, and housed than the hand-workers whose place they take, and that every increase in the efficiency and complexity of machinery is attended by a rise in real wages. The best machinery requires for its economical use a fair standard of living among the workers who co-operate with it, and with the further development of machinery in each industry we may anticipate a further rise of this standard, though we are not entitled to assume that this natural and necessary progress of comfort among machine-workers has no fixed limit, and that it is equally applicable to all industries and all countries.

It might, therefore, appear that as one industry after another fell under machine-production, the tendency of machine-development must necessarily make for a general elevation of the standard of comfort among the working classes. It may very well be the case that the net influence of machinery is in this direction. But it must not be forgotten that the increased spread of machine-production does not appear to engage a larger proportion of the working population in machine-tending. Indeed, if we may judge by the recent history of the most highly-evolved textile industries, we are entitled to expect that, when machinery has got firm hold of all those industries which lend themselves easily to routine production, the proportion of the whole working population engaged directly in machine-tending will continually decrease, a larger and larger proportion being occupied in those parts of the transport and distributing industries which do not lend themselves conveniently to machinery, and in personal services. If this is so, we cannot look upon the evolution of machinery, with its demand for intenser and more efficient labour, as an adequate guarantee of a necessary improvement in the standard of comfort of the working classes as a whole. To put the matter shortly, we have no evidence to show that a rise in the standard of material comfort of shopmen, writing clerks, school-teachers, 'busmen, agents, warehousemen, dockers, policemen, sandwich-men, and other classes of labour whose proportion is increasing in our industrial society, will be attended by so considerable a rise in the efficiency of their labour as to stimulate a series of such rises. The automatic movement which Schulze-Gaevernitz and others trace in the typical machine-industries is not shown to apply to industry as a whole, and if the tendency of machine-development is to absorb a larger proportion of the work but a smaller proportion of the workers, it is not possible to found large hopes for the future of the working classes upon this movement of the earning of high wages in machine-industry.

§ 9. But though the individual self-interest of the producer cannot be relied upon to favour progressive wages, except in certain industries and up to a certain point, the collective interest of consumers lends stronger support to "the economy of high wages." We have seen that the possession of an excessive proportion of "power to consume" by classes who, because their normal healthy wants are already fully satisfied, refuse to exert this power, and insist upon storing it in unneeded forms of capital, is directly responsible for the slack employment of capital and labour. If the operation of industrial forces throw an increased proportion of the "power to consume" into the hands of the working classes, who will use it not to postpone consumption but to raise their standard of material and intellectual comfort, a fuller and more regular employment of labour and capital must follow. If the stronger organisation of labour is able to raise wages, and the higher wages are used to demand more and better articles of consumption, a direct stimulus to the efficiency of capital and labour is thus applied. The true issue, however, must not be shirked. If the power of purchase now "saved" by the wealthier classes passed into the hands of the workers in higher money wages, and was not spent by them in raising their standard of comfort, but

was "invested" in various forms of capital, no stimulus to
industry would be afforded; the "savings" of one class
would have fallen into the hands of another class, and their
excess would operate to restrict industry precisely as it now
operates. Though we would gladly see in the possession of
the working classes an increased proportion of those forms
of capital which are socially useful, this simple act of
transfer, however brought about, would furnish no stimulus
to the aggregate industry. From the standpoint of the
community nothing else than a rise in the average standard
of current consumption can stimulate industry. When it is
clearly grasped that a demand for commodities is the only
demand for the use of labour and of capital, and not merely
determines in what particular direction these requisites of
production shall be applied, the hope of the future of our
industry is seen to rest largely upon the confident belief
that the working classes will use their higher wages not to
draw interest from investments (a self-destructive policy) but
to raise their standard of life by the current satisfaction of
all those wholesome desires of body and mind which lie
latent under an "economy of low wages." The satisfaction
of new good human desires, by endowing life with more hope
and interest, will render all intelligent exertion more effective, by distributing demand over a larger variety of commodities will give a fuller utilisation both of natural and
human resources, and by redressing the dislocated balance
of production and consumption due to inequality of purchasing power, will justify high wages by increased fulness
and regularity of work. But it must be clearly recognised
that however desirable "saving" may seem to be as a moral
virtue of the working classes, any large practice of saving
undertaken before and in preference to an elevation of
current consumption, will necessarily cancel the economic
advantages just dwelt upon. Just as the wise individual will
see he cannot afford to "save" until he has made full
provision for the maintenance of his family in full physical
efficiency, so the wise working class will insist upon utilising
earlier accesses of wages in promoting the physical and
intellectual efficiency of themselves and their families before
they endeavour to "invest" any considerable portion of
their increased wages. Mr. Gould puts this point very
plainly and convincingly: "Where economic gains are small,

savings mean a relatively low plane of social existence. A parsimonious people are never progressive, neither are they, as a rule, industrially efficient. It is the man with many wants—not luxurious fancies, but real legitimate wants— who works hard to satisfy his aspirations, and he it is who is worth hiring. Let economists still teach the utility and the necessity of saving, but let the sociologist as firmly insist that to so far practise economy as to prevent in the nineteenth century a corresponding advance in civilisation of the working with the other classes is morally inequitable and industrially bad policy. I am not sorry that the American does not save more. Neither am I sure but that if many working-class communities I have visited on the Continent were socially more ambitious, there would not be less danger from Radical theories. One of the most intelligent manufacturers I ever met told me a few years ago he would be only too glad to pay higher wages to his working people, provided they would spend the excess legitimately and not hoard it. He knew that in the end he should gain thereby, since the ministering to new wants only begets others."[1] If there are theoretic economists who still hold that "a demand for commodities is not a demand for labour," they may be reminded that a paradox is not necessarily true. In fact, this particular paradox is seen to be sustained by a combination of slipshod reasoning and moral prejudice. The growing opinion of economic students is veering round to register in theory the firm empirical judgment from which the business world has never swerved, that a high rate of consumption is the surest guarantee of progressive trade. The surest support of the "economy of high wages" is the conviction that it will operate as a stimulus to industry through increased consumption. The working classes, especially in the United States and in England, show a growing tendency to employ their higher wages in progressive consumption. Upon the steady operation of this tendency the economic future of the working classes, and of industry in general, largely depends.

[1] E. R. L. Gould, *Contemporary Review*, January 1893.

CHAPTER XI.

SOME EFFECTS OF MODERN INDUSTRY UPON THE WORKERS AS CONSUMERS.

§ 1. *How far the different Working Classes gain from the Fall of Prices.*

§ 2. *Part of the Economy of Machine-production compensated by the growing Work of Distribution.*

§ 3. *The Lowest Class of Workers gains least from Machine-production.*

§ 1. In considering the effect of machine-production upon a body of workers engaged in some particular industry we are not confined to tracing the effects of improvements in the arts and methods of that single branch of production. As consumers they share in the improvements introduced into other industries reflected in a fall of retail prices. Insomuch as all English workers consume bread they are benefited by the establishment of a new American railway or the invention of new milling machinery which lowers the price of bread; as all consume boots the advantage which the introduction of boot-making machinery confers upon the workers is not confined to the higher wages which may be paid to some operatives in the boot factory, but is extended to all the workers who can buy cheaper boots.

How far do methods of modern capitalist production tend to benefit the labourer in his capacity as consumer?

Economic theory is in tolerably close accord with experience in the answer it gives to this question. Each portion of the working classes gains in its capacity of consumer from improved methods of production in proportion to the amount by which its income exceeds the bare subsistence wage of unskilled workers. The highly-paid mechanic gains most, the sweated worker least. The worker earning forty shillings per week gains much more than twice as much as the worker earning twenty shillings from each general cheapening in the cost of production. There are several reasons why this is so.

1. Where there exists a constant over-supply of labour competing for what must be regarded at any particular time as a fixed quantity of employment, wages are determined with tolerably close reference to the lowest standard of living among that class of workers, and not by any fixed or customary money wage. This is particularly the case in the "sweating" trades of large towns. Here such improvements in machinery and methods of industry as lower the price of articles which fall within the "standard of living" of this class are liable to be speedily reflected in a fall of money wages paid for such low-skilled work. In other words, a "bare subsistence wage" does not gain by a fall in the price of the articles which belong to its standard of comfort.

Even in the lowest kinds of work there is no doubt some tendency to stick to the former money wage and thus to raise somewhat the standard of real wages, but where the competition is keenest this *vis inertiæ* is liable to be overborne, and money wages fall with prices. As we rise to the more highly skilled, paid, and organised grades of labour, we come to workers who are less exposed to the direct constant strain of competition, where there is not a chronic over-supply of labour. Here a fall of retail prices is not necessarily or speedily followed by any corresponding fall of money wages, and the results of the higher real wages enjoyed for a time impress themselves in a higher habitual standard of comfort and strengthen the resistance which is offered to any attempt to lower money wages, even though the attempt may be made at a time when an over-supply of labour does exist.

In proportion as a class of workers is highly paid, educated, and organised, it is able to gain the benefit which improved machinery brings to the consumer, because it is better able to resist the economic tendency to determine wages by reference to a standard of comfort independent of monetary considerations. So far as the lowest waged and most closely competing labourers have gained by the fall of prices, it has been due to the pressure of sentiment on the part of the better class of employers and of the public against the lowering of money wages, even where the smaller sum of money will purchase as much as a larger sum previously.

2. The smaller the income the larger the proportion of it that is spent upon commodities whose expense of production and whose price is less affected by machinery. Machine-production, by the fall of prices it brings, has benefited people in direct proportion to their income. The articles which have fallen most rapidly in price are those comforts and luxuries into which machine-production enters most largely. The aristocracy of the working classes, whose standard of comfort includes watches, pianos, books, and bicycles, has gained much more by the fall of prices than those who are obliged to spend all their wages on the purchase of bare necessaries of life. The gain of the former is manifold and great, the benefit of the latter is confined to the cheapening of bread and groceries—a great benefit when measured in terms of improved livelihood no doubt, but small when compared with the increase of purchasing power conferred by modern production upon the Lancashire factory family, with its £3 or £4 a week, and in large measure counterbalanced by the increased proportion of the income, which, in the case of town operatives, goes as rent and price of vegetables, dairy produce, and other commodities which have risen in price.

3. The highly-paid operatives generally work the shortest hours, the low-paid the longest. So far as this is not compensated by an increased intensity of labour on the part of those working short hours, it implies an increased capacity of making the most out of their wages. Longer leisure enables a worker to make the most of his consumption, he can lay out his wages more carefully, is less tempted to squander his money in excesses directly engendered by the reaction from excessive labour, and can get a fuller enjoyment and benefit from the use of the consumables which he purchases. A large and increasing number of the cheapest and the most intrinsically valuable commodities, of an intellectual, artistic, and spiritual character, are only open to the beneficial consumption of

those who have more leisure at their command than is
yet the lot of the low-skilled workers in our towns.

§ 2. If we compare the statistics of wages we shall find
that the largest proportionate rise of money wages has been
in the highly-organised machine industries, and that the
benefit which machinery confers upon the workers in the
capacity of consumers falls chiefly to the same workers.

It must not, however, be assumed that improved methods
of production yield their full benefit through competition
to the consuming public.   On the contrary, much of the
economy of machine-production fails to exercise its full
influence upon retail prices.   There are two chief reasons
for this failure.   To one of these adequate attention has
been already drawn, the growth of definite forms of capitalist monopoly, which secure at some point or other in the
production of a commodity, as higher profits, that which
under free competition would pass to the consumer through
lower shop prices.   The second consists in the abnormal
growth of the distributive classes, whose multiplication is
caused by the limitation which the economy of machinery
imposes upon the amount of capital and labour which can
find profitable employment in the extractive and manufacturing processes.   A larger and larger number of industrial workers obtain a living by a subdivision of the work of
distribution carried to a point far beyond the bounds of
social utility.   For, on the one hand, when competition of
manufacturers and transporters is more and more confined
to a small number of large businesses which, because their
united power of production largely transcends the consumption at profitable prices, are driven into closer competition, a larger amount of labour is continually engaged
in the attempt of each firm to secure for itself the largest
share of business at the expense of another firm.   On the
other hand, shut out from effective or profitable competition in the manufacturing industries, a larger amount
of capital and labour seeks to engage in those departments
of the distributive trade where new-comers have a better
chance, and where by local settlement or otherwise they
have an opportunity of sharing the amount of distribution
that is to be done.   Hence a fall of wholesale prices is
usually not reflected in a corresponding fall of retail prices,
for competition in retail trade, as J. S. Mill clearly recog-

nised, " often, instead of lowering prices, merely divides the gains of the high price among a greater number of dealers."[1]

§ 3. The wide difference between the economic position of the skilled mechanic and the common labourer shows how fallacious is that treatment of the influence of machinery upon the condition of the working classes which is commonly found in treatises of political economy. To present a comparative picture of the progress of the working classes during the last half century, which assigns to them an increase of money wages, obtained by averaging a number of rises in different employments, and reduces this increase to real wages without any reference to the different use of wages by different classes, is an unscientific and mischievous method of dealing with one of the most important economic questions. The influence of machine-production appears to be widely different upon the skilled mechanic and the common labourer considered both as producers and consumers, and tends to a wide difference in standard of comfort between the two classes. This difference is further enhanced by the indirect assistance which machinery and large-scale industry gives to the skilled workers to combine and thus frequently to secure wages higher than are economically requisite to secure their efficient work. On the other hand, growing feelings of humanity and a vague but genuine feeling of social justice in an ever larger portion of the public often enable the low-skilled worker to secure a higher standard of comfort than the operation of economic competition alone would enable him to reach. But after due allowance is made for this, the conclusion is forced upon us that the gain of machine-production, so far as an increase in real wages is concerned, has been chiefly taken by the highly-skilled and highly-waged workers, and that as the character of work and wages descends, the proportionate gain accruing from the vast increase of productive power rapidly diminishes, the lowest classes of workers obtaining but an insignificant share.

[1] *Principles of Political Economy*, Bk. ii., chap. iv. § 3.

CHAPTER XII.

WOMEN IN MODERN INDUSTRY.

§ 1. *Growing Employment of Women in Manufacture.*
§ 2. *Machinery favours Employment of Women.*
§ 3. *Wages of Women lower than of Men.*
§ 4. *Causes of Lower Wages for Women.*
§ 5. *Smaller Productivity or Efficiency of Women's Labour.*
§ 6. *Factors enlarging the scope of Women's Wage-work.*
§ 7. *"Minimum Wage" lower for Women—Her Labour often subsidised from other sources.*
§ 8. *Woman's Contribution to the Family Wages—Effect of Woman's Work upon Man's Wages.*
§ 9. *Tendency of Woman's Wage to low uniform level.*
§ 10. *Custom and Competition as determinants of Low Wages.*
§ 11. *Lack of Organisation among Women—Effect on Wages.*
§ 12. *Over-supply of Labour in Women's Employments the root-evil.*
§ 13. *Low Wages the chief cause of alleged Low "Value" of Woman's Work.*
§ 14. *Industrial Position of Woman analogous to that of Low-skilled Men.*
§ 15. *Damage to Home-life arising from Women's Wage-work.*

§ 1. Modern manufacture with machinery favours the employment of women as compared with men. Each census during the last half century shows that in England women are entering more largely into every department of manufacture, excepting certain branches of metal work, machine-making and shipbuilding, etc., where great muscular strength is a prime factor in success.

The following table,[1] indicating the number of males and

---

[1] The figures for the periods 1841 to 1881 are drawn from Mr. Charles Booth's *Occupations of the People*. The figures for 1891 are drawn from the Census Report, and arranged as nearly as possible in accordance with Mr. Booth's classification.

	M. 1841.	F.	M. 1851.	F.	M. 1861.	F.	M. 1871.	F.	M. 1881.	F.	M. 1891.	F.
Earthenware .	23,600	7,400	34,800	11,700	42,500	13,400	49,700	17,700	52,300	19,700	64,300	23,800
Fuel, Gas, Chemicals .	6,890	300	16,400	1,700	24,800	1,500	34,900	4,100	44,000	4,000	66,400	6,300
Fur, Leather, Glue .	31,600	2,400	44,500	6,500	47,300	8,300	43,400	10,200	49,400	12,300	59,100	18,200
Wood Furniture, Carriages, etc. .	147,500	4,900	180,200	8,900	202,200	14,100	214,200	19,500	221,600	18,400	253,000	23,300
Paper, Floorcloth, Waterproof, etc. .	8,900	3,200	13,600	8,300	14,000	10,700	20,300	13,400	24,000	22,300	28,600	34,200
Textiles, Dyeing .	346,200	257,600	462,400	472,100	439,700	526,500	414,500	555,500	396,400	566,200	430,500	555,600
Dress .	343,600	177,200	397,500	471,200	378,000	550,900	303,300	552,700	341,700	609,300	353,500	681,300
Food, Drink, Smoking .	82,700	8,000	120,900	12,400	133,400	15,600	145,700	18,500	162,300	28,900	173,100	60,200
Watches, Instruments, Toys .	19,000	800	23,500	1,200	32,800	2,000	35,900	3,000	41,700	3,400	44,600	5,600
Printing, Bookbinding, etc. .	21,100	1,500	30,400	3,800	41,300	6,200	57,000	8,600	75,000	13,100	102,100	19,100
TOTAL .	1,030,600	463,600	1,324,200	997,000	1,357,200	1,150,100	1,385,500	1,203,200	1,401,000	1,299,500	1,576,100	1,447,600

females employed in the leading groups of manufactures at
decennial points since 1841, clearly indicates the nature
and extent of the industrial advance of woman.

From this table we perceive that while the number of
males engaged in these manufactures has increased by 53
per cent. during the half century 1841 to 1891, the number
of females has increased by 221 per cent.   This movement,
which must be regarded partly as a displacement of male
by female labour, partly as an absorption of new manufactures by female labour, proceeded with great rapidity from

TEXTILE WORKERS.

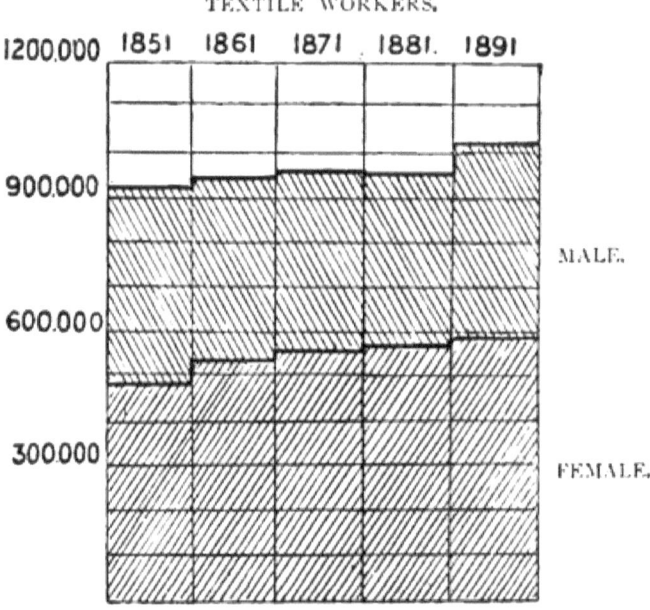

the beginning of the period up to 1881.   The check apparent
in the last decennium, in which the number of males employed seems to have increased faster than that of the
females, does not, however, indicate a reversal or even a
suspension of the industrial movement.   It is attributable
to an abnormal change in a single great industry—the
cotton trade; excluding this, the employment of females
in each group of manufactures has grown faster than that
of males.

If we confine our survey to adults (excluding males and females below fifteen) the rapid and regular advance of female employment as compared with male is still more striking.

When we turn to the textile industries and to dress, the change of proportionate employment among the sexes is very noteworthy. In textiles and dyeing there was a continuous decline in the absolute numbers of adult male

DRESS WORKERS.

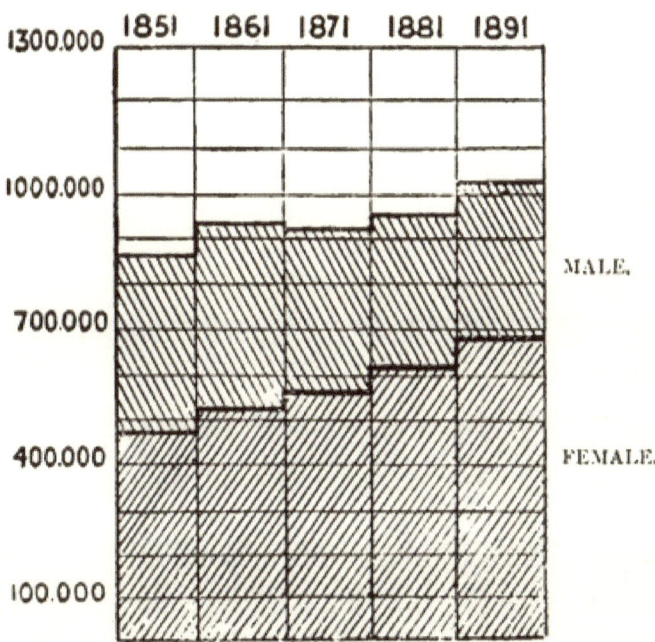

workers and a continuous increase of female workers up to 1881. In 1851 there were 394,400 men employed, in 1881 the number had fallen to 345,900, while the women had risen during the same period from 390,800 to 500,200. The census figures for 1891 mark a decided check in this movement. Adult male workers show an increase of 34,000 upon the 1881 figures in the textile industries, while the increase of female workers is only 15,000. This is due, on the one hand, to the feverish and disordered expansion of

the cotton industry, which offers a larger proportion of male
employment than other textile branches ; on the other hand,
to the alarming decay of the lace and linen industries, which
show an absolute decline of female employment amounting
to nearly 13,000.   So likewise in the dress industries 377,400
men were employed in 1851, and 335,900 in 1881, while

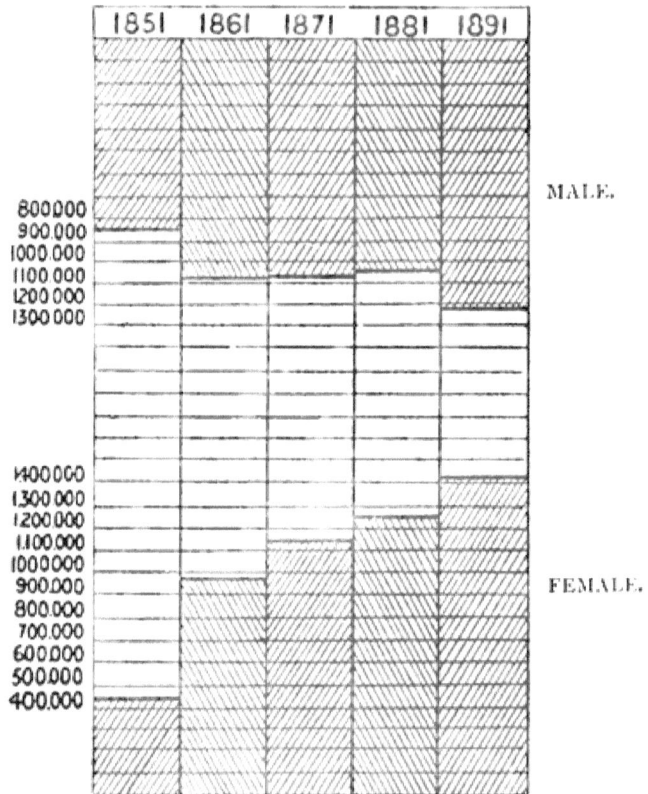

the number of women employed had increased from
441,000 to 589,000.[1]

<hr />

[1] Here also the figures for 1891 give a result slightly divergent from
the above.   While the number of women employed continues to increase,
reaching 691,441, the number of men employed are greater than in
1881, amounting to 408,392, a large proportionate increase, though
less than that of the women.

These figures chiefly indicate a displacement of male by female labour. But the movement is by no means peculiar to the textile and dress industries which may appear specially adapted to the faculties of women. Wherever women have got a firm footing in a manufacture a similar movement is traceable; the relative rate of increase in the employment of women exceeds that of men, even where the numbers of the latter do not show an absolute decline. Such industries are wood furniture and carriages; printing and book-binding; paper, floorcloths, waterproof; feathers, leather, glues; food, drink, smoking; earthenware, machinery, tools.[1] Women have also obtained employment in connection with other industries which are still in the main "male" industries, and in which no women, or very few, were engaged in 1841. Such are fuel, gas, chemicals; watches, instruments, toys. The only group of machine industries in which their numbers have not increased more rapidly than those of men since 1851 are the metal industries. Over some of these, however, they are obtaining an increased hold. In the "more mechanical portions" of the growing "cycle" industry, hollow-ware, and in certain departments of the watchmaking trade, they are ousting male labour, executing with machinery the work formerly done by male hand-workers.[2]

From this and similar evidence relating to the statistics of employment in modern industrial countries, the following conclusions seem justified:—

(1.) That the tendency of modern industry is to increase the quantity of wage-work given to women as compared with that given to men.

In qualification of this tendency consideration should be taken of the greater irregularity of women's work, and of

---

[1] The recent statistics of tailoring and shoemaking, which are becoming more and more machine industries, mark this movement strongly. In the tailoring trade, while male workers increase from 107,668 in 1881 to 119,496 in 1891, female workers increase from 52,980 to 89,224. In the boot and shoe trade, while men increase from 180,884 to 202,648, women increase from 35,672 to 46,141. In Leicestershire and Northamptonshire, where boots and shoes are a machine-industry, 40 women are employed to 100 men, though the proportion for the whole industry is only 23 women to 100 men.

[2] *Report to Commission of Labour on Employments of Women*, pp. 142, 146.

the fact that a large number of women returned as industrial workers give only a portion of their working-day to industry.

(2.) That this tendency is specially operative in manufacturing industries. The increase of female employment in the "dealing" industries and in "industrial service" is not larger than the increase of male employment between 1851 and 1881.

(3.) That in the manufacturing industries, omitting a few essentially male industries where even under machinery the muscles are severely taxed, the increased rate of female employment is greatest in those industries where machinery has been most highly developed, as for example in the textile industries and dress.

Out of 1,840,898 women placed in the industrial class in 1891 no fewer than 1,319,441 were engaged in textile industries and dress, though under the latter head there is of course still a good deal of hand industry.

It seems evident that modern improvements in machinery under normal circumstances favour the employment of women rather than of men. There is some reason to suppose that machinery also favours the employment of children as compared with adults, where the economic forces are allowed free play. In the textile industries of the United States the work of women and children predominates even more largely than in England; in 1880 the number of women and children employed were 112,859 as compared with 59,685 men, while in Massachusetts out of 61,246 work-people only 22,180 were adult males. So far as legislation and public opinion do not interfere, the tendency is strongly in favour of employing children. Mr. Wade says, in *Fibre and Fabric*, "The tendency of late years is towards the employment of child labour. We see men frequently thrown out of employment owing to the spinning mule being displaced by the ring-frame, or children spinning yarn which men used to spin. In the weave-shops, girls and women are preferable to men, so that we may reasonably expect that in the not very distant future all the cotton manufacturing districts will be classed in the category of she-towns."[1]

---

[1] Quoted Wells, *Contemporary Review*, 1887, p. 392.

§ 2. In modern machinery a larger and larger amount of inventive skill is engaged in adjusting machine-tending to the physical and mental capacity of women and children. The evolution of machinery has not moved constantly in this direction. In cotton-spinning, for example, the earlier machines—Hargreave's jennies and Arkwright's water-frames—were generally worked by women and children, the women who had been engaged in the use of the older instruments—the distaff, spindle, hand-wheel—coming into the mills. But the growing complexity and size of the mule made it too cumbrous for women and children, and spinning for a while became a male occupation in England. In the United States the difficulty of procuring male labour stimulated the invention of the ring spinning-frame, some sixty years ago, which could be worked by woman's labour. The limitations and imperfections of this mode of spinning retarded its adoption in England for upwards of half a century. But recent improvements have led to a rapid increase of the adoption of the ring-frame in Lancashire. In the low medium and low counts it is rapidly displacing the mule, and in countries where fine counts are little spun it will probably be the dominant machine.[1] In Lancashire it does not, however, seem at all likely to be rendered capable of displacing the mule in finer counts. The ring-frame throws spinning once more into the hands of women and of children, who in some Lancashire towns are quickly displacing the labour of the men.

So far as children are concerned, the economic tendency to adjust machine-tending to their limited strength is in some measure defeated by the growth of strong public feeling and legislative protection of younger children. Had full and continued licence been allowed to the purely "economic" tendencies of the factory system in this country and in America, there can be little doubt but that almost the whole of the textile industry and many other large departments of manufacture would be administered by the cheap labour of women and young children. The profits attending this free exploitation of cheap labour would have been so great that invention would have been

---

[1] Marsden, *Cotton Spinning*, p. **296**, etc. S. Andrew, *Fifty Years Cotton Trade*, p. **7**.

concentrated, even more than has been the case, upon spreading out the muscular exertion and narrowing the technical skill so as to suit the character of the cheaper labour. It is quite possible that some of the oppressive conditions of our early factory system, the exhausting hours of labour, the cruelty of overseers, the utter neglect of all sanitation, the bad food, might have been found opposed to the true interests of economy and efficiency, and that the more developed factory might have been managed more humanely. But if we may judge by the progress made in the employment of weaker labour where it has had free scope, it seems reasonable to believe that, had no Factory Acts been passed, and had public feeling furnished no opposition, the great mass of the textile factories of this country would have been almost entirely worked by women and children.

We have seen already that the advantages attending efficient labour furnish no guarantee that it will be most profitable to employ the most efficient labour at the highest wages. The evidence of industrial history shows that it will often be most profitable to employ less efficient labour provided that labour can be got "cheap." The increasing employment of women in machine-industry is in nearly all cases directly traceable to the "cheapness" of woman's labour as compared with man's

§ 3. Thus we are brought to the discussion of the important question which underlies all understanding of the position of woman in modern industry—"Why are women paid less wages than men?"

In almost all kinds of work in which both men and women are engaged, the women earn less than the men. Where men and women are engaged in the same industries but in different branches, the wage level of the woman's work is nearly always lower than that of the men. A general survey of industry shows that the highly-paid industries are almost invariably monopolised by men, the lowly-paid industries by women. This applies not only to unskilled and skilled manual work, but to routine-mental, intellectual, and artistic work,[1] wherever custom or com-

---

[1] This fourfold classification—(1) manual, (2) routine-mental, (3) artistic, (4) intellectual—is a serviceable suggestion of Mr. Sidney Webb in his paper upon woman's wages (*Economic Journal*, vol. i., 1881).

petition are the chief direct determinants of wages.
Certain exceptions to this rule, which readily suggest themselves, are explained by the fact that the wages of the
labour in question are determined not by custom or
competition, but by some other law. Where the product
is of the highest intellectual or artistic quality, sex makes
no difference in the price;' "the rent of ability" of
George Eliot or Madame Patti is determined by the law of
monopoly values. In certain employments, as, for instance,
the stage, sexual attractions give women a positive advantage, which in certain grades of the profession assist them
to secure a high level of remuneration. So also in a few
cases governments or private employers pay women as
highly as men for the same work, though women could be
got to work for less. But even in those occupations where
women would seem to be most nearly upon an economic
equality with men, in literature, art, or the stage, the scale
of pay for all work, save that where special skill, personal
attraction, or reputation secures a "fancy" price, is lower
for women than for men.

§ 4. It is easy to find answers to the question, "Why are
women paid less than men?" which evidently contain an
element of truth. Three answers leap readily to the lips:
"Because women cannot work so hard or so well,"
"Because women can live upon less than men," "Because
it is more difficult for a woman to get wage-work." Each
of these answers comprises not one reason but a group of
reasons why women get low wages, and the difficulty lies in
relating the different reasons in these different groups so as
to yield something that shall approach an accurate solution
of the problem. Setting these groups in somewhat more
exact language, we may classify the causes as—

a. Causes relating to "productivity" or efficiency of
labour.
b. Causes relating to "needs" or standard of comfort.
c. Causes relating to character and intensity of competition.

§ 5. *a.* Women do not on the average work so hard or so
well as men, so that if wages were paid with sole reference
to quantity and quality of the product of labour women
would get less. This inferiority in the net efficiency of
women's labour is partly due to physical, partly to social

causes. The following are the leading factors in this inferiority of efficiency:—

(1) The physical weakness of woman, as compared with man, closes many occupations to her. In manufactures the metal industries have been almost entirely closed to women, and most branches of the mining and railway industries. In England and America the rougher work of agriculture is almost wholly given over to male labour, and in several continental countries there is a growing tendency to spare women the kinds of labour which tax the muscular forces most severely. The growing consideration for the duties of maternity, operating through public opinion and legislation, favour this curtailment of woman's sphere of activity. Further, in all employments where physical strength is an important factor, the net productivity of woman's labour tends to fall below man's, although in some cases superior deftness or lightness of hand related to physical fragility may compensate. Even in modern textile factories the superior force of man's muscles often gives him a great advantage. In fustian and velvet cutting, where the same piece-wages are paid to men and women, the actual takings of the men are about double. "Every person has two long frames upon which the cloth is stretched ready for cutting, and while women are unable to cut more than one piece at a time, men can cut two pieces without difficulty."[1]

Where physical strength is not a prime factor it may enter incidentally. So even in weaving women are under some disadvantage through inability to work the heavy Jacquard looms, and to "tune" their looms.[2]

Where manual work is concerned brute strength and endurance form an important ingredient in what is called manual skill, and affect the quality of the work as well as the pace and regularity of the output. Though, as we have seen, a chief object of modern machinery is to diminish the importance of this element, it plays no inconsiderable part in affecting the quantity of work turned out by women as compared with men even in industries where the direct strain upon the muscles is less severe.

(2) But even when we take those kinds of work where

---

[1] *Report to Commission of Labour on Employment of Women*, p. 141.
[2] Webb, *Economic Journal*, vol. i. p. 658.

skill seems least dependent upon physical force, men have generally some advantage in productivity, though a smaller one. There are cases in which this does not seem to be the case, as in the weaving industries of Lancashire and part of Yorkshire, where women not merely receive the same piece wages, but earn weekly wages which, after making allowance for sickness and irregularity, indicate that in quantity and quality of work they are upon a level with the men.[1] In certain branches of low-skilled mental work the same holds true, as in the Savings Bank Department of the Post Office. But generally, even where the "skill" is of a purely technical order, the man has the advantage. Where the elements of design, resource, judgment, enter in, the superiority of male labour is unquestioned, and in occupations which demand these qualities women are confined generally to the lower routine portions of the work. This is the case in the Post Offices where women are largely used as sorting clerks and telegraphists, and in numerous offices of private business firms. How far these defects of manual and intellectual skill, which generally prevent women from successfully competing in the higher grades of labour, are natural, how far the results of defective education and industrial training, we are not called upon here to consider. The fact stands that women do not work so well.

(3) The reluctance of male workers to allow women to qualify for and to undertake certain kinds of work which men choose to regard as "their own," though sometimes defensible when all the terms of competition are taken into account,[2] must be held to confine and lessen the average

[1] I am informed, however, in Lancashire, that the strongest and ablest male workers will not undertake weaving, finding it tedious and monotonous.

[2] Women sometimes abuse the superior competitive powers contained in their lower standard of subsistence, and the smaller number of those dependent on them, to undersell male labour. In Sheffield file-making, where women are paid the same list of prices as men, it is said that they practise sweating in their homes to the detriment of male workers. So in carpet-weaving at Halifax; recently when the men struck against a reduction upon their wage of 35s., women took the work at 20s. (Lady Dilke, "Industrial Position of Women," *Nineteenth Century*, Oct. 1893.) In watch-making, "the hand-work for which men were paid about 18s. a-week is now done by women with machinery for about 12s." (*Report to Labour Commission on Women's Employments*, p. 146.)

productivity of female labour in certain departments of industry. Closely allied to this is the social feeling, partly based upon the recognition of a real difference of physical and mental vigour, partly upon prejudice, which bars women from the highly-paid and responsible posts of superintendence and control in industries where both sexes are employed. In a general comparison of the male and female wage in a highly organised industry, the fact that women are held disqualified for all posts of high emolument and responsibility has a material effect upon the average of wages. Where men and women work in the same industry, the women are commonly confined to the less productive work, and where they do the same work they seldom reach man's level in quantity and quality.

(4) This inferior efficiency is not solely attributable to these reasons. Woman's incentive to acquire industrial efficiency is not so great as man's. A large number of women-workers do not enter an industrial occupation as the chief means of support throughout their life. The influence of matrimony and domestic life operates in various ways upon women's industry. The expectation of marriage and a release from industrial work must lessen the interest of women in their work. The fact that even while unmarried a large proportion of women-workers are not dependent upon their earnings for a livelihood will have the same result. A larger proportion of the woman's industrial career is occupied in acquiring the experience which makes her a valuable worker, and the probability that, after she has acquired it, she may not need to use it, diminishes both directly and indirectly the net value of her industrial life ; the element of uncertainty and instability prevents the advancement of competent women to posts where fixity of tenure is an important factor.

Where married women are engaged in industrial work either in factories or at home, domestic work of necessity engages some of their strength and interest, and is liable to trench upon the energy which otherwise might go into industry. Even unmarried women have frequently some domestic work to do which is added to their industrial work. Thus the incentive to efficiency is weaker in woman, her industrial position is less stable and her industrial life shorter, while part of her energy is diverted to other than industrial channels.

(5) There is conclusive evidence to show that women are more often absent from work owing to sickness and other claims upon their time than men.[1] Though closely related to the former factors this may be treated separately in assessing the net productiveness of women, because it is distinctly measurable. But in touching this point it should be remarked that weaker muscular development does not necessarily imply more sickness. The loss of working time sustained by women could probably be reduced considerably by more attention to physical training and exercise and by a higher standard of diet.

(6) Although the limitations of law and custom, which limit the hours of labour for women in many of their industrial occupations and forbid them to undertake night-work, cannot be reasonably held to reduce the net efficiency of women's labour taken as an aggregate, they must be allowed to diminish the direct net productiveness of women in certain employments as compared with men, and either to bar them out of these employments or engage them upon lower wages. In certain textile factories where goods of some special pattern are woven at short notice, and where overtime is essential, women cannot be employed. In the Post Office, where night-work is required at certain seasons, women are at a disadvantage, which is doubtless reflected in the lower wages they receive.

(7) Lastly, the inferior mobility of woman as compared with man has an influence in reducing the average efficiency of her labour. On the one hand, women are more liable to have the locality of their home fixed by the requirements of the male worker·in the family ; on the other hand, they are physically less competent to undertake work far from their home. Hence they are far more narrowly restricted in their choice of work than men. They must often choose not that work they like best, or can do best, or which is most remunerative, but that which lies near at hand. This

---

[1] Dr. Bertillon (*Journal de la Société de Statistique de Paris*, Oct.-Nov. 1892) shows that among the Lyons silkworkers (1872-89) and in the Italian Societies (1881-85) the sickness of women is considerably greater than of men. In Lyons 9.39 days as compared with 7.81 for men; in Italy 8.5 as compared with 6.6.

restriction implies that large numbers of women undertake low-skilled, low-paid, ineffective, and irregular work at their own homes or in some neighbouring work-room, instead of engaging in the more productive and more remunerative work of the large factories.   Every limitation in freedom of choice of work signifies a reduction in the average effectiveness of labour.

§ 6.   These elements of inferior physique and manual skill, lower intelligence and mental capacity, lack of education and knowledge of life, irregularity of work, more restricted freedom of choice, must in different degrees contribute to the inferior productivity of woman's industrial labour.

In regarding this influence the experienced student of industrial questions hardly requires to be reminded that these must be regarded not merely as causes of low wages, but also as effects.   This constant recognition of the interaction of the phenomena we are regarding as cause and effect is essential to a scientific conception of industrial society.   Women are paid low wages because they are relatively inefficient workers, but they also are inefficient workers because they are paid low wages.

While this smaller productivity diminishes the maximum wage attainable by women as compared with men, it is evident that many forces are at work which tend to equalise the productivity of men and women in industry : the evolution of machinery adapted to the weaker physique of women ; the breakdown of customs excluding women from many occupations ; the growth of restrictions upon male adult labour with regard to the working-day, etc., correspondent with those placed upon women ; improved mobility of women's labour by cheaper and more facile transport in large cities ; the recognition by a growing number of women that matrimony is not the only livelihood open to them, but that an industrial life is preferable and possible.   These forces, unless counteracted by stronger moral and social forces, seem likely to raise the average productivity of women's industrial labour, and to incite her more and more to undertake industrial wage-work.

§ 7.   As the maximum wage may be said to vary with productivity, so the minimum wage is said to vary with the "wants" of the worker.   Women are said to "want" less than man, and therefore the stress of competition can drive their wages to a lower level. It is possible that a woman can sustain the smaller quantity of physical energy required for her work somewhat more cheaply than a man can sustain the energy required for his work, and that the early increments of material comfort above the bare subsistence line may be attended by a larger increase of productivity in the man than in the woman. If this is so, then the minimum subsistence wage and the wage of true economic efficiency, the smallest wage a wise employer in his own interest will consent to pay, are lower in the case of women than of men. But this difference furnishes no adequate explanation of the difference between the male and the female minimum wage. The wage of the low-skilled male labourer enables him to consume certain things which do not belong strictly to his "subsistence"—to wit, beer and tobacco; the wage of the low-skilled female labourer often falls below what is sufficient with the most rigid economy to provide "subsistence." We are not then concerned with a difference which refers primarily to the quantity of food, etc., required to support life. The wages of the low-skilled labourer in regular employ would, if properly used, suffice to furnish him more than a bare physical subsistence; the wages of the lowest-paid women workers in factories would not suffice to maintain them in the physical condition to perform their work.[1]

It is not then precisely with the "standard of comfort" of male and female workers that we are concerned. The economic relation in which men and women workers stand to other members of their family is a more important factor. The wage of a male worker must be sufficient to support not only himself but the average family dependent upon him, in the standard of comfort below which he will not consent to work. When little work is available for his wife and children, or where his "standard of comfort" requires them not to undertake wage-work, his minimum wage must suffice to keep some four persons. His standard of comfort may be beaten down by stress of circumstances, his

---

[1] This holds, for example, of many branches of the fur, trimmings, stays, umbrella, match-box trades, and the "finishing" departments of the trousers and shirt trades in East London. Cf. Miss Collet in *Labour and Life of the People*, vol. i.

family may be driven to take what work they can get, but
in any case his wage must be above the "subsistence" of a
single man. When the man is the sole wage-earner, or is
only assisted slightly by his family, as, for example, in the
metal and mining and building industries, average male
wages are much higher than in the textile industries, where
the women and children share largely in the work.[1]

Women workers, on the other hand, have not in most
cases a family to support out of their wages. In the majority
of instances their own "sustenance" does not or need not
fall entirely upon the wages they earn. They are partly
supported by the earnings of a father or a husband or other
relative, upon some small unearned income, upon public or
private charity. Where married women undertake work in
order to increase the family income, or where girls not
obliged to work for a living enter factories or take home
work to do, there is no ascertainable limit to the minimum
wage in an industry. Grown-up women living at home will
often work for a few shillings a week to spend in dress and
amusements, utterly regardless of the fact that they may be
setting the wage below starvation-point for those unfortunate
competitors who are wholly dependent on their earnings for

[1] In the United States the general standard of money wages for
working women in cities is considerably higher than in England. The
average wage throughout the country was recently estimated to amount to
$5.24 per week, or just under 21s. But the divergences from this average
are much wider than in England. The lowest wages fall almost to the
lowest English level, for some 3 per cent. of the number averaged were
earning less than 8s. a week. About 20 per cent. were earning between
14s. and 19s. per week. The earnings in the chief textile industries
show wide variations, yielding, however, a rough average of about 20s.
weekly wages in cotton mills, and about 22s. in woollen mills. A
general comparison would yield a standard of some 15s. as the customary
wage corresponding to the 10s. in England (*Report of the Commissioner
of Labour*, 1888, chap. iii. and Table xxix.). Some allowance, however, must be made for the more expensive living in American cities.
However, in spite of the fact that organised action is almost unknown
among women workers in America, the real wages are higher than in
England. This is partly owing to the general insistence upon a higher
standard of consumption, partly to the fact that a larger number of
employments are open to women than in England, and partly to the
higher skill and intelligence they put into their work. Thus the
maximum wage, measured by productivity, is higher, the minimum,
measured by "wants," is higher, while the terms of competition do not
so generally keep down actual wages to the minimum.

a living. Even where girls living at home pay to their parents the full cost of their keep, the economy of family life may enable them to keep down wages to such a point that another girl who has to keep herself alone may be sorely pressed, while a woman with a family to support cannot get a living.

Miss Collet, in her investigation of women workers in East London, remarked of the shirt-finishers, one of the lowest-paid employments—"These shirt-finishers nearly all receive allowances from relatives, friends, and charitable societies, and many of them receive outdoor relief."[1] This is true of most of the low-paid work of women. Even in the textile factories, with the exception of weaving, most of the scales of wages are below what would suffice to keep the recipient in the standard of comfort provided by the family wage.

§ 8. The relation of a worker to other persons in the family is such that, in determining the minimum wage for any member, it is right to take the standard of comfort of the family as the basis, and to consider the mutual relations of the several workers upon this basis. We shall find that not merely is the wage of the woman affected by the industrial condition of the adult male worker, but that the wage of the latter is affected by women's wages, while the wages of child labour exercise an influence upon each. The problem is one of the distribution of work and wages among the several working members of a family, how much of the family work and how much of the family wage shall fall to each. As the children, and in many cases the women, are not free agents in the transaction, it may often happen that they are employed for wages which represent neither the cost of subsistence nor any other definite amount but the prevalent opinion of the dominant male of the family. A "little piecer" in a Lancashire mill may get wages more than sufficient for his keep, while many a farm boy or errand boy could not keep himself in food out of the earnings he brings home. This element of economic unfreedom in the lives of many women and most children must not be left out of sight in a consideration of the comparative statistics of wages for men, women, and children.

---

[1] *Labour and Life of the People*, vol. 1. p. 410.

Men workers often fail to recognise that by encouraging their wives and driving their children to the mills or other industrial work, they are helping to keep down their own wages. Men's wages in all the textile industries of the world are low as compared with those prevalent in industries demanding no higher skill or intelligence, but in which women take no important part. If the male textile workers used their rising intelligence and education to keep their women and children out of the mills, men's wages must and would distinctly rise.[1] The low wages paid to both men and women in many branches of textile work as compared with wages in other industries on approximately the same level of skill, goes for the most part to the consuming public in reduced prices of textile wares. It is true the Lancashire and certain of the Yorkshire textile operatives often enjoy a fairly high family wage, but they give out a more than correspondent aggregate of productive energy.

American statistics yield some striking evidence in illustration of the depressing influence exercised upon male wages by the labour of women and children. "Among factory operatives, all branches taken together, the wives and children who contribute to the support of the family are, on an average, as one and a quarter to each family, while among those employed in the building trades the average of wives and children who work is only one to every four families. Hence in the building trades the wages of the man supply about 97½ per cent. of the total cost of the family's living, while among the factory operatives the wages of the man only supply 66 per cent., or two-thirds, of the cost of the family's living, because the other one-third is furnished by the labour of the wife or children. Nor is this because the cost of living of the factory operative family is greater than that of the labourer in the building trades, for while the average family in the building trades contains 4½ persons, that of the factory operative contains 5⅞ persons.[2]

---

[1] It must, however, be borne in mind that the results of such a policy followed by Lancashire, or any other single part of the textile industry of the world, would be qualified or even negatived if the example was not followed by their competitors.

[2] This effect of industrial opportunities for women and children in promoting early and more fruitful marriages is also illustrated in Lancashire; the average family of the factory operative is considerably higher than the average for the working classes as a whole.

The total cost of living in the former is about $50 a year more than in the latter, and the wages of the man in the former are nearly $250 a year more than those of the latter."[1] Similar evidence is tendered from other trades, the gist of which is summed up in the Report of the Labour Bureau of Massachusetts in the following words:—"Thus it is seen that in neither of the cases where the man is assisted by his wife or children does he earn as much as other labourers. Also that in the case where he is assisted by both wife and children he earns the least."[2]

§ 9. But though the minimum wage of women and children is, strictly speaking, not to be measured by any ascertainable standard of subsistence, so far as the factory work of adult women is concerned 10s. may be said to be a standard wage. Factory wages, excepting for cotton-weavers, seldom vary widely from this sum. Differences of difficulty, disagreeability, or skill have little power to raise wages much above 10s., or to depress them much below. Moreover, fluctuations of trade and prices have very little effect upon this wage. Though women are largely employed in industries where improvements in machinery and methods have immensely increased the productivity of labour, their wages are very little higher than they were half a century ago. Since this rate prevails in many industries where an adequate supply of women's labour cannot be drawn from married or "assisted" women, and where the wage must be sufficient to tempt women who have to keep themselves, 10s. may be said to be the "bare subsistence" wage for women. The wide prevalence of this wage and its independence of conditions of locality, time, nature of work, have made it generally recognised as a "customary wage," and for any casual work, or any new employment requiring ordinary feminine skill or exertion, 10s. is regarded as sufficient remuneration for a woman. The basis of this custom is the knowledge that women can always be induced to work for a bare subsistence measured at 10s. or thereabouts, or for extra comforts procurable by this sum regarded as a subsidiary income.[3]

---

[1] Gunton, *Wealth and Progress*, p. 169.

[2] *Report of the Statistics of Labour*, p. 71.

[3] Dr. Smart has a valuable treatment of the subject in his pamphlet, *Women's Wages*, pp. 22-25.

It appears that the wages of bare subsistence and the wages of extra comforts have a certain tendency to equality in some of the low-paid factory trades of London, though accompanied by a difference in the quality and intensity of the labour involved.

The following diagram exhibits the uniformity of factory wages in East End women's industries :—

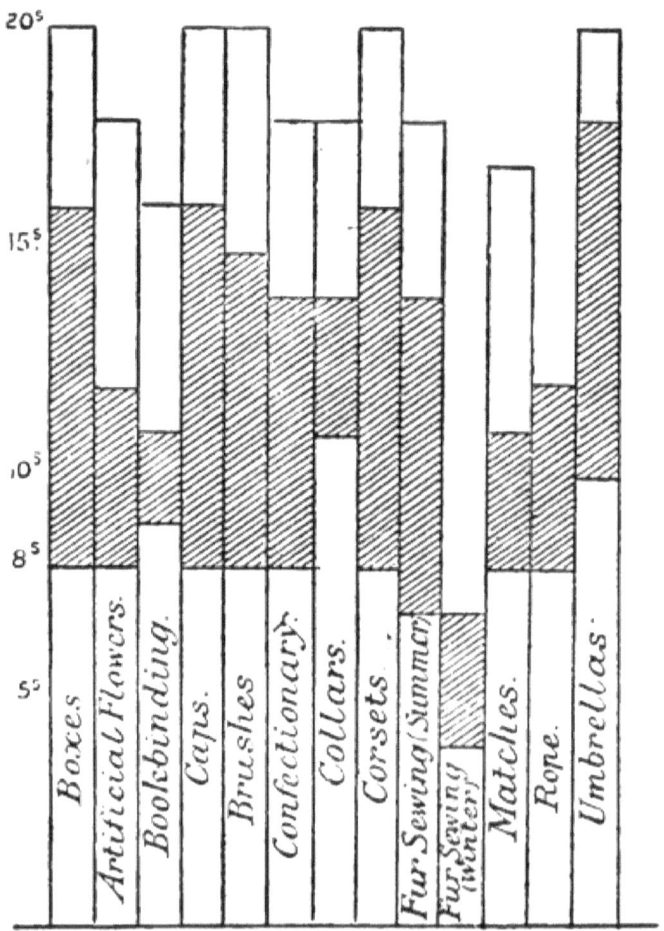

Upon this table Miss Collet bases the following opinion:—"The most striking feature is the uniformity of maximum wages and the difference in the skill required, and I believe it to be the fact that the match girls and the jam girls, who are at the bottom of the social scale, do not have to work so hard for their money as, for example, the capmakers and bookbinders, who, in the majority of cases, belong to a much higher social grade. And whereas the bookfolder or booksewer who earns 11s. a week exercises greater skill, and gives a closer attention to her work, than the jam or match girl who earns the same amount, that sum which would be almost riches to the dock-labourer's daughter represents grinding poverty to the daughter of the clerk or bookbinder, with a much higher standard of decency, if she is by any chance obliged to depend on herself. How is it that this uniformity prevails, and that efficiency brings with it nothing but the privilege of working harder for the same money?"[1]

Miss Collet's reply to the question is, that while the match and jam girls pay the full price of home, board, and lodging, the others often pay nothing, spending all they get upon dress and amusement. This, taken along with the influence of the competition of home-workers in the bookfolding and booksewing trades, explains the fact that the harder and higher-skilled work gets no higher wages.

§ 10. A knowledge of the productivity of labour as measuring the maximum wage-level, and of "wants" or standard of comfort as measuring the minimum wage-level, does not enable us to determine even approximately the actual wage-level in any industry. The actual wage may be fixed at any point between the two extremes. So far as competition is an active determinant, everything will depend upon the quantitative relation between supply and demand for labour. When there is a short supply of labour available for any work, wages may rise to the maximum; when there is more labour available than is required, wages will fall towards the minimum. But, as we have already admitted, competition works very slowly and inadequately in many of the industries in which women and children are engaged. The force of custom, assisted by ignorance of the labour market, prevents women from taking advantage of an increased demand or a decreased supply of labour

---

[1] *Labour and Life of the People*, vol. i. p. 469.

to lift this wage above the customary level towards the level of productivity. Women are more contented to live as they have lived than men. As Miss Collet says, "the contentment of women themselves, when they have obtained enough for their standard of living, is another reason why competition is so ineffective among highly-skilled workers."[1]

This "contentment" or apathy, partly the result of ignorance, partly the result of sex feebleness, enhanced by the exhausting burden of present industrial conditions, is alluded to by the several reports of the sub-commissioners to the Labour Commission as a chief difficulty in the effective organisation of women workers, even when the work is conducted in large factories.

In other ways, woman is less of a purely "economic" creature than man. The flow of labour from one occupation to another, which tends to equalise the net advantages amongst male occupations, is far feebler among women workers, notwithstanding that trade union barriers and the vested interests of expensively-acquired skill are less operative in woman's work. The reluctance of women to freely communicate to one another facts regarding their wage and conditions of labour is particularly noted as a barrier to united action.

Those who have investigated the conditions of women workers in towns are agreed as to the enormous influence of class and æsthetic feelings in narrowing the competition. "The girl who makes seal-skin caps at a city warehouse does not wish to work for an East End chamber-master, even though she could make more at the commoner work ; just as a soap-box maker would not care to make match-boxes, even though skilled enough to make more by it."[2] This sensitiveness of social distinction in industrial work, based partly upon consideration of the class and character of those employed, partly upon the skill and interest of the work itself, is a widespread and powerful influence among women workers. It tends to bring about that equalisation of wages in skilled and unskilled industries which, as we have seen, practically exists, for if there is an economic rise

---

[1] *Labour and Life of the People*, vol. i. p. 460.
[2] *Ibid.*, vol. i. p. 459; cf. also p. 469.

of wages in the lower grades of work, it does not tempt the competition of high-skilled workers, while a corresponding rise in the wages of the higher grades would draw competitors from the lower grades to qualify themselves for undertaking work which would at once give them more money and more social respect. The lower wages often paid for more highly-skilled work simply mean that the women take out a larger portion of their wage in "gentility." This influence, which is operative amongst men, reducing the wages of routine-mental labour to the level of common unskilled manual labour, is powerful in all ranks of women, rising perhaps in its potency with the social status of the woman. Considerations of "gentility" enable us to obtain "teachers" for board schools at an average "salary" of £75 per annum, as compared with £119 for men, the fixed scale of women teachers in the same grade being 16 per cent. less than for men.

Thus custom, ignorance, contentment, social prejudices operate in different ways and in different degrees to prevent women workers from claiming in higher wages that share of the increased capacity of the community for making wealth which men workers have been able to procure.

§ 11. The above-mentioned forces operate chiefly as barriers of free economic competition. But women are equally at a disadvantage when and in so far as they do compete for work and wages. Weak, unorganised units of labour, they are compelled to make terms with large organised masses of capital. By the organised action of trade unionism the majority of skilled working men have been able to raise their wages far above the bare subsistence minimum, and to hold it at the higher level until a firm standard of higher comfort is formed to be a platform for further endeavour. With a few significant exceptions, skilled women workers have been unable to do the same. Instead of presenting a firm, united front to their employers in their demand for higher wages, or their resistance of a fall, they are taken singly and compelled to submit to any terms which the employers choose to impose, or custom appears to sanction. The consequence is that in most instances skilled women workers are paid very little higher wages than unskilled women workers. The high value due to their skill goes either to the employer in high profits, or, where keen competition operates, to the consumer in low prices ; the woman who puts out skill is paid not according to her worth but according to her wants. Yet the possession of technical skill is the basis of trade organisation. Wherever a number of women workers possess a particular skill and experience, and are engaged in fairly stable employment, the requisites of effective trade organisation exist. By combination these women can wield an economic power, measured by the difficulty and cost of dismissing them *en masse* and replacing them by less skilled and experienced labour, which they can use as a lever to raise their wages and other conditions of employment by a series of steps until they approach the maximum limit imposed by their productivity. That such action is feasible is proved by experience. Concerted action of factory women in several minor trades, both in London and in the provincial towns, has been attended with success. The examples of the cigar-makers at Nottingham, the women at Messrs. Bryant & May's, the rope-makers in a large East London factory, show what can be done by determined combination, even confined to workers in a single factory. But the crucial case is furnished again by the textile industries. In the Lancashire weaving, where men and women are working side by side in the same sheds, and are members of the same trades unions, we find the one notable exception to the low wages of women. Here women's weekly earnings are nearly the same as men's. The weaving is unquestionably skilled work, but so also is a great deal of other textile work not nearly so well paid. It is beyond doubt the power of the joint union of male and female weavers that alone maintains these wages for women. The same is the explanation of the equality of wages paid to men and women in the Sheffield file-making.

"But what if the Union should break down? It is as certain as anything based on experience can be, that in a few weeks, or even days, it would be possible for the employers to reduce the wages of the women-weavers ; that rather than lose their work, women would consent to the reduction; that as they accepted lower wages, men would drop off to other industries, and would cease to compete for the same work; and that in a comparatively short time power-loom weaving would be left, like its sister, cotton-spinning, to women workers exclusively, and wages fall to the general level of women's wages."[1] Where these conditions of strong combination in trades unions do not exist we find that women's weekly wages fall considerably below men's in the weaving trades. This is so in most of the woollen industries of Yorkshire, and still more in the minor and more scattered textile work in other counties.[2] In the spinning-mills of Lancashire the women, combined in unions of their own, are able to obtain wages considerably higher than those which prevail elsewhere for similar work, though not so high as that of weavers. The following table, in which spinning and weaving and other departments are "pooled" for purposes of wages, is sufficient to indicate the advantage Lancashire women enjoy from their strong industrial position, as compared on the one hand with average factory work and wages, on the other hand with the less favourably placed worsted and linen industries, and even with the woollen.

[1] Smart, *Woman's Wages*, p. 23.

[2] In some cases where women are found getting the same rate of wages as men, the industry is a woman's industry in which a few lower-skilled or inferior male workers are employed. The woman's scale dominates, the men who are employed descending to it. This is the case in some weaving trades where men work still almost entirely with hand-looms, leaving women with a practical monopoly of power-loom work. (*Report of Woollen Manufactures in Miscellaneous English Towns*, pp. 98, 99.) Where both men and women are freely engaged in the same class of work, the men are always (save in the area of the Lancashire trade unions) paid at higher rates : where the same rates are paid they are determined upon the woman's scale. The comparison between Huddersfield and other cloth-making towns in Yorkshire establishes this point. "In the cloth mills of these three districts, Bradford, Huddersfield, and Leeds, men and women engaged upon the same work at the looms receive the same pay. In the Huddersfield district the proportion of men to women among the weavers is much greater than it is in the districts of Bradford, Halifax, or Leeds, and in the Huddersfield districts alone there is a weaver's scale, according to which women are paid from 15 to 50 per cent. below men. The proportion of women is, however, rapidly increasing; and I found many firms where the scale is not in operation. At some places men and women were paid alike *upon the woman's scale*. At other firms men were paid at a slightly higher rate than women, the women's scale being the basis of calculation for all classes of work." (Miss Abraham in *Reports on Employment of Women to the Labour Commission*, p. 100.)

	Weekly Wages.			Average.
	Cotton.	Woollen.	Worsted.	Linen.
	s. d.	s. d.	s. d.	s. d.
Men . . .	25 3	23 2	23 4	19 9
Lads and boys .	9 4	8 6	6 6	6 3
Women . .	15 3	13 3	11 11	8 11
Girls . . .	6 10	7 5	6 2	4 11 [1]

Thus we see that whereas men's wages are nearly the same in the three chief English industries, women's wages vary widely, yielding a very great advantage to the Lancashire cotton-workers.

§ 12. It cannot, however, reasonably be maintained that the whole of this economic advantage owned by weavers and other women workers in Lancashire is due directly to organisation. It is no doubt partly due to the conditions which also make Trade Unionism effective, an abundant demand for female labour in relation to the supply. In the less concentrated woollen industries of the West of England, where a large supply of female labour is available beyond the demand, the difference between men's and women's wages is far greater than it is even in those parts of Yorkshire where women are but slightly organised. This brings us to the most vital point in the problem of the industrial position of women. When there is an over-supply of labour qualified to compete for any work, wages must fall to the minimum of "wants" unless those in possession of the work are so strongly organised as to prevent outsiders from effectively competing. In a highly-skilled trade the workers may often have a practical monopoly of the skill, which gives them both power to organise and power when organised. But in a low-skilled trade, or where employers are able to introduce unlimited numbers of girls into the trade, there exists no such power to organise. Those who most need organisation are least able to organise. This is the crux for low-skilled male labour, and the great mass of women's industries are in the same economic condition, because the kind of skill required is possessed or easily attainable by a much larger number of competitors for work than are sufficient to meet the demand at a decent wage. The deep abiding difficulty in the way of organising women workers lies here. Cut out as they are, by

[1] *Report on Principal Textile Trades*, p. xxv.

physical weakness, by lack of the means of technical training, in some cases by organised opposition of male workers,
or by social prejudices, from competing in a large number
of skilled industries, their competition within the permitted
range of occupations is keener than among men : not merely
in the unskilled but in the skilled industries the available
supply of labour is commonly far in excess of the demand,
for the skill is generally such as is common to or easily
attainable by a large number of the sex.   To this must be
added the consideration that a larger proportion of women's
industries are concerned with the production of luxuries
which are peculiarly subject to fluctuation of trade by the
elements of season, weather, fashion, and rise or fall of
incomes.   Finally, a much larger proportion of women's
work is done in small factories, in workshops, and in the
home, under conditions which are inimicable to the
effective organisation of the workers.   Until out-work is
much diminished, and effective inspection and limitation of hours in small workshops drives a much larger
proportion of women workers into large factories, where
closer social intercourse can lay the moral foundation of
trade organisation in mutual acquaintance, trust, and regard,
there is little prospect of women being able to raise their
"customary" wage considerably above its present subsistence level, or to obtain any considerable alleviation of the
burdensome conditions of excessive hours of labour, insanitary surroundings, unjust fines, etc., from which many
women workers suffer.

Women cannot in most of their industries organise
effectively under present conditions.   In each trade, therefore, the workers employed are surrounded by a permanent
mass of potential "black legs" willing to take their labour
from urgent need, ignorance, or thoughtlessness, and possessing or able to attain the small skill required.   In men's
industries, save in the most unskilled, there is not a constant
over-supply of labour, in most women's industries there is.

§ 13. Comparing women's wages with men's we are now
able to sum up as follows :—The smaller productivity of
woman's work makes the possible maximum wage lower ;
the smaller wants of women make the possible minimum
wage lower ; the greater weakness of women as competitors,
arising chiefly from excess of supply of labour, makes their

actual wage approximate to the lower rather than to the higher level.

In regarding productivity as a measure of maximum wage it is necessary to guard carefully against one misapprehension. So far as we are comparing the wage of men and women engaged upon the same work, the smaller wages of the latter may easily be seen to have some relation to the smaller product of their labour. But when productivity is expressed in terms of the selling value of the work no such measurement is open to us. We are thus thrown back on market value and are told that the reason women get so little is that what they make fetches so low a price. But the circularity of this argument will appear on revising the question and asking, "Why do women's products sell so cheap?" the obvious answer being, "Because the cost of labour in them is so little,"—*i.e.*, because women receive low wages. But if we refuse to take selling prices as the measure of productivity, what measure have we? No accurate measure of effort, skill, or efficiency is open if we refuse the scale of the market itself. Yet if we consider the conditions of wages and prices in such "sweated" trades as shirt-making, we cannot but conclude that the consumer gets the advantage of the "sweating"; that is to say, a certain portion of the productivity of the workers passes to the consumer through the agency of low prices. That which might have gone to the shirt-makers in decent wages has gone to the purchaser. This criticism of course posits a measurement of productivity at variance with that afforded by competition, or, more strictly speaking, it discounts the abnormal terms of the competition in the sweated industry. If we say that 1s. 11½d. as the retail price of a shirt is a "sweating" or unfair price, we mean that the skill and effort embodied in this product would, if there were absolute equality of competition and absolute fluidity of labour, be measured at say 3s. It is true that no such measurement is open to us, and all such estimates are guesswork. But the idea which underlies the sentiment against "sweating" is a true one, although it has no exact practical embodiment so long as our only meaning of "value" is value in exchange at present competitive rates. It is therefore not inaccurate to represent productivity as forming the maximum wage, though we may have no exact measure

of productivity at hand. The fact that any increase in
productivity of labour is liable under certain circumstances
of competition to pass away entirely to the consumer, is no
reason for denying that an increase of productivity has
taken place which might under other circumstances of competition have gone to the producer as higher wages. Though
productivity as a measure of maximum wages is more or
less of an unknown quantity, it is none the less true that as
this "unknown" fluctuates so the possibility of high wages
fluctuates.

§ 14. If the above analysis is correct it is not difference of
sex which is the chief factor in determining the industrial
position of woman. Machinery knows neither sex nor age,
but chooses the labour embodied in man, woman, or child,
which is cheapest in relation to the degree of its efficiency.
Thus the causes which depress woman's industry are chiefly
the same which depress the industry of low-skilled men and
children. In each case the limits of productivity and
" wants " are lower than for skilled men workers, while the
terms of their competition keep their wages to the lower
level and check the full incentive to efficiency. Setting
aside the case of children, who are protected in some
degree from the full effects of competition upon the conditions of their employment, the industrial case of women is
closely analogous to that of low-skilled men. The physical
weakness of the one corresponds with the technical weakness of the other so far as efficiency is concerned ; in both
cases the low standard of wants gives a low minimum wage,
while the excessive supply of labour, rendering concerted
action almost impossible, keeps wages close to the minimum.

§ 15. The displacement of male adult labour which is going
on by female, and, when permitted, by child labour, does not
necessarily imply that women and children are doing more
work and men less than they used to do. Before the
industrial revolution women were quite as busily and
numerously engaged in industry as now, and the children
employed in textile and other work were often worked in
their own homes with more cruel disregard to health and
happiness than is now the case. Even now the longest
hours, the worst sanitary conditions, the lowest pay, are in
the domestic industries of towns which still survive under
modern industry. But though the regular factory women

and the half-timers are generally better off in all the terms of their industry than the uninspected women and children who still slave in such domestic industries as the trimmings and match-box trades, the growing tendency of modern industry to engage women and children away from their homes is fraught with certain indirect important consequences. When industry was chiefly confined to domestic handicrafts, the claims of home life constantly pressed in and tempered the industrial life. The growth of factory work among women has brought with it inevitably a weakening of home interests and a neglect of home duties. The home has suffered what the factory has gained. Even the shortening of the factory day, accompanied as it has been by an intensification of labour during the shorter hours, does not leave the women competent and free for the proper ordering of home life. Home work is consciously slighted as secondary in importance and inferior, because it brings no wages, and if not neglected is performed in a perfunctory manner, which robs it of its grace and value. This narrowing of the home into a place of hurried meals and sleep is on the whole the worst injury modern industry has inflicted on our lives, and it is difficult to see how it can be compensated by any increase of material products. Factory life for women, save in extremely rare cases, saps the physical and moral health of the family. The exigencies of factory life are inconsistent with the position of a good mother, a good wife, or the maker of a home. Save in extreme circumstances, no increase of the family wage can balance these losses, whose values stand upon a higher qualitative level.

The direct economic tendency of machine-industry to take women and children away from the home to work must be looked upon as a tendency antagonistic to civilisation.[1] In the case of children, factory legislation of increasing severity has been necessary to prevent the spread or continuance of the evil.[2] The factory regulations restricting and protecting women are directly continuous with this policy, and may be regarded in the light of a protection of the home against the

---

[1] The evidence adduced by Dr. Arlidge in his *Diseases of Occupations* regarding the effects of factory life upon the physique of children is conclusive. See p. 38, etc.

[2] See Appendix on Factory Legislation.

undue encroachments of the machine. How far further restrictions may be left to voluntary action and the growth of a saner estimate of values, or how far further legal protection of the home may be required, it remains for history to determine.

APPENDIX.

THE following Table of Factory Legislation is constructed to illustrate the lines along which State protection of labour has advanced in this century in England. Four laws of development are clearly discernible :—

1. Movement along the line of strongest human feeling. Weakest workers are protected first, pauper children who are the least "free" parties in a contract, then protection advances to other children, young persons, women, men.

2. Protective legislation moves from the more highly organised to the less highly organised structures of industry. Cotton-mills are sole subjects of earliest Factory Acts, then woollen, then other textile trades, trades subsidiary to textile industries, non-textile factories, larger workshops, domestic workshops, retail trade, domestic service.

3. Growing complexity of aims and of legislative machinery. Primarily Factory Acts aim at regulation of quantity of labour. Reductions of the working-day forms a backbone of this legislation. A twelve-hour day, ten, nine, eight, covering wider classes of workers and applied to a larger number of industries, marks the line of movement. With each advance the basis of protection is broadened, other considerations of machine-fencing, sanitation, education, etc., entering more largely into the Acts.

4. Increased effectiveness of legislation with growth of centralised control. Local initiative and control proves ineffective, yields to State inspection, the number of inspectors growing, and their power increasing. Improvements in the mechanism of central control, an increased number of inspectors, working men and women inspectors, are the distinguishing features of recent State protection of labour.

21

Date.	Industries affected.	Class of Workers chiefly protected.	Nature of Regulations.	Mode of Administration.	Effectiveness.
1802	Cotton and 'other mills' (applied exclusively to cotton).	Apprenticed Pauper Children.	12 Hours Day. Night-work regulated. Education, sanitation.	Local Justices to appoint visitors.	Virtually inoperative.
1819 } 1820 }	Do. Do.	Children (not Paupers).	Prohibition of work under 9 years. Young persons (under 16) a 12 hour day. Regulation for meal-time. Amendment of 1802 Act.	Do.	Do.
1825	Do.	Do.	Shortened Saturday labour. Penalties provided for breach of Factory Regulations.	Do. (Millowners and relatives prevented from acting on the Bench in reference to Factory Acts.)	Generally evaded.
1833 } 1834 }	All Textile Industries.	Children and Young Persons.	48 Hours Week for Children (9-13). 69 Hours for Young Persons (13-18). Prohibits night-work for Young Persons. Children in Silk Mills, 10 Hours Day.	Government Inspectors (4).	1 out of every 11 millowners convicted in 1834, in spite of defiant attitude of magistrates.
1842	Mines.	Children and Women.	No underground work.	Mine Inspectors.	
1844 to 1846 }	Printworks.	Children, Young Persons, Women.	Factory Acts applied. 'False relay' system for children checked. 6½ Hours Day for Children. Female Young Persons age raised to 21. 12 Hours Day for Women. No night-work for women	Government Inspectors.	Improved administration, but 'false relay' system re-established. Fines inadequate.
1847 to 1850 }	Textile Factories, Printworks, etc.	Do.	10 Hours Day, afterwards 10½ Hours Day for Young Persons and Women, practically for Men.	Increased Staff of Government Inspectors.	Largely defied or evaded for some time.
1860	Bleaching and Dyeing.	Do.	Do., with special regulations for overtime.		
1860	Coal and Iron Mines.	All Workers.	Restriction on male labour under 12. Safety, ventilation, etc.	Mine Inspectors.	

Date.	Industries affected.	Class of Workers chiefly protected.	Nature of Regulations.	Mode of Administration.	Effectiveness.
1863	Finishing processes in Bleaching and Dyeing, Bakehouses, Alkali Works.	Children, Young Persons, Women.	} Factory Acts generally applied.		
1864	Non-textile Factories, (Earthenware, Fustian Cutting, Cartridges, Lucifer Matches, Paperstaining).	Do.			
1867	All Factories & Workshops.	Do.	Factory Acts Extension Act. Workshops Regulation Act, applying to Workshops. Factory rules affecting hours, education, etc., in modified form.	Workshops Act left at first to local authorities, brought under Factory Inspectors, 1871.	Workshops Act dead letter in 1868-69. Later, fines inadequate. Inspectors inadequate.
1867	Agriculture.	Children, Women.	Act for Suppression of Agricultural Gangs fixing minimum age at 8, regulating employment of Women.		
1870	Printworks, Bleaching, Dyeing.	Children, Young Persons, Women.	Application of chief provisions of 1867 Factory Act.		
1871	Brickworks and Fields.	Children and Young Female Persons.	Forbids employment. Improved conditions for Women.		
1873	Agriculture.	Children.	Minimum age raised to 10.		
1878	Factories, Workshops, Agriculture.	Children, Young Persons, Women, (incidentally Men).	Consolidation of Factories & Workshops Act (extending some provisions to agriculture).	Increased Staff of Inspectors.	
1891	Do.	Do.	Amendment of Factories & Workshops Act. Age for Children raised to 11. Protection in dangerous trades.	Board of Trade power to schedule dangerous trades.	
1892	Shops.	Children, Young Persons.	Limits working-day.		
1893	Various Trades.	All workers.	Restrictions on dangerous trades.	Appointment of working men and women Inspectors. Increased number of Inspectors.	
1893	Railways.	Adult males	Restrictions on hours of labour.		

CHAPTER XIII.

MACHINERY AND THE MODERN TOWN.

§   1. *The Modern Industrial Town as a Machine-product.*
§   2. *Growth of Town as compared with Rural Population in the Old and New Worlds.*
§   3. *Limits imposed upon the Townward Movement by the Economic Conditions of World-industry.*
§   4. *Effect of increasing Town-life upon Mortality.*
§   5   *The impaired quality of Physical Life in Towns.*
§   6. *The Intellectual Education of Town-life.*
§   7. *The Moral Education of Town-life.*
§   8. *Economic Forces making for Decentralisation.*
§   9. *Desirability of Public Control of Transport Services to effect Decentralisation.*
§ 10. *Long Hours and Insecurity of Work as Obstacles to Reforms.*
§ 11. *The Principle of Internal Reform of Town-life.*

§ 1. In the last few chapters we have examined some of the influences of modern machine-production upon men and women in the capacity of producers, in relation to character, duration, intensity, regularity of employment, the remuneration of labour, and the economic relations which subsist between workers and employers. It remains to give special consideration to one factor in the environment of modern industrial life, which is of paramount importance upon the public, both in its working and living capacity.

The biggest, and in some respects the most characteristic of machine-products is the modern industrial town. Steam-power is in a most literal sense the maker of the modern town. When the motive-power of industrial work was chiefly confined to the forces stored in man, the economy obtained by collecting larger numbers of men to work in close proximity to one another was comparatively small, and was commonly outweighed by the difficulty of securing for them a sufficient supply of food and other commodities, and by the greater immobility of labour at a time when fixed local associations were a strong binding force, and transport was slow and expensive. When the earlier machinery drew its motive-power chiefly from water, the local attachment and wide distribution of this power prevented the concentration of industry from advancing very far. Only in proportion as steam-power became the dominating agent did the economies of factory-production drive the workers to crowd ever more densely in the districts where coal and water for generating steam were most accessible, and to throng together for the most economical use of steam-power in industry.

This rapid appreciation of the economies of centralised production, heedless of all considerations, sanitary, æsthetic, moral, found a hasty business expression in these huge hideous conglomerations of factory buildings, warehouses, and cheap workmen's shelters, which make the modern industrial town. The requirements of a decent, healthy, harmonious individual or civic life played no appreciable part in the rapid transformation of the mediæval residential centre, or the scattered industrial village into the modern manufacturing town. Considerations of cheap profitable work were paramount; considerations of life were almost utterly ignored. So swift, heedless, anarchic has this process been, that no adequate provisions were made for securing the prime conditions of healthy, physical existence required to maintain the workers in the most profitable state of working efficiency. Only of recent years in a few of the larger manufacturing towns has some slow revival of the idea of civic life, as distinct from the organised manipulation of municipal affairs for selfish business purposes, begun to manifest itself. The typical modern town is still a place of workshops, not of homes.

Transport-machinery, the railway and the steamship, have been almost as important factors in the making of towns as manufacturing-machinery. By easily, quickly, and cheaply bringing food from a distance, they make town work and

town life upon a large scale possible ; by imparting increased
fluidity to capital and labour, they continually increase the
economic advantages of highly concentrated industry. In
the opening up of new countries like the United States and
Australia, the railway is the literal maker of the town, in
older countries it is the chief alimental channel.

The pace at which this concentration of population in
large towns proceeds is the most serviceable measurement
of the progress which the various parts of the industrial
world are making in machine-industry.

There are changes other than those of industrial method
which help the townward movement. The spirit of curiosity
and enterprise stimulated by education and the newspaper
press, a desire for freer and more varied social intercourse,
a love of sensation and amusement, a seeking after culture
and intellectual development, in some cases the mere
promptings of idleness, discontent, or even criminal desires,
drive an increasing proportion of the younger rural population towards the towns. But it is the combination of
industrial changes in which machinery plays the central
part—the increased application of machinery to agriculture
reducing the demand for agricultural labour, the development of manufacturing industries in towns, the labour of
transport and distribution requiring centralised machinery—
that makes this movement physically and economically
feasible. The shift in the proportionate demand for labour
in towns and in country attributable to machine-production
is a principal direct agent in the movement.

§ 2. In England, *par excellence* the manufacturing country,
the growth of the town as compared with the country is
strongly marked during the last thirty years.

	1861.	1871.	1881.	1891.
Urban Population[1] ...	62.3	64.8	66.6	71.7
Rural ,, ...	37.7	35.2	33.4	28.3

During the decennium 1881-91 there was a considerable check in the immigration from the country into the

---

[1] According to Arthur Young, in 1770 half the population was already
urban. But though the townward drift, owing in large measure to the
land-hunger of the aristocracy and wealthy merchant class, and the
labour-saving economy of large farming, was clearly visible before the
development of machine-industry, it is probable that Young's estimate
goes beyond the facts.

large towns, though the proportion of townsfolk to country folk grew even more rapidly than in the preceding ten years.[1]

In Holland and Belgium, notwithstanding a large migration to foreign lands, the towns grow far quicker than the total population. Thus in Holland in the period 1870-79 the towns increased 17.25, while the rural districts only increased 6.8. In Belgium, where the emigration across the border is still larger, there is a tide of migration of the

GROWTH OF FRENCH POPULATION.

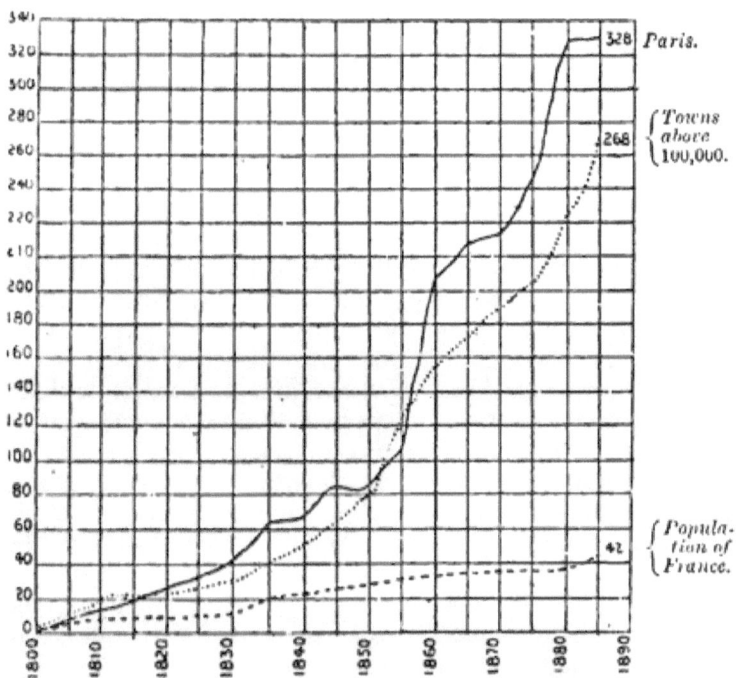

parochial or country population continually setting towards Antwerp, Brussels, and Liege.[2]

This flow of population to the towns is not affected to

[1] Mr. Cannan points out that this is due on the one hand to the healthier conditions of the towns whose natural increase is larger: on the other hand, to an increased migration from the rural parts to foreign countries. ("The Decline of Urban Immigration," *National Review*, January 1894.)

[2] Ravenstein, *Statistical Journal*, June 1889.

any considerable extent either by the rate of growth of the population itself or by the small stake in the land possessed by the bulk of the agricultural population in such a country as England. For in France, where the growth of population during the last half century has been extremely slow, and where the majority of the agriculturists have a definite stake in the soil, the growth of the town population is most remarkable. In Germany also, where peasant-proprietors are very numerous, the towns continually absorb a larger proportion of the population. In 1871 the urban population of the empire was 36.1 per cent. of the total, in 1885 it was 41.8 per cent. In Austria, Hungary, Sweden, Italy, a similar movement is clearly traceable. The above diagram relating to movements of French population indicates that Paris has been growing more rapidly than other French towns. In other industrial countries also it is found that the pace of growth varies for the most part directly with the size of the town. In England, it is true that the largest cities show during the last decennium a certain slackening in the pace of growth. But the towns between 20,000 and 100,000 are still growing far more rapidly than those between 5,000 and 20,000, while those below 5,000 fail to keep pace with the general rise of population. This fact obtains the clearest recognition in the preliminary report of the census of 1891.[1] "The urban population increases then very much more rapidly than the rural population. And not only so, but the larger, or rather the more populous the urban districts,[2] and the more decided therefore its urban character, the higher, generally speaking and with many individual exceptions, is the rate of growth."

The movement is then not merely to town life, but to large-town life. The following diagram shows the rate of growth of the chief European centres of population during the present century :—

[1] *Preliminary Report* (c. 6422), p. 23.
[2] It is often pointed out that an Urban Sanitary District is not always a town. But if rural areas are sometimes classed as towns, many large outskirts of towns, practically partaking of the character of the towns, are not included. The figures cited above may there-fore be regarded as a fairly accurate account of the growth of town life.

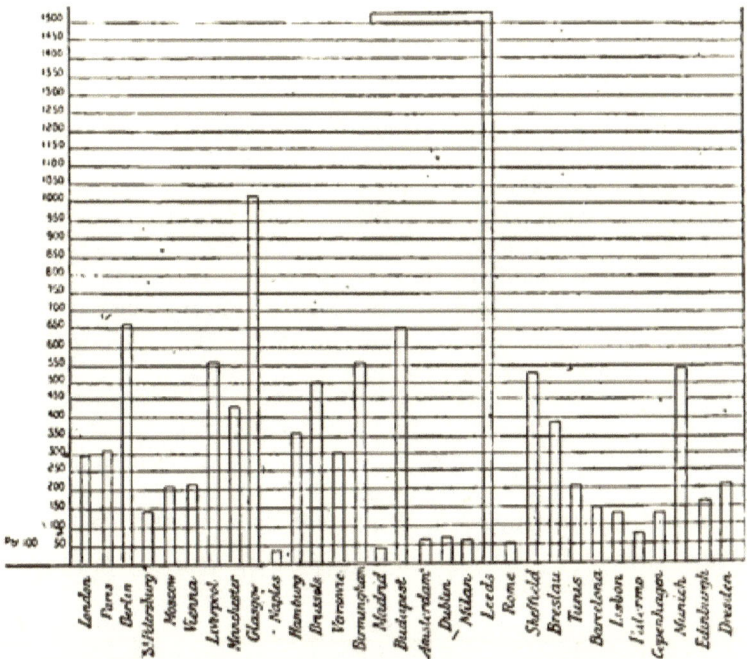

The figures relating to Germany are peculiarly instructive upon this point :—

GERMANY—RATE OF INCREASE OF GOVERNMENT DISTRICTS.[1]

Per Cent.	Times in which such rate occurred.	
	Town Districts.	Rural Districts.
Increase.		
30	3	——
25-30	2	——
20-25	10	1
15-20	33	2
11-15	65	——
9-11	55	4
5-9	50	35
3-5	8	69
1-3	——	56
0-1	1	28
Decrease.		
1-0	1	18
3-1	——	22
5-3	——	3
0-5	——	4

[1] Longstaff, " Rural Depopulation," *Jour. of Stat. Soc.*, Sept. 1893.

German Empire.	1871.	1886	Rate of Increase.
Towns over 100,000	1,968,000	3,327,000	69 per cent.
,, ,, 20,000	3,147,000	4,147,000	31 ,,
,, ,, 5,000	4,588,000	5,694,000	24 ,,
,, .. 2,000	5,086,000	5,734,000	12 ,,
Rural Population .	26,219,000	26,318,000	3 ,,

But the movement is by no means confined to the densely-populated countries of Europe. If we turn to the "new world" we find it illustrated still more remarkably. In the United States of America, long before the population approached its present height, and while large tracts of fertile land still remained to be parcelled out, the towns began to absorb more and more of the population. The following diagram will show this movement to have been continuous, and with a gathering momentum as the century moved on :—

GROWTH OF CITY POPULATION IN THE UNITED STATES.

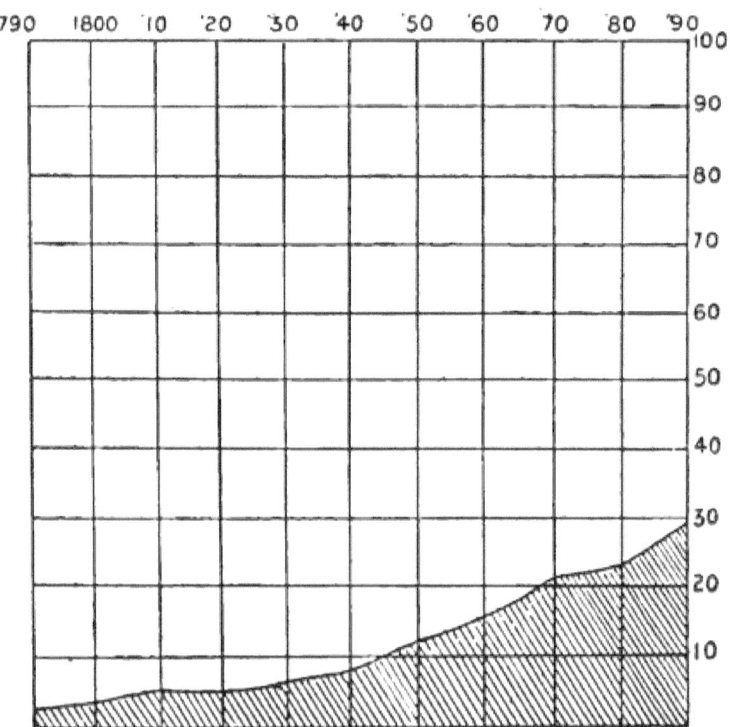

What holds of the United States holds also of the newly settled countries with small populations, as New South Wales, Victoria, Canada, and even Manitoba,[1] Argentina, and Uruguay. Nearly one-third of the whole population of New South Wales is resident in Sydney, and a fourth of the population of Queensland in Brisbane. Victoria presents the most striking case. In 1881 its four largest towns contained more than two-fifths of the whole population, Melbourne alone holding one-third.

In Canada there is the same diminution of rural and growth of town population. New Brunswick contains 14 counties; in the decade 1871-81 · only one of these showed a slight diminution, but not less than 7 in the decade 1881-91. The 18 counties of Nova Scotia all showed an increase in 1871-81, 8 showed a decrease in 1881-91. Quebec contains 61 counties, 10 of which showed a decrease in 1871-81, 26 in 1881-91. Ontario has 48 counties, only 4 of which showed slight decrease in 1871-81; 20 showed a much more rapid decrease in 1881-91.

The following table shows that the accelerating decrease of the rural parts is accompanied by a correspondingly accelerating increase of the chief towns:—

	1871.	1881.	1891.
Kingston [2] . .	12,407	14,091	19,264
London . . .	15,826	26,266	31,977
Ottawa . . .	21,545	31,307	44,154
Hamilton . .	26,717	35,961	48,980
Toronto . . .	56,092	96,196	181,220
	132,586	203,821	325,595

The portentously rapid growth of the largest cities is of course not wholly attributable to economic causes. To form the capital cities of the New World, political and social influences have co-operated with industrial. Nor can these causes be ignored in explaining the rapid growth of certain

[1] Cf. Longstaff, *Studies in Statistics*, p. 157.
[2] These Canadian statistics are quoted from Dr. Longstaff's paper in *Journal of Statistical Society*, Sept. 1893.

European capitals, especially Berlin, Paris, London, and Vienna. But the effective operation of these forces is largely dependent on the modern machinery of transport, and in the main these great centres must be regarded as manufacturing and commercial towns.

Though the lack of any common statistical basis prevents us from being able to trace with exactitude the comparative pace of this movement in different countries, we know enough to justify the general conclusion that this centralising tendency varies directly with the degree of material civilisation attained in the several countries by the mass of the population. In England, France, United States, Australia, where steam engines, electric light, newspapers, and all the most highly elaborated mechanical contrivances are available in towns, the growth of town life is most rapid ; in Russia, Turkey, India, Egypt, where mechanical development is still far behind, the townward march is far slower. As the area of machine-industry spreads, so this movement of population will become more general, and as towns grow larger so it would appear that this power to suck in the rural population is stronger and more extensive.

§ 3. These facts and figures do not, however, of themselves justify the conclusion that a larger proportion of the world's population is moving into towns. In all the advanced industrial countries a smaller proportion of the population is engaged in those extractive and domestic industries which belong to rural life, a larger proportion in the manufacturing and distributive industries which belong to towns. But this movement is made possible by the fact that an increasing proportion of the food and the raw materials of manufacture used in these countries is drawn from the labour of the more backward countries. The increase of the area of the industrial world is effecting such a division of labour as hands over an ever-increasing proportion of the agricultural work to the inhabitants of those countries which do not rank as civilised industrial countries. The known growth of certain large trading centres in India, China, Egypt, South Africa, etc., does not justify us, in the absence of careful statistical inquiry, in assuming that an increased proportion of the inhabitants of these and other more backward portions of the globe is passing into town life. Unless agricultural machinery and improved agricultural methods are advancing more rapidly in these great "growing areas" than we have a right to suppose, it would seem that there must be some increased demand for agricultural and other rural labour which shall, partially, at any rate, compensate for the diminished demand for such kinds of labour in the more advanced industrial communities. For although a large number of the industries subsidiary to agriculture, the making of tools, waggons, gates, fencing, etc., have now passed from the country to the towns, while the economies of machinery and improved cultivation have advanced so far that it is alleged that three men working on soil of average quality can raise food for one thousand, still the growth of population with a constantly rising standard of material consumption seems likely to prevent any net diminution in the proportion of labour engaged upon the soil in the industrial world. So long as modern methods of production and consumption in civilised countries require an ever-increasing quantity of raw materials, it would seem *à priori* unlikely that a smaller proportion of the whole industry of the world should be devoted to agricultural and other extractive industries, and a larger amount to the manufacturing and distributive industries, where the chief economies of machine-production are so largely applied.

Since this growth of town population is quicker in the advanced industrial communities, slower in the less advanced, so it may well be the case that, in the countries which are but slightly and indirectly affected by modern industry, it does not exist at all. There exist, however, no satisfactory data upon which a judgment may be formed upon this point.

§ 4. The effects of this concentration of population upon the character and life of the people are multifarious. For convenience in grouping facts, these effects may be considered in relation to (*A*) physical health, (*B*) intelligence, (*C*) morals, though it will be evident that the influences placed under these respective heads act and react upon one another in many intricate and important ways.

(*A*) The best test of the effect of town life upon the population is afforded by a comparison of the rates of mortality of town and country population respectively.

DEATH-RATE IN TOWN AND COUNTRY DISTRICTS OF
ENGLAND, 1851-90.[1]

Years.	Annual Deaths per 1000.			Deaths in Town Districts to 100 Deaths in Country in equal numbers living.
	England and Wales.	Town.	Country.	
1851-60	22.2	24.7	19.9	124
1861-70	22.5	24.8	19.7	126
1871-80	21.4	23.1	19.0	122
1881	18.9	20.1	16.9	119
1882	19.6	20.9	17.3	121
1883	19.5	20.5	17.9	115
1884	19.5	20.6	17.7	117
1885	19.0	19.7	17.8	111
1886	19.3	20.0	18.0	111
1887	18.8	19.7	17.2	115
1888	17.8	20.9	17.4	114
1889	17.9	19.3	16.4	118
1890		20.9	17.4	120

But as matters stand at present the statistics above quoted do not mark the full extent of the difference of healthfulness in town and country. When allowance is made for age and sex distribution in town and country population, the difference in death-rate appears much greater. For in the towns are found (*a*) a much larger proportion of females; (*b*) a larger proportion of adults of both sexes in the prime of life; (*c*) a much smaller proportion of very aged persons:[2] hence if conditions of health were equal in town and country, the town death-rate would be lower instead of higher than that of the country. The *Report of the Census of 1881*[3] calls special attention to this point, which is commonly ignored in comparing death-rates of town and country. "If we take the mean (1871-80) death-rates in England and Wales at each age-period as a standard, the death-rate in an urban population would be 20.40 per 1000, while the death-rate in the rural

[1] *Report of Commissioners, etc.,* vol. xxx. p. 65.
[2] Newsholm, *Vital Statistics,* p. 137. (Sonnenschein.)
[3] Vol. iv. p. 23.

population would be 22.83. Such would be their respective death-rates on the hypothesis that the urban districts and the rural districts were equally healthy. We know, however as a matter of fact that urban death-rates, instead of being lower than rural death-rates, are much higher. The difference of healthiness, therefore, between the two is much greater than the difference between their death-rates."

The same facts come out in comparing Paris with the rest of France. At each age the death-rate for Paris is higher than for France.

Age.[1]	Paris. 1886.	France. 1877-80.
0 to 1 year	230?	170?
1 to 5 years	58.2	28
15 to 20 ,,	9.1	6
30 to 40 ,,	13.6	10
60 to 70 ,,	51.2	41

The English statistics indicate a slight and by no means constant tendency towards a diminution of the difference between town and rural mortality, due no doubt to improvements in city sanitation and to some general elevation of the physical environment and standard of living among a large section of the working classes. The same slight tendency is visible in France. During the period 1861-65 the urban death-rate was 26.1, as compared with 21.5, the rural death-rate; during the period 1878-82 the rates were respectively 24.3 and 20.9.[2]

Such indications of hygienic progress in our towns are not, however, sufficient to justify any expectation that the life of industrial towns will be made as healthy as that of the country. It is not possible to ignore the fatal significance of the continuous flow of an increasing proportion of the younger, healthier, and more vigorous part of the country population into town life. Dr. Ogle, who has collected much evidence upon this subject, sums up as follows:—
"The combined effect of this constantly higher mortality of the towns, and of the constant immigration into it of the pick of the rural population, must clearly be a gradual deterioration of the whole, inasmuch as the more energetic and vigorous members of the community are consumed

---

[1] Levasseur, vol. ii. p. 402.   [2] *Ibid.*, vol. ii. p. 155.

more rapidly than the rest of the population. The system is one which leads to the survival of the unfittest."

§ 5. Not only is life on an average of shorter duration in the towns, but it is of inferior physical quality while it lasts. The lowering of the townsman's physique not merely renders him less able to resist definite assaults of disease but injures his general capacity of work and enjoyment. This progressive deterioration of physique accounts for the unceasing flow of fresh country blood into the towns. In spite of the advantage of possession and knowledge of the town, the townsman cannot hold his own in the competition for town work; the new-comer jostles the old-comer from the best posts, and drives him to depend upon inferior and more precarious occupations for a living. Economic conditions, acquired social tastes, and impaired powers of physical labour prevent the feeble town blood from flowing back into the country to recruit its vigour. Hence the *impasse* which forces problems of town poverty and incapacity ever more prominently upon the social reformer.

In dealing with the diseases of occupations, Dr. Arlidge says, "It is a most difficult problem to solve, especially in the case of an industrial town population, how far the diseases met with in it are town-made and how far trade-made; the former almost always predominate."[1]

It is not indeed possible to clearly distinguish the two classes of effects. Since machinery makes the industrial town, it makes it as a place to work in and a place to live in, and though certain trade conditions will operate more directly upon the inhabitants as workers, their effects will merge with and react upon the life-conditions of the town. The special characteristics of town work which cause ill-health and disease are—

(*a*) The predominance of indoor occupations, involving unwholesome air.

(*b*) The sedentary character of most work in factories or workrooms, or otherwise the lack of free play of physical activities.

(*c*) The wear and tear of nerve fibre (*e.g.*, in boiler-making, weaving sheds, etc.).

(*d*) The wearisome monotony and lack of interest attend-

---

[1] *Diseases of Occupations*, p. 33.

ing highly specialised and sub-divided machine-industry, producing physical lassitude.[1]

(e) Injuries arising from dust fumes, or other deleterious matter, or from the handling of dangerous material or tools.

Much valuable work has been done of recent years by French, German, and English physicians and statisticians, throwing light upon the specific diseases appertaining to various industries, and giving some measurement of their extent. But though certain specifically industrial qualities have a considerable place in swelling the mortality of towns, Dr. Arlidge is fully justified in his opinion that in industrial centres more of the diseases are town-made than trade-made. The statistics of infant mortality are conclusive upon this point. In comparing the death-rates for town and country, the difference is far wider for children below the industrial age than for adults engaged in industrial work. Mr. Galton has calculated that in a typical industrial town the number of children of artisan townsfolk that grow up are little more than half as many as in the case of the children of labouring people in a healthy country district.[2] The figures quoted above from M. Levasseur relating to France point to a similar conclusion. Many of the evils commonly classified as belonging to specific industries, in particular the foul atmosphere, imperfect sanitation, and overcrowding, which are found in many factories and most city workshops, are rightly regarded as town-made rather than trade-made, for they are the normal and often the necessary accompaniments of a congested industrial population. In qualification of this, having regard to the effects of machine-development, we must remember that the worst hygienic conditions of town work are found in those branches of industry which have lagged behind in industrial evolution, while the best hygienic conditions are found in the most highly-organised branches of textile industry. "Generally speaking, the more elaborate and costly the machinery, the more excellent the architecture. Thus in textile works machinery acquires its maximum of importance, and by its dimensions necessitates commodious shops, buildings of

---

[1] Dr. Arlidge, pp. 25, 26.
[2] Quoted by Professor Marshall, *Principles of Political Economy*, p. 258. Cf. also *Statistical Society*, March 1873, for U.S.A. statistics.

great size, and well-ordered arrangements to facilitate the performance of the mutually dependent series of operations carried on." [1]

Legal restrictions upon unhealthy and dangerous employments, shorter working hours, adequate inspection, the stimulus given by such measures to a more rapid application of highly-developed machinery, may succeed in reducing considerably the physical evils directly arising from town industries. But the town will still remain a more unhealthy place to live in than the country, and as on the one hand the fundamental and paramount importance of a healthy physical environment receives fuller recognition, and on the other hand larger leisure and opportunities of enjoyment and development make life more valuable to the mass of the workers than it is at present, the pressure of this problem of town life will grow apace.

§ 6. (*B*) That town life, as distinguished from town work, is educative of certain intellectual and moral qualities, is evident. Setting aside that picked intelligence which flows to the town to compete successfully for intellectual employment, there can be no question but that the townsman has a larger superficial knowledge of the world and human nature. He is shrewd, alert, versatile, quicker, and more resourceful than the countryman. In thought, speech, action, this superiority shows itself. The townsman has a more developed consciousness, his intelligence is constantly stimulated in a thousand ways by larger and more varied society, and by a more diversified and complex economic environment. While there is reason to believe that town work is on the average less educative than country work, town life more than turns the scale. The social intercourse of the club, the trade society, the church, the home, the public-house, the music-hall, the street, supply innumerable educative influences, to say nothing of the ampler opportunities of consciously organised intellectual education which are available in large towns. If, however, we examine a little deeper the character of town education and intelligence certain tolerably definite limitations show themselves. School instruction, slightly more advanced than in the country, is commonly utilised to sharpen industrial competi-

----

[1] Dr. Arlidge, p. 30.

tion, and to feed that sensational interest in sport and crime which absorbs the attention of the masses in their non-working hours; it seldom forms the foundation of an intellectual life in which knowledge and taste are reckoned in themselves desirable. The power to read and write is employed by the great majority of all classes in ways which evoke a minimum of thought and wholesome feeling. Social, political, and religious ·prejudices are made to do the work which should be done by careful thought and scientific investigation.

Scattered and unrelated fragments of half-baked information form a stock of "knowledge" with which the townsman's glib tongue enables him to present a showy intellectual shop-front. Business smartness pays better in the town, and the low intellectual qualities which are contained in it are educated by town life. The knowledge of human nature thus evoked is in no sense science, it is a mere rule-of-thumb affair, a thin mechanical empiricism. The capable business man who is said to understand the "world" and his fellow-men, has commonly no knowledge of human nature in the larger sense, but merely knows from observation how the average man of a certain limited class is likely to act within a narrow prescribed sphere of self-seeking. Town life, then, strongly favours the education of certain shallow forms of intelligence. In actual attainment the townsman is somewhat more advanced than the country-man. But the deterioration of physique which accompanies this gain causes a weakening of mental fibre: the potentiality of intellectual development and work which the countryman brings with him on his entry to town life is thwarted and depressed by the progressive physical enfeeble-ment. Most of the best and strongest intellectual work done in the towns is done by immigrants, not by town-bred folk.

§ 7. (C) This intellectual weakness of town life is best expressed in terms which show the intimate relation between intelligence and morals. A lack of "grit," pertinacity of purpose, endurance, "character," marks the townsman of the second generation as compared with the countryman. As the intellectual powers of the townsman, though quantitatively impaired, are more highly developed than those of the countryman, so it is with his "morals." In positive attainments of conscience, virtue, and vice, the townsman shows considerable advance. This point is commonly misunderstood. The annals of crime afford irrefutable evidence of the greater criminality of the towns. London, containing less than one-fifth of the population of England and Wales, is responsible for more than one-third of the annual number of indictable crimes.[1] In France the criminality of the urban population is just double that of the rural population.[2] In 1884-86, out of each 100,000 city population sixteen were charged with crimes; out of each 100,000 rural population only eight. It is indeed commonly recognised in criminology that, other things being equal, crime varies with the density of population. There is no difficulty in understanding why this should be so. The pressure of population and the concentration of property afford to the evil-disposed individual an increased number of temptations to invade the person or property of others; for many sorts of crime the conditions of town life afford greater security to the criminal; social and industrial causes create a large degenerate class not easily amenable to social control, incapable of getting regular work to do, or of doing it if they could get it.

If the town were a social organism formed by men desirous of living together for mutual support, comfort, and enjoyment in their lives, it might reasonably be expected that a wholesome public feeling would be so strongly operative as to outweigh the increased opportunities of crime. But, as we have seen, the modern town is a result of the desire to produce and distribute most economically the largest aggregate of material goods: economy of work, not convenience of life, is the object. Now, the economy of factory co-operation is only social to a very limited extent; anti-social feelings are touched and stimulated at every point by the competition of workers with one another, the antagonism between employers and employed, between sellers and buyers, factory and factory, shop and shop.

Perhaps the most potent influence in breaking the strength of the *morale* of the town worker is the precarious

---

[1] W. D. Morrison, "The Study of Crime," *Mind*, vol. i. N.S., No. 4.

[2] Levasseur, vol. ii. p. 456.

and disorderly character of town work. That element of monotonous order, which we found excessive in the education afforded by the individual machine to the machine-tender, is balanced by a corresponding defect in machine-industry taken as a whole. Town work, as we have seen, is more irregular than country work, and this irregularity has a most pernicious effect upon the character of the worker. Professor Foxwell has thus strikingly expressed the moral influences of this economic factor: "When employment is precarious, thrift and self-reliance are discouraged. The savings of years may be swallowed up in a few months. A fatalistic spirit is developed. Where all is uncertain and there is not much to lose, reckless over-population is certain to be set at. These effects are not confined to the poorer classes. The business world is equally demoralised by industrial speculation, careful pre-vision cannot reckon upon receiving its due return, and speculation of the purest gambling type is thereby en-couraged. But the working class suffers most."[1]

The town as an industrial structure is at present inade-quate to supply a social education which shall be strong enough to defeat the tendencies to anti-social conduct which are liable to take shape in criminal action. The intellectual training given by town life does not, as we have seen, assist in stimulating higher intellectual and moral interests whose satisfaction lies above the plane of material desire. There is indeed some evidence that the meagre and wholly rudimentary education given to our town-dwellers is, by reason of its inadequacy, a direct feeder of town vices. The lower forms of music-hall entertainment, the dominant popular vice of gambling, the more degraded kinds of printed matter, owe their existence and their financial success to a public policy which has confined the education of the people to the three R's, making it generally impos-sible, always difficult, for them to obtain such intellectual training as shall implant higher intellectual interests with whose pursuit they may occupy their leisure. But, in taking count of the criminality and vice of large towns it is not just to ignore a certain counter-claim which might be made. If our annals of virtue were kept as carefully as our annals

[1] *Claims of Labour*, p. 196.

of vice, we might find that town life stood higher in the one than in the other. There are more opportunities to display positive goodness and positive badness in the town; life is more crowded and more rapid, and it is likely that acts of kindness, generosity, self-denial, even of heroic self-sacrifice, are more numerous in the town than in the country. The average townsman is more developed morally as well as intellectually for good and for evil. That the good does not more signally predominate is in no small measure due to the feeble social environment. Public opinion is generally a little in advance of the average morality of the individuals who compose the public. Here is a mighty lever for raising the masses. But where the density of population is determined by industrial competition, rather than by human-social causes, it would seem that the force of sound public opinion is in inverse proportion to the density of population, being weakest in the most crowded cities. In spite of the machinery of political, religious, social, trade organisations in large towns, it is probable that the true spiritual cohesiveness between individual members is feebler than in any other form of society. If it is true that as the larger village grows into the town, and the town into the ever larger city, there is a progressive weakening of the bonds of moral cohesion between individuals, that the larger the town the feebler the spiritual unity, we are face to face with the heaviest indictment that can be brought against modern industrial progress, and the forces driving an increased proportion of our population into towns are bringing about a decadence of *morale* which is the necessary counterpart of the deterioration of national physique.

So far as we are justified in regarding the modern town and the tendency to increased town life as results of machinery and industrial evolution, there can be little doubt of the validity of these accusations. The free play of economic forces under the guidance of the selfish instincts of commercial individuals, or groups of individuals, is driving an increased proportion of the population of civilised countries into a town life which is injurious to physical and moral health, and provides no security for the attainment of an intellectual life which is worth living.

§ 8. But powerful as these centralising forces have been during the last century and a half, we are not justified in

assuming that they will continue to operate with gathering
momentum in the future, and that the results which are
assigned to them will increase in magnitude.   Such an
assumption would ignore two groups of counteracting forces
which are beginning to manifest themselves in the more
advanced industrial communities.

The first of these groups consists of a number of directly
counteracting or decentralising forces.

As a town grows in size the value of the ground on
which it stands grows so rapidly that it becomes economically available only for certain classes of industrial undertaking, in which the occupation of central space is an
element of prime importance.   In all large commercial
cities the residential quarters are driven gradually farther
and farther away from the centre by incessant encroachments of business premises.   The city of London and
the "down town" quarter of New York are conspicuous
examples of this displacement of residential buildings by
commercial.   The richer inhabitants are the earliest and
quickest to leave.   As the factory or the shop plants itself
firmly among the better-class dwelling-houses, these inhabitants pass in large numbers to the outskirts of the town,
forming residential suburbs which, for some time at any
rate, are free from the specific evils of congestion.   This
encroachment of the factory and the shop at first has little
effect, if any, in thinning the residential population of the
district.   While the shopkeepers and their employees live in
the neighbourhood, and the factory workers can afford to
pay the rent for houses or lodgings near their work, the
central population will grow denser than before.   But as
the city grows in size and commercial importance, an increasing number of the most central sites will pass from
manufactory premises and shops into use for warehouses
and business offices, and for other work in connection with
distribution and finance.   The workers on these premises
will, in the case of the wealthier, be unwilling, in the case
of the poorer be unable, to live near their work; where
factories and shops remain, the great mass of the employees
will not be able to afford house-rents determined by this
competition of a more valuable commercial use of land.
So we find that the number of inhabitants of the city of
London diminishes in each recent census, and the same is

true as regards the most valuable portions of Paris, New
York, and other large cities. This decentralising force is,
however, only in full operation in the very centre of the
largest cities. The first effect of the competition of commercial with living premises is to raise house-rents and to
drive the poorer population into narrower, less commodious,
and less sanitary dwellings. Where ground landowner and
builder have a free hand the market value of central ground
for small, lofty, cheap-built slums can be made to hold its
own for a long time with the business premises which
surround them. Even when ground value has risen so
high as to displace many of these slums, the tendency is
for the latter to spring up and thicken in districts not far
removed from the centre. Thus in London the densest
population is found in Whitechapel and St. George's in
the East. Indeed, there is evidence that these districts
have already reached "saturation point," that is to say,
the pressure of business demands for ground, the increased
competition of the dwellers themselves, and the growing
restrictions imposed by law and public opinion upon the
construction of the most "paying" forms of house property,
prevent any further growth of population in these parts.
As this saturation point is reached in one district, the growth
of dense population goes on faster in the outlying districts,
and, with forms which vary with local conditions, the same
economic forces manifest themselves with similar results
over a wider area. The poorer population shifts as short
a distance as it can, and then only when driven by a rise
of rents. Even when it moves somewhat farther out it
seldom gets far enough to escape the centralising forces.
Residential working-class districts like West Ham become
rapidly congested by the constant flow of population from
more central places. Moreover, the same decentralising
forces are set up in the large suburban districts, by
the planting there of factories and other industrial works
designed to take advantage of a large supply of labour
close at hand, and land procurable at a lower rental. This
applies also to many of the suburbs originally chosen as
residential quarters of the well-to-do classes. The whole
western district of London, comprised by Kensington,
Notting Hill, Hammersmith, etc., contains large and
designed areas of dense poverty and overcrowding. So

far as the mass of poorer workers in London and other large cities are concerned, it would appear that their endeavour to escape beyond the limits of congested city life has hitherto been unavailing : the decentralising forces of rising ground rents, uncomfortable and insanitary dwellings, are ever at work, but the centralising forces set up by any large number who seek an outlet in the same direction, with close spacial limitations to their migrating tendency, are too strong. High rents, a fuller appreciation of the hygienic advantages of more space, and of proximity to country air and country scenes, have induced an increasing number of the " middle " classes, and even of those who, in a pecuniary sense, form the upper working class, to incur the expenditure of time, trouble, and railway fares involved in living sufficiently far from the centre to avoid the centralising pressure. The most important practical problem of social reform to-day is how to secure this option of extra-city life for the mass of city workers. If the economies of low ground rent and slightly cheaper labour were sufficiently large to induce the establishment of manufactories at considerable distances from large centres of population, we might look in time to see the large industrial town give place to a number of industrial villages, gathered round some single large factory or " works." The growing facilities of communication with large towns at increased distances, afforded by recent expansions of railway service, and by improvements in telegraphic and telephonic media, have done something towards this form of decentralisation. Round Manchester and other larger northern manufacturing towns an increasing number of factories are springing up ; in the United States the same phenomenon is still commoner. Smaller rents, cheaper living, lower wages, especially in textile mills where women are largely employed, and lastly, more submissive labour, are everywhere the economic stimuli of this decentralisation of manufacture. Assuming that some more cheaply and easily transmissible motor-power can be found for manufacture, and that a cheap and readily available transport service by steam or electricity is widely spread, it seems not unlikely that the economies of decentralised manufacture may widely or even universally outweigh the primary centralising economies which created

our great manufacturing towns. Whether a wide diffusion
of industrial villages, which might be of a size and structure
to reproduce in a somewhat less virulent form many of the
physical and moral vices of the larger towns, and which
possibly might retard or nullify some of the educative and
elevating influences springing from the organisation and co-
operative action of large masses of workers, can be regarded
as a desirable substitute or remedy for our congested city
life, is open to grave doubt. A whole country like England,
thickly blotched at even intervals by big industrial villages
comprised of a huge factory or two with a few rectangular
streets of small, dull, grimy, red-brick cottages, and one or
two mansions standing inside their parks at the side remote
from the factories, would, from an æsthetic point of view, be
repulsive to the last degree ; and out of a country, the whole
of which was thus ordered for pure purposes of industrial
economy, it is difficult to believe that any of the higher
products of human effort could proceed. But the possibility of some such outcome of the decentralising forces
already visible must not be ignored. It is even likely that
the labour movement, advancing as it does more rapidly in
large manufacturing centres than elsewhere, may, by increasing the freedom and power of labour associated upon a large
scale, apply an additional stimulus to the *entrepreneur* to place
his business undertakings so as to make strongly combined
action of labourers more difficult. American manufacturers
are distinctly actuated by this motive in selecting the
locality of their factories, and have been able in many
cases to maintain a despotic control over the workers which
would be quite impossible were their factories planted in
the middle of a large city.[1]

§ 9. This method of partial decentralisation depends in
large measure, it is evident, upon such progress in the transport services for persons, goods, and intelligence as shall
minimise the inconvenience of a less central position, rendering the location of the business a matter of comparative
indifference. But it is to improved transport services that
we may look to facilitate a kind of decentralisation, the net

---

[1] One of the specific advantages in America has been the absence of
any serious endeavour on the part of legislation to put down Truck.
The grossest abuses of Truck appear in country manufacturing towns
of the United States.

gain of which is less dubious than that arising from the substitution of a large number of industrial villages for a small
number of industrial towns. Is it not possible for more
town-workers to combine centralised work with decentralised
life—to work in the town but to live in the country? May
not this advantage, at present confined to the wealthier
classes, be brought within the reach of the poorer classes?
Some small progress has been made of recent years towards
the realisation of this ideal. Three chief difficulties stand
in the way of success: the length of the working-day, which
makes the time required for travelling to and from a distant
home a matter of serious consideration; the defective
supply of convenient, cheap, and frequent trains or other
quick means of conveyance; the irregularity and uncertainty of tenure in most classes of labour, which prevents
the establishment of a settled house chosen with regard to
convenient access to a single point of industry. Some
recent progress has been made in large cities, such as
Vienna, Paris, and London, in providing workmen's trains
and by the cheapening of train and 'bus fares; but such
experiments are generally confined within too narrow an
area to achieve any satisfactory amount of decentralisation,
for the interests of private carrying companies demand that
the largest number of passengers shall travel from the
smallest number of stations. It would appear that considerable extension of direct public control over the means
of transport will be required, in order to secure to the people
the full assistance of modern mechanical appliances in
enabling them to avoid the mischief of over-crowded dwellings. For such purposes the railway has now replaced the
high-road, and we can no more afford to entrust the public
interest in the one case to the calculating self-interest of
private speculation than in the other case. A firm public
control in the common interest over the steam and electric
railways of the future seems essential to the attainment of
adequate decentralisation for dwelling purposes. Private
enterprise in transport, working hand in hand with private
ownership of land, will only substitute for a single mass of
over-crowded dwellings a number of smaller suburban areas
of over-crowded dwellings. The bicycle alone, among
modern appliances of mechanical speed, can safely be
entrusted to the free private control of individuals, and, if

one may judge by the remarkable expansion of its use, it
seems likely to afford no trifling assistance to the decentralising tendencies.

§ 10. The removal of the other two barriers belongs to
that joint action of labour organisation and legislation which
aims at building up a condition of stable industrial economy.
One of the most serviceable results of that shortening of the
working-day, upon which public attention is so powerfully
concentrated, would be the assistance it would render to
enable workmen and workwomen to live at a longer distance from their work. So long, however, as a large proportion of city workers have no security of tenure in their
work, are liable at a day's or a week's notice, for no fault of
their own, to be obliged to seek work under another
employer in a distant locality, or if employed by the same
master to be sent to a distant job, now to find themselves
without any work at all, at another time to have to work all
hours to make up a subsistence wage, it is evident that
these schemes of decentralisation can be but partial in their
application. An increased stability both in the several
trades and in the individual businesses within the trade is a
first requisite to the establishment of a fixed healthy home
for the industrial worker and his family.

§ 11. It is, however, unlikely that any wide or lasting
solution of the problem of congested town life will be
found in a sharp local severance of the life of an industrial
society which shall abandon the town to the purposes of a
huge workshop, reserving the country for habitation. The
true unity of individual and social life forbids this abrupt
cleavage between the arts of production and consumption,
between the man and his work. It is only in the case
of the largest and densest industrial cities, swollen to an
unwieldy and dangerous size, that such methods of decentralisation can in some measure be applied. In these
monstrous growths machinery of decentralisation may be
evoked to undo in part at any rate the work of centralising
machinery. In smaller towns, where the circumference
bears a larger proportion to the mass, a spreading of the
close-packed population over an expanded town-area will be
more feasible, and will form the first step in that series of
reforms which shall humanise the industrial town. The
congestion of the poorer population of our towns, and the

struggle for fresh air and elbow-room which it implies, is the most formidable barrier to the work of transforming the town from a big workshop into a human dwelling-place, with an individual life, a character, a soul of its own. The true reform policy is not to destroy the industrial town but to breathe into it the breath of social life, to temper and subordinate its industrial machine-goods-producing character to the higher and more complex purposes of social life. An ample, far-sighted, enlightened, social control over the whole area of city ground, whether used for dwellings or for industrial purposes, is the first condition of the true municipal life. The industrial town, left for its growth to individual industrial control, compresses into unhealthily close proximity large numbers of persons drawn together from different quarters of the earth, with different and often antagonistic aims, with little knowledge of one another, with no important common end to form a bond of social sympathy. The town presents the single raw material of local proximity out of which municipal life is to be built. The first business of the municipal reformer then is to transform this excessive proximity into wholesome neighbourhood, in order that true neighbourly feelings may have room to grow and thrive, and eventually to ripen into the flower of a fair civic life. "A modern city," it has been well said, "is probably the most impersonal combination of individuals that has ever been formed in the world's history."[1] To evoke the personal human qualities of this medley of city workers so as to reach within the individual the citizen, to educate the civic feeling until it take shape in civic activities and institutions, which shall not only safeguard the public welfare against the encroachments of private industrial greed, but shall find an ever ampler and nobler expression in the æsthetic beauty and spiritual dignity of a complex, common life—all this work of transformation lies in front of the democracy, grouped in its ever-increasing number of town-units.

[1] J. S. Mackenzie, *An Introduction to Social Philosophy*, p. 101.

CHAPTER XIV.

CIVILISATION AND INDUSTRIAL DEVELOPMENT.

§ 1. *Imperfect Adjustment of Industrial Structure to its Environment.*

§ 2. *Reform upon the Basis of Private Enterprise and Free Trade.*

§ 3. *Freedom and Transparency of Industry powerless to cure the deeper Industrial Maladies.*

§ 4. *Beginnings of Public Control of Machine-production.*

§ 5. *Passage of Industries into a public Non-competitive Condition.*

§ 6. *The "raison d'être" of Progressive Collectivism.*

§ 7. *Collectivism follows the line of Monopoly.*

§ 8. *Cases of "Arrested Development:" the Sweating Trades.*

§ 9. *Retardation of rate of Progress in Collective Industries.*

§ 10. *Will Official Machine-work absorb an Increasing Proportion of Energy?*

§ 11. *Improved Quality of Consumption the Condition of Social Progress.*

§ 12. *The Highest Division of Labour between Machinery and Art.*

§ 13. *Qualitative Consumption defeats the Law of Decreasing Returns.*

§ 14. *Freedom of Art from Limitations of Matter.*

§ 15. *Machinery and Art in production of Intellectual Wealth.*

§ 16. *Reformed Consumption abolishes Anti-Social Competition.*

§ 17. *Life itself must become Qualitative.*

§ 18. *Organic Relations between Production and Consumption.*

§ 19. *Summary of Progress towards a Coherent Industrial Organism.*

§ 1. Modern industrial societies have hitherto secured to a very inadequate extent the services which modern machinery and methods of production are capable of rendering. The actual growth of material wealth, however great, has been by no means commensurate with the enormously increased powers of producing material commodities afforded by the discoveries of modern science, and the partial utilisation of these discoveries has been attended by a very unequal distribution of the advantages of this increase in the stock of common knowledge and control of nature. Moreover, as an offset against the growth of material wealth, machinery has been a direct agent in producing certain material and moral maladies which impair the health of modern industrial communities.

The unprecedented rapidity and irregularity of the discovery and adoption of the new methods made it impossible for the structure of industrial society to adjust itself at once to the conditions of the new environment. The maladies and defects which we detect in modern industry are but the measure of a present maladjustment.

The progressive adjustment of structure to environment in the unconscious or low-conscious world is necessarily slow. But where the conscious will of man, either as an individual or as a society, can be utilised for an adjusting force, the pace of progress may be indefinitely quickened. A strongly-rooted custom in a man yields very slowly to the pressure of changed circumstances which make it useless or harmful, unless the man consciously recognises the inutility of the custom and sets himself to root it out and plant another custom in its place. So the slowness of this work of industrial adjustment has been in no small measure due to the lack of definite realisation by the members of modern communities of the need and importance of this adjustment. A society which should bring its conscious will to bear upon the work of constructing new social and industrial forms to fit the new economic conditions, may make a progress which, while rapid, may yet be safe, because it is not a speculative progress, but one which is guided in its line of movement by precedent changes of environment.

Regarding, then, this conscious organised endeavour, enlightened and stimulated by a fuller understanding of

industrial forces in their relation to human life, as a determinant of growing value in the industrial evolution of the
future, it may properly belong to a scientific study of
modern industry to seek to discover how the forces of
conscious reform can reasonably work in relation to the
economic forces whose operations have been already investigated.

In other words, what are the chief lines of economic
change required to bring about a readjustment between
modern methods of production and social welfare?   The
answer to this question requires us to amplify our interpretation of the industrial evolution of the past century, by
producing into the future the same lines of development,
that they may be justified by the appearance of consistency
with some rational social end.   The most convenient,·and
perhaps the safest way to meet this demand is to indicate,
with that modesty which rightly belongs to prophecy, some
of the main reforms which seem to lie upon the road of
industrial progress, rendered subordinate to larger human
social ends.

§ 2. So far as the waste of economic maladjustment
consists in the excessive or defective application of various
kinds of productive force at different points of industry,
upon the existing basis of individual initiative and control,
the reforms which are desirable must be considered as
contributing to the more complete establishment of "free"
competition in industry.

The complete breakdown of all barriers which impede
the free flow of commerce and the migration of capital and
labour, the fullest and widest dissemination of industrial
information, are necessary to the attainment of the individualistic ideal of free trade.   Perfect transparency of
industrial operations, perfect fluidity of labour and of wealth
would effect incalculably great economies in the production
of commercial wealth.   The free-trader, in his concentration
upon the achievement of the latter economy, has generally
failed to do full justice to the importance of the former.
He has indeed to some limited extent recognised the value
of accurate and extended industrial information as the
intellectual basis of free trade.   But, in common with most
economists, he has failed to carry this consideration far
enough.   It is generally admitted that the increased pub-

lication of accounts and quotations of stock, springing out
of the extension of joint-stock enterprise, the growth of
numerous trade journals, the collection and dissemination
of industrial facts by government bureaux and private
statisticians, are serviceable in many ways. But the extreme
repugnance which is shown towards all endeavours to
extend the compulsory powers of acquiring information by
the state, the extreme jealousy with which the rights of
private information are maintained, show how inadequately
the true character of modern industry is grasped. In the
complexity of modern commerce it should be recognised
that there is no such thing as a "self-regarding" or a private
action. No fact bearing on prices, wages, profits, methods
of production, etc., concerns a single firm or a single body
of workers. Every industrial action, however detailed in
character, however secretly conducted, has a public import,
and necessarily affects the actions and interests of innumerable persons. Indeed it is often precisely in the knowledge
of those matters regarded as most private, and most carefully
secreted, that the public interest chiefly lies. Yet so firmly
rooted in the business mind is the individualistic conception
of industry, that any idea of a public development of those
important private facts upon which the credit of a particular
firm is based, would appear to destroy the very foundation
of the commercial fabric. But, although in the game of
commerce a single firm which played its hand openly while
others kept theirs well concealed might suffer failure, it is
quite evident that the whole community interested in the
game would gain immensely if all the hands were on the
table. Many, if not most, of the great disasters of modern
commercial societies are attributable precisely to the fact that
the credit of great business firms, which is pre-eminently an
affair of public interest, is regarded as purely private before
the crash. As industry grows more and more complex, so
the interest of the public and of an ever-wider public in
every industrial action grows apace, and a correspondingly
growing recognition of this public interest, with provision
for its security, will be found necessary. So far as the
natural changes of industrial structure in the private business fail to provide the requisite publicity, the exercise of
direct public scrutiny must come to be enforced. The
reluctance shown alike by bodies of employers and of

workers to divulge material facts is in large measure due to
the false ideas they have conceived as to the nature of
industrial activity, which education can do something to
remove, but which, if not removed, must be over-ruled in
the public interest.

§ 3. It must not, however, be supposed that the most
thorough transparency of industry, any more than the
removal of the political barriers which prevent Free Trade,
would tend to bring about the desirable adjustment between
the healthy social organism and the environment of machine-
production. Full free trade would supply, quicken, and
facilitate the operation of those large economic forces which
we have seen at work : the tendency of capital to gravitate
into larger and fewer masses, localised where labour can
be maintained upon the most economical terms : a correspondent but slower and less complete organisation of labour
in large masses : the flow of labouring population into towns,
together with a larger utilisation of women and (where permitted) children for industrial work : a growing keenness
of antagonism as the mass of the business-unit is larger,
and an increased expenditure of productive power upon
aggressive commercial warfare : the growth of monopolies
springing from natural, social, or economic sources, con-
ferring upon individuals or classes the power to consume
without producing, and by their consumption to direct the
quantity and character of large masses of labour.

The complete realisation of full free trade in all directions
has no power whatever to abate the activity of these forces,
and would only serve to bring their operation into more
signal and startling prominence.

For the waste of periodic over-production visible in trade
depression, for the sufferings caused by ever larger oscillations in prices and greater irregularity of employment of
capital and labour, for the specific evils of long hours or
excessive intensity of labour, dangerous and unwholesome
conditions of employment, increased employment of women
and children, and growth of large-city life, freedom of trade
conjoined with publicity of business operations can furnish
no remedies.

It has been seen that these injuries to individuals and
groups of individuals, and through them to society, arise
naturally and necessarily from the unfettered operation of

the enlightened self-interest of individuals and groups of individuals engaged in obtaining for themselves, by the freest use of industrial means available, the largest quantity of money.

So far as these evils are in form or in magnitude the peculiar products of the last two centuries, they are in large measure traceable to methods of production controlled by machinery, and to the social estimate of machine-products which gives machinery this controlling power.

If this is so, such progress as shall abate these evils and secure for humanity the uses of machinery without the abuses will lie in two directions, each of which deserves consideration : (1) an adequate social control over machine-production ; (2) an education in the arts of consumption such as may assign proper limits to the sphere of machine-production.

§ 4. That machinery subject to the unrestricted guidance of the commercial interests of an individual or a class cannot be safely trusted to work for the general welfare, is already conceded by all who admit the desirability or necessity of the restrictive legislation of Factory Acts, Mines Regulation Acts, and the large growth of public provisions for guarding against economic, hygienic, and other injuries arising from the conditions of modern industrial life.

These provisions, whether designed directly to secure the interests of a class of employees, as in the case of Factory Acts, or to protect the consuming public, as in the case of Adulteration Acts, must be regarded as involving an admission of a genuine antagonism between the apparent interests of individuals and of the whole community, which it is the business of society to guard against.

All this legislation is rightly interpreted as a restriction of the freedom of individual industry under modern methods of production, required in the public interest. Uncontrolled machine-production would in some cases force children of six or eight years to work ten hours a day in an unhealthy factory, would introduce suddenly a host of Chinese or other "cheap" workers to oust native labour accustomed to a higher standard of comfort, would permit an ingenious manufacturer to injure the consumer by noxious adulteration of his goods, would force wages to be paid by orders upon shops owned or controlled by employers, would oblige workers to herd together in dens of infection, and to breed physical and moral diseases which would injure the body politic. The need of a growing social control over modern machine-production, in cases where that production is left in the main to the direction of individual enterprise, is admitted on every side, though the development of that control has been uneven and determined by the pressure of concrete grievances rather than by the acceptance of any distinct theory of public responsibility.

Other limitations upon individual freedom of industry imply a clearer recognition of the falsehood of the *laissez faire* position. The undertaking by the State or the Municipality, or other units of social life, of various departments of industry, such as the railways, telegraphs, post-offices, is a definite assertion that, in the supply of the common services rendered by these industries, the competition of private interests cannot be relied upon to work for the public good.

§ 5. The industries which the State either limits or controls in the interest either of a body of workers or of the consuming public may be regarded as passing from a private competitive condition to a public non-competitive condition. If therefore we wish to ascertain how far and in what directions social control of modern production will proceed, we shall examine those industries which already exhibit the collective character. We shall find that they are of two kinds—(1) industries where the size and structure of the "business" is such that the protection afforded by competition to the consuming public and to the workers has disappeared, or is in frequent abeyance, (2) industries where the waste and damage of excessive competition outweighs the loss of enterprise caused by a removal or restriction of the incentive of individual gain. As we have seen in the analysis of "trusts," these two characteristics, wasteful competition and monopoly, are often closely related, the former signifying the process of intense struggle, the object and ultimate issue of which is to reach the quiet haven of monopoly. Generally speaking, social control in the case of over-competing industries is limited to legislative enactments regarding conditions of employment and quality of goods. Only those industries tend to pass under public administration where the monopoly is of an article of general and necessary consumption, and where, therefore, a raising of prices considerably above the competition rate would not succeed in evoking effective competition. Since the general tendency of industry, so far as it falls under modern economies of machinery and method, is either towards wasteful competition or towards monopoly, it is to be expected that there will be a continual expansion of State interference and State undertakings. This growing socialisation of industry must be regarded as the natural adjustment of society to the new conditions of machine-production. As under the economies of machine-production the business-unit, the mass of capital and labour forming a single "firm" or "business," grows larger in size and more potent in its operations, the social disturbances which it can occasion by its private activity, the far-reaching and momentous results of its strain of competition, the probability of an anti-social exercise of "monopolic" power over the whole or part of its market-area, will of necessity increase. The railway and shipping industries, for example, in countries like England and the United States, have already reached a stage of industrial development when the social danger arising from an arbitrary fixing of rates by a line or a "pool" of lines, from a strike or lock-out of "dockers" or railway men, is gaining keener recognition every year. The rapidly growing organisation of both capital and labour, especially in the fundamental industries of coal, iron, and machine-making, in the machine-transport industries, and the most highly evolved manufactories, gives to a body of employers or employed, or to a combination of both, the power at any moment to paralyse the whole or a large portion of the entire trade of a country in pursuit of some purely private interest or resentment, or in the acquisition of some strategical position, which shall enable them to strengthen their competing power or gain a monopoly. Although the organisation of masses of capital and of labour may, as is often urged, make industrial strife less frequent, the effects of such strife upon the wider public, who have no opportunity of casting a vote for war or peace, are more momentous. Moreover, as these private movements of capital and labour proceed, the probability of combined action between employers and employed in a particular industry, to secure for themselves some advantages at the public expense, will be a factor of increasing importance in industrial evolution.

The Trade Union movement and the various growths of Industrial Partnership, valuable as they are from many points of view, furnish no remedies against the chief forms of economic monopoly and economic waste; they can only change the personality and expand the number of monopolists, and alter the character, not the quantity, of economic waste. Society has an ever-deepening and more vital interest in the economical management of the machinery of transport, and this interest is no whit more secure if the practical control of railways and docks were in the hands of the Dockers' Union or the Amalgamated Society of Railway Servants, or of a combined board of directors and trade union officials, than it is under present circumstances. On the contrary, an effective organisation of capital and labour in an industry would be more likely to pursue a policy opposed to the interests of the wider public than now, because such a policy would be far more likely to succeed.

§ 6. When it is said that modern industry is becoming essentially more collective in character and therefore demands collective control, what is meant is that under modern industrial development the interest of the industrial society as a whole, and of the consuming public in each piece of so-called private enterprise, is greater than it was ever before, and requires some guarantee that this interest shall not be ignored. Where the industry is of such a kind, and in such a stage of development, that keen competition without undue waste survives, this public interest can commonly be secured by the enactment of restrictive legislation. Where such partial control is insufficient to secure the social interest against monopoly or waste, State management, upon a national, municipal, or such other scale as is economically advisable, must take the place of a private enterprise which is dangerous to society. This necessity becomes obvious as soon as the notion of a business as being purely "private" or "self-regarding" in its character is seen to be directly negatived by an understanding of the complex social nature of every commercial act. So soon as the idea of a social industrial organism is grasped, the question of State interference in, or State assumption of, an industry becomes a question of social expediency—that is, of the just interpretation of the facts relating to the particular case. In large measure this social control is to be regarded, not as a necessary protection against the monopolic power of individuals, but as necessary for the security of individual property within the limits prescribed by social welfare. Modern machine-evolution, as is seen, permits and encourages the wanton invasion and destruction of forms of capital by the competition of new savings employed in an anti-social way. It likewise tends to the frequent destruction of the value of that labour power which is the sole property of the mass of workers. " The property which every man has in his own labour, as it is the original foundation, so it is the most sacred and inviolable."[1]

There are certain wastes of economic power involved in all competition ; there are certain dangers of monopoly attaching to all private conduct of industry. Collective control deals with these wastes and dangers, adjusting itself to their extent and character.

§ 7. To the question how far and how rapidly may this extension of collective control proceed, no more definite answer is possible than this, that as a larger and larger amount of industry passes into the condition of the most highly evolved machine-industries of to-day, and develops along with the corresponding economies, corresponding dangers and wastes, larger portions will pass under restrictive legislation or State management.

The evolution in the structure of capitalist enterprise, while it breeds and aggravates the diseases of trade depression, sweating, etc., likewise prepares the way and facilitates the work of social control. It is easier to inspect a few large factories than many small ones, easier to arbitrate where capital and labour stands organised in large masses, easier to municipalise big joint-stock businesses in gas, water, or conveyance. Every legislative interference, in the way of inspection or minor control, quickens the evolution of an industry, and hastens the time when it acquires the position of monopoly which demands a fuller measure of control, and finally passes into the ranks of public industry.

Thus it would follow that, unless proceeding *pari passu* with this evolution there was a springing up or an expansion

---

[1] *Wealth of Nations*, p. 110.

of other industries not so amenable to large machine production and therefore not prone to the dangers and wastes
which appertain to it, collectivism would absorb an ever-
increasing proportion of industrial effort.

§ 8. At present it appears that there are two great classes
of productive work which have not fallen under machine-
industry and capitalism in its typical form. There is that
work which machinery is technically competent to perform,
but which it cannot economically undertake so long as
large quantities of very cheap labour are available. This
class comprises the bulk of what are commonly called the
"sweating" trades, the cheap low-skilled domestic workshop
labour. The other class consists of artistic and intellectual
work which cannot be successfully undertaken by machinery.
The first of these classes is universally admitted to comprise
cases of arrested development. The irregular working of
the more highly-evolved industries, the successive supplanta-
tion of branches of skilled labour by machinery, the blind
migration of labour from distant parts, keeps the large
industrial centres supplied with a quantity of unskilled and
untrained labour, which can be bought so cheaply that in
the lowest branches of many trades it does not pay the
entrepreneur to incur the initial cost of setting up expensive
machinery and the risk of working it. The social and
moral progress of industrial nations requires, as a first
condition of orderly progress, that these cases of arrested
growth shall be absorbed into the general mass of machine-
industry. These problems of "the sweating system," the
unemployed, the pauper class, the natural products of the
working of a system of competition where the competitors
start from widely different lines of opportunity, can never be
solved by the private play of enlightened self-interest, unless
that enlightenment take a far more altruistic form than is
consistent with the continuance of competitive industry.
This is the fundamental paralogism of that school of
reformers who find the cure of industrial maladies in
the humanisation of the private employer. A whole class
of employers sufficiently humane and far-sighted to consistently desire the welfare of their employees (and no
fewer than the whole class would suffice, for otherwise the
less benevolent will undersell and take the business from
the more benevolent) would be so highly civilised that

they would no longer be willing to compete with one another so as to injure one another's business : they would out of pure goodwill organise into a " monopoly," and working this monopoly for the exclusive interest of themselves and their employees, rack-rent the consuming public ; or if their benevolence extended to all their customers they would socialise their business, conducting it for the greatest good of all society. Such a form of socialised industry, dependent upon the moral character of perishable individuals, would possess all the weaknesses charged against State socialism without any of the educative advantages or the security and stability of that system. The " captain of industry " remedy is a sentimental and not a scientific one. Once regard " sweating " as a case of arrested development and the true line of progress will be seen to lie in the absorption of these backward industries into the main current of industrial movement, leaving them to pass through the necessary phases of machine-production and to be subjected to an increasing pressure of social control until they are ripe for society to undertake. Then there will remain outside of capitalist machine-industry only that class of work which is artistic and therefore individualistic in character.

§ 9. We now stand face to face with the main objection so often raised against all endeavours to remedy industrial and social diseases by the expansion of public control. Competition and the zest of individual gain, it is urged, furnish the most effective incentive to enterprise and discovery. Assuming that society were structurally competent to administer industry officially, the establishment of industrial order would be the death-blow to industrial progress. The strife, danger, and waste of industrial competition are necessary conditions to industrial vitality.

How much force do these objections contain in the light of the information provided by our study of industrial evolution? It should be recognised at the outset that the economic individualist is not a conservative, defending an established order and pointing out the dangers attending proposed innovations. Our analysis of the structure of modern industry shows the progressive socialisation of certain classes of industry as a step in the order of events, equally natural and necessary with the earlier steps by which

machine-industry superseded handicraft and crystallised in
ever larger masses with changing relations to one another.
The indictment against social control over industry is an
indictment against a natural order of events, on the ground
that nature has taken a wrong road of advancement.   It
is only possible to regard the legislative action by which
public control over industry is established as "unnatural"
or "artificial" by excluding from "Nature" those social
forces which find expression in Acts of Parliament, an
eminently unscientific mode of reasoning.

   But though this growing exercise of social control cannot be regarded as "fighting against the constitution of
things,"[1] it may be considered by those who hold we have
no guarantee of the future development of the human race, as
one of the lines of action in which the advancing enfeeble-
ment of man may express itself : the abandonment of
individual strife in commerce may be regarded as a mark of
diminishing vitality, which seeks immunity from effort and
an equable condition of material comfort, in preference to
the risks and excitement of a more eventful and arduous
career.   Order will be purchased at the price of progress :
the abandonment of individual enterprise in industry is part
of the decadence of humanity.   This is the interpretation
which Dr. Pearson, in his *National Life and Character*,
places upon the socialistic tendencies of the age : the sup-
pression of competitive industry in order to cure poverty,
physical misery, and social injustice, will produce a society
which is "sensuous, genial, fibreless."   The validity of such
a judgment rests upon two assumptions : first, that social
control of industry necessarily crushes the spirit of individual enterprise and checks industrial progress ; second,
that extension of State control over capitalist industry
necessarily implies a diminished scope of individual control
in the production of wealth.

   The first assumption is open to a number of criticisms
which must be held to greatly modify its force, and which
may be summarised as follows :—

   (1) Much individual enterprise in industry does not make
for industrial progress.   A larger and larger proportion of
the energy given out in trade competition is consumed in

---

[1] Spencer, *Contemporary Review*, March 1884.

violent warfare between trade rivals, and is not represented either in advancement of industrial arts or in increase of material wealth.

(2) History does not show greed of gain as the motive of the great steps in industrial progress. The love of science, the pure delight of mechanical invention, the attainment of some slight personal convenience in labour, and mere chance, play the largest part in the history of industrial improvements. These motives would be as equally operative under state-control as under private enterprise.

(3) Such personal inducements as may supply a useful stimulus to the inventive faculty could be offered in socially-controlled industry, not merely publicity and honour, but such direct material rewards as were useful.

Industrial history shows that in modern competitive industry the motive of personal gain is most wastefully applied. On the one hand, the great mass of intelligent workers have no opportunity of securing an adequate reward for any special application of intelligence in mechanical invention or other improvement of industrial arts. Few great modern inventors have made money out of their inventions. On the other hand, the *entrepreneur*, with just enough business cunning to recognise the market value of an improvement, reaps a material reward which is often enormously in excess of what is economically required to induce him to apply his " business " qualities to the undertaking.

(4) The same charges of weakened individual interest, want of plasticity and enterprise, routine torpidity, are in a measure applicable to every large business as compared with a smaller. Adam Smith considered them fatal barriers to the growth of joint-stock enterprise outside a certain narrowly-defined range. But the economies of the large business were found to outweigh these considerations. So a well-ordered state-industry may be the most economical in spite of diminished elasticity and enterprise.

But while these considerations qualify the force of the contention that state-control would give no scope for industrial progress, they do not refute it. The justification of the assumption by the State of various functions, military, judicial, industrial, is that a safe orderly routine in the conduct of these affairs is rightly purchased by a loss of elasticity and a diminished pace of progress. The arts of war and of justice would probably make more advance under private enterprise than under public administration, and there is no reason to deny that postal and railway services are slower to adopt improvements when they pass under government control.

It may be generally admitted that, as the large modern industries pass from the condition of huge private monopolies to public departments, the routine character will grow in them, and they will become less experimental and more mechanical. It is the nature of machines to be mechanical, and the perfection of machine-industries, as of single machines, will be the perfection of routine. Just in proportion as the machine has established its dominancy over the various industries, so will they increase in size, diminish in flexibility, and grow ripe for admission, as routine businesses, into the ranks of state-industry. If the chief object of society was to secure continual progress in military arts and to educate to the utmost the military qualities, it would be well to leave fighting to private enterprise instead of establishing state monopolies in the trade of war. It sacrifices this competition, with the progress it induces and the personal fitness it evolves, in order that the individual enterprise of its members may be exercised in the competition of industrial arts, inducing industrial progress and evolving industrial fitness. The substitution of industrialism for warfare is not, however, understood to imply a diminution of individual enterprise, but an alteration in its application.

If, starting from this point of view, we regard human life as comprising an infinite number of activities of different sorts, operating upon different planes of competition and educating different human "fitnesses," we shall understand how the particular phase of industrial evolution we are considering is related to the wider philosophic view of life. All progress, from primitive savagedom to modern civilisation, will then appear as consisting in the progressive socialisation of the lower functions, the stoppage of lower forms of competition and of the education of the more brutal qualities, in order that a larger and larger proportion of individual activity may be engaged in the exercise of higher functions, the practice of competition upon higher planes, and the education of higher forms of fitness.

If the history of past civilisation shows us this, there is an
à priori presumption that each further step in the repression
of individual enterprise and in the extension of state-control
does not mean a net diminution in individual activity or
any relaxation of effort in self-assertion, but merely an elevation of the plane of competition and of the kind of human
qualities engaged.   This is, in fact, the philosophical defence
of progressive socialism, that human progress requires that
one after another the lower material animal functions shall
be reduced to routine, in order that a larger amount of
individual effort may be devoted to the exercise of higher
functions and the cultivation by strife of higher qualities.

To suppose that the reduction of all machine-industry to
public routine services, when it becomes possible, will imply
a net diminution in the scope of individual self-expression,
rests upon the patent fallacy of assigning certain fixed
and finite limits to human interest and activity, so that
any encroachment from the side of routine lessens the
absolute scope of human spontaneity and interest.   If, as
there is reason to believe, human desires and the activities
which are engaged in satisfying them are boundless, the
assumption that an increase in the absolute amount of
state-control or routine-work implies a diminution of the
field for individual enterprise is groundless.   The under-
lying motive, which alone can explain and justify each
step in progressive socialism, is the attainment of a net
economy of individual effort, which, when it is released
from exercise upon a lower plane of competition, may
be devoted to exercise upon a higher.   If the result of
extending social control over industry were merely to bring
about a common level of material comfort, attended by
spiritual and intellectual torpor and contentment, the movement might be natural and necessary, but could hardly be
termed progress.

But such a view is based upon a denial of the axiom that
the satisfaction of one want breeds another want.   Experience does not teach the decay but the metamorphosis of
individuality.   Under socialised industry progress in the
industrial arts would be slower and would absorb a smaller
proportion of individual interest, in order that progress in the
finer intellectual and moral arts might be faster, and might
engage a larger share of life.   To future generations of more

highly evolved humanity the peculiar barbarism of our age will consist in the fact that the major part of its intelligence, enterprise, genius, has been devoted to the perfection of the arts of material production through mechanical means. If it is desirable that more of this individual energy should be engaged in the production of higher forms of wealth by competition upon higher planes, this can only be achieved by the process of reducing to routine the lower functions. Higher progress can only be purchased by an economy of the work of lower progress, the free, conscious expression of higher individuality by the routine subordination of lower individuality. Industrial progress would undoubtedly be slower under state-control, because the very object of such control is to divert a larger proportion of human genius and effort from these occupations in order to apply them in producing higher forms of wealth. It is not, however, right to assume that progress in the industrial arts would cease under state-industry; such progress would be slower, and would itself partake of a routine character— a slow, continuous adjustment of the mechanism of production and distribution to the slowly-changing needs of the community.

§ 10. A most important misunderstanding of the line of industrial development arises from a conviction that all production of wealth embodied in matter tends to pass under the dominion of machinery, that an increasing number of workers in the future will become machine-tenders, and that the state-control of machine-industry would bring the vast majority of individuals into the condition of official machine-workers. This, however, is by no means a reasonable forecast. In competitive machine-industry, although it is to the interest of the individual business to "save" as much labour as possible, the play of competition causes to be made and worked a much larger quantity of machinery than is enough to maintain the current rate of consumption, and thus keeps in the ranks of manufacture a much larger quantity of labour than is socially necessary. Yet in a typical manufacturing country like England statistics show that the proportion of the working population engaged in machine manufactures is not increasing. If, then, by the gradual elimination of competition in the machine-industries, the quantity of machine-work were kept down to the social requirements of the community's consumption, the proportion of machine-workers would be less than it is, assuming the demand for machine-made goods continued the same.

But what, it may be said, will become of the increasing proportion of the workers not required by machinery? will they go to swell indefinitely the ranks of distributors? Will the number of merchants, jobbers, speculators, shopkeepers, agents, middlemen of various sorts, grow without limit? Assuming that the work of distribution were left to competitive enterprise, and that the quantity and quality of consumption remained the same as now, this result would seem necessarily to follow. The labour saved in manufacture would pass, as it does now, to intensify the competition of the distributive trades and to subdivide into needlessly small fragments the necessary but limited amount of distributive work. But these assumptions are not necessarily correct. If, as seems likely, the increased intensity of competition forced the growth of strong monopolies in certain departments of distribution, the anti-social power thus bestowed upon individuals would necessitate the extension of state-control to them also. The work of distribution would thus pass into routine-industry administered by the public for the public interest. Thus the area of socialised industry would extend until it absorbed one after another all industries possessing the machine-character and capable of administration by routine. It might thus appear that, after all, the forebodings of the individualist would be verified, the work of life would be reduced to a dull monotonous mechanism grinding out under bureaucratic sway an even quantity of material comforts for a community absorbed in the satisfaction of its orderly behaviour.

This goal seems inevitable if we assume that no change takes place in the quantity and quality of the consumption of the community, that individual consumers save or try to save the same proportion of their incomes as now, and apply the portion that they spend to the purchase of increased quantities of ever-cheapening machine-made goods.

But are we justified in considering it necessary, or even probable, that consumption will in amount and character remain unchanged?   In proportion as the large industries pass into the condition of monopolies, whether under private or public control, the area of safe and profitable investment for the average "saving" man will be more restricted.   Thus some of the useless "saving" which takes the shape of excessive plant, machinery, and other forms of capital will be prevented.   In other words, the quantity of consumption will increase, and this increase will give fuller employment to the machinery of production and to the labour engaged in working it and in distributing the increased product.   If, however, increased consumption merely took the form of consuming increased quantities of the same material goods as before, the gain would be limited to the rise of material comfort of the poorer classes, and this gain might be set off by the congested and torpor-breeding luxury of the better-to-do.   A mere increase in quantity of consumption would do nothing to avert the drifting of industry into a bureaucratic mechanism.

§ 11.   It is to improved quality and character of consumption that we can alone look for a guarantee of social progress. Allusion has been already made to the class of artistic and intellectual work which cannot be undertaken by machinery. It must never be forgotten that art is the true antithesis of machinery.   The essence of art in this wide sense is the application of individual spontaneous human effort.   Each art-product is the repository of individual thought, feeling, effort, each machine-product is not.   The "art" in machine-work has been exhausted in the single supreme effort of planning the machine ; the more perfect the machine the smaller the proportion of individual skill or art embodied in the machine-product.   The spirit of machinery, its vast rapid power of multiplying quantities of material goods of the same pattern, has so over-awed the industrial world that the craze for quantitative consumption has seized possession of many whose taste and education might have enabled them to offer resistance.   Thus, not only our bread and our boots are made by machinery, but many of the very things we misname "art-products." Now a just indictment of this excessive encroachment of machinery is not based upon the belief, right or wrong, that machinery cannot produce things in themselves as fit or beautiful as art.   The true inadequacy of machine-

products for human purposes arises from the fact that
machine-products are exactly similar to one another, whereas
consumers are not. So long as consumers consent to sink
their individuality, to consume articles of precisely the same
shape, size, colour, material, to assimilate their consumption
to one another, machinery will supply them. But since no
two individuals are precisely similar in physical, intellectual,
or moral nature, so the real needs of no two will be the
same, even in the satisfaction of ordinary material wants.
As the dominance of machinery over the workers tends to
the destruction of individuality in work, obliging different
workers to do the same work in the same way with a
premium upon the mere capacity of rapid repetition, in the
same way it tends to crush the individuality of consumers
by imposing a common character upon their consumption.
The progressive utilisation of machinery depends upon the
continuance of this indiscriminate consumption, and the
willingness of consumers to employ every increase of income
in demanding larger and larger quantities of goods of the
same pattern and character. Once suppose that consumers
refuse to conform to a common standard, and insist more
and more upon a consumption adjusted to their individual
needs and tastes, and likewise strive to follow and to satisfy
the changing phases of their individual taste, such individuality in consumption must impose a corresponding individuality in production, and machinery will be dethroned
from industry. Let us take the example of the clothing trade. Provided the wearing public will consent to
wear clothes conforming to certain common patterns and
shapes which are only approximate "fits," machinery can be
used to make these clothes , but if every person required
his own taste to be consulted, and insisted upon an exactitude of fit and a conformity to his own special ideas of
comfort, the work could no longer be done by machinery,
and would require the skill of an "artist." It is precisely
upon this issue that the conflict of machine *versus* hand-
labour is still fought out. The most highly-finished articles
in the clothing and boot trades are still hand-made ; the
best golf-clubs, fishing-rods, cricket bats, embody a large
amount of high manual skill, though articles of fair average
make are turned out chiefly by machinery in large quantities.
These hand-made goods are produced for a small portion of

24

the consuming public, whose education and refinement of taste induces them to prefer spending their money upon a smaller quantity of commodities adjusted in character to their individual needs, than upon a larger quantity of common commodities.

Assuming that industrial evolution places an increasing proportion of the consuming public in secure possession of the prime physical necessaries of life, it is surely possible that they too may come to value less highly a quantitative increase in consumption, and may develop individuality of tastes which require individual production for their satisfaction. In proportion as this happens, hand-work or art must play a more important part in these industries, and may be able to repel the further encroachments of machinery, or even to drive it out of some of the industrial territory it has annexed. But although the illustration of the present condition of the clothing trades serves to indicate the nature of the contest between machinery and art in the region of ordinary material consumption, it is not suggested that social progress will, or ought to, expel machinery from most of the industries it controls, or to prevent its application to industries which it has not yet reached. The luxury and foppish refinement of a small section of "fashionable" society, unnaturally relieved of the wholesome necessity of work, cannot be taken as an indication of the ways in which individuality or quality of consumption may or will assert itself, in a society where social progress is based upon equality of opportunity, and the power to consume has some just relation to ability and merit. It seems reasonable to expect that on the whole machinery will retain, and even strengthen and extend, its hold of those industries engaged in supplying the primitive needs of man—his food, clothing, shelter, and other animal comforts. In a genuinely progressive society the object will be so to order life as to secure, not merely the largest amount of individual freedom or self-expression, but the highest quality. If an undue amount of individuality be devoted to the production and consumption of food, clothing, etc., and the conscious, refined cultivation of these tastes, higher forms of individual expression in work and life will be neglected. The just economy of individuality will therefore relegate certain branches of production to machinery, in order that the energy saved by such

routine-work may be set free for higher individual endeavour.
The satisfaction of the primary animal wants—hunger, thirst,
cold, etc.—are common to all; in these purely physical
demands there is less qualitative difference in different men;
as the needs are the same the consumption will be the same.
The absence of wide individual differences of taste marks
out the commodities for routine or machine-production. As
individuals are nearest alike in their prime physical needs,
so, as they gradually develop higher material wants, and,
after these are satisfied, æsthetic, intellectual, moral wants,
their individualism becomes more and more marked. It is
therefore in the most highly developed, or, as they are sometimes called, the more "artificial" wants of man, that the
diversity of individual nature shows itself most strongly, and
demands a satisfaction peculiar to itself which only art can
give. In a highly evolved society it is likely that many
physical needs, and even some intellectual needs, will be
common to all, and will engage little individual attention.
These may be graded as routine wants, and may be satisfied
by machine-made goods. As a society, safely ordered in
the supply of ordinary physical comforts, continued to
develop, a less and less diversity would show itself in the
ordinary aspect of its material civilisation, because the
individuality which once found expression there is raised
to a higher plane of activity. The enrichment and enlargement of human life in such a society would undoubtedly
manifest itself in a greater likeness between the individual
members in the lower modes of life, but the extent of individual difference in the higher modes would be ever widening. The object of the levelling in the lower processes of
life would be that higher individual differences might have
opportunity to assert themselves. In a progressive society
thus conceived, where socialisation and individuation grow
inseparably related and reacting on one another, there is
evidently no fixed limit to the progress of machinery. As
each higher want is educated, some lower want will drop
into the position of a routine-want, and will pass into the
rightful province of machinery. But though a large proportion of material commodities would doubtless be made by
machinery, it is not signified that art will be banished from
what are commonly called the industrial arts. On the contrary, art may be in many ways the friend and co-operator

of machinery, the latter furnishing a routine foundation for the display of individual taste and of individual satisfaction in the consumer. One of the most hopeful signs of the last few years is the growing intrusion of art into the machine-industries,—the employment of skilled designers and executants who shall tempt and educate the public eye with grace of form and harmony of colour. In pottery, textile wares, hardware, furniture, and many other industries, the beginnings of public taste are operating in demand for variety and ornament. May not this be the beginning of a cultivation of individual taste which shall graft a fine-art upon each machine-industry, apportioning to machinery that work which is hard, dull, dangerous, monotonous, and uneducative, while that which is pleasant, worthy, interesting, and educative is reserved for the human agent?

§ 12. Machinery is thus naturally adapted to the satisfaction of the routine wants of life under social control. The character of machine-production, as has been shown, is essentially collective. The maladies of present machine-industries are due to the fact that this collective character is inadequately recognised, and machinery, left to individual enterprise and competition, oppresses mankind and causes waste and commercial instability. In a word, the highest division of labour has not been yet attained, that which will apportion machinery to the collective supply of the routine needs of life, and art to the individual supply of the individual needs. In this way alone can society obtain the full use of the "labour-saving" character of machinery, minimising the amount of human exertion engaged in tending machinery and maximising the amount engaged in the free and interesting occupations. Engaged in satisfying the steady, constant needs of society under social regulation, machinery would no longer be subject to those fearful oscillations of demand which are liable unforeseen to plunge whole masses of workers into unemployment and poverty, and to waste an infinite amount of "saving." Where the fluctuations in consumption were confined to the region of individual taste, the changes of taste and growing variety of consumption would furnish the education of the artist, who will acquire skill and flexibility by freely following and directing the changing tastes of consumers.

In such a forecast it is of course useless to endeavour to

predict how far art will continue to occupy itself with
industry, or how far, set free by machinery, it will be
absorbed in the creation of finer intellectual or spiritual
products, or in what are now termed the fine arts. This
must depend upon the nature of the harmonious development of human capacities of effort and enjoyment under
conditions of individual freedom, and the interaction of the
free development of individuals in a society founded upon an
equality of the material means of life. The study of the
qualitative development of consumption in modern society
is only just beginning to be recognised as the true starting-
point of economic science, for although many of the older
economists did verbal homage to the importance of this
branch of study, it has been reserved for recent thinkers
to set about the work.[1]

§ 13. It is hardly too much to say that the whole of social
progress depends upon the substitution of qualitative for
quantitative methods of consumption. In so far as individuals apply their growing ability to consume in order
to demand increased quantities of the same articles they
consumed before, or flash variety of fashionable goods in
no wise adjusted to individual need or taste, they extend
the dominion of machinery. In so far as they develop
individual taste, delicacy rather than quantity of satisfaction,
they give wider scope to work which embodies conscious
human skill and deserves the name of art.

But there is another bearing of this point of equal significance. Political economists have a dismal formula called
the Law of Diminishing Returns, which casts a dark shadow
upon industrial progress as it is commonly conceived. The
more food and clothing, fuel, and other material goods we
require, the further we have to go for the material, and the
harder it is to get: we must plough inferior lands yielding
smaller crops, we must sink deeper shafts for our coal and
iron. As our population grows ever larger, and this larger
number wants more and more pieces of the earth to feed

---

[1] Professor Jevons' work upon this branch of Economics was marred
by an attempt to treat it purely mathematically, that is to reduce qualitative to quantitative differences—an impossibility. Among recent
writers, Professor Patten, of Pennsylvania University, has made by far
the most important contributions towards a systematic treatment of
the economics of consumption.

its machines and to turn out the increased quantity of goods, the drain upon natural resources is constantly increasing. The material world is limited; in time Nature will become exhausted, and, long before this happens, the quantity of human labour required to raise the increased supply of raw material in the teeth of the Law of Diminishing Returns will far exceed the economies attending large-scale machine-production.

This danger will also be found to result entirely from the quantitative estimate of human wealth and human life.

Confining our view for the moment to that branch of production which is engaged in providing food, to which the Law of Diminishing Returns is held to apply with special rigour, we can see without difficulty how, by a progressive differentiation of consumption, we can mitigate or even utterly defeat the operation of this law. If the inhabitants of a country persist in maintaining a single narrow standard of diet, and use the whole of their land for growing wheat and raising sheep, not merely do they waste all other fine productive qualities belonging to certain portions of the cultivated or uncultivated soil, but every increase in their narrow consumption drives them to worse soil, obliges them to put more labour into a quarter of wheat or a sheep, and increases the proportion of their aggregate product which goes as rent.[1] If, on the other hand, a community cultivates a varied consumption and seeks to utilise each portion of its soil for whatever form of food it can grow best, instead of grading its land exclusively according to its wheat or sheep-raising capacity, it is able to defeat the "niggardliness of nature" which asserts itself when the community insists upon a continual extension of the same demands. For land which may be very bad for wheat-growing or grazing, which may even be "below the margin of cultivation" for these purposes, may be well adapted for producing other commodities. A large variety of alternative uses will enable us to get the largest net amount of utilities out of Nature, and a community which, in lieu of an extension of demand for the same commodities, asserts its civilisation in the education of new demands and a greater complexity in

---

[1] Patten's *Premises of Political Economy*, chap. iv.

the standard of its comfort, may draw from the land an indefinite increase of wealth without putting forth more labour or paying higher rent. It is simply one more example of the economy attainable by division of labour and specialisation of function.

§ 14. What applies to food will equally apply to the use of the earth for providing the raw material of all other forms of material wealth. A people with growing variety of consumption is ever finding new and more profitable uses for slighted or neglected capacities of nature. The social progress of nations must be chiefly determined by the amount of their intelligent flexibility of consumption. Mere variety of consumption in itself is not sufficient to secure progress. There must be a progressive recognition of the true relations, between the products which can be most economically raised upon each portion of the soil, and the wholesome needs of mankind seeking the full harmonious development of their faculties in their given physical environment. A progressive cultivation of taste for a variety of strong drinks, though it might provide an increased number of alternative uses for the soil, and might enhance the aggregate market-values of the wealth produced, would not, it is generally held, make for social progress. That nation which, in its intelligent attainment of a higher standard of life, is able to thoroughly assimilate and harmonise the largest variety of those products for which their soil and climate are best adapted, will be foremost in industrial progress and in the other arts of civilisation which spring out of it.

The case is a simple one. A mere increase in the variety of our material consumption relieves the strain imposed upon man by the limits of the material universe, for such variety enables him to utilise a larger proportion of the aggregate of matter. But in proportion as we add to mere variety a higher appreciation of those adaptations of matter which are due to human skill, and which we call Art, we pass outside the limits of matter and are no longer the slaves of roods and acres and a law of diminishing returns. So long as we continue to raise more men who demand more food and clothes and fuel, we are subject to the limitations of the material universe, and what we get ever costs us more and benefits us less. But when we cease to demand more, and

begin to demand better, commodities, more delicate, highly
finished and harmonious, we can increase the enjoyment
without adding to the cost or exhausting the store. What
artist would not laugh at the suggestion that the materials
of his art, his colours, clay, marble, or what else he wrought
in, might fail and his art come to an end? When we are
dealing with qualitative, *i.e.* artistic, goods, we see at once
how an infinite expenditure of labour may be given, an
infinite satisfaction taken, from the meagrest quantity of
matter and space. In proportion as a community comes to
substitute a qualitative for a quantitative standard of living,
it escapes the limitations imposed by matter upon man.
Art knows no restrictions of space or size, and in proportion
as we attain the art of living we shall be likewise free.

§ 15. So far the consideration of reformed qualitative
consumption has been confined to material goods. But a
people moving along the line of progress, seeking ever a
more highly qualitative life, will demand that a larger proportion of their energy shall be given to the production and
consumption of intellectual goods.

This world likewise is at present largely under the
dominion of Machinery and a Law of Diminishing Returns.
By making of our intellectual life a mere accumulation of
knowledge, piling fact upon fact, reading book upon book,
adding science to science, striving to cover as much intellectual ground as possible, we become mere worshippers
of quantity. It is not unnatural that our commercial life
should breed such an intellectual consumption, and that
the English and American nations in particular, who have
beyond others developed machine-production and the
quantitative genius for commerce, should exhibit the same
taste in their pursuit after knowledge. Pace, size, number,
cost, are ever on their lips. To visit every European capital
in a fortnight, see acres of pictures, cathedrals, ruined castles,
collect out of books or travel the largest mass of unassorted
and undigested information, is the object of such portion of
the commercial life as can be spared from the more serious
occupations of life, piling up bale after bale of cotton goods
and eating dinner after dinner of the same inharmoniously
ordered victuals.

Our schools and colleges are engaged in turning out year
by year immense quantities of common intellectual goods.

Our magazines, books, and lectures are chiefly machine-products adjusted to the average reader or hearer, and are reckoned successful if they can drive a large number of individuals to profess the same feelings and opinions and adopt the same party or creed, with the view of enabling them to consume a large number of copies of the same intellectual commodities which can be turned out by intellectual machinery, instead of undergoing the effort of thinking and feeling for themselves. This danger, connected with the rapid spread of printed matter, is a grave one. Happily there are visible here also counteracting influences, forces that tend to individualise intellectual consumption. and thus to stimulate the higher arts of intellectual production. In a progressive community it will be more fully recognised that it is not sufficient to induce people to give more time and attention to intellectual consumption; they must demand intellectual goods vitally adjusted to their individual needs.

§ 16. To the increased regard for quality of life we must likewise look to escape the moral maladies which arise from competition. For what is the cause of anti-social competition? It is the limitation of quantity. Two dogs are after one bone. Two persons wish to consume one commodity at the same time. Now, even in material goods, the more qualitative consumption becomes, and the more insistent each individual is upon the satisfaction of his peculiar tastes, the smaller will be the probability that two persons will collide in their desires, and struggle for the possession of the self-same commodity. Even in art-objects which are still bounded by matter, among genuine lovers of art the individuality of each stands out in mitigation of the antagonism of competition, for no two will have precisely the same tastes or estimates, or will seek with equal avidity the same embodiments of art. As we rise to purely intellectual or moral enjoyments, competition gives way to generous rivalry in co-operation. In the pursuit of knowledge or goodness the rivalry is no longer antagonism—what one gains another does not lose. One man's success is not another's failure. On the contrary, the enrichment of one is the enrichment of all. Both in the production and the consumption of the highest goods of Science, Art, and Virtue, social, not anti-social, motives are the chief

stimulus. In the highest forms of consumption, the practice
of the noblest arts of life, the enjoyment of the finest
intellectual and spiritual goods, there is no purely selfish
consumption. For though the highest individuality is then
attained, the enjoyment of one individual requires the enjoyment of others. The attainment of the highest reaches
of knowledge is impossible for the individual without the
constant and increasing aid of other minds and the inspiring
"spirit of the age"; the enjoyment of such knowledge is in
an even wider communication. The practice and enjoyment of the arts of goodness are necessarily social, because
the good life can only be lived in a good society. Spinoza
has summed up the truth in saying—"The highest good is
common to all, and all may equally enjoy it." So it appears
that the highest goods are essentially at once individual
and social, pointing once more the attainment of the higher
synthesis in which the antagonism of the "one" and the
"all," which shows itself in the lower planes of competing
effort and enjoyment, disappears.

§ 17. One necessary condition of this progressive life
cannot be ignored. Human life itself must become more
qualitative, not only in its functional activities, but in its
physical basis. The greatness and worth of a community
must be seen more clearly to consist not in the numbers,
but in the character of its members. If the number of
individuals in a society continually increases, no reform in
methods of consumption can prevent the constant increase
in the proportion of human energy which must be put into
the production of the prime material necessaries of physical
life which are, and in spite of all improved methods of
treating nature will remain, ultimately subject to a law of
diminishing returns : so, less and less energy can be spared
for the life of varied and delicate consumption, high individuality and intellectual and moral growth. Professor
Geddes has well expressed the importance of this truth :
"The remedy lies in higher and higher individuation—
i.e., if we would repress excessive multiplication, we must
develop the average individual standard throughout society.
Population not merely tends to out-run the means of subsistence, but to degenerate below the level of subsistence,
so that without steadily directing more and more of our
industry from the production of those forms of wealth

which merely support life to those which evoke it, from the increase of the fundamental necessities of animal life to that of the highest appliances of human culture, degeneration must go on."[1]

§ 18. One final consideration remains. Modern large-scale industry has enlarged and made more distinct an unnatural and injurious separation of the arts of production and the arts of consumption. Work has become more and more differentiated from enjoyment, and in a twofold way. Modern machine-industry has in the first place sharpened the distinction between the "working classes," whose name indicates that their primary function is to labour and not to live, and the comfortable classes, whose primary function is to live and not to labour, which private enterprise in machine-industry has greatly enlarged. The extremes of these large classes present the divorcement of labour and life in startling prominence. But since work and enjoyment are both human functions, they must be organically related in the life of every individual in a healthy community. It must be recognised to be as essential to the consumer to produce as for the producer to consume. The attempt on the part of an individual or a class to escape the physical and moral law which requires the output of personal exertion as the condition of wholesome consumption can never be successful. On the plane of physical health, Dr. Arlidge, in his book upon *The Diseases of Occupations*, points the inevitable lesson in the high rate of disease and mortality of the "unoccupied class" in that period of their life when they have slaked their zest for volunteer exertion and assume the idle life which their economic power renders possible. The man of "independent means" cannot on the average keep his life in his body nearly so long as the half-starved, ill-housed agricultural labourer, from whose labour he draws the rents which keep him in idleness. The same law applies in the intellectual world. The dilettante person who tries to extract unceasing increments of intellectual or æsthetic enjoyment from books or pictures or travel, without the contribution of steady, painful intellectual effort, fails to

---

[1] Professor Patrick Geddes, *Claims of Labour*. Cf. *The Evolution of Sex*, chap. xx. (Contemporary Science Series: Walter Scott).

win an intellectual life, for the mere automatic process of collecting the knowledge of others for personal consumption without striving to enlarge the general stock, congests and debilitates the mind and prevents the wholesome digestion and assimilation.

The same necessary evil arises from the sharp separation of the processes of production and consumption in the individual life of the worker Industry which is purely monotonous, burdensome, uninteresting, uneducative, which contains within itself no elements of enjoyment, cannot be fully compensated by alternate periods of consumption or relaxation. The painful effort involved in all labour or exertion should have linked with it certain sustaining elements of related interest and pleasure. It is the absence of this which condemns machine-tending from the human standpoint, it is the presence of this which distinguishes every art. Hence in a progressive society we must look to see not the abolition of machinery, but the diminution of machine-tending which attends the growing perfection of machinery, in order that the arts may be able to absorb a larger share of human exertion.

The arts of production and consumption will, in the evolution of a wholesome industrial society, be found inseparable: not merely will they be seen to be organically related, but rather will appear as two aspects of the same fact, the concave and the convex of life. For the justly ordered life brings the identification of life, a continuous orderly intake and output of wholesome energy. This judgment, not of "sentimentalism" but of science, finds powerful but literally accurate expression in the saying of a great living thinker, "Life without work is guilt, work without art is brutality." Just in proportion as the truth of the latter phrase finds recognition the conditions which make "life without work" possible will disappear. Everything in human progress will be found to depend upon a progressive realisation of the nature of good "consumption." Just in proportion as our tastes become so qualitative that we require to put our own spontaneity, our sense of beauty and fitness, our vital force, into whatever work we do, and likewise require the same elements of spontaneity and individuality in all we enjoy, the economic conditions of a perfect society will be attained.

§ 19. This forecast of the social and industrial goal seems justified by a thoughtful interpretation of the tendencies visible in the development of modern industry. How fast may be the progress towards such an ideal, or how far such progress may be frustrated or impaired by the appearance of new or the strengthening of old antagonistic forces, lies beyond the powers of legitimate speculation. The endeavour to test industrial evolution by reference to the wider movements of human life brings into prominence two great tendencies whose operations, attested not dimly by modern history, are in close accord with the general trend of the development of social and individual life and the relations subsisting between the two.

As modern industrial societies develop they disclose certain material wants which are common to all or most members, and are less subject to fluctuations in quantity or quality of demand than others. These routine wants, representing that part of consumption which is common, can be supplied most economically by highly organised machinery and highly concentrated methods of production. But so long as the machinery for the satisfaction of the common wants remains outside the common control, and is worked for the benefit of sections of the community whose interests conflict, both with one another and with the general interest, an immense amount of waste and danger arises from the working of the machinery, and grave social maladies are engendered. These maladies evoke in the best ordered and most intelligent communities an increasing pressure of public control. This public control is strengthened and extended in proportion as the highly evolved structure of the industry enables its administrators to exercise powers of monopoly either in relation to the treatment of its employees, or in relation to the price or quality of the commodities it supplies to the public. Such industries as develop these economic powers of monopoly in the highest degree, and in relation to the supply of prime necessaries or comforts of common life, pass gradually into the condition of public industries organised for the public good. It seems likely that all the important machine industries engaged in satisfying common routine wants will gradually develop the monopolic characteristics which accrue to large production, and will pass by degrees through the different phases of public control until they become merged in public industry.

This so-called socialistic movement in industry represents the growing cohesiveness of modern societies. At all times there is a strong natural tendency to supply common wants by common efforts. So long as the common wants in their wider significance only extend to protection of the person and of certain forms of personal property, state-work is confined within these protective limits, and the work of producing common wealth, so far as it exists, is left to village communities or other small units of social organisation. As the elements of steady common consumption grow in number, the common organisation of activity to supply them will grow, and where the supply has at first been left to private enterprise, the abuse of power and growing inconvenience of competition will drive them into public industry. But since the very *raison d'être* of this increased social cohesiveness is to economise and enrich the individual life, and to enable the play of individual energy to assume higher forms out of which more individual satisfaction may accrue, more and more human effort will take shape in industries which will be left to individual initiative and control, the arts in which the freedom of personal spontaneity will find scope in the expression of physical or moral beauty and fitness and the attainment of intellectual truth. The infinite variety which these forms of artistic expression may assume, fraught with the individuality of the artist, will prevent them from ever passing into "routine" or "common" industries, though even in the fine arts there will be certain elements which, as they become part of the common possession, will become relatively void of individual interest, and will thus pass into a condition of routine activity. The idea of continuity in human progress demands this admission. But since each encroachment of routine into the "finer arts" is motived by a prior shifting of the interest of the consumer into forms of higher refinement, there will be a net gain and not a loss in the capacity of individual exercise in artistic work. In every form of human activity the progress of routine industry will be the necessary condition of the expansion of individual freedom of expression. But while the choice and control of each higher form of "industry" will remain individualistic, in proportion as the moral bonds of society obtain fuller conscious recognition, the work of the "artist" likewise will be dedicated more and more to the service of his fellow-men. Thus will the balance of the social and individual work in the satisfaction of human wants be preserved, while the number of tnose wants increase and assume different values with the progress of the social and individual life.

INDEX.

ABRAHAM, *Report on Employment of Women*, 315

Adjustment in progressive industry, 351

Agriculture, 32, 41, 102 ; agricultural labour, 333

Andrew, S., *Fifty Years' Cotton Trade*, 297

Apprentices, statute of, 26

Arkwright, 50, 56

Arlidge, Dr., 252, 255, 320, 336, 337, 379

Art in industry, 371-378

Ashley, Professor, *Economic History*, 38

BABBAGE, *Economy of Manufactures*, 50-51, 236, 249

Baines, *History of Cotton Manufacture*, 23, 37

Baker, *Monopolies and the People*, 128, 134, 139, 147

Board of Trade Journal, 241

Balance of trade, 15

Banking, 42

Bertillon, 303

Birtwistle, T., 248

Böhm-Bawerk, *Positive Theory of Capital*, 101, 196.

Booth, Charles, *Labour and Life of the People*, 41 ; *Occupations of the People*, 226, 228, 290

Bowley, A. L., *England's Foreign Trade*, 174

Brassey, *Foreign Work and English Wages*, 265-266

Brentano, *Uber die Ursachen der heutigen Not*, 58 ; *Hours and Wages in Relation to Production*, 78, 91, 270

Burnley, *Wool and Wool-Combing*, 33, 51, 94

Business, evolution of the, 10, 35, 40, 88, 92

CAIRNES, J. E., *Logical Method of Political Economy*, 8 ; *Some Leading Principles of Political Economy*, 211

Canada, town population, 331

Canals, 25

Cannan, E., *Production and Consumption*, 214 ; *Decline of Urban Immigration*, 327 (note)

Capital, meaning of, 5 ; fixed, 40 ; growing size of, 92-93 ; excessive forms of, 170, etc. ; definitions of, 209-215 ; concentration of, 117-122

Capitalism, 4, 40 ; factors in growth of, 73-81, 101

Carding, 57

Cartwright, 58, 75

Census, occupations of the people, 71, 228 ; town population, 328 ; mortality in towns, 334

Chalmers, *Estimate*, 23

Chartered companies, 18

Child-workers, in domestic industry, 32 ; in factory, 297, 307, 319 ; legal protection of, 322-323 ; child mortality, 337

Climate, 73, 109

Clothier, 39, 40, etc.

Collet, 305, 307, 311, 312

Competition, 104, 108, 118, 120, etc. ; "unfair," 146

Consumption, insufficient quantity, 180, etc ; progressive, 284 ; quality of, 368

Concentration of industry, 38, 101

Cooke-Taylor, *The Modern Factory System*, 36, 37, 50, 66, 251-252, 255

Corner, 127, 129

Cotton, 24, 37, 55, 63, 105; consumption of, 80; machinery, 90, 247; statistics, 228; spinning labour, 246; factory legislation, 322

Cournot, *Recherches sur les Principes Mathématiques de la Theorie des Richesses*, 97

Crime in towns, 340

Crompton, 56

Cunningham, *History of English Industry*, 14, 19, 42, 55; *Uses and Abuses of Money*, 236, 251

Custom, in women's industries, 311

DECENTRALISATION, 345

Defoe, *Tour*, 25, 28, 32, 33, 38, 40

Depression of trade, 171, 206, etc.

Dilke, Lady, 301 (note)

Differentiation, 106

Diminishing returns, law of, 374

Dodd, C. S. T., *Ten Years of the Standard Oil Trust*, 130, 144

Domestic industry, 35, 69, 78

Dress trades, 293, 294

"Driving," 248, 249

ECONOMY of competitive power, 118; of high wages, 261-286

Ellison, T., *History of the Cotton Trade*, 76, 228

Europe, growth of towns, 329

FACTOR, 41

Factory, 37, 39, 57; system, 50, 319, 320; legislation, 321-323

Fairs, 30, 105

Foreign trade, in England, 13, 73; Europe, 20, 106

Foxwell, H. S., *The Claims of Labour*, 341

Foundational industries, 102

France, English trade with, 16; machine-development, 74; employments, 233; town population, 328, 335; treaty, 63

Free trade, 63, 79, 352-354

GAS-TAR, 53

Geddes, Professor Patrick, *The Evolution of Sex*, 379; *The Claims of Labour*, 379

Germany, 79; cotton trade in, 77-78, 81; town population, 329

Giffen, R., *Essays in Finance*, 175

Gould, 272, 284

Gunton, G., *The Economic and Social Aspect of Trusts*, 138, 149, 153; *Wealth and Progress*, 271, 309

Guyot, Yves, *Principles of Social Economy*, 219

HARGREAVES, 56

Halifax, 31, 33, 41, 301 (note)

Hearn, *Plutology*, 211

Hodge, evidence before House of Lords, 57

Holland, trade of, 16, 17, 26; towns in, 327

IMMIGRATION, 19, 326-331

India, 108, 270, 280

Industrial organism, 11, 20, 105

International trade, 14, 75

Invention, "heroic" view of, 57; by small increments, 58-59

Iron trade, 23, 28, 72, 84; growth of, 64-66

JAMES, *History of Worsted Manufacture*, 36

Jenks, J. W., 137, 150

Jevons, W. S., *Theory of Political Economy*, 185, 209, 373

Joint-stock company, 42, 121, 353

KAY, fly-shuttle, 56

Keynes, *Scope and Method of Political Economy*, 212

King, Gregory, 22, 72

LABOUR organisations, 152, 317, 357

Lancashire, 29, 55, 81, 111, 183, 184, 270, 297, 314

Leeds, 31, 41

Levasseur, M. S., *La Population Française*, 233, 335

Levi, Leone. *Work and Pay*, 222

Linen manufacture, 24, 63

Lloyd, H. D., 153

Localisation of industry, 109, 111-115

Lombe, 55, 61, 68

Longstaff, *Rural Depopulation*, 329; *Studies in Statistics*, 331

MACHINERY, place of, in modern industry, 6; definition of, 45, etc.; evolution of, 60; machine-making, 66, 67; laws of application, 68-70; relation to trade depression, chap. vii.; productivity of, 173; effects on demand for labour, chap. viii.; effects on character of labour, chap. ix.; education of, 257; gain to workers from, 281; machine-goods, 287; social control over, 355; economic limits of, 369; intellectual, 376
Macpherson, *Annals of Commerce*, 12, 13, 20, 23, 32
Mackenzie, *Introduction to Social Philosophy*, 349
Malthus, *Principles of Political Economy*, 210
Market, 10, 96, 99; towns, 30
Marsden, *Cotton Spinning*, 297
Marshall, *Principles of Economics*, 5 (note), 29, 96, 97, 211, 221 (note), 236, 245, 251, 254, 259, 337
Marx, *Capital*, 45, 46, 66, 244
Middleman, 41
Mill, J. S., *Principles of Political Economy*, 185, 189-191, 197, 210, 289
Mill, James, *Elements of Political Economy*, 210
Money, 7, 97, 98
Monopolies, 89, 124, 356; economic powers of, chap. vi.; monopoly-prices, 156, etc.; monopoly wages, 299
Morrison, *The Study of Crime*, 340
Motor, 45, 66, 67
Mulhall, *Dictionary of Statistics*, 251

NAVIGATION, risks of, 14; acts, 17
Newsholm, *Vital Statistics*, 334
Nicholson, J. S., *Effects of Machinery on Wages*, 235, 238, 239, 249

OVER-CONSUMPTION, 215-219
Over-production, 169, 171; economic diagnosis of, 176-190

Over-crowding, 344
Owen, Robert, 263

PARASITIC industries, 113
Patten, S. N., *Theory of Dynamic Economics*, 104, 251, 373; *Premises of Political Economy*, 374
Physiocrats, 261
Playfair, Sir L., 53, 170, 173
Population, English, 22, 77; statistics of, 326-332; population question, 378
Porter, *Progress of the Nation*, 62, 63, 77, 105, 129, 226, 250
Portugal, English trade with, 16
Potter, *The Co-operative Movement*, 129
Power, 38
Price, Bonamy, *Practical Political Economy*, 211, 215
Prices, fall of, 285; fluctuations of, 176
Protection, 18, 77, 79
Publicity in business, 353

RAILWAYS, comparative statistics, 82, 139, 140, 112, 174, 231, 232, 347
Ravenstein, *Statistical Journal*, 327
Retail trade, 114, 115, 229; multiplication of retailers, 288
Ricardo, D., 210
Ring-spinning, 127
Robertson, J. M., *Fallacy of Saving*, 187
Rogers, Thorold, *Political Economy*, 211, 236
Ruskin, J., *Unto this Last*, 199
Russia, 73, 79, 270

SAVING, analysis of, 185-190, 198-201
Schoenhof, *Economy of High Wages*, 81, 275
Schulze-Gaevernitz, *Der Grossbetrieb*, 24, 29, 54, 55, 70, 76, 78, 81, 108, 111, 247, 250, 267-270, 276; *Zum Socialen Frieden*, 91
Scrivener, *History of Iron Trade*, 28, 52, 64, 74
Secondary industries, 103
Shaftoe, 224

Sheffield, 29
Sherman, R., *The Standard Oil Trust*, 130, 132
Shipping, 83, 173, 233
Sidgwick, *Principles of Political Economy*, 185, 211
Silk trade, 23, 55, 61-63, 238, 240
Smart, Dr., *Women's Wages*, 309, 315
Smith, Adam, *Wealth of Nations*, 11, 18, 26, 30, 32, 43, 63, 185, 209, 255, 262, 359, 363
Smith, *Memoirs of Wool*, 12, 24, 35, 41, 262
Socialism, 356-361; in relation to competition, 364, 365; in relation to individualism, 370, etc.
Specialisation, local, 28, etc., 33, 93
Spencer, H., *Principles of Sociology*, 106, 362
Spinning, 56, 57; statistics of, 79, 268, 269; ring-spinning, 296, 297
Spinoza, 378
Staffordshire, 29
Standard Oil Trust, 131-137, 144
Statistical abstract, 90
Steam power, 85, 86
Supply and demand, 68, 162-166; applied to invention, 59
Sweating 286, 307, 310, 318, 360, 361
Sympathy in trades, 104
Syndicates, 89, 126, 128

Textiles, protected, 17, domestic industry, 32, 54, 68, 112; statistics, 228, 296; wages, 242, 316; men and women in, 292, 303
Towns, as machine-products, 324, etc.; growth of town populations, 326-332; mortality in, 334; physique in, 336; intelligence in, 338; morals in, 339, 340
Toynbee, *The Industrial Revolution*, 24, 42, 79
Trade unions, 357; among women, 313, 317
Transport, machinery of, 173, 325; monopolies in, 139, 140, cheapening of, 347
Truck, 152, 346

Trust, 126, 141; definition of, 130, 131; Standard Oil, 131-137; conditions of, 139 etc.; economic power of, chap. vi.

Under-consumption, 182, etc.
Unemployment, 241
United States of America, 75, 76, 81, 91, 93, 130, 140, 141, 172, 231, 269, 274, 275, 296; colonial policy, 67; women's wages in, 306 (note), 308, 309; growth of town life, 330
Ure, *History of the Cotton Manufacture*, 36, 37, 55, 63, 64, 77, 79; *Philosophy of Manufacture*, 258, 262, 263, 274

Wade, *Fibre and Fabric*, 296
Wages, "natural," 261; economy of low, 264, 298; economy of high, 266-275; women's, 299, etc.
Walker, F., *Political Economy*, 211
Waste, utilisation of, 52
Watch-making, 94, 96, 301 (note)
Watt, 65, 75
Weaving, 32, 56; power-loom, 63; survival of hand weaving, 70, 236; comparative statistics of, 81, 268, 269; labour in weaving, 248, 276; women and children in, 297, 300
Webb, S., *Economic Journal*, 298, 300
Wells, D. A., *Contemporary Review*, 91, 171, 173, 254, 296
Women, employment of, 259, 290-321
Woollen trade, 23, 26, 34, 54-57, 61, 73; report of committee on manufacture 39; statistics for Great Britain, 90
Working classes, condition of, 289, 379; legal protection of, 322, 323
Wright, Carroll D., *Report on Industrial Depressions*, 171, 224

Yeats, *The Growth and Vicissitudes of Commerce*, 72, 74; *The Golden Gates of Trade*, 106, 109
Young, Arthur, *Tours*, 22, 25, 39, 262, 326